GUIDE

SOC 1® – SOC for Service Organizations: ICFR   JANUARY 1, 2017

Reporting on an Examination of Controls at a Service Organization Relevant to User Entities' Internal Control Over Financial Reporting (SOC 1®)

AICPA®

20974-349

3 4 5 6 7 8 9 0 AAP 1 9 8

ISBN 978-1-94354-664-0

Preface

About AICPA Guides

This AICPA Guide *Reporting on an Examination of Controls at a Service Organization Relevant to User Entities' Internal Control Over Financial Reporting (SOC 1®),* has been developed by the AICPA Service Organizations Guide Task Force to assist practitioners engaged to examine and report on controls at a service organization that are likely to be relevant to user entities' internal control over financial reporting.

This guide is recognized as an *interpretive publication,* as described in AT-C section 105, *Concepts Common to All Attestation Engagements* (AICPA, *Professional Standards*). Interpretative publications are recommendations on the application of Statements on Standards for Attestation Engagements (SSAEs) in specific circumstances, including engagements for entities in specialized industries. The SSAEs are also known as the attestation standards.

Interpretive publications are issued under the authority of the Auditing Standards Board (ASB) after all ASB members have been provided an opportunity to consider and comment on whether the proposed interpretive publication is consistent with the SSAEs. The members of the ASB have found the attestation guidance in this guide to be consistent with the SSAEs.

Although interpretive publications are not attestation standards, AT-C section 105 requires the practitioner to consider applicable interpretive publications in planning and performing an attestation engagement because interpretive publications are relevant to the proper application of the SSAEs in specific circumstances. If the practitioner does not apply the attestation guidance included in an applicable AICPA Guide, the practitioner should be prepared to explain how he or she complied with the SSAE provisions addressed by such attestation guidance.

AICPA Guides may include certain content presented as "Supplement," "Appendix," or "Exhibit." A supplement is a reproduction, in whole or in part, of authoritative guidance originally issued by a standard-setting body (including regulatory bodies) and is applicable to entities or engagements within the purview of that standard setter, independent of the authoritative status of the applicable AICPA Guide. Both appendixes and exhibits are included for informational purposes and have no authoritative status.

Purpose and Applicability

This guide provides guidance to practitioners engaged to examine and report on a service organization's controls over the services it provides to user entities when those controls are likely to be relevant to user entities' internal control over financial reporting. In April 2016, the ASB issued SSAE No. 18, *Attestation Standards: Clarification and Recodification,*[1] which includes AT-C section 320, *Reporting on an Examination of Controls at a Service Organization Relevant to User Entities' Internal Control Over Financial Reporting* (AICPA,

---

[1] Statement on Standards for Attestation Engagements No. 18, *Attestation Standards: Clarification and Recodification* (AICPA, *Professional Standards*), is effective for service auditor's reports dated on or after May 1, 2017.

Professional Standards). AT-C section 320 establishes the requirements and application guidance for reporting on controls at a service organization that are likely to be relevant to user entities' internal control over financial reporting. The controls addressed in AT-C section 320 are those that a service organization implements to prevent, or detect and correct, misstatements[2] in the information it provides to user entities. A service organization's controls are relevant to a user entity's internal control over financial reporting when they are part of the information and communications component of the user entity's internal control maintained by the service organization.[3] In the attestation standards, a CPA performing an attestation engagement is ordinarily referred to as a *practitioner*. In AT-C section 320, a CPA who reports on controls at a service organization is known as a *service auditor*.

The attestation standards enable a practitioner to report on subject matter other than historical financial statements. In the case of AT-C section 320, the subject matter is the fairness of the presentation of management's description of the service organization's system,[4] the suitability of the design of the service organization's controls relevant to user entities' internal control over financial reporting, and in a type 2 engagement, the operating effectiveness of those controls.

This guide also assists service auditors in understanding the kinds of information auditors of the financial statements of user entities (user auditors) need

---

[2] Paragraph .10 of AT-C section 105, *Concepts Common to All Attestation Engagements* (AICPA, *Professional Standards*), defines a misstatement as

> A difference between the measurement or evaluation of the subject matter by the responsible party and the proper measurement or evaluation of the subject matter based on the criteria. Misstatements can be intentional or unintentional, qualitative or quantitative, and include omissions. In certain engagements, a misstatement may be referred to as a *deviation, exception*, or *instance of noncompliance*.

In this guide,

- the term *misstatement* is used to refer to an error or omission in the description of the service organization's system, and may be used in the generic sense to refer to a deficiency in the design of a control or a deficiency in the operating effectiveness of a control.
- the term *deviation* or *exception* refers to an instance in which a test of controls indicates that the control was not operating effectively to achieve the control objective.
- the term *deficiency in the design of controls* is used when (*a*) a control necessary to achieve the control objective is missing, or (*b*) an existing control is not properly designed so that, even if the control operates as designed, the control objective would not be achieved.
- the term *deficiency in the operating effectiveness of a control* is used when a properly designed control does not operate as designed or when the person performing the control does not possess the necessary authority or competence to perform the control effectively.

[3] Controls may also be relevant when they are part of one or more of the other components of a user entity's internal control over financial reporting. The components of an entity's internal control over financial reporting are described in detail in appendix B, "Internal Control Components," of AU-C section 315, *Understanding the Entity and Its Environment and Assessing the Risks of Material Misstatement* (AICPA, *Professional Standards*).

[4] AT-C section 320, *Reporting on an Examination of Controls at a Service Organization Relevant to User Entities' Internal Control Over Financial Reporting*, defines the term *service organization's system* as

> The policies and procedures designed, implemented, and documented by management of the service organization to provide user entities with the services covered by the service auditor's report. Management's description of the service organization's system identifies the services covered, the period to which the description relates (or in the case of a type 1 report, the date to which the description relates), the control objectives specified by management or an outside party, the party specifying the control objectives (if not specified by management), and the related controls.

from a service auditor's report. AU-C section 402, *Audit Considerations Relating to an Entity Using a Service Organization* (AICPA, *Professional Standards*), addresses the user auditor's responsibility for obtaining sufficient appropriate audit evidence in an audit of the financial statements of a user entity.

Defining Professional Responsibilities in AICPA *Professional Standards*

AICPA *Professional Standards* applicable to attestation engagements use the following two categories of professional requirements, identified by specific terms, to describe the degree of responsibility they impose on a practitioner:

- *Unconditional requirements.* The practitioner must comply with an unconditional requirement in all cases in which such requirement is relevant. The attestation standards use the word *must* to indicate an unconditional requirement.

- *Presumptively mandatory requirements.* The practitioner must comply with a presumptively mandatory requirement in all cases in which such requirement is relevant; however, in rare circumstances, the practitioner may judge it necessary to depart from the requirement. The need for the practitioner to depart from a relevant presumptively mandatory requirement is expected to arise only when the requirement is for a specific procedure to be performed and, in the specific circumstances of the engagement, that procedure would be ineffective in achieving the intent of the requirement. In such circumstances, the practitioner should perform alternative procedures to achieve the intent of that requirement and should document the justification for the departure and how the alternative procedures performed in the circumstances were sufficient to achieve the intent of the requirement. The attestation standards use the word *should* to indicate a presumptively mandatory requirement.

References to *Professional Standards*

In citing attestation standards and their related interpretations, references to standards that have been codified use section numbers within the codification of currently effective SSAEs rather than the original statement number.

Attestation Clarity Project

In April 2016, the ASB issued SSAE No. 18 to address concerns about the clarity, length, and complexity of the attestation standards. To make the standards easier to read, understand, and apply, the ASB adopted the following clarity drafting conventions in redrafting the attestation standards:

- Establishing objectives for each clarified section

- Including a definitions section, when relevant, in each clarified section

- Separating requirements from application and other explanatory material

- Numbering application and other explanatory material paragraphs using an A- prefix and presenting them in a separate section that follows the requirements section
- Using formatting techniques, such as bulleted lists, to enhance
  readability

Changes to the Attestation Standards Introduced by SSAE No. 18

Restructuring of Attestation Standards

The attestation standards provide for three types of services—examination, review, and agreed-upon procedures engagements. SSAE No. 18 restructures the
attestation standards so that the applicability of any AT-C section to a particular engagement depends on the type of service provided and the subject matter
of the engagement.

AT-C section 105 contains requirements and application guidance applicable
to any attestation engagement. AT-C section 205, *Examination Engagements*,
AT-C section 210, *Review Engagements*, and AT-C section 215, *Agreed-Upon
Procedures Engagements* (AICPA, *Professional Standards*), each contain incremental requirements and application guidance specific to the level of service
performed. The applicable requirements and application guidance for an engagement to report on any of these subject matters are contained in three AT-C
sections: AT-C section 105; AT-C section 205, 210, or 215, depending on the level
of service provided; and the applicable subject matter section.

To avoid repetition, the requirements and application guidance in AT-C section
105 are not repeated in the level of service sections or in the subject matter
sections, and the requirements and application guidance in the level of service
sections are not repeated in the subject matter sections, with the exception of
a repetition of the basic report elements for the particular subject matter.

Practitioner Is Required to Request Written Assertion

In all attestation engagements, the practitioner is required to request from the
responsible party a written assertion about the measurement or evaluation
of the subject matter against the criteria. In examination and review engagements, when the engaging party is also the responsible party, the responsible
party's refusal to provide a written assertion requires the practitioner to withdraw from the engagement when withdrawal is possible under applicable laws
and regulations. In examination and review engagements, when the engaging
party is not the responsible party, the responsible party's refusal to provide a
written assertion requires the practitioner to disclose that refusal in the practitioner's report and restrict the use of the report to the engaging party. In an
agreed-upon procedures engagement, the responsible party's refusal to provide
a written assertion requires the practitioner to disclose that refusal in the practitioner's report.

Risk Assessment in Examination Engagements

SSAE No. 18 incorporates a risk assessment model in examination engagements. In examination engagements, the practitioner is required to obtain an
understanding of the subject matter that is sufficient to enable the practitioner

to identify and assess the risks of material misstatement in the subject matter and provide a basis for designing and performing procedures to respond to the assessed risks.

Incorporates Certain Requirements in Auditing Standards

SSAE No. 18 incorporates a number of detailed requirements that are similar to those contained in the Statements on Auditing Standards (SASs), such as the requirement to obtain a written engagement letter and to request written representations. SSAE No. 18 includes these requirements based on the ASB's belief that a service that results in a level of assurance similar to that obtained in an audit or review of historical financial statements should generally consist of similar requirements.

Separate Discussion of Review Engagements

SSAE No. 18 separates the detailed procedural and reporting requirements for review engagements from their counterparts for examination engagements. The resulting guidance more clearly differentiates the two services.

Convergence

It is the ASB's general strategy to converge its standards with those of the International Auditing and Assurance Standards Board (IAASB). Accordingly, the foundation for AT-C section 105, 205, and 210 is International Standard on Assurance Engagements (ISAE) 3000 (Revised), *Assurance Engagements Other Than Audits or Reviews of Historical Financial Information*. Many of the paragraphs in SSAE No. 18 have been converged with the related paragraphs in ISAE 3000 (Revised), with certain changes made to reflect U.S. professional standards. Other content included in this statement is derived from the extant SSAEs. The ASB decided not to adopt certain provisions of ISAE 3000 (Revised); for example, a practitioner is not permitted to issue an examination or review report if the practitioner has not obtained a written assertion from the responsible party, except when the engaging party is not the responsible party. In the ISAE, an assertion (or representation about the subject matter against the criteria) is not required in order for the practitioner to report.

ISAE 3402, *Assurance Reports on Controls at a Service Organization*, is the IAASB's assurance standard that addresses reporting on controls at a service organization. Appendix F, "*Comparison of Requirements in AT-C Section 320, Reporting On an Examination of Controls at a Service Organization Relevant to User Entities' Internal Control Over Financial Reporting, with Requirements of International Standard on Assurance Engagements 3402,* Assurance Reports on Controls at a Service Organization," of this guide highlights substantive differences between AT-C section 320 and ISAE 3402, and appendix G, "*Illustrative Service Auditor's Report When Reporting Under Both AT-C Section 320, Reporting on an Examination of Controls at a Service Organization Relevant to User Entities' Internal Control Over Financial Reporting, and ISAE 3402,* Assurance Reports on Controls at a Service Organization" contains an illustrative service auditor's report that may be used when a practitioner is reporting under both AT-C section 320 and ISAE 3402.

Changes From AT Section 801, *Reporting on Controls at a Service Organization*, to AT-C Section 320

Prior to the issuance of SSAE No. 18, the requirements and application guidance for service auditors were codified in AT section 801, *Reporting on Controls at a Service Organization* (AICPA, *Professional Standards*). In SSAE No. 18, the requirements and application guidance for service auditors are codified in AT-C section 320. AT-C section 320 includes the following changes from AT section 801:

- Paragraph .08 of AT-C section 320 revises the definition of *complementary user entity controls* to indicate that such controls are limited to controls that are necessary to achieve the control objectives stated in management's description of the service organization's system. The definition of complementary user entity controls in AT section 801 includes user entity controls that are necessary to achieve the control objectives stated in management's description of the system as well as those that are not.

- Paragraph .08 of AT-C section 320 introduces the term *complementary subservice organization controls* and defines that term. This term replaces the term *controls at a subservice organization* and its definition.

- Paragraph .08 of AT-C section 320 deletes the qualifier "in all material respects" from the description of management's assertion in the definitions of *Management's description of a service organization's system and a service auditor's report on that description and on the suitability of the design and operating effectiveness of controls* and *Management's description of a service organization's system and a service auditor's report on that description and on the suitability of the design of controls*.

- Paragraph .23 of AT-C section 320 adds a requirement for the service auditor to read the reports of the internal audit function and regulatory examinations that relate to the services provided to user entities and the scope of the engagement.

- If the application of complementary subservice organization controls is necessary for the service organization to achieve the related control objectives stated in management's description of the service organization's system, paragraphs .40*l*v–.41*l*iv of AT-C section 320 require the service auditor to add a statement to that effect in the service auditor's opinion.

- The elements of the service auditor's report in paragraphs .40–.41 of AT-C section 320 and the illustrative service auditor's report in paragraph .A75 of AT-C section 320 are revised to conform with the requirements for an examination report in AT-C section 205.

- Paragraph .A18 of AT-C section 320 clarifies that management's assertion may be attached to management's description of the service organization's system or may be included in the description if it is clearly segregated from the description.

- Paragraph .A52 of AT-C section 320 provides examples of information produced by the service organization that is commonly used by the service auditor.

- Paragraph .A62 of AT-C section 320 adds application guidance indicating that the service auditor may include in the description of tests of controls and results the procedures the service auditor performed to verify the completeness and accuracy of information provided by the service organization.

- AT-C section 320, unlike AT section 801 does not contain most of the requirements and application guidance on using the work of the internal audit function because under the restructured attestation standards, the requirements and application guidance on this topic are in AT-C section 205.

Examinations of System and Organization Controls: SOC Suite of Services

In 2017, the AICPA introduced the term *system and organization controls* (SOC) to refer to the suite of services practitioners may provide in connection with system-level controls of a service organization and system or entity-level controls of other organizations. Formerly, SOC referred to *service organization control*. By redefining that acronym, the AICPA enables the introduction of new internal control examinations that may be performed (*a*) for other types of organizations, in addition to service organizations and (*b*) on either system-level or entity-level controls of such organizations. The following are designations for four such examinations in the SOC suite of services and the source of the guidance for performing and reporting on each:

- *SOC 1®—SOC for Service Organizations: ICFR.* The performance and reporting requirements for an examination of controls at a service organization that are likely to be relevant to user entities' internal control over financial reporting are found in AT-C section 320. AICPA Guide *Reporting on an Examination of Controls at a Service Organization Relevant to User Entities' Internal Control Over Financial Reporting (SOC 1®)* contains application guidance for practitioners.

- *SOC 2®—SOC for Service Organizations: Trust Services Criteria.* The performance and reporting requirements for an examination of controls at a service organization relevant to security, availability, processing integrity, confidentiality, and privacy are found in AT-C section 205. AICPA Guide *Reporting on Controls at a Service Organization Relevant to Security, Availability, Processing Integrity, Confidentiality, or Privacy (SOC 2®)* contains application guidance for practitioners.

- *SOC 3®—SOC for Service Organizations: Trust Services Criteria for General Use Report.* The performance and reporting requirements for an examination of controls at a service organization relevant to security, availability, processing integrity, confidentiality, and privacy resulting in a general use report are found in AT-C section 205. AICPA Guide *Reporting on Controls at a Service Organization Relevant to Security, Availability, Processing Integrity, Confidentiality, or Privacy (SOC 2®)* discusses reporting on such examinations.

- *SOC for Cybersecurity.* The performance and reporting requirements for an examination of an entity's cybersecurity risk management program and related controls are found in AT-C section 205. AICPA Guide *Reporting on an Entity's Cybersecurity Risk Management Program and Controls* contains application guidance for practitioners.

In 2018, the AICPA plans to introduce a new examination service and attestation guide related to SOC for vendor supply chains. The guide will provide application guidance to practitioners engaged to examine and report on system-level controls in vendor supply chains. The purpose of such an examination is to enable entities to better understand and manage external risks, including cybersecurity risk, related to their vendors and distribution networks.

Guidance Considered in This Edition

This edition of the guide has been modified by AICPA staff to include certain changes necessary due to the issuance of authoritative guidance since the guide was originally issued and other revisions as deemed appropriate. Relevant guidance issued through January 1, 2017, has been considered in the development of this edition of the guide.

In particular, this guide has been updated to reflect SSAE No. 18. The changes made to this edition of the guide are pervasive.

This guide does not include all attestation requirements that may be applicable to the types of engagements covered by this guide. This guide is intended to be used in conjunction with all applicable sources of relevant guidance. In determining the applicability of recently issued guidance, the effective date of the guidance should also be considered.

Applicability of Quality Control Standards

QC section 10, *A Firm's System of Quality Control* (AICPA, *Professional Standards*), addresses a CPA firm's responsibilities for its system of quality control for its accounting and auditing practice.[5] A system of quality control consists of policies that a firm establishes and maintains to provide it with reasonable assurance that the firm and its personnel comply with professional standards, as well as applicable legal and regulatory requirements. The policies also provide the firm with reasonable assurance that reports issued by the firm are appropriate in the circumstances.

QC section 10 applies to all CPA firms with respect to engagements in their accounting and auditing practice. In paragraph .06 of QC section 10, an accounting and auditing practice is defined as "a practice that performs engagements

---

[5] Paragraph .13 of QC section 10, *A Firm's System of Quality Control* (AICPA, *Professional Standards*), defines an *accounting and auditing practice* as

   a practice that performs engagements covered by this section, which are audit, attestation, compilation, review, and any other services for which standards have been promulgated by the AICPA Auditing Standards Board (ASB) or the AICPA Accounting and Review Services Committee (ARSC) under the "General Standards Rule" (ET sec.1.300.001) or the "Compliance With Standards Rule" (ET sec. 1.310.001) of the AICPA Code of Professional Conduct. Although standards for other engagements may be promulgated by other AICPA technical committees, engagements performed in accordance with those standards are not encompassed in the definition of an *accounting and auditing practice.*

covered by this section, which are audit, attestation, compilation, review, and any other services for which standards have been promulgated by the ASB or the AICPA Accounting and Review Services Committee under the "General Standards Rule" (ET sec.1.300.001) or the "Compliance With Standards Rule" (ET sec. 1.310.001) of the AICPA Code of Professional Conduct. Although standards for other engagements may be promulgated by other AICPA technical committees, engagements performed in accordance with those standards are not encompassed in the definition of an *accounting and auditing practice*."

In addition to the provisions of QC section 10, readers should be aware of other sections within AICPA *Professional Standards* that address quality control considerations, including the following provisions that address engagement-level quality control matters for various types of engagements that an accounting and auditing practice might perform:

- AT-C section 105, *Concepts Common to All Attestation Engagements*

- AU-C section 220, *Quality Control for an Engagement Conducted in Accordance With Generally Accepted Auditing Standards* (AICPA, *Professional Standards*)

- AR-C section 60, *General Principles for Engagements Performed in Accordance With Statements on Standards for Accounting and Review Services* (AICPA, *Professional Standards*)

Paragraphs .32–.33 of AT-C section 105 address the practitioner's specific responsibilities regarding quality control procedures for an attestation engagement. When applicable, paragraph .42 of AT-C section 105 addresses the responsibilities of the engagement quality control reviewer.

AU-C section 220 addresses the auditor's specific responsibilities regarding quality control procedures for an audit of financial statements. When applicable, it also addresses the responsibilities of the engagement quality control reviewer.

Paragraphs .19–.23 of AR-C section 60 address engagement level quality control in an engagement performed in accordance with Statements on Standards for Accounting and Review Services.

Because of the importance of engagement quality, we have added a new appendix, appendix H, *Overview of Statements on Quality Control Standards*, of this guide. Appendix H summarizes key aspects of the quality control standards. This summarization should be read in conjunction with AICPA QC section 10, AU-C section 220, AT-C section 105, AR-C section 60, and the quality control standards issued by the PCAOB, as applicable.

AICPA.org Website

The AICPA encourages you to visit its website at www.aicpa.org and the Financial Reporting Center at www.aicpa.org/FRC. The Financial Reporting Center supports members in the execution of high-quality financial reporting. Whether you are a financial statement preparer or a member in public practice, this center provides exclusive member-only resources for the entire financial reporting process and provides timely and relevant news, guidance, and examples in areas including accounting, preparing financial statements, and performing compilation, review, audit, attest, or assurance and advisory engagements. Certain content on the AICPA's websites referenced in this guide may be restricted to AICPA members only.

Recognition

Auditing Standards Board
(2016–2017)

Michael J. Santay, *Chair*	Alan Long
Gerry Boaz	Richard Miller
Dora Burzenski	Daniel D. Montgomery
Joseph Cascio	Steven Morrison
Lawrence Gill	Richard N. Reisig
Steven M. Glover	Catherine M. Schweigel
Gaylen Hansen	Daniel J. Hevia
Tracey Harding	Jere G. Shawver
Ilene Kassman	Chad Singletary

Service Organizations Task Force

Joseph G. Griffin, *Chair*	James R. Merrill
Robert F. Dacey	David L. Palmer
Chris K. Halterman	Kirt Seale
Craig P. Linnell	Sheryl K. Skolnik
Suzanne K. Nersessian	

AICPA Staff

Charles E. Landes *Vice President Professional Standards and Services*	Judith M. Sherinsky *Senior Technical Manager Audit and Attest Standards*

TABLE OF CONTENTS

Chapter 1

Introduction and Background

> This chapter provides examples of service organizations, describes how a service organization's controls may affect a user entity's internal control over financial reporting, and identifies other engagements performed under Statements on Standards for Attestation Engagements that involve reporting on controls.

1.01 Many entities outsource aspects of their business activities to organizations that provide services ranging from performing a specific task under the direction of the entity to replacing entire business units or functions of the entity. Many of the services provided by such organizations are integral to their customers' business operations. However, not all of those services are relevant to their customers' internal control over financial reporting and, therefore, to an audit of financial statements.

1.02 AT-C section 320, *Reporting on an Examination of Controls at a Service Organization Relevant to User Entities' Internal Control Over Financial Reporting* (AICPA, *Professional Standards*), uses the term *service organization* to refer to an entity to which services are outsourced. AT-C section 320 defines a service organization as "an organization or segment of an organization that provides services to user entities, which are likely to be relevant to those user entities' internal control over financial reporting." The entities that use the services of a service organization are termed *user entities*.

1.03 Services performed by service organizations and controls related to these services may affect a user entity's internal control over financial reporting. When this situation occurs, an auditor performing an audit of a user entity's financial statements (a user auditor) is required to perform risk assessment procedures to obtain an understanding of how the user entity uses the services of a service organization.

1.04 An example of the service organizations addressed by AT-C section 320 and this guide is a health insurance company that processes medical claims for other companies that have self-insured health plans. When the medical claims processing function is outsourced, the participants in the self-insured health plan are instructed to submit their claims directly to the medical claims processor. The medical claims processor processes the claims for the self-insured health plans based on rules established by the companies with the self-insured health plans, for example, rules related to eligibility and the amount to be paid for each service. The medical claims processor provides claims data to the companies that have self-insured health plans, such as the cost of claims paid during the period under examination and the cost of claims incurred during the examination period but not recorded until after the examination period. The self-insured companies use this data to record their claims expense and the related liability. That information flows through to the self-insured companies' financial statements. Controls at the claims processor will affect the quality of the data provided to the self-insured health plans. Therefore, controls at the service organization (medical claims processor) are relevant to user entities' (companies with a self-insured health plan) internal control over financial reporting.

1.05 The following are some additional examples of service organizations that perform functions that are relevant to user entities' internal control over financial reporting:

- *Trust departments of banks.* The trust department of a bank may serve as custodian of an employee benefit plan's assets, maintain records of each participant's account, allocate investment income to the participants based on a formula in the trust agreement, and make payments to the participants. If an employee benefit plan engages a service organization to perform some or all of these tasks, the services provided by the service organization generate information that is included in the plan's financial statements.

- *Custodians for investment companies.* Custodians for investment companies are responsible for the receipt, delivery, and safekeeping of an investment company's portfolio securities; the receipt and disbursement of cash resulting from transactions in these securities; and the maintenance of records of the securities held for the investment company. The custodian may also perform other services for the investment company, such as collecting dividend and interest income and distributing that income to the investment company. The custodian is a service organization to the investment company.

- *Mortgage servicers or depository institutions that service loans for others.* Investor entities may purchase mortgage loans or participation interests in such loans from thrifts, banks, or mortgage companies. These loans become assets of the investor entities, and the sellers may continue to service the loans. Mortgage servicing activities generally include collecting mortgage payments from borrowers, conducting collection and foreclosure activities, maintaining escrow accounts for the payment of property taxes and insurance, paying taxing authorities and insurance companies as payments become due, remitting monies to investors (user entities), and reporting data concerning the mortgage to user entities. The user entities may have little or no contact with the mortgage servicer other than receiving the monthly payments and reports from the mortgage servicer. The user entities record transactions related to the underlying mortgage loans based on data provided by the mortgage servicer.

- *Application service providers (ASPs).* ASPs provide packaged software applications and a technology environment that enables customers to process financial and operational transactions. An ASP may specialize in providing a particular software package solution to its users, may perform business processes for user entities that the user entities had traditionally performed themselves, or may provide some combination of these services. As such, an ASP may be a service organization if it provides services that are part of the user entity's information system.

- *Regional transmission organizations (RTOs).* These are entities in the electric utility industry (also referred to as independent system operators) that are responsible for the operation of a centrally dispatched electric system or wholesale electric market. They are also responsible for initiating, recording, billing, settling, and reporting transactions, as well as collecting and remitting cash from participants based on the transmission tariff or other governing rules. These services may be part of a participant's information system, therefore making the RTO a service organization.

1.06 Some service organizations provide services and implement controls that are relevant to subject matter other than user entities' internal control over financial reporting. Paragraph .04 of AT-C section 320 indicates that, although AT-C section 320 focuses on controls at service organizations likely to be relevant to user entities' internal control over financial reporting, the guidance in AT-C section 320 may also be helpful to a practitioner performing an engagement under AT-C section 205, *Examination Engagements* (AICPA, *Professional Standards*), to report on controls at a service organization other than those that are likely to be relevant to user entities' internal control over financial reporting. An example of such an engagement is an examination of controls over the security, availability, or processing integrity of a system or the confidentiality or privacy of the information processed by the system performed under AT-C section 205 and the AICPA Guide *Reporting on Controls at a Service Organization Relevant to Security, Availability, Processing Integrity, Confidentiality, or Privacy (SOC 2®)*. Paragraph 1.09 of this guide contains a table that provides examples of engagements to report on controls other than those relevant to user entities' internal control over financial reporting and the professional standard or interpretive guidance that addresses or provides a framework for each engagement.

1.07 AU-C section 402, *Audit Considerations Relating to an Entity Using a Service Organization* (AICPA, *Professional Standards*), addresses the user auditor's responsibility for obtaining sufficient appropriate audit evidence in an audit of the financial statements of a user entity that uses one or more service organizations. User auditors should be aware that paragraph .05 of AU-C section 402 indicates that AU-C section 402 does not apply to the following:

- Services that are limited to processing an entity's transactions that are specifically authorized by the entity, such as the processing of checking account transactions by a bank or the processing of securities transactions by a broker (that is, when the user entity retains responsibility for authorizing the transactions and maintaining the related accountability)

- The audit of transactions arising from an entity that holds a proprietary financial interest in another entity, such as a partnership, corporation, or joint venture, when the partnership, corporation, or joint venture performs no processing on behalf of the entity

1.08 In addition to controls that affect user entity's internal control over financial reporting, a service organization implements controls that are relevant to its own internal control over financial reporting, not to the services it provides to user entities. This guide focuses only on those controls at service organizations that are likely to be relevant to user entities' internal control over financial reporting, whether or not they may be relevant to the service organization's own financial reporting objectives.

©2017, AICPA   AAG-ASO 1.08

Other Types of Internal Control Engagements

1.09 Many attestation engagements that involve reporting on controls or internal control are not performed under AT-C section 320. Table 1-1 is intended to assist practitioners in determining the applicable attestation standard or interpretive guidance to be used when reporting on controls in a variety of circumstances.

Table 1-1

Determining the Applicable Attestation Standard or Interpretive Guidance When Reporting on Controls

Nature of the Engagement	Professional Standard or Other Guidance	Restrictions on the Use of the Report

Reporting on controls at a service organization relevant to user entities' internal control over financial reporting:
 	
• Controls were not designed by the service organization, and
 	
• Management of the service organization
 	
  — will not provide an assertion regarding the suitability of the design of the controls
 	
  — will provide an assertion regarding the fairness of the presentation of the description and the operating effectiveness of the controls
	Report on the fairness of the presentation of the description under AT-C section 205, *Examination Engagements* (AICPA, *Professional Standards*), using the description criteria in paragraph .15 of AT-C section 320, *Reporting on an Examination of Controls at a Service Organization Relevant to User Entities' Internal Control Over Financial Reporting* (AICPA, *Professional Standards*), and adapting the relevant requirements and guidance therein.	Use of this report is restricted to management of the service organization, user entities, and the auditors of the user entities' financial statements.

Determining the Applicable Attestation Standard or Interpretive Guidance When Reporting on Controls—*continued*

Nature of the Engagement	Professional Standard or Other Guidance	Restrictions on the Use of the Report
This examination report includes management's description of the service organization's system[1] and a description of the service auditor's tests of controls and results.	Report on an examination of the operating effectiveness of the controls under AT-C section 205 or	AT-C section 205 Use of this report is restricted to management of the service organization, user entities, and the auditors of the user entities' financial statements.
The agreed-upon procedures report includes a description of the agreed-upon procedures performed by the practitioner and the practitioner's findings.	Report on the agreed-upon procedures performed under AT-C section 215, *Agreed-Upon Procedures Engagements* (AICPA, *Professional Standards*).	AT-C section 215 Use of this report is restricted to the specified parties that agreed upon the sufficiency of the procedures for their purposes.
Reporting on controls at a service organization relevant to user entities' internal control over financial reporting: • Controls were not designed by the service organization and	Report on the fairness of the presentation of the description of the service organization's system, the suitability of the design of the controls, and in a type 2 report,[2] the operating effectiveness of the controls under AT-C section 320	Use of this report is restricted to management of the service organization, user entities, and the auditors of the user entities' financial statements.

(continued)

---

[1] AT-C section 320, *Reporting on an Examination of Controls at a Service Organization Relevant to User Entities' Internal Control Over Financial Reporting* (AICPA, *Professional Standards*), defines the term *service organization's system* as

> The policies and procedures designed, implemented, and documented by management of the service organization to provide user entities with the services covered by the service auditor's report. Management's description of the service organization's system identifies the services covered, the period to which the description relates (or in the case of a type 1 report, the date to which the description relates), the control objectives specified by management or an outside party, the party specifying the control objectives (if not specified by management), and the related controls.

[2] See paragraph 2.12 of this guide for a definition of the term *Management's description of a service organization's system and a service auditor's report on that description and on the suitability of the design and operating effectiveness of controls*, which is referred to as a *type 2 report*.

Determining the Applicable Attestation Standard or Interpretive Guidance When Reporting on Controls—*continued*

Nature of the Engagement	Professional Standard or Other Guidance	Restrictions on the Use of the Report
• Management of the service organization will provide an assertion regarding the suitability of the design of the controls (in addition to its assertion regarding the fairness of the presentation of the description of the service organization's system and the operating effectiveness of the controls).		
Reporting on controls at a service organization relevant to security availability, processing integrity, confidentiality, or privacy This report includes management's description of the service organization's system, and in a type 2 report, includes a description of service auditor's tests of controls and results (SOC 2® engagement)	Report on the fairness of the presentation of the description of the service organization's system; the suitability of the design of the controls at a service organization relevant to security, availability, processing integrity, confidentiality, or privacy; and in a type 2 report, the operating effectiveness of those controls under AT-C section 205 and the AICPA Guide *Reporting on Controls at a Service Organization Relevant to Security, Availability, Processing Integrity, Confidentiality, or Privacy (SOC 2®)*	Use of this report is restricted to parties that are knowledgeable about • the nature of the service provided by the service organization. • how the service organization's system interacts with user entities, subservice organizations, and other parties. • internal control and its limitations. • the criteria and how controls address those criteria. • complementary user entity controls and how they interact with related controls at the service organization.

Determining the Applicable Attestation Standard or Interpretive Guidance When Reporting on Controls—*continued*

Nature of the Engagement	Professional Standard or Other Guidance	Restrictions on the Use of the Report
Reporting on controls at a service organization relevant to security, availability, processing integrity, confidentiality, or privacy. The examination report does not include a description of the service organization's system or a description of the practitioner's tests of controls and results (SOC 3® engagement)	Report on whether the entity has maintained effective controls over its system with respect to security, availability, processing integrity, confidentiality, or privacy under AT-C section 205 and TSP section 100, *Trust Services Principles and Criteria for Security, Availability, Processing Integrity, Confidentiality, and Privacy* (AICPA, *Trust Services Principles and Criteria*)	This is a general-use report.[3]
Reporting on a service provider's controls to achieve compliance control objectives relevant to SEC Rule 38a-1, "Compliance Procedures and Practices of Certain Investment Companies,"[4] and SEC Rule 206(4)-7, "Compliance Procedures and Practices"[5]		

(continued)

---

[3] The term *general use* refers to reports for which use is not restricted to specified parties.

[4] Code of Federal Regulations (CFR), Title 17, Section 270.38a-1.

[5] 17 CFR 275.206(4)-7.

Determining the Applicable Attestation Standard or Interpretive Guidance When Reporting on Controls—*continued*

Nature of the Engagement	Professional Standard or Other Guidance	Restrictions on the Use of the Report
Reporting on the suitability of the design and operating effectiveness of a service provider's controls over compliance that may affect user entities' compliance This examination report does not include a description of the service organization's system or a description of the practitioner's tests of controls and results.	Report under AT-C section 205 and Statement of Position (SOP) 07-2, *Attestation Engagements That Address Specified Compliance Control Objectives and Related Controls at Entities that Provide Services to Investment Companies, Investment Advisers, or Other Service Providers* (AICPA, *Professional Standards*, AUD section 40)	Use of this report is restricted to chief compliance officers, management, boards of directors, and independent auditors of the service provider and of the entities that use the services of the service provider.
Performing agreed-upon procedures as referred to in paragraph .05 of AT-C section 320		
Performing and reporting on the results of agreed-upon procedures related to the controls of a service organization or to transactions or balances of a user entity maintained by a service organization This agreed-upon procedures report does not include a description of the service organization's system. It does include a description of the agreed-upon procedures performed by the practitioner and the practitioner's findings.	Report under AT-C section 215	Use of this report is restricted to the specified parties that agreed upon the sufficiency of the procedures for their purposes.

Determining the Applicable Attestation Standard or Interpretive Guidance When Reporting on Controls—*continued*

Nature of the Engagement	Professional Standard or Other Guidance	Restrictions on the Use of the Report
Reporting on controls over compliance with laws and regulations		
Reporting on the effectiveness of an entity's internal control over compliance with the requirements of specified laws, regulations, rules, contracts, or grants. This examination report does not include a description of the service organization's system or a description of the practitioner's tests of controls and results.	Report under AT-C section 205	Use of this report is restricted in the following circumstances: *a.* The practitioner determines that the criteria used to evaluate the subject matter are appropriate only for a limited number of parties who either participated in their establishment or can be presumed to have an adequate understanding of the criteria. *b.* The criteria used to evaluate the subject matter are available only to specified parties. *c.* The engaging party is not the responsible party, and the responsible party does not provide the written representations required by paragraph .50 of AT-C section 205, but does provide oral responses to the practitioner's inquiries about the matters in paragraph .50 of AT-C section 205, as provided for in paragraphs .51 and .56*a* of AT-C section 205. In this case, the use of the practitioner's report should be restricted to the engaging party.

(continued)

Determining the Applicable Attestation Standard or Interpretive Guidance When Reporting on Controls—*continued*

Nature of the Engagement	Professional Standard or Other Guidance	Restrictions on the Use of the Report
Performing and reporting on the results of applying agreed-upon procedures related to an entity's internal control over compliance with specified requirements	Report under the applicable paragraphs of AT-C section 315, *Compliance Attestation* (AICPA, *Professional Standards*)	Use of this report is restricted to the specified parties that agreed upon the sufficiency of the procedures for their purposes.
Reporting on an entity's internal control over financial reporting in an integrated audit		
Reporting on the design and operating effectiveness of an entity's internal control over financial reporting that is integrated with an audit of financial statements	Report under AU-C section 940, *An Audit of Internal Control Over Financial Reporting That Is Integrated With an Audit of Financial Statements* (AICPA, *Professional Standards*)	This is a general-use report.
This audit report does not include a description of the entity's system of internal control or a description of the auditor's tests of controls and results.		

Chapter 2

Understanding How a User Auditor Uses a Type 1 or Type 2 Report

> This chapter is intended to provide service auditors with an understanding of how a user auditor uses a type 1 or type 2 report in auditing the financial statements of a user entity. Knowing how a user auditor uses such reports helps the service auditor in evaluating management's description of the service organization's system and in determining whether the service organization's control objectives are reasonable in the circumstances. In addition, this chapter may aid user auditors in understanding how to use a given type 1 or type 2 report in an audit of a user entity's financial statements.

Obtaining an Understanding of the Entity and Its Environment, Including the Entity's Internal Control When the Entity Uses a Service Organization

2.01 AU-C section 315, *Understanding the Entity and Its Environment and Assessing the Risks of Material Misstatement*, and AU-C section 330, *Performing Audit Procedures in Response to Assessed Risks and Evaluating the Audit Evidence Obtained* (AICPA, *Professional Standards*), require the auditor to obtain an understanding of the entity being audited, including its internal control relevant to the audit, sufficient to identify and assess the risks of material misstatement and design and perform further audit procedures responsive to those risks. AU-C section 402, *Audit Considerations Related to an Entity Using a Service Organization* (AICPA, *Professional Standards*), expands on how a user auditor applies AU-C sections 315 and 330 when auditing the financial statements of an entity that uses one or more service organizations.

2.02 Paragraph .03 of AU-C section 402 indicates that services provided by a service organization are relevant to an audit of a user entity's financial statements when those services and the controls over them affect the user entity's information system, including related processes relevant to financial reporting. Paragraph .19 of AU-C section 315 states that an auditor should obtain an understanding of the information system, including the related business processes relevant to financial reporting, including the following areas:

    a. The classes of transactions in the user entity's operations that are significant to the user entity's financial statements

    b. The procedures within both IT and manual systems, by which the user entity's transactions are initiated, authorized, recorded, processed, corrected as necessary, transferred to the general ledger, and reported in the financial statements

    c. The related accounting records, supporting information, and specific accounts in the user entity's financial statements that are used to initiate, authorize, record, process, and report the user entity's transactions. This includes the correction of incorrect information and how information is transferred to the general ledger; the records may be in either manual or electronic form

   d. How the user entity's information system captures events and conditions, other than transactions, that are significant to the financial statements

   e. The financial reporting process used to prepare the user entity's financial statements, including significant accounting estimates and disclosures

   f. Controls surrounding journal entries, including nonstandard journal entries used to record nonrecurring, unusual transactions, or adjustments

If a service organization's services affect any of the areas listed in items (*a*)–(*f*), those services are part of the user entity's information system.

2.03 Other controls at a service organization may be relevant to the audit, such as controls over the safeguarding of assets. However, services that do not affect the areas described in paragraph 2.02 are not part of a user entity's information system and service providers that provide such services would not be considered service organizations for the purpose of AT-C section 320, *Reporting on an Examination of Controls at a Service Organization Relevant to User Entities' Internal Control Over Financial Reporting* (AICPA, *Professional Standards*).

Service Organization Services to Which AU-C Section 402 Does Not Apply

2.04 Paragraph .05 of AU-C section 402 indicates that the section does not apply to services provided by a service organization that are limited to processing an entity's transactions that are specifically authorized by the entity, such as the processing of checking account transactions by a bank or the processing of securities transactions by a broker (that is, when the user entity retains responsibility for authorizing the transactions and maintaining the related accountability). AU-C section 402 also does not apply to the audit of transactions arising from an entity that holds a proprietary financial interest in another entity, such as a partnership, corporation, or joint venture, when the partnership, corporation, or joint venture performs no processing on behalf of the entity.

Understanding Whether Controls at a Service Organization Affect a User Entity's Internal Control

2.05 When a user entity uses a service organization, transactions that affect the user entity are subjected to policies and procedures (controls) that are, at least in part, physically and operationally separate from the user entity. A user auditor may need to understand controls at the service organization in order to understand the entity being audited, including its internal control relevant to the audit.

2.06 When auditing an entity that uses one or more service organizations, the user auditor is required by AU-C section 402 to obtain an understanding of how the user entity uses the services of a service organization in the user entity's operations, including the following:

a. The nature of the services provided by the service organization and the significance of those services to the user entity, including their effect on the user entity's internal control

b. The nature and materiality of the transactions processed or accounts or financial reporting processes affected by the service organization

c. The degree of interaction between the activities of the service organization and those of the user entity

d. The nature of the relationship between the user entity and the service organization, including the relevant contractual terms for the activities undertaken by the service organization

2.07 Paragraph .A1 of AU-C section 402 indicates that information about the nature of the services provided by a service organization may be available from a wide variety of sources including user manuals; system overviews; technical manuals; the contract or service level agreement between the user entity and the service organization; reports by service organizations, internal auditors, or regulatory authorities on controls at the service organization; and reports by the service auditor, if available.

2.08 When obtaining an understanding of internal control relevant to the audit, the user auditor should evaluate the design and implementation of relevant controls at the user entity that relate to the services provided by the service organization, including those that are applied to the transactions processed by the service organization. Interaction between a service organization and a user entity relates to the extent to which a user entity is able to monitor the activities of the service organization and implement controls over those activities. For example, when a user entity initiates transactions and the service organization executes, processes, and records those transactions, a high degree of interaction exists between the activities at the user entity and those at the service organization. In these circumstances, the user entity could implement effective controls over those transactions. For example, an entity that uses a payroll processing service organization could establish controls over the submission and receipt of information from the service organization, such as comparing the data submitted to the service organization with reports received from the service organization after the data has been processed, or recalculating a sample of the payroll amounts for clerical accuracy and reviewing the amount of the payroll for reasonableness. These controls may be tested by the user auditor and may enable the user auditor to conclude that the user entity's controls are operating effectively for some or all of the related assertions, regardless of the controls in place at the service organization. In these situations, the user auditor is not likely to request a service auditor's report or other information from the service organization.

2.09 In contrast, when a service organization initiates, executes, and does the processing and recording of the user entity's transactions, a lower degree of interaction exists, and it may not be practicable or possible for the user entity to implement effective controls for those transactions. An example would be a user entity that authorizes a broker-dealer to purchase and sell securities for it, based on a trust agreement (a discretionary account). In this case, the service organization is initiating the transactions and also maintaining the accountability for the transactions. The user entity records all of its securities transactions based on the monthly statements or daily advices provided by the broker-dealer.

2.10 User auditors should determine whether they have obtained an understanding of the nature and significance of the services provided by the service organization and their effect on the user entity's internal control relevant to the audit that is sufficient to provide a basis for the identification and assessment of risks of material misstatement.

2.11 If the user auditor is unable to obtain a sufficient understanding of these matters from the user entity, the user auditor should obtain that understanding from one or more of the following procedures:

a. Obtaining and reading a type 1 or type 2 report on the service organization's system, if available

b. Contacting the service organization, through the user entity, to obtain specific information

c. Visiting the service organization and performing procedures that will provide the necessary information about the relevant controls at the service organization

d. Using another auditor to perform procedures that will provide the necessary information about the relevant controls at the service organization

Generally, a service organization will want to minimize the number of user auditors or other auditors performing their own tests of controls at the service organization. However, allowing user auditors or other auditors to conduct tests of controls at the service organization may be a practical option if the service organization has few user entities or conducts a number of specific procedures and controls for each user entity.

Types of Service Auditor's Reports

2.12 Paragraph .08 of AT-C section 320 defines the following two types of reports:

Management's description of a service organization's system and a service auditor's report on that description and on the suitability of the design of controls (referred to in this section as a *type 1 report*). A service auditor's report that comprises the following:

a. Management's description of the service organization's system

b. A written assertion by management of the service organization about whether, based on the criteria

i. management's description of the service organization's system fairly presents the service organization's system that was designed and implemented as of a specified date

ii. the controls related to the control objectives stated in management's description of the service organization's system were suitably designed to achieve those control objectives as of the specified date *c.* A report that expresses an opinion on the matters in *bi*–ii.[1]

Management's description of a service organization's system and a service auditor's report on that description and on the suitability of the design and operating effectiveness of controls (referred to in this section as a *type 2 report*). A service auditor's report that comprises the following:

     a. Management's description of the service organization's system

     b. A written assertion by management of the service organization about whether, based on the criteria

         i. management's description of the service organization's system fairly presents the service organization's system that was designed and implemented throughout the specified period

         ii. the controls related to the control objectives stated in management's description of the service organization's system were suitably designed throughout the specified period to achieve those control objectives

         iii. the controls related to the control objectives stated in management's description of the service organization's system operated effectively throughout the specified period to achieve those control objectives

     c. A report that

         i. expresses an opinion on the matters in *bi*–iii

         ii. includes a description of the tests of controls and the results thereof

Paragraph .08 of AT-C section 320 defines control objectives as "the aim or purpose of specified controls at the service organization" and indicates that "control objectives address the risks that controls are intended to mitigate."

User Auditor Obtains Evidence of the Operating Effectiveness of Controls at a Service Organization

2.13 The user auditor may determine that it is necessary to test controls at the service organization, either because the auditor's risk assessment includes an expectation that controls at the service organization are operating effectively or because it is not possible or practicable to obtain sufficient appropriate audit evidence from substantive procedures alone. In these circumstances, the user auditor should obtain audit evidence about the operating effectiveness of those controls from one or more of the following procedures:

     a. Obtaining and reading a type 2 report, if available

     b. Performing appropriate tests of controls at the service organization

---

[1] The term *service auditor's report* in this guide means the service auditor's letter in which he or she expresses an opinion on management's description of the service organization's system, the suitability of the design of the controls included in the description, and in a type 2 report, the operating effectiveness of the controls.

    c. Using another auditor to perform tests of controls at the service organization on behalf of the user auditor

2.14 Because a type 1 report does not include tests of the operating effectiveness of controls, a type 1 report would not meet the user auditor's needs. In practice, most user auditors will need evidence of the operating effectiveness of controls at the service organization. Accordingly, to minimize the number of visits by user auditors, especially if the service organization has a large number of user entities, a service organization would likely need to provide a type 2 report.

2.15 The user auditor should evaluate whether the period covered by a given type 2 report is appropriate for the user auditor's purposes. To provide evidence in support of the user auditor's risk assessment, the period covered by the type 2 report would need to overlap a substantial portion of the period covered by the user entity's financial statements being audited.

2.16 In evaluating the appropriateness of the period covered by the tests of controls, the user auditor keeps in mind that the shorter the period covered by a specific test and the longer the time elapsed since the performance of the test, the less evidence the test may provide. For example, a report on a nine-month testing period that covers only one or two months of the user entity's financial reporting period offers less support than a report in which the testing covers eight months of the user entity's financial reporting period. If the service auditor's testing period is completely outside the user entity's financial reporting period, the user auditor is unable to rely on such tests to conclude that the user entity's controls are operating effectively because the tests do not provide current audit period evidence of the effectiveness of the controls, unless other procedures are performed, such as those described in paragraphs .13–.14 of AU-C section 330. Based on paragraph .15 of AU-C section 330, if a user auditor plans to rely on a service organization's controls over a risk the user auditor has determined to be a significant risk, evidence of the operating effectiveness of those controls should be based on tests of those controls in the current period. Considering this, the service organization may choose to provide type 2 reports with sufficient frequency and covering sufficient periods to meet user auditor needs.

2.17 The service organization may consider the following examples when determining an appropriate test period for a type 2 report.

    Example 1. The majority of user entities have calendar year-ends. The service organization may want to provide a type 2 report for the period January 1, 20X0, to December 31, 20X0, to maximize the usefulness of the report to user entities and their auditors.

    Example 2. User entities have year-ends that span all months of the year. The service organization determines that issuing a report each quarter (or more often than annually) with tests of operating effectiveness that cover twelve months is most likely to maximize the usefulness of the report to user entities and their auditors.

2.18 Included in the criteria in paragraph .15 of AT-C section 320 for evaluating the fairness of the presentation of management's description of the service organization's system is a criterion regarding whether the description includes relevant details of changes to the service organization's system during the period covered by the description. Paragraph .29 of AT-C section 320 requires the service auditor to determine whether changes that the service auditor believes are significant have been included in management's description of the service organization's system. In addition, if superseded controls are relevant to the achievement of the control objectives stated in the description, the service auditor should, if possible, test the superseded controls before the change. The service auditor's description of tests of controls and results would describe tests of the controls and results of the tests for the period before the change and for the period after the change.

Information That Assists User Auditors in Evaluating the Effect of a Service Organization on a User Entity's Internal Control

2.19 In performing a service auditor's engagement, the following additional information may assist user auditors in evaluating the effect of the service organization on the user entities' internal control:

- Information about controls at user entities and subservice organizations that management of the service organization assumes, in the design of the service organization's system, will be implemented by user entities and subservice organizations because they are necessary to achieve the control objectives stated in management's description of the service organization's system (complementary user entity controls and complementary subservice organization controls). The criteria for a description of a service organization's system in paragraph .15*a*vii of AT-C section 320 requires that complementary user entity controls and complementary subservice organization controls be identified in the description. The user auditor should determine whether complementary user entity controls identified by the service organization are relevant in addressing the risks of material misstatement relating to the relevant assertions in the user entity's financial statements, and if so, the user auditor should obtain an understanding of whether the user entity has designed and implemented such controls. Likewise, the user auditor should determine whether complementary subservice organization controls are relevant in addressing the risks of material misstatement related to the relevant assertions in the user entity's financial statements, and if so, the user auditor should perform procedures to determine whether the subservice organization(s) have designed and implemented such controls. For example, the user entity auditor may review a SOC 1® report on the subservice organization's system to determine whether it addresses the complementary subservice organization controls.

- The cause of deviations[2] in the results of tests of controls if the service auditor has identified them. Such information may be included in the service auditor's description of tests of controls and results.

- Incidents of noncompliance with laws or regulations, fraud, or uncorrected misstatements attributable to management or other service organization personnel that are not clearly trivial and that

---

[2] In this guide, the term *exceptions* is used interchangeably with the term *deviations*.

may affect one or more user entities. If the service auditor becomes aware of such matters, the service auditor should determine their effect on management's assertion, management's description of the service organization's system, the achievement of the control objectives, and the service auditor's report. Additionally, the service auditor should determine whether this information has been communicated appropriately to affected user entities. If the information has not been so communicated and management of the service organization refuses to do so, the service auditor should take appropriate action, which may include the following:

— Obtaining legal advice about the consequences of different courses of action

— Communicating with those charged with governance of the service organization

— Disclaiming an opinion, modifying the service auditor's opinion, or describing the matter in a separate paragraph in the practitioner's report

— Communicating with third parties, for example, a regulator, when required to do so

— Withdrawing from the engagement

— Considering the nature of the user entities and how the services provided by the service organization are likely to affect them, for example, the predominant types of user entities, and whether the user entities are regulated by government agencies

— Reading contracts with user entities to gain an understanding of the service organization's contractual obligations

2.20 If a user auditor is unable to obtain sufficient appropriate audit evidence regarding the services provided by the service organization relevant to the audit of the user entity's financial statements, the user auditor should consider the effect on the user auditor's report, including considering whether to modify the opinion in the user auditor's report in accordance with AU-C section 705, *Modifications to the Opinion in the Independent Auditor's Report* (AICPA, *Professional Standards*).

Chapter 3

Planning a Service Auditor's Engagement

> This chapter discusses the responsibilities of management of the service organization and the service auditor and matters to be considered and procedures to be performed by the service auditor in planning a service auditor's engagement. It also identifies the required elements of management's description of a service organization's system and management's written assertion. This guide may not address all of the requirements and application guidance relevant to an engagement performed under AT-C section 320, *Reporting on an Examination of Controls at a Service Organization Relevant to User Entities' Internal Control Over Financial Reporting* (AICPA, *Professional Standards*); therefore, it should be read in conjunction with AT-C section 105, *Concepts Common to All Attestation Engagements*, AT-C section 205, *Examination Engagements* (AICPA, *Professional Standards*), and AT-C section 320.

Understanding the Responsibilities of Management of the Service Organization

3.01 During the engagement, management of the service organization is responsible for the following:

- Defining the scope of the engagement (paragraph 3.02)[1]

- Determining the type of engagement to be performed (a type 1 or type 2 engagement) (paragraphs 3.03–.07)

- Determining the period to be covered by the report or, in the case of a type 1 report, the specified "as of" date of the report (paragraphs 3.08–.13)

- Determining whether services provided to a service organization by other entities are likely to be relevant to user entities' internal control over financial reporting, and if so, identifying these other entities as subservice organizations (paragraphs 3.14–.18)

- Determining whether subservice organizations will be carved out or included in the description of the service organization's system (paragraphs 3.19–.23)

- Selecting the criteria to be used, stating them in the assertion, and determining that the criteria are appropriate for management's purposes (paragraph 3.24)

- Preparing the description of the service organization's system, including the completeness, accuracy, and method of presentation of the description (paragraphs 3.25–.67)

---

[1] Unless otherwise noted, the parenthetical paragraph references within this list indicate the paragraph or paragraphs of this guide where a topic is discussed.

- Specifying the control objectives; stating them in the description of the service organization's system; and if the control objectives are specified by law, regulation, or another party (for example, a user group or a professional body), identifying in the description the party specifying the control objectives (paragraphs 3.68–.76)

- Identifying the risks that threaten the achievement of the control objectives stated in the description of the service organization's system and designing, implementing, and documenting controls that are suitably designed and operating effectively to provide reasonable assurance that the control objectives stated in the description will be achieved (paragraphs 3.77–.78)

- Preparing a written assertion (including the completeness, accuracy, and method of presentation of the assertion) that accompanies management's description of the service organization's system, both of which will be provided to user entities (paragraphs 3.79–.81)

- Having a reasonable basis for management's assertion (paragraph 3.82)

- Providing the service auditor with written representations at the conclusion of the engagement (When the inclusive method[2] is used, management of the service organization and management of the subservice organization agree to provide and do provide such representations. Paragraphs 4.178–.191 of this guide discuss the service auditor's responsibility for requesting written representations; appendix B, "Illustrative Type 2 Reports—Inclusive Method, Including Illustrative Management Representation Letters," includes illustrative representation letters for management of the service organization and management of the subservice organization when the inclusive method is used; and appendix C, "Illustrative Management Representation Letters," includes representation letters for type 1 and type 2 engagements.)

- If the service auditor plans to use internal auditors to provide direct assistance, providing the service auditor with written acknowledgment that internal auditors providing direct assistance to the service auditor will be allowed to follow the service auditor's instructions, and that the service organization will not intervene in the work the internal auditors perform for the service auditor (This is discussed in paragraph 3.93 under the heading "Agreeing on the Terms of the Engagement," because such written acknowledgment is commonly included in the engagement letter.)

- Providing the service auditor with access to all information, such as records, documentation, service level agreements, and internal audit or other reports, that management is aware of and that are relevant to the description of the service organization's system and management's assertion (paragraph .25*b*iii(1) of AT-C section 105)

- Providing the service auditor with access to additional information that the service auditor may request from management for

---

[2] The term *inclusive method* is defined in paragraph 3.19 of this guide.

the purpose of the examination engagement (paragraph .25*b*iii(2) of AT-C section 205)

- Providing the service auditor with unrestricted access to personnel within the service organization from whom the service auditor determines it is necessary to obtain evidence relevant to the service auditor's engagement (paragraph .25*b*iii(3) of AT-C section 205)

- Disclosing to the service auditor the following:

  — Incidents of noncompliance with laws and regulations, fraud, or uncorrected errors attributable to management or other service organization personnel that are clearly not trivial and that may affect one or more user entities and whether such incidents have been communicated appropriately to affected user entities

  — Knowledge of any actual, suspected, or alleged intentional acts by management or the service organization's employees that could adversely affect the fairness of the presentation of management's description of the service organization's system or the completeness or achievement of the control objectives stated in the description

  — Any deficiencies in the design of controls of which management is aware

  — All instances in which controls have not operated as described

  — Any events subsequent to the period covered by management's description of the service organization's system, up to the date of the service auditor's report, that could have a significant effect on management's assertion (Appendix B includes illustrative representation letters for management of the service organization and management of the subservice organization when the inclusive method is used, and appendix C includes representation letters for type 1 and type 2 engagements. This representation is required by paragraph .50 of AT-C section 205.)

Defining the Scope of the Engagement

3.02 In defining the scope of a service auditor's engagement, management of the service organization considers which services (including the classes of transactions processed), functions performed, business units, functional areas, or applications are likely to be relevant to user entities' internal control over financial reporting. Management also considers whether the service organization has any contractual obligations to provide a type 1 or type 2 report to one or more of its user entities, including the frequency with which such a report is to be issued and the period that will be covered by the report. In the case of a recurring or existing engagement, the prior report provides a useful starting point for defining the scope of the engagement.

Determining the Type of Engagement to Be Performed

3.03 Management of a service organization is responsible for determining whether the service auditor will perform a type 1 or type 2 engagement and the period to be covered by the report (or in the case of a type 1 report, the specified as-of date). To provide a report that is likely to be useful to user entities and their auditors, management of the service organization may find the guidance for user auditors in AU-C section 402, *Audit Considerations Relating to an Entity Using a Service Organization* (AICPA, *Professional Standards*), helpful. Chapter 2, "Understanding How a User Auditor Uses a Type 1 or Type 2 Report," of this guide presents information to assist service auditors in understanding how a user auditor uses a type 1 or type 2 report in auditing the financial statements of a user entity.

3.04 Because user auditors may need evidence of the operating effectiveness of controls at a service organization, the service organization generally will choose to provide a type 2 report rather than a type 1 report. If a type 2 report is not available, user auditors may need to obtain evidence about the operating effectiveness of controls by visiting the service organization and performing tests of the controls there or requesting that another practitioner perform such tests. When a service auditor's report is not available, a greater likelihood exists that user auditors will visit the service organization to perform their own tests or will request that another practitioner perform such tests, likely increasing the demands placed on management and others at the service organization.

3.05 Typically, a type 1 engagement may be appropriate in either of the following instances:

- User entities are able to exercise effective user entity controls over the services performed by the service organization.

- The service organization is issuing a report on controls at the service organization for the first time and the service auditor is unable to perform the procedures necessary to issue a type 2 report.

3.06 A type 1 engagement enables the service organization to provide user auditors with a report on the fairness of the presentation of the description of the service organization's system and the suitability of the design of controls. Such a report is designed to meet the user auditor's needs for planning the audit of a user entity's financial statements.

3.07 In a type 1 engagement, the service auditor does not obtain assurance that the control objectives stated in management's description of the service organization's system were achieved because the service auditor's objective in a type 1 engagement does not include obtaining evidence about the operating effectiveness of controls. The discussion in this guide focuses on type 2 reports, given their predominance in practice.

Determining the Period to Be Covered by the Report

3.08 Paragraph .A49 of AT-C section 320 states that, generally, a type 2 report "is most useful to user entities and their auditors when it covers a substantial portion of the period covered by the user entity's financial statements being audited," for example, a report that covers at least nine months of the period covered by the audit of the user entity's financial statements.

3.09 To increase the likelihood that the report will be useful to user entities and their auditors, if circumstances permit, management of the service organization may wish to determine from the user entities their financial reporting periods so that management of the service organization can select a period that corresponds with the financial reporting period of the majority of its user entities.

3.10 Management and the service auditor may wish to discuss other strategies for identifying a period to be covered by the report that best meets the needs of user entities. For example, ABC Company, which is one of XYZ Service Organization's two largest user entities, has a fiscal year ending June 30, 20X2, and DEF Company, the other of the two largest user entities, has a fiscal year ending December 31, 20X2. By selecting a reporting period of January 1, 20X2, through December 31, 20X2, the service organization minimizes the usefulness of the report for ABC Company because, although ABC Company's user auditor may use the service auditor's report for the year ending December 31, 20X1, as a source of evidence for the first six months of ABC Company's financial reporting period, the service auditor's report that covers the last six months of ABC Company's financial reporting period will most likely not be available in time for the audit of ABC Company's financial statements. One strategy for the service organization to address this problem is to provide semiannual reports that cover contiguous six-month periods.

3.11 Certain circumstances may warrant a longer period than the period initially contemplated by management of the service organization. This might occur when the period initially contemplated would result in a gap between the end of the period covered by one report and the beginning of the period covered by the following report, for example, when one report covers the period January 1, 20X1, to September 30, 20X1, and the subsequent report covers the period January 1, 20X2, to September 30, 20X2. In these circumstances, the description may exclude key controls such as annual controls or significant changes in controls that occur during the gap period that are likely to be relevant to user entities' internal control over financial reporting. In such situations, the service auditor may discuss with management of the service organization the effect of the gap between the periods covered by the reports on the information needs of user entities and their auditors, and may recommend that management expand the period covered by the report to include the gap period. In some circumstances, management's refusal to expand the period could result in a scope limitation and modification of the service auditor's opinion.

3.12 Certain circumstances, such as the following, may result in a situation in which a service organization is unable to provide a type 2 report that covers a substantial portion of the period covered by its user entities' financial statements:

- The service auditor is engaged close to the date by which the report is needed and evidence of the operating effectiveness of controls cannot be obtained retroactively.

- For example, testing the control requires that the service auditor observe the control being performed.

- The service organization's system or controls have been in operation for less than a substantial portion of the period covered by the user entities' financial statements.

- Significant changes have been made to the controls and it is not practical to (a) wait to issue a report until a substantial portion of the user entities' financial reporting periods has passed or (b) issue a report that covers the system before and after the changes.

- The service organization is issuing a report on controls at the service organization for the first time.

- A new or modified law or regulation has an effective date that results in a report that covers a period that is less than a substantial portion of the period covered by the user entities' financial statements in the first year of the law or regulation's enactment.

3.13   When any of the circumstances in paragraph 3.12 exist, management of the service organization may decide to expand subsequent reporting periods to cover a substantial portion of the period covered by its user entities' financial statements.

Determining Whether Services Provided to a Service Organization by Other Entities Are Likely to Be Relevant to User Entities' Internal Control Over Financial Reporting

Determining Whether the Service Organization Uses a Subservice Organization

3.14   Paragraph .08 of AT-C section 320 defines a *subservice organization* as "a service organization used by another service organization to perform some of the services provided to user entities that are likely to be relevant to those user entities' internal control over financial reporting." In the following examples of subservice organizations, certain controls at the subservice organization are likely to be relevant to the user entities' internal control over financial reporting:

- An entity that hosts key applications used by a service organization and is responsible for general IT controls that are likely to be relevant to user entities' internal control over financial reporting, such as controls related to logical access, program changes, and computer operations

- An entity that processes a subset of the transactions that are part of the services provided by the service organization that are likely to be relevant to user entities' internal control over financial reporting, for example,

  — a claims processing entity that processes a subset of the claims processed by the service organization

  — an entity that has custody over certain types of securities (a subcustodian) that is part of the custodial services provided by the service organization

3.15   Subservice organizations may be separate entities that are external to the service organization or may be entities related to the service organization, for example, a subservice organization that is a subsidiary of the same company that owns the service organization.

3.16   During planning, management of the service organization determines whether it uses any subservice organizations as defined in paragraph .08 of AT-C section 320. As part of making that determination, management considers whether controls over the functions performed by the entity from which it has contracted services are likely to be relevant to the user entities' internal control over financial reporting.

Determining Whether an Organization That Provides Services to a Service Organization Is a Vendor or a Subservice Organization

3.17 In this guide, organizations that provide services to a service organization that are not considered subservice organizations are referred to as *vendors*. This distinction is important because, if an organization that provides services to a service organization is not a subservice organization, AT-C section 320 is not applicable. Table 3-1 presents matters to consider in determining whether an organization used by a service organization is a vendor or a subservice organization. This table does not contain a comprehensive list of matters to be considered and is presented for illustrative purposes only. In any engagement, when determining whether an organization is a vendor or a subservice organization, the service auditor should use professional judgment, based on the particular facts and circumstances of the engagement.

Table 3-1

Determining Whether an Organization That Provides Services to a Service Organization Is a Vendor or a Subservice Organization

1	2	3
What service does the organization provide to the service organization?	*Is the service provided by the organization relevant to user entities' internal control over financial reporting?*	*Is the organization a vendor or a subservice organization?*
Report printing and mailing This organization prints the service organization's electronic files containing financial reports for user entities and mails the reports to the user entities. The information in the reports is incorporated into the user entities' financial statements. The organization is responsible for controls over the completeness and accuracy of the reports.	Yes. The service provided by this organization is relevant to user entities' internal control over financial reporting because the information in the reports is incorporated into the user entities' financial statements.	Subservice organization

(continued)

Determining Whether an Organization That Provides Services to a Service Organization Is a Vendor or a Subservice Organization—*continued*

1	2	3
What service does the organization provide to the service organization?	*Is the service provided by the organization relevant to user entities' internal control over financial reporting?*	*Is the organization a vendor or a subservice organization?*
Report printing and mailing This organization prints the service organization's electronic files containing financial reports for user entities and mails the reports to the user entities. The information in the reports is incorporated into the user entities' financial statements. The organization prints and mails the statements but the service organization retains responsibility for the completeness and accuracy of the reports.	No. Because the service organization retains responsibility for controls over the completeness and accuracy of the reports, controls at this organization are not likely to be relevant to user entities' internal control over financial reporting.	Vendor
Document storage and record retention This organization picks up boxes of documents from the service organization and stores them at its facility.	No. Although this service is important to the service organization's business and enables the service organization to meet certain regulatory requirements, document storage and record retention services do not relate to user entities' internal control over financial reporting.	Vendor
Electric power This organization provides electric service to the service organization.	No. Although important for the service organization's continuing operations, the electric service does not relate to user entities' internal control over financial reporting	Vendor

Determining Whether an Organization That Provides Services to a Service Organization Is a Vendor or a Subservice Organization—*continued*

1	2	3
What service does the organization provide to the service organization?	*Is the service provided by the organization relevant to user entities' internal control over financial reporting?*	*Is the organization a vendor or a subservice organization?*
Pharmacy claims processing This organization processes pharmacy claims for a medical claims processing service organization. Pharmacy claims are a subset of all the claims the medical claims processing service organization receives. The information in the reports provided by the organization are incorporated in the financial statements of user entities that submit pharmacy claims to the medical claims processor.	Yes. The processing performed by the pharmacy claims processor is relevant to the internal control over financial reporting of user entities that submit pharmacy claims to the organization for processing.	Subservice organization
Application hosting This organization manages all of the IT systems for the service organization.	Yes. The service provided by the application hosting organization relates to user entities' internal control over financial reporting because controls at the application hosting organization are necessary for the service organization's application controls to operate effectively.	Subservice organization
Software development The service organization outsources the development of its application changes to a software development organization. This organization receives the authorized changes from	No. In this scenario the organization would be considered a vendor because the service organization's controls alone are sufficient to meet the needs of a user entity's internal control over financial reporting.	Vendor

(continued)

Determining Whether an Organization That Provides Services to a Service Organization Is a Vendor or a Subservice Organization—*continued*

1	2	3
What service does the organization provide to the service organization?	*Is the service provided by the organization relevant to user entities' internal control over financial reporting?*	*Is the organization a vendor or a subservice organization?*
the service organization, develops the changes, and sends them back to the service organization. The service organization authorizes all changes to be developed, reviews the accuracy of the changes, performs all user acceptance testing, and approves all changes prior to implementing them in production.		
Cloud-based data processing The service organization operates its Internet sales application at a cloud-based data processing entity. Although the service organization implements certain controls over the functions performed by the cloud-based data processing entity, the service organization's controls alone are not sufficient to enable the service organization to achieve the related control objectives because it relies on the effectiveness of certain controls at the cloud-based data processing entity, specifically, the IT general controls.	Yes. The services provided by the cloud-based data processing entity are relevant to user entities' internal control over financial reporting because controls at the data-processing entity are necessary for the service organization's controls to operate effectively.	Service organization

3.18 As noted in table 3-1, controls at an entity that provides services to a service organization may appear to be relevant to a user entity's internal control over financial reporting. However, if the service organization's controls alone are sufficient to meet the needs of the user entity's internal control over financial reporting (that is, achievement of the control objectives is not dependent on the entity's controls), management may conclude that the entity is not a subservice organization. In these circumstances, management of the service organization would not need to, but may, indicate in its description of the service organization's system and in management's assertion that it uses the services of another entity. Likewise, the service auditor would not be required to disclose the services provided by the other entity or refer to the other entity in the service auditor's report.

Determining Whether Subservice Organizations Will Be Carved Out or Included in the Description

3.19 Management of the service organization determines whether the functions performed by a subservice organization are likely to be relevant to user entities' internal control over financial reporting and whether to use the inclusive method or the carve-out method to present information about the services provided by the subservice organization in its description of the service organization's system. Paragraph .08 of AT-C section 320 contains the following definitions of the terms *carve-out method* and *inclusive method*:

> **Carve-out method.** Method of addressing the services provided by a subservice organization, whereby management's description of the service organization's system identifies the nature of the services performed by the subservice organization and excludes from the description and from the scope of the service auditor's engagement the subservice organization's relevant control objectives and related controls. (When using the carve-out method, controls at the subservice organization are not subject to the service auditor's examination procedures.)

> **Inclusive method.** Method of addressing the services provided by a subservice organization whereby management's description of the service organization's system includes a description of the nature of the services provided by the subservice organization as well as the subservice organization's relevant control objectives and related controls. (When using the inclusive method, controls at the subservice organization are subject to the service auditor's examination procedures.)

Factors for Management to Consider in Determining Whether Services Provided by a Subservice Organization Should Be Presented Using the Carve-Out or Inclusive Method

3.20 Although the inclusive method provides more information for user auditors than the carve-out method does, the inclusive method may not be appropriate or feasible in all circumstances. Factors that are relevant in determining which approach to use include the following:

    a. The nature and extent of the information about the subservice organization that user auditors may need

    b. The challenges entailed in implementing the inclusive method, which are described in paragraphs 3.23 and 3.53 of this guide *c.* Whether the service auditor is independent of the subservice organization (In an inclusive method engagement, the service auditor's report covers the service organization and the subservice organization, and the service auditor would need to be independent of both entities.)

    d. The availability of a type 1 or type 2 service auditor's report on the subservice organization that meets the needs of user entities[3] and their auditors

3.21 An inclusive report generally is most useful in the following circumstances:

- The services provided by the subservice organization are extensive.

- A type 1 or type 2 report that meets the needs of user entities and their auditors is not available from the subservice organization.

- Information about the subservice organization is not readily available from other sources.

3.22 The inclusive method is facilitated if the service organization and the subservice organization are related parties or if the contract between the service organization and the subservice organization provides for an inclusive description of the service organization's and subservice organization's system and report by the service auditor.

3.23 The inclusive method is frequently difficult to implement and for a number of reasons may not be feasible in certain circumstances. The approach entails extensive planning and communication between the service auditor, the service organization, and the subservice organization. Both the service organization and the subservice organization would need to agree on the inclusive approach before it is adopted.

Selecting the Criteria to Be Used

3.24 Management of the service organization is responsible for selecting the criteria to be used in preparing the description of the service organization's system. Paragraph .15 of AT-C section 320 identifies the attributes of suitable criteria for preparing and evaluating management's description of the service organization's system; paragraphs .16–.17 of AT-C section 320 identify the attributes of suitable criteria for evaluating the design and operating effectiveness of the service organization's controls. Additional criteria may be needed, for example, to meet a regulatory requirement. Paragraphs 3.25–.73 of this guide provide additional information about the criteria for the description of the service organization's system. Paragraphs 3.26–.34 and paragraphs 3.71–.74 of this guide address matters related to how the content of the description is affected when a service organization uses a subservice organization.

---

[3] Paragraph .A70 of AT-C section 320, *Reporting on an Examination of Controls at a Service Organization Relevant to User Entities' Internal Control Over Financial Reporting* (AICPA, *Professional Standards*), indicates that a user entity is also considered a user entity of the service organization's subservice organizations if controls at subservice organizations are relevant to internal control over financial reporting of the user entity. In such a case, the user entity is referred to as an *indirect* or *downstream* user entity of the subservice organization. Consequently, an indirect or downstream user entity may be included in the group to whom use of the service auditor's report is restricted if controls at the service organization are relevant to internal control over financial reporting of such indirect or downstream user entity.

Preparing the Description of the Service Organization's System and Management's Assertion

3.25 Management of the service organization is responsible for preparing the description of the service organization's system, including the completeness, accuracy, and method of presentation of the description. The description of the service organization's system is intended to provide user auditors and user entities with information about the service organization's system that may be relevant to the user entities' internal control over financial reporting. Aspects of a service organization's system are considered relevant to user entities' internal control over financial reporting if they affect any of the items discussed in paragraphs 2.02–.03 of this guide.

3.26 Management is responsible for documenting the service organization's system. Paragraph .A14 of AT-C section 320 indicates that no one particular form of documenting the service organization's system is prescribed and the extent of the documentation may vary depending on the size and complexity of the service organization and its monitoring activities. The description may be presented using various formats, such as narratives, flowcharts, tables, or graphics, or a combination thereof. The description of the service organization's system is intended to

- provide sufficient information for user auditors to understand how the service organization's processing (or the function performed by the service organization) affects user entities' financial statements and

- enable user auditors to assess the risks of material misstatements in the user entities' financial statements.

3.27 A complete and accurate description should not omit or distort information relevant to the service organization's system. However, management's description of the service organization's system is prepared to meet the common needs of a broad range of user entities and their user auditors and may not, therefore, include every aspect of the service organization's system that each individual user entity and its user auditor may consider important in a particular environment.

3.28 Paragraph .A37 of AT-C section 320 states, in part, that the description need not address every aspect of the service organization's processing or the services provided to user entities. Certain aspects of the processing or the services provided may not be relevant to user entities' internal control over financial reporting or may be beyond the scope of the engagement. For example,

- a service organization that provides five different applications to user entities may engage a service auditor to report on only three of those applications.

- a trust department that has separate organizational units providing personal trust services and institutional trust services may engage a service auditor to report on only the institutional trust services.

In these situations, the description of the service organization's system would address only the controls pertaining to those applications or organizational units included in the scope of the engagement.

3.29 The degree of detail included in the description generally is equivalent to the degree of detail a user auditor would need if the user entity were performing the outsourced service itself. However, the description need not be so detailed that it would allow a reader to compromise the service organization's security or other controls.

3.30 The description of the service organization's system can be organized in a variety of ways. For example, the description may be organized by the components of internal control (the control environment, risk assessment process, information and communications, control activities, and monitoring processes). The description should permit a user entity or its auditor to understand the flow of transactions or information through the service organization's system. To accomplish this, a description may contain narratives that describe the processes and controls that the service organization has placed in operation to control risk associated with those processes. Diagrams or flowcharts may be used to supplement the narratives contained in the description.

Content of the Description

3.31 Paragraph .15 of AT-C section 320 identifies the attributes of suitable criteria for evaluating whether management's description of the service organization's system is fairly presented. Those criteria are also included in paragraph 4.04 of this guide.

3.32 In order for management's description of the service organization's system to be fairly stated, it should address all of the description criteria[4] in paragraph .15 of AT-C section 320, unless specified criteria are not applicable.

3.33 Paragraph .15ai of AT-C section 320 requires that the description include the types of services provided, including, as appropriate, the classes of transactions processed. Examples of classes of transactions are

- distributions (lump-sum payments, periodic payments, forfeitures, loans),
- the method by which trade instructions are received (mail, fax, voice response unit [VRU], web, telephone), and
- program changes (new releases, emergency changes, patches).

The description need not necessarily describe every individual transaction type—just those classes of transactions that are relevant to user entities' financial statements.

3.34 To be useful to user entities and user auditors, when describing a service organization's controls, the description should include information about the frequency with which a control is performed or the timing of its occurrence, the person or parties responsible for performing the control, the activity being performed, and the source of the information to which the control is applied. The following control description is an example that includes all of these elements:

> The Cash Reconciliation Group (*persons responsible for performing the control*) reconciles (*activity performed*) money movement reflected in the ABC application output report (*source of the information*) to the

---

[4] Suitable description criteria have all of the attributes in paragraph .A42 of AT-C section 105, *Concepts Common to All Attestation Engagements* (AICPA, *Professional Standards*), and in paragraph .15 of AT-C section 320.

fund's custodian bank report (*source of the information*) on a monthly basis (*frequency*).

3.35 Deficiencies in certain IT general controls may affect both the proper operation of programmed control procedures and the effectiveness of certain manual controls. For example, a service organization may have a small IT staff and therefore assigns responsibility for migrating changes to production to the lead programmer. Without any oversight by other individuals responsible for reviewing, testing, and approving the changes, the lead programmer could make unauthorized or inaccurate changes to the software and migrate those changes into the production environment. If such deficiencies exist, it is helpful to user entities and their auditors if the description of the service organization's system identifies

- the deficiencies,
- the effect of the deficiencies on key programmed procedures,
- relevant manual controls performed by service organization personnel, and
- any complementary user entity controls that user entities would be expected to perform.

Complementary User Entity Controls

3.36 Paragraph .15*a*vii of AT-C section 320 indicates that the description should include, among other things, the specified control objectives and the controls designed to achieve those control objectives including, as applicable, complementary user entity controls. Complementary user entity controls are controls that management of the service organization assumes, in the design of the service organization's system, will be implemented by user entities and are necessary to achieve the control objectives stated in management's description of the service organization's system. It is important that the description indicate that the user entities are responsible for implementing those complementary user entity controls.

3.37 Some examples of typical complementary user entity controls are controls at user entities over

- logical access to the service organization's application by user entity personnel.
- the completeness and accuracy of input submitted to the service organization.
- the completeness, accuracy, and authorization of output received by the user entity, for example, reconciling input reports to output reports.

Content of the Description When the Service Organization Uses the Carve-Out Method

3.38 Based on the criteria for the description of a service organization's system in paragraphs .15*a*vi and the application guidance in paragraph .A37 of AT-C section 320, when the carve-out method is used, the description should include the nature of the services performed by the subservice organization but would not describe the detailed processing or controls at the subservice organization. The description of the service organization's system carves out those control objectives for which related controls operate only or primarily at the subservice organization. However, the description should contain sufficient information concerning the carved-out services to enable user entities and their auditors to

- understand the significance and relevance of the subservice organization's services to user entities' internal control over financial reporting and
- determine what additional information they may need to obtain from the subservice organization to assess the risks of material misstatement of the user entity's financial statements.

3.39   When the carve-out method is used, AT-C section 320 is silent about whether disclosure of the identity of the subservice organization is required. However, typically that information would be needed by user auditors in order to obtain information and perform procedures related to the subservice organization. If the description does not disclose the identity of the subservice organization, the service auditor may discuss this matter with management of the service organization and explain why such information is needed by user auditors.

3.40   The purpose of the description of the services provided by the subservice organization is to

- alert user entities and their auditors to the fact that another entity (the subservice organization) is involved in the processing of the user entities' transactions and that such services may affect the user entities' internal control over financial reporting,
- identify the services the subservice organization provides,
- identify the types of controls that management of the service organization assumes will be implemented by the subservice organization and are necessary to achieve the control objectives stated in management's description of the service organization's system (complementary subservice organization controls).

3.41   The description of the services provided by a subservice organization when using the carve-out method should be prepared at a level of detail that could reasonably be expected to provide a broad range of user auditors with sufficient information to obtain an understanding of internal control in accordance with AU-C section 402. The following are some examples of such descriptions and how they might be revised to make them more useful.

> *Scenario 1.* Trust Group Service Organization uses XYZ Pricing Subservice Organization to obtain market values for all exchange-traded securities. The description of the service organization's system states the following:
>
>> Trust Group uses XYZ Pricing Subservice Organization to obtain market values of securities.
>
> Because the description does not identify which securities the subservice organization prices, user entities and their auditors may be unable to determine the significance of the service provided by the subservice organization. A better description would be the following:
>
>> Trust Group uses XYZ Pricing Subservice Organization to obtain market values for all exchange-traded securities.
>
> *Scenario 2.* Trust Group Service Organization hosts its Trust System at Computer Outsourcing Subservice Organization, which provides

the computer processing infrastructure. The description of the service organization's system states the following:

> Trust Group Service Organization outsources aspects of its computer processing to Computer Outsourcing Subservice Organization.

This description is not specific enough to enable user entities and their auditors to determine the significance of the services provided by the subservice organization. The following is a more detailed description that provides the necessary information:

> Trust Group Service Organization hosts its Trust System at Computer Outsourcing Subservice Organization. Trust Group maintains responsibility for application changes and user access, and Computer Outsourcing Subservice Organization provides the computer processing infrastructure and changes thereto.

Complementary Subservice Organization Controls

3.42 When using the carve-out method, instances may exist in which the achievement of one or more control objectives is dependent on one or more controls at the subservice organization. Such controls are termed *complementary subservice organization controls* and are defined in paragraph .08 of AT-C section 320 as "controls that management of the service organization assumes, in the design of the service organization's system, will be implemented by the subservice organizations and are necessary to achieve the control objectives stated in management's description of the service organization's system." In such a situation, paragraph .15*a*vii of AT-C section 320 requires that management's description of the service organization's system identify such complementary subservice organization controls. Because complementary subservice organization controls are necessary to achieve certain control objectives, it is important that the description of the service organization's system describe the subservice organization's responsibilities for implementing those complementary subservice organization controls and also indicate that the related control objectives can be achieved only if the complementary subservice organization's controls are suitably designed and operating effectively throughout the period. To be meaningful to user entities and their auditors, complementary subservice organization controls should be specific to the services provided but may be presented as broad control categories or objectives. The service organization may wish to include a table in the description that identifies those instances in which control objectives are met solely by the service organization and those in which controls at the service organization and complementary subservice organization controls are needed to meet the control objectives.

3.43 Some examples of complementary subservice organization controls are the following:

- Controls relevant to the completeness and accuracy of transaction processing performed by the subservice organization on behalf of the service organization

- Controls relevant to the completeness and accuracy of specified reports provided to and used by the service organization

- General IT controls relevant to the processing performed for the service organization

3.44   Alternatively, the service organization may be able to exclude from the description the elements of the control objectives that are achieved through complementary subservice organization controls and include in the description only those elements of the control objectives that are achieved by controls at the service organization. In this circumstance, the description would include the nature of the services provided by the subservice organization and exclude from the description and from the scope of the service auditor's engagement the subservice organization's relevant control objectives and related controls. In certain circumstances, user entities of the service organization may request and obtain from the subservice organization a copy of the subservice organization's type 1 or type 2 report as indirect or downstream users, as discussed in paragraph .A70 of AT-C section 320.

3.45   A service organization may obtain a copy of a type 1 or type 2 report from the subservice organization if one is available. If the subservice organization's type 1 or type 2 report identifies the need for complementary user entity controls at the service organization, the service organization's description should describe the processes and controls the service organization has implemented to address the complementary user entity controls identified in the subservice organization's description of its system. In addition to describing the services provided by the subservice organization, the service organization may indicate in its description whether the subservice organization's report is a type 1 or type 2 report.

3.46   If the service organization uses the carve-out method and obtains the subservice organization's type 1 or type 2 report that identifies the need for complementary user entity controls, during planning, management of the service organization considers how to address that information in its description of the service organization's system. For example, a service organization that outsources aspects of its technology infrastructure to a subservice organization may find that the subservice organization's description of its systems includes the following complementary user entity control:

> User entities should have controls in place to provide reasonable assurance that access to system resources and applications is restricted to appropriate user entity personnel.

To address the complementary user entity control included in the subservice organization's description, the service organization would include a control objective, such as the following, in its description of the service organization's system:

> Controls provide reasonable assurance that access to system resources and applications is restricted to appropriate service organization personnel.

3.47   When using the carve-out method, management of the service organization would carve out those control objectives for which related controls operate only at the subservice organization. For example, a service organization that is responsible for restricting logical access to its system to properly authorized individuals may adopt the carve-out method for a computer processing subservice organization that hosts the user entity's applications and computers. In this situation, the service organization would include a control objective that addresses restricting logical access to the system to properly authorized individuals, but would not include a control objective related to physical security. To provide useful information to users of a type 1 or type 2 report, the service organization may wish to identify in its description those control objectives related to the service performed by the service organization for which the carved-out subservice organization is responsible.

Content of the Description When the Service Organization Uses the Inclusive Method

3.48 As indicated in paragraph .11 of AT-C section 320, when the inclusive method is used, the service auditor should apply the requirements in AT-C sections 105, 205, and 320 to the services provided by the subservice organization, as applicable, including the requirement to obtain management of the service organization's acknowledgment and acceptance of responsibility for the matters described in paragraph .10*b* of AT-C section 320 as they relate to the subservice organization, which includes providing a written assertion. Paragraph .16 of AT-C section 105 (shown after this paragraph) provides guidance in determining whether a requirement is applicable to a subservice organization.

> .16 Subject to paragraph .20, the practitioner should comply with each requirement of the AT-C sections that is relevant to the engagement being performed, including any relevant subject matter AT-C section, unless, in the circumstances of the engagement,
>
> > *a.* the entire AT-C section is not relevant, or
> >
> > *b.* the requirement is not relevant because it is conditional, and the condition does not exist.

3.49 In most inclusive engagements, the service organization is the only engaging party (not the service organization and the subservice organization). When a subservice organization is not an engaging party, the condition of being an engaging party does not exist for the subservice organization, and therefore, any requirements related only to an engaging party do not apply to the subservice organization—for example, the requirement in paragraph .07 of AT-C section 205 for the practitioner to agree upon the terms of the engagement with the engaging party. A non-engaging party subservice organization in an inclusive engagement has no contractual relationship with the service auditor. When using the inclusive method in these circumstances, the service organization and the subservice organization determine who will be responsible for providing each entity's description and integrating the descriptions.

3.50 As such, when the inclusive method is used, the subservice organization should provide the service auditor with a written assertion covering the services performed by the subservice organization, which accompanies management's description of the service organization's system and is provided to user entities by the subservice organization. Service organization management should include the assertion in, or attach it to, the description of the service organization's system. If management's assertion is included in the description rather than accompanying the description it should be clearly segregated from the description, for example, through the use of headings, because it is not a part of the description and the service auditor is not reporting on management's assertion.

3.51 During planning, the service auditor should determine whether it will be possible to obtain evidence that supports the portion of the opinion that addresses the subservice organization and obtain a written assertion from the subservice organization.

3.52 If management of the service organization wishes to use the inclusive method of presentation, but management of the subservice organization refuses to provide a written assertion, the service organization will not be able to use the inclusive method but may be able to use the carve-out method instead.

3.53 The service organization generally coordinates the use of the inclusive method with the subservice organization. If the inclusive method is used, matters to be agreed upon or coordinated by the service organization and the subservice organization include the following:

- The scope of the examination and the period to be covered by the service auditor's report
- Acknowledgment from management of the subservice organization that it will provide the service auditor with a written assertion and representation letter (Both management of the service organization and management of the subservice organization are responsible for providing the service auditor with a written assertion and representation letter.)
- The planned content and format of the inclusive description
- The representatives of the subservice organization and the service organization, and who will be responsible for
  — providing each entity's description
  — integrating the descriptions
- For a type 2 report, the timing of the tests of controls

3.54 When the service organization uses the inclusive method to present the services provided by a subservice organization, management of the service organization is responsible for evaluating the service organization's description of its system as well as the subservice organization's description of its system.

3.55 As indicated in paragraph 3.48 of this guide, if the service organization uses the inclusive method, management of the subservice organization is required to provide a written assertion. This assertion ordinarily would be expected to address the fairness of presentation of the description, the suitability of the design of the controls, and the operating effectiveness of the controls. However, in some circumstances, the achievement of a control objective may be dependent on a combination of the service organization's controls and the subservice organization's controls. In such circumstances, if the service organization designed the controls for the subservice organization, it may be possible when using the inclusive method for the service organization to take responsibility for the fair presentation of the description and for the suitability of the design of its own controls and the subservice organization's controls. If the service organization includes an assertion about the fair presentation of the description and suitability of the design of the subservice organization's controls in its assertion, the subservice organization's assertion may be limited to the operating effectiveness of its controls.

3.56 Using the inclusive method becomes more complex when the service organization uses multiple subservice organizations. When the services of more than one subservice organization are likely to be relevant to user entities' internal control over financial reporting, management of the service organization may use the inclusive method for one or more subservice organizations and the carve-out method for other subservice organizations. In these instances, management's description needs to clearly state which subservice organizations and related functions are included in the description and which are carved out. The presentation of any subservice organizations should adhere to the approach that the service organization has selected, whether that approach is the inclusive or carve-out method.

3.57 If the inclusive method is used, the description includes the nature of the services provided by the subservice organization and the relevant control objectives and related controls performed by the subservice organization. Relevant controls at the subservice organization may also include aspects of the subservice organization's control environment, risk assessment process, information and communications, and monitoring activities. Based on paragraph .A37 of AT-C section 320, the description should separately identify controls at the service organization and controls at the subservice organization. However, no prescribed format exists for differentiating between controls at the service organization and controls at the subservice organization.

3.58 If the description includes organizations that provide services to the service organization that are considered vendors in addition to organizations that provide services to the service organization that are considered subservice organizations, it may be helpful if the description distinguishes between vendors and subservice organizations because AT-C section 320 is not applicable to vendors as that term is described in paragraph 3.17 of this guide.

Other Aspects of the Service Organization's Internal Control Components

3.59 Paragraph .15*a*viii of AT-C section 320 requires that the service organization's description include other aspects of the service organization's internal control components (control environment, risk assessment process, information and communications [including the related business processes], control activities, and monitoring activities) that are relevant to the services provided. Aspects of these components of internal control may affect the achievement of specific control objectives. If that is the case, they generally would be included with the description of the controls designed to achieve those control objectives. Controls related to these components of internal control that are included in the description of the service organization's system should be limited to the specific aspects of those internal control components that are necessary to achieve the control objective. For example, to achieve a control objective related to logical security, a monitoring control might be "On a monthly basis, the service organization's internal audit function monitors the effectiveness of controls over the authorization of user access by validating user access for a sample of users." An entire internal control component typically would not be included in the description because it would likely include controls that are not necessary to achieve the specified control objectives. When using the inclusive method, management should consider whether the other aspects of the subservice organization's internal control components are relevant to the services provided to user entities.

3.60 A service organization may decide to present such aspects of its control environment, risk assessment process, information and communications, and monitoring components of internal control as separate control objectives when aspects of those components of internal control relate to the control objectives. In general, most service organizations do not take this approach in presenting these components of internal control because doing so may introduce detail that is not particularly useful to user auditors. Information about deficiencies in such components of internal control, alone, are of less interest to user auditors than they would be if these deficiencies were specifically associated with other control objectives because user auditors are focusing on controls at the service organization that are relevant to the services provided to user entities (for example, processing user entities' transactions) and need to understand how deficiencies in these components of internal control might affect the user entities' financial statement assertions.

Effect on the Description of a Service Organization's Monitoring Activities

3.61 As required by paragraphs .15*a*viii and explained in paragraph .A27 of AT-C section 320, management's description of the service organization's system and the scope of the service auditor's engagement includes controls at the service organization that monitor the effectiveness of controls at the subservice organization, which may include some combination of ongoing monitoring to determine that potential issues are identified timely and separate evaluations to determine that the effectiveness of internal control is maintained over time. Management's description of the service organization's system when using the inclusive method generally includes controls at the service organization designed to monitor services provided by the subservice organization, such as the following:

- Reviewing and reconciling output reports
- Holding periodic discussions with the subservice organization
- Making regular site visits to the subservice organization
- Testing controls at the subservice organization by members of the service organization's internal audit function
- Reviewing type 1 or type 2 reports on the subservice organization's system prepared pursuant to AT-C section 320 or AT-C section 205
- Monitoring external communications, such as customer complaints relevant to the services provided by the subservice organization

Management's description of the service organization's system should include a description of the design of such monitoring controls and the persons responsible for performing them.

3.62 The following is a brief description of the components of a service organization's internal control, other than its control activities, that may be relevant to user entities' internal control over financial reporting and, as a result, may be necessary for the achievement of specified control objectives.

- *Control environment.* The control environment sets the tone of an organization, influencing the control consciousness of its people. It is the foundation for all the other components of internal control, providing discipline and structure. Aspects of a service organization's control environment may affect the services provided to user entities. For example, management's hiring and training practices generally would be considered an aspect of the control environment that may affect the services provided to user entities because those practices affect the ability of service organization personnel to provide services to user entities. Paragraph .A79 of AU-C section 315, *Understanding the Entity and Its Environment and Assessing the Risks of Material Misstatement* (AICPA, *Professional*

Standards), presents the following as elements of the control environment that may be relevant when obtaining an understanding of the control environment:

— Communication and enforcement of integrity and ethical values

— Commitment to competence

— Participation by those charged with governance

— Management's philosophy and operating style

— Organizational structure

— Assignment of authority and responsibility

— Human resource policies and practices

● *Risk assessment.* Aspects of a service organization's risk assessment process may affect the services provided to user entities. How management of a service organization addresses identified risks could affect its own financial reporting process as well as the financial reporting processes of user entities. The following is a list of risk assessment factors and examples of how they might relate to a service organization:

— *Changes in the operating environment.* If a service organization provides services to user entities in a regulated industry, a change in regulations may necessitate a revision to existing processing. Revisions to existing processing may create the need for additional or revised controls.

— *New personnel.* New personnel who are responsible for executing manual controls that affect user entities may increase the risk that controls will not operate effectively.

— *New or revamped information systems.* A service organization may incorporate new functions into its system that could affect user entities.

— *Rapid growth.* If a service organization gains a substantial number of new customers, the operating effectiveness of certain controls could be affected.

— *New technology.* A service organization may implement a cloud-based version of software that was previously run on a mainframe. Although the new software may perform similar functions, it may operate so differently that it affects user entities.

— *New business models, products, or activities.* The diversion of resources to new activities from existing activities could affect certain controls at a service organization.

— *Corporate restructurings.* A change in ownership or internal reorganization could affect reporting responsibilities or the resources available for services to user entities.

— *Expanded foreign operations.* A service organization that uses personnel in foreign locations to maintain programs used by domestic user entities may have difficulty responding to changes in user requirements.

— *New accounting pronouncements.* The implementation of relevant accounting pronouncements in a service organization's software and controls could affect user entities.

— *Changes in economic conditions.* Slowing growth in the economy may cause the service organization to curtail or reduce the range of services provided to user entities.

- *Information and communications.* Activities of a service organization that may represent part of a user entity's information and communications component of internal control include the following:

  — The information system relevant to financial reporting objectives, consisting of the procedures—whether automated or manual—and records established by the service organization to initiate, authorize, record, process, and report a user entity's transactions (as well as events and conditions) and maintain accountability for the related assets, liabilities, and equity

  — Communication, which involves how the entity communicates financial reporting roles and responsibilities and significant matters relating to financial reporting, including communications between management and those charged with governance and external communications, such as those with regulatory authorities. This may include the extent to which service organization personnel understand how their activities relate to the work of others (including user entities) and the means for reporting exceptions to an appropriate higher level within the service organization and to user entities.

- *Monitoring.* Many aspects of monitoring may be relevant to the services provided to user entities. For example, a service organization may employ internal auditors or other personnel to evaluate the effectiveness of controls over time, through ongoing activities, periodic evaluations, or various combinations of the two. The service organization's monitoring of the subservice organization's activities that affect user entities' internal control over financial reporting is another example of monitoring. This form of monitoring may be accomplished through visits to the subservice organization or, alternatively, by obtaining and reading a type 1 or type 2 report on the subservice organization. Monitoring external communications, such as customer complaints and communications from regulators, generally would be relevant to the services provided to user entities. These monitoring activities are frequently included as control activities for achieving a specific control objective.

3.63 Relevant aspects of all the components of internal control should be included in management's description of the service organization's system. However, in describing the controls intended to meet specified control objectives, management should use judgment in determining what aspects of the other components of internal control should be included in the description, depending on the unique facts and circumstances.

Consideration of the 2013 COSO Framework

3.64 Various frameworks can be used as established criteria for designing, implementing, and evaluating the effectiveness of internal control. One such framework that may be used is the *Internal Control—Integrated Framework* (2013 COSO framework),[5] which was updated in May 2013 by the Committee of Sponsoring Organizations of the Treadway Commission (COSO) and supersedes the 1992 COSO framework. The 2013 COSO framework retains the five components of internal control included in the 1992 framework (and in paragraphs .15–.25 of AU-C section 315) and formalizes the concepts into 17 principles associated with the components. The five components and 17 principles of the 2013 COSO framework are shown in table 3-2.

Table 3-2

Summary of Control Components and Principles

Control Environment	Risk Assessment	Control Activities	Information and Communication	Monitoring Activities
1. Demonstrates commitment to integrity and ethical values.	6. Specifies suitable objectives.	10. Selects and develops control activities.	13. Uses relevant, quality information.	16. Conducts ongoing or separate evaluations, or both.
2. Exercises oversight responsibility.	7. Identifies and analyzes risk.	11. Selects and develops general controls over technology.	14. Communicates internally.	17. Evaluates and communicates deficiencies.
3. Establishes structure, authority, and responsibility.	8. Assesses fraud risk.	12. Deploys control activities through policies and procedures.	15. Communicates externally.	
4. Demonstrates commitment to competence.	9. Identifies and analyzes significant change.			
5. Enforces accountability.				

3.65 The attestation standards are not based on a specific internal control framework; therefore, the service auditor is not required to consider the 17 principles in the 2013 COSO framework when evaluating the design, implementation, or operating effectiveness of relevant controls in an engagement performed under AT-C section 320 (nor is management of a service organization required to use the 17 principles when designing and implementing internal control). However, the service auditor may find it useful to consider the principles included in the 2013 COSO framework, especially when one or more of the user entities uses the 2013 COSO framework to evaluate their internal control over financial reporting. In such cases, user entity management may be looking to the service organization's description of its system to provide information relevant to those principles that may affect the user entity's adherence to the 2013 COSO framework requirements. Therefore, during planning, the service auditor may discuss requirements of user entities with management of the service organization to determine whether and how the service

---

[5] © 2013, Committee of Sponsoring Organizations of the Treadway Commission (COSO). All rights reserved. Used by permission. See www.coso.org.

organization will communicate relevant aspects of the principles in the description of the service organization's system.

Changes to the System During the Period

3.66 The criterion in paragraph .15*b* of AT-C section 320 addresses whether the description of the service organization's system in a type 2 engagement includes relevant details of changes to the service organization's system during the period covered by the description. Changes would be included in the description if they are likely to be relevant to the user entities' internal control over financial reporting, for example, the service organization's migration to a cloud infrastructure.

Changes to the System That Occur Between the Periods Covered by a Type 1 or Type 2 Report

3.67 In some cases, type 1 or type 2 reports do not cover a continuous period and there is a gap between the periods covered by type 1 or type 2 reports. If a significant change occurs during the gap period, management of the service organization may decide that such changes are likely to be considered significant to user entities and their auditors, and management may include a description of such changes in the type 2 report for the period following the gap period in the section of the type 2 report titled, "Other Information Provided by the Service Organization." An example of such a change is a conversion to a new computer system or application during the gap period that results in (*a*) new or additional controls that are considered significant to user entities and (*b*) controls over the conversion process that were not tested by the service auditor.

Specifying the Control Objectives and Stating Them in the Description

3.68 The criterion for the description of the service organization's system in paragraph .15*a*vii of AT-C section 320 requires that the description of the service organization's system include the specified control objectives and controls designed to achieve those objectives, including, as applicable, complementary user entity controls and complementary subservice organization controls assumed in the design of the service organization's controls. Control objectives assist the user auditor in determining how the service organization's controls affect the user entity's financial statement assertions. In determining the control objectives to be included in the description, management of the service organization selects control objectives that relate to the types of assertions commonly embodied in the broad range of user entities' financial statements.

3.69 There are multiple formats for presenting the controls and control objectives in management's description of the service organization's system and no one format is required. A frequently used format is the placement of a three-column matrix (or matrixes) in the section of the type 2 report that is usually reserved for the service auditor's description of tests of controls and results (usually identified as section 4, "Service Organization's Control Objectives and Related Controls, and Independent Service Auditor's Description of Tests of Controls and Results"). A separate matrix is presented for each control objective, and the control objective is identified above the matrix. The controls that management has identified to achieve that control objective are placed in the first column of the matrix. Both the control objective and the controls to achieve that objective are considered an extension of management's description of the service organization system (usually identified as section 3). Columns 2 and 3 of the matrix belong to the service auditor and include a description of the service auditor's tests of controls and the results of those tests, respectively. A note placed in the description of the service organization's system indicating that management's controls and control objectives are included in section 4 and are part of management's description of the service organization's system incorporates these controls and control objectives in the description by reference. This obviates the need to repeat the controls and control objectives in section 3 and again in section 4. For clarity, the matrix(es) in section 4 would also indicate that the controls and control objectives are part of management's description of the service organization's system and that the descriptions of tests of controls and results are provided by the service auditor. Exhibit 3-1 and the illustrative type 2 reports in appendix A, "Illustrative Type 2 Reports," and appendix B illustrate a format for including the service organization's controls and control objectives in the section of a type 2 report that ordinarily contains only the description of the service auditor's tests of controls and results.

Exhibit 3-1

Format for Including the Service Organization's Controls and Control Objectives in the Description of the Service Auditor's Tests of Controls and Results

Section 4:

Service Organization's Control Objectives and Related Controls, and Independent Service Auditor's Description of Tests of Controls and Results

The controls in column 1 and the control objective above the matrix are part of management's description of the service organization's system (usually designated as section 3). The description of tests of controls and results in columns 2 and 3, respectively, are provided by the service auditor and are part of section 4.

Control Objective 1: Controls provide reasonable assurance that...

1	2	3
Management's Description of the Service Organization's Controls to Achieve the Related Control Objective	Service Auditor's Description of Tests of Controls	Service Auditor's Description of the Results of Tests

Attributes of Control Objectives That Are Reasonable in the Circumstances

3.70 Paragraph .25*a* of AT-C section 320 requires the service auditor to evaluate whether the control objectives stated in management's description of the service organization's system are reasonable in the circumstances. Paragraph .A39 of AT-C section 320 indicates that control objectives that are reasonable in the circumstances "relate to the types of assertions commonly embodied in the broad range of user entities' financial statements to which controls at the service organization could reasonably be expected to relate." Examples of such assertions are assertions about existence and accuracy that are affected by access controls that prevent, or detect, unauthorized access to the system. Although the service auditor ordinarily will not be able to determine how controls at a service organization specifically relate to the assertions embodied in individual user entities' financial statements, the service auditor considers matters such as the following when identifying the types of assertions to which the controls are likely to relate:

- The types of services provided by the service organization, including the classes of transactions processed
- The contents of reports and other information prepared for user entities
- The information used in the performance of procedures
- The types of significant events other than transactions that occur in providing the services
- Services performed by a subservice organization, if any
- The responsibility of the service organization to implement controls, including responsibilities established in contracts and agreements with user entities
- The risks to a user entity's internal control over financial reporting arising from IT used or provided by the service organization

3.71 The following is an example of a description of the services that an illustrative service organization provides to its customers, followed by examples of control objectives specified by the service organization and the types of assertions in the user entities' financial statements to which they relate:

> *Example*: Example Trust Organization provides fiduciary services to institutional, corporate, and personal trust customers. Example Trust Organization has engaged a service auditor to report on a description of its system related to the processing of transactions for user entities of the institutional trust division. Example Trust Organization has discretionary authority over investment activities, maintains the detailed records of investment transactions, and records investment income and expense. Reports are provided to user entities for use in preparing their financial statements. The service organization has specified control objectives that it believes relate to assertions in the user entities' financial statements and that are consistent with its contractual obligations. Table 3-3, "Examples of Assertions in User Entities' Financial Statements and Related Service Organization Control Objectives," identifies some of the control objectives specified by the service organization and the types of assertions in the user entities' financial statements to which they relate.

Table 3-3

Examples of Assertions in User Entities' Financial Statements and Related Service Organization Control Objectives

Assertions in User Entities' Financial Statements	Control Objectives of the Service Organization
	Controls provide reasonable assurance that—
Completeness	investment purchases and sales are recorded completely, accurately, and on a timely basis.
Valuation or allocation	investment income is recorded accurately and timely.
Rights and obligations	the service organization's records accurately reflect securities held by third parties, for example, depositories or subcustodians.

3.72 Paragraph .A39 of AT-C section 320 also indicates that control objectives that are reasonable in the circumstances are complete. Although a complete set of control objectives can provide a broad range of user auditors with a framework to assess the effect of controls at the service organization on assertions commonly embodied in user entities' financial statements, the service organization ordinarily will not be able to determine how controls at a service organization specifically relate to the assertions embodied in individual user entities' financial statements and cannot, therefore, determine whether control objectives are complete from the viewpoint of individual user entities or user auditors. Paragraph .A39 of AT-C section 320 points out that it is the responsibility of individual user entities or user auditors to assess whether the service organization's description addresses the particular control objectives that are relevant to their needs.

3.73 Whether a particular set of control objectives is complete will depend on the services provided to the user entities. For example, consider a service organization that provides computer services primarily to user entities in the financial services industry. Its application software enables user entities to process savings, mortgage loan, consumer loan, commercial loan, and general ledger transactions. The following are illustrations of how the service auditor evaluates the completeness of the control objectives for this service organization.

> *Example 1.* Example Service Organization has provided its user entities with a type 2 report that addresses the savings application and the related underlying IT general controls, but the report does not address any of the other applications provided by Example Service Organization. In evaluating whether the control objectives are complete, the service auditor determines that most user entities use only the savings application. As such, the report contains a complete set of control objectives for user entities that use only the savings application.

Example 2. Example Service Organization includes only those control objectives related to the savings application and excludes control objectives and controls that address the underlying IT general controls. The control objectives related to IT general controls should be included because of their relevance to user entities' internal control over financial reporting. The service auditor would conclude that the control objectives are not complete because IT general controls and the related control objectives are critical to the achievement of the control objectives relevant to the savings application and would be relevant to user entities that use the savings application. (See paragraph 5.51 for a separate illustrative paragraph that would be added to the service auditor's report when the description omits control objectives and related controls required for other controls to be suitably designed and operating effectively.)

Example 3. One of Example Service Organization's control objectives is "Controls provide reasonable assurance that savings and withdrawal transactions received from user entities are recorded completely and accurately." This control objective does not address timeliness and no other control objective addresses timeliness. The service auditor would conclude that the control objectives were incomplete because the timeliness with which transactions are recorded would be likely to be relevant to user entities' internal control over financial reporting. (See paragraph 5.61 for a separate illustrative paragraph that would be added to the service auditor's report when the service organization's description of its system includes an incomplete control objective.)

3.74 Having suitable criteria is one of the preconditions for performing an attestation engagement. In an engagement performed under AT-C section 320, the control objectives serve as part of the criteria for determining whether the controls are suitably designed and operating effectively. Paragraph .25*b*ii of AT-C section 105 indicates that suitable criteria have each of the following attributes:

- *Relevance.* Control objectives are relevant to the subject matter.
- *Objectivity.* Control objectives are free from bias.
- *Measurability.* Control objectives permit reasonably consistent measurements, qualitative or quantitative, of subject matter.
- *Completeness.* Control objectives are complete when they do not omit relevant factors that could reasonably be expected to affect decisions of the intended users made on the basis of the control objectives.

3.75 Paragraph .A39 of AT-C section 320 addresses the relevance and completeness of suitable criteria but does not address the objectivity and measurability of suitable criteria. A discussion of objectivity and measurability follows.

3.76 As indicated in paragraph .A42 of AT-C section 105, one of the characteristics of suitable criteria is objectivity (the criteria are free from bias). If a service organization drafts its control objectives so that the results of evaluating the fairness of the presentation of the description and suitability of the design and operating effectiveness of the controls would always be positive for that particular service organization, the control objectives would not have the attribute of objectivity. Also, as indicated in paragraph 3.74, suitable criteria are measureable, which means they permit reasonably consistent conclusions about whether the control objectives have been achieved. For example, the following control objective would not be measureable:

> Controls provide reasonable assurance that physical access to computer equipment, storage media, and program documentation is adequate.

This objective could be reworded as follows to meet the measurability attribute of suitable criteria:

> Controls provide reasonable assurance that physical access to computer equipment, storage media, and program documentation is limited to authorized personnel.

Another example of a control objective that is not measureable is the following:

> Controls provide reasonable assurance that logical security policies and procedures adhere to management's intentions.

User entities would have no way of knowing what management's intentions are, and the service auditor would have no basis for determining whether the control objective had been achieved. The service auditor would conclude that this control objective is worded in a manner that would not permit report users to arrive at reasonably similar conclusions about the achievement of the control objective and would ask the service organization to modify the wording of the control objective. Paragraph 5.58 of this guide presents an example of a separate paragraph that would be added to the service auditor's report when the description includes a control objective that is not measureable.

Identifying Risks That Threaten the Achievement of the Control Objectives

3.77 Control objectives relate to the risks that controls seek to mitigate. Paragraph .16a of AT-C section 320 indicates that one of the criteria for evaluating whether controls stated in management's description of the service organization's system are suitably designed is whether management has identified the risks that threaten the achievement of the control objectives. For example, the risk that a transaction is recorded at the wrong amount or in the wrong period can be addressed by the following control objective:

> Controls provide reasonable assurance that contribution and withdrawal transactions received from user entities are initially recorded completely and accurately.

3.78 Paragraph .A17 of AT-C section 320 discusses various approaches that management of the service organization may employ to identify relevant risks. Management may have a formal or informal process for identifying relevant risks that threaten the achievement of the control objectives. A formal process may include estimating the significance of identified risks, assessing the likelihood of their occurrence, and developing action plans to address them. Because the control objectives relate to the risks that controls seek to mitigate, thoughtful identification of control objectives by management when designing, implementing, and documenting the service organization's system may itself represent an informal but effective process for identifying the relevant risks.

Preparing Management's Written Assertion

3.79 Paragraph .10bvi of AT-C section 320 indicates that one of the preconditions for a service auditor to accept or continue an engagement to report on controls at a service organization is that management of the service organization acknowledge and accept responsibility for providing the service auditor with a written assertion[6] that accompanies management's description of the service organization's system. The service organization's assertion may be attached to the description of the service organization's system or may be included in the description if it is clearly segregated from the description, for example, through the use of headings. Management's assertion is segregated from the description because it is not part of the description and the service auditor is not reporting on management's assertion. Exhibit B, "Illustrative Assertions by Management of a Service Organization," of AT-C section 320 includes illustrative management assertions for type 1 and type 2 engagements. In addition, appendixes A and B of this guide include illustrative assertions for other situations, for example, when a service organization uses the inclusive method to present a subservice organization.

3.80 The service auditor's report indicates that management is responsible for preparing the description of the service organization's system and its assertion, including the completeness, accuracy, and method of presentation of the description and assertion. Management's assertion generally would be expected to reflect any modifications to the service auditor's opinion, such as modifications resulting from misstatements in management's description of the service organization's system or deficiencies in the design or operating effectiveness of controls. Paragraph 5.96 of this guide contains an example of a modified assertion related to the fairness of the presentation of the description, and paragraph 5.97 contains an example of a modified assertion related to the operating effectiveness of controls.

3.81 Management's assertion would also be expected to reflect any modifications to the service auditor's opinion for situations in which complementary user entity controls or complementary subservice organization controls are necessary to achieve the service organization's control objectives. This guide includes the following examples of modified assertions that reflect various modifications of the service auditor's opinion:

Location of Illustrative Modified Assertion in This Guide	Modification of the Service Auditor's Opinion
Paragraph 5.96	The service auditor's opinion is modified because the description of the service organization's system is not fairly presented.
Paragraph 5.97	The service auditor's opinion is modified because controls were not operating effectively.
Example 1 of appendix A, "Illustrative Type 2 Reports"	Complementary user entity controls are required to achieve the control objectives.

---

[6] Generally, management's assertion is placed on the service organization's letterhead. AT-C section 320 does not require that management's assertion be signed.

Location of Illustrative Modified Assertion in This Guide	*Modification of the Service Auditor's Opinion*
Example 2 of appendix A	The service organization uses the carve-out method for the subservice organization; complementary user entity controls and complementary subservice organization controls are required to achieve the control objectives.
Example 1 of appendix B, "Illustrative Type 2 Reports—Inclusive Method, Including Illustrative Management Representation Letters."	The service organization uses the inclusive method to present the subservice organization; complementary user entity controls are required to achieve the control objectives.
Example 2 of appendix B	The service organization uses • the inclusive method for one subservice organization; complementary user entity controls are required to achieve the control objectives. • the carve-out method for another subservice organization; complementary user entity controls and complementary subservice organization controls are required to achieve the control objectives.

Having a Reasonable Basis for Its Assertion

3.82 Paragraph .10*b*ii of AT-C section 320 states that a service auditor should accept or continue an engagement only if, among other things, management of the service organization acknowledges and accepts responsibility for having a reasonable basis for its written assertion. The work performed by the service auditor as part of a type 1 or type 2 engagement would not be considered a basis for management's assertion because the service auditor is not part of the service organization's internal control. AT-C section 320 does not include requirements for the service auditor to perform procedures to determine whether management has a reasonable basis for its assertion. However, paragraph .A15 of AT-C section 320 states the following:

> **.A15** Management's monitoring activities may provide evidence of the design and operating effectiveness of controls in support of management's assertion. Monitoring of controls is a process to assess the effectiveness of internal control performance over time. It involves assessing the effectiveness of controls on a timely basis, identifying and reporting deficiencies to appropriate individuals within the service organization, and taking necessary corrective actions. Management accomplishes monitoring of controls through ongoing activities, separate evaluations, or a combination of the two. Ongoing monitoring

activities are often built into the normal recurring activities of an entity and include regular management and supervisory activities. Internal auditors or personnel performing similar functions may contribute to the monitoring of a service organization's activities. Monitoring activities may also include using information communicated by external parties, such as customer complaints, which may indicate problems or highlight areas in need of improvement. The greater the degree and effectiveness of ongoing monitoring, the less need for separate evaluations. Usually, some combination of ongoing monitoring and separate evaluations will ensure that internal control maintains its effectiveness over time. The service auditor's report on controls is not a substitute for the service organization's own processes to provide a reasonable basis for its assertion.

Responsibilities of the Service Auditor

3.83 During planning, the service auditor is responsible for the following:

- Determining whether to accept or continue an engagement for a particular client (paragraphs 3.84–.90)[7]
- Establishing an understanding with management of the service organization regarding the services to be performed and the responsibilities of management and the service auditor, which ordinarily is documented in an engagement letter (paragraphs 3.91–.94)
- Assessing the suitability and availability of the criteria management has used in preparing the description (paragraphs 3.95–.96)
- Obtaining an understanding of the service organization's system (paragraphs 3.97–.105)
- Assessing the risk of material misstatement (paragraphs 3.106–.109)
- Requesting a written assertion about whether the subject matter is in accordance with or based on the criteria (paragraph .10 of AT-C section 205 and paragraph .13 of AT-C section 320)

Client and Engagement Acceptance and Continuance

3.84 With respect to the acceptance and continuance of client relationships and specific engagements, paragraph .27 of QC section 10, *A Firm's System of Quality Control* (AICPA, *Professional Standards*), states that the firm should establish policies and procedures for the acceptance and continuance of client relationships and specific engagements, designed to provide the firm with reasonable assurance that it will undertake or continue relationships and engagements only when the firm

a. is competent to perform the engagement and has the capabilities, including time and resources, to do so;

b. can comply with legal and relevant ethical requirements; and

c. has considered the integrity of the client and does not have information that would lead it to conclude that the client lacks integrity.

---

[7] Unless otherwise noted, the parenthetical paragraph references in this list indicate the paragraphs within this guide where a more detailed discussion of a particular topic can be found.

3.85 Quality control policies and procedures related to the acceptance and continuance of client relationships and specific engagements help the firm to mitigate risks, such as association risk, which is the risk that the service auditor will be associated with management of a service organization that does not possess the appropriate ethical and moral character, thereby damaging the service auditor's professional reputation.

3.86 Some of the matters that are relevant when the service auditor is determining whether to accept or continue an engagement include the scope of the description, the nature of the user entities, how subservice organizations are used, how information about subservice organizations will be presented, the control objectives, the risks that threaten the achievement of the control objectives, and the period covered by the report. The following are examples of a service auditor's consideration of matters that might affect the decision to accept or continue an engagement:

> *Example 1.* The service organization has requested a type 2 report for a period that is not a substantial portion of the period covered by user entities' internal control over financial reporting because the service organization or the system has been in operation for less than six months and it is not feasible to wait six months to issue a report or to issue a report covering both the system that existed before the new system was implemented and the new system. The service auditor may determine that there is an appropriate basis for undertaking an engagement with a specified period of less than six months.

> *Example 2.* The service organization has requested a type 2 report for the five-month period February 1, 20X1, to June 30, 20X1, because a significant problem related to the operating effectiveness of controls, which was intentionally not communicated by the service organization to the user entities, occurred in January 20X1. The service auditor may question accepting this engagement.

> *Example 3.* The service organization has requested a type 2 report for the five-month period February 1, 20X1, to June 30, 20X1, because a certain user group needs a report for only that period. Important controls operate on dates that are not included in the five-month period. The service auditor suggests that the period covered by the report be extended to include the dates on which the controls operate. If management of the service organization decides not to expand the five-month period, the service auditor should consider whether or not to accept the engagement. If the service auditor decides to accept the engagement, the service auditor should determine the effect, if any, on the service auditor's report and whether to modify the opinion.

3.87 The "Independence Rule" (AICPA, *Professional Standards*, ET section 1.200.001) requires that a member in public practice be independent in the performance of professional services as required by standards promulgated by bodies designated by the AICPA Council. For attestation engagements, those standards are Statements on Standards for Attestation Engagements (attestation standards). Paragraph .24 of AT-C section 105 states that "the practitioner must be independent when performing an attestation engagement in accordance with the attestation standards unless the practitioner is required by law or regulation to accept the engagement and report on the subject matter or assertion." When the practitioner is not independent but is required by law or regulation to accept the engagement and report on the subject matter, the service auditor should disclaim an opinion and should specifically state that the practitioner is not independent. The practitioner is neither required to provide, nor precluded from providing, the reasons for the lack of independence; however, if the practitioner chooses to provide the reasons for the lack of independence, the practitioner should include all the reasons therefor.

3.88 A firm's independence assessment process may address matters such as scope of services, fee arrangements, firm and individual financial relationships, firm business relationships, and alumni and familial relationships. The "Independence Rule" is followed by interpretations of the rule that assist the service auditor in assessing independence.

3.89 In performing a service auditor's engagement, the service auditor need not be independent of each user entity.

3.90 Paragraph .23 of AT-C section 105 states that "the engagement partner should be satisfied that appropriate procedures regarding the acceptance and continuance of client relationships and attestation engagements have been followed and should determine that conclusions reached in this regard are appropriate."

Agreeing on the Terms of the Engagement

3.91 Paragraph .07 of AT-C section 205 requires the practitioner to agree upon the terms of the engagement with the engaging party in sufficient detail in an engagement letter or other suitable form of written agreement. Such a written agreement reduces the risk that either the service auditor or management of the service organization may misinterpret the needs or expectations of the other party. For example, it reduces the risk that management of the service organization may rely on the service auditor to protect the service organization against certain risks or to perform certain management functions.

3.92 Paragraph .08 of AT-C section 205 states that the agreed-upon terms of the engagement should include the following:

  a. The objective and scope of the engagement

  b. The responsibilities of the practitioner

  c. A statement that the engagement will be conducted in accordance with attestation standards established by the American Institute of Certified Public Accountants

  d. The responsibilities of the responsible party and the responsibilities of the engaging party, if different

  e. A statement about the inherent limitations of an examination engagement

  f. Identification of the criteria for the measurement, evaluation, or disclosure of the subject matter

  g. An acknowledgment that the engaging party agrees to provide the practitioner with a representation letter at the conclusion of the engagement

3.93 Paragraph .41 of AT-C section 205 indicates that, if the service auditor plans to use internal auditors to provide direct assistance, prior to doing so, the service auditor should obtain written acknowledgment from the responsible party (management of the service organization) that internal auditors providing direct assistance to the service auditor will be allowed to follow the service auditor's instructions and that the responsible party will not intervene in the work the internal auditors perform for the service auditor. If the engaging party is the responsible party, the service auditor may wish to include this matter in the engagement letter.

3.94 Although not required by the attestation standards, the service auditor would ordinarily expect the engaging party to sign the engagement letter. The engaging party's refusal to sign the engagement letter would be a relevant factor in the service auditor's consideration of the integrity of the client and the service auditor's decision about whether to accept or continue the engagement.

Assessing the Suitability of Criteria

3.95 Paragraph .14 of AT-C section 320 indicates that the service auditor should assess whether management has used suitable criteria in preparing its description of the service organization's system, in evaluating whether the controls included in the description were suitably designed, and in a type 2 engagement, in evaluating whether the controls operated effectively throughout the specified period to achieve the control objectives stated in the description. The attributes of suitable criteria for an engagement performed under AT-C section 320 are identified in paragraphs .15–.17 of AT-C section 320.

3.96 Having suitable criteria is one of the preconditions for an attestation engagement. If the service auditor determines after the engagement has been accepted that suitable criteria were not used, paragraph .28 of AT-C section 105 requires the service auditor to discuss the matter with the appropriate party (usually management), which would ordinarily include requesting that management revise the criteria. The service auditor should determine whether

- the matter can be resolved,

- it is appropriate to continue with the engagement, and

- if the matter cannot be resolved but it is still appropriate to continue with the engagement, whether, and if so how, to communicate the matter in the service auditor's report.

Obtaining an Understanding of the Service Organization's System

3.97 Paragraph .20 of AT-C section 320 states that the service auditor should obtain an understanding of the service organization's system, including controls that are included in the scope of the engagement. That understanding should include service organization processes used to

a. prepare the description of the service organization's system, including the determination of control objectives;

b. identify controls designed to achieve the control objectives;

c. assess the suitability of the design of the controls; and

d. in a type 2 report, assess the operating effectiveness of controls.

3.98 According to paragraph .14 of AT-C section 205, the service auditor's understanding should be sufficient to

a. enable the service auditor to identify and assess the risks of material misstatement in the subject matter and *b.* provide a basis for designing and performing procedures to respond to the assessed risks and to obtain reasonable assurance to support the service auditor's opinion.

3.99 Obtaining an understanding of the service organization's system, including related controls, assists the service auditor in the following:

- Identifying the boundaries of the system and how it interfaces with other systems
- Assessing whether management's description of the service organization's system fairly presents the service organization's system that has been designed and implemented
- Understanding which controls are necessary to achieve the control objectives stated in management's description of the service organization's system, whether controls were suitably designed to achieve those control objectives, and, in the case of a type 2 report, whether controls were operating effectively throughout the specified period to achieve those control objectives
- When a separate type 1 or type 2 report exists for a subservice organization, whether management has identified controls that are necessary, either at the service organization or at user entities, to address relevant complementary user entity controls identified in the carved-out subservice organization's description of its system

3.100 In obtaining an understanding of the subject matter, paragraph .15 of AT-C section 205 states that the service auditor should obtain an understanding of internal control over the preparation of the subject matter, which, in the case of a service auditor's engagement, focuses on evaluating the suitability of the design of controls over the preparation of the description of the service organization's system and determining whether the controls have been implemented by performing procedures in addition to inquiry of the personnel responsible for the description. In a service auditor's engagement, the evaluation of the fair presentation of the description of the service organization's system and the suitability of the design and operating effectiveness of controls included in the description is performed as part of the service auditor's response to the assessed risks of material misstatement of the subject matter.

3.101 The service auditor's procedures to obtain the understanding may include the following:

- Inquiring of management and others within the service organization who, in the service auditor's judgment, may have relevant information
- Observing operations and inspecting documents, reports, and printed and electronic records of transaction processing
- Inspecting a selection of agreements between the service organization and user entities to identify their common terms
- Reperforming the application of a control

3.102 One or more of the preceding procedures may be accomplished through the performance of a walkthrough. Paragraph .21 of AT-C section 320 states that, if the service organization has an internal audit function, part of the service auditor's understanding of the service organization's system should include the following (also see paragraphs 3.110–.127):

    a. The nature of the internal audit function's responsibilities and how the internal audit function fits in the service organization's organizational structure

    b. The activities performed, or to be performed, by the internal audit function as it relates to the service organization

3.103 Management of a service organization may use either a formal or an informal process to prepare the description of the service organization's system. For example, a small service organization that prepares only one report per year is likely to have an informal process in which a few employees with personal knowledge of the operation of the system are assigned responsibility for drafting the description of the service organization's system and the draft is reviewed by senior management. A large service organization with many interrelated services and multiple reports that address systems that span many functional units is more likely to have a formal process. Such a process is likely to include a project management role that coordinates preparation of the description by different functional areas and review of the description by key executives across the organization. These two different types of processes are likely to be subject to different sources of misstatement. An understanding of the service organization's process for preparing the description may assist the service auditor in

- identifying possible sources of material misstatement in the description,
- determining the likelihood of such misstatements, and
- designing procedures to evaluate the fairness of the presentation of the description.

3.104 An understanding of management's process for determining the risks that would prevent the control objectives from being achieved, and for designing and implementing controls to address those risks, may assist the service auditor in identifying deficiencies in the design of controls. Many service organizations have a formal risk assessment process based on the 2013 COSO framework. In those circumstances, the service auditor may be able to inspect the risk assessment and controls documentation prepared by management to obtain an understanding of this process.

3.105 Often management's system of internal control includes monitoring activities and system reports for management that permit management to continuously, as well as periodically, monitor the operating effectiveness of controls. Management may also make use of internal audit evaluations as part of its assessment of the effectiveness of controls. Finally, management may perform specific procedures to assess the effectiveness of controls periodically through controls self-assessment programs and functions that are responsible for periodically testing the effectiveness of controls. In most cases, management will use a combination of the various assessment techniques. Most controls assessment techniques include documentation of their performance, permitting the service auditor to inspect the documentation as part of obtaining an understanding of the system.

Assessing the Risk of Material Misstatement

3.106 Based on the service auditor's understanding of the service organization's system, paragraph .22 of AT-C section 320 states that the service auditor should assess the risk of material misstatement. In a type 1 or type 2 engagement, the risk of material misstatement relates to the risk that, in all material respects, based on the criteria in management's assertion,

    a. management's description of the service organization's system is not fairly presented;

    b. the controls are not suitably designed to provide reasonable assurance that the control objectives stated in management's description of the service organization's system would be achieved if the controls operated effectively; and

    c. in the case of a type 2 report, the controls did not operate effectively throughout the specified period to achieve the related control objectives stated in management's description of the service organization's system.

3.107   Because the subject matter of a service auditor's engagement relates to the fair presentation of management's description of the service organization's system and the suitability of the design and operating effectiveness of a service organization's controls, risk assessment principally focuses on inherent risks that affect the preparation of the description of the service organization's system and the effectiveness of the service organization's controls. Paragraph .A10*a*i of AT-C section 105 defines inherent risk as the susceptibility of the subject matter to a material misstatement before consideration of any related controls. Inherent risks related to a service auditor's engagement may include those related to new or changed controls, system changes, significant changes in processing volume, new personnel or significant changes in key management or personnel, new types of transactions, or new products or technologies. They may also include inherent risks arising from subservice organizations.

3.108   In addition, paragraph .32*a* of AT-C section 205 requires the service auditor to consider whether risk assessment procedures and other procedures related to understanding the subject matter indicate risk of material misstatement due to fraud or noncompliance with laws or regulations. For example, fraud risks related to a service organization might include management override of controls at the service organization, misappropriation of user entity assets by service organization personnel, and creation by service organization personnel of false or misleading documents or records of user entity transactions processed by the service organization.

3.109   Paragraph .23 of AT-C section 320 states that "the service auditor should read the reports of the internal audit function and regulatory examinations that relate to the services provided to user entities and the scope of the engagement, if any, to obtain an understanding of the nature and extent of the procedures performed and the related findings. The findings should be taken into consideration as part of the risk assessment and in determining the nature, timing, and extent of the tests."

Planning to Use the Work of Internal Auditors

3.110   The internal audit function of an entity performs assurance and consulting activities designed to evaluate and improve the effectiveness of the entity's governance, risk management, and internal control processes. Using the work of internal auditors includes (*a*) using the work of the internal audit function in obtaining evidence and (*b*) using internal auditors to provide direct assistance.

3.111 Internal audit activities that are relevant to a service auditor's engagement are those that provide information or evidence about the services provided to user entities, the fair presentation of the description of the service organization's system, or suitability of the design or operating effectiveness of the service organization's controls that are likely to be relevant to user entities' internal control over financial reporting. Certain internal audit activities may not be relevant to a service auditor's engagement, for example, the internal audit function's procedures to evaluate the efficiency of certain management decision-making processes.

3.112 Paragraph .39 of AT-C section 205 indicates that when the service auditor expects to use the work of the internal audit function in obtaining evidence or to use internal auditors to provide direct assistance, the service auditor should determine whether the work can be used for purposes of the examination by evaluating

a. the level of competence of the internal audit function or the individual internal auditors providing direct assistance;

b. the extent to which the internal audit function's organizational status and relevant policies and procedures support the objectivity of the internal audit function or, for internal auditors providing direct assistance, the existence of threats to the objectivity of those internal auditors and the related safeguards applied to reduce or eliminate those threats; and

c. when using the work of the internal audit function, the application by the internal audit function of a systematic and disciplined approach, including quality control.

3.113 *Objectivity* refers to the ability to perform tasks without allowing bias, conflict of interest, or undue influence of others to override professional judgments. Factors that may affect the service auditor's evaluation of objectivity include the following:

a. Whether the organizational status of the internal audit function, including the function's authority and accountability, supports the ability of the function to be free from bias, conflict of interest, or undue influence of others to override professional judgments (for example, whether the internal audit function reports to those charged with governance or an officer with appropriate authority, or if the function reports to management, whether it has direct access to those charged with governance)[8]

b. Whether the internal audit function is free of any conflicting responsibilities (for example, having managerial or operational duties or responsibilities that are outside of the internal audit function)

c. Whether those charged with governance oversee employment decisions related to the internal audit function, for example, determining the appropriate remuneration policy

---

[8] As indicated in paragraph .A18 of AT-C section 105, management and governance structures vary by entity, reflecting influences such as size and ownership characteristics. Such diversity means that it is not possible for the attestation standards to specify for all engagements the person(s) or groups at a particular entity with specified responsibilities. Identifying the appropriate management personnel or those charged with governance to whom the internal audit function should report may require the exercise of professional judgment.

    d. Whether any constraints or restrictions placed on the internal audit function by management or those charged with governance exist, for example, in communicating the internal audit function's findings to the service auditor

    e. Whether the internal auditors are members of relevant professional bodies and their memberships obligate their compliance with relevant professional standards relating to objectivity or whether their internal policies achieve the same objectives

3.114 The competence of the internal audit function refers to the attainment and maintenance of knowledge and skills of the function as a whole at the level required to enable assigned tasks to be performed diligently and with the appropriate level of quality. Factors that may affect the service auditor's evaluation of competence include the following:

- Whether the internal audit function is adequately and appropriately resourced relative to the size of the service organization and the nature of its operations.

- Whether established policies for hiring, training, and assigning internal auditors to internal audit engagements exist.

- Whether the internal auditors have adequate technical training and proficiency in auditing. Relevant criteria that may be considered by the service auditor in making the assessment may include, for example, the internal auditors' possession of a relevant professional designation and experience.

- Whether the internal auditors possess the required knowledge relating to the service organization's services, system, and controls over that system and whether the internal audit function possesses the necessary skills (for example, industry-specific knowledge) to perform work related to the service organization's services.

- Whether the internal auditors are members of relevant professional bodies or have certifications that oblige them to comply with the relevant professional standards, including continuing professional education requirements.

3.115 Factors that may affect the service auditor's determination of whether the internal audit function applies a systematic and disciplined approach include the following:

- The existence, adequacy, and use of documented internal audit procedures or guidance covering such areas as risk assessments, work programs, documentation, and reporting, the nature and extent of which is commensurate with the nature and size of the internal audit function relative to the complexity of the service organization.

- Whether the internal audit function has appropriate quality control policies and procedures (for example, those relating to leadership, human resources, and engagement performance) or quality control requirements in standards set by relevant professional bodies for internal auditors. Such bodies may also establish other appropriate requirements, such as conducting periodic external quality assessments.

3.116 The service auditor's determination of whether the internal audit function applies a systematic and disciplined approach is intended to address the risk that the service auditor inappropriately uses internal audit-like work performed in an informal, unstructured, or ad hoc manner. However, the level of formality of an acceptable approach may vary depending on the nature and size of the internal audit function relative to the complexity of the service organization.

3.117 Activities similar to those performed by an internal audit function may be conducted by functions with other titles within a service organization. Some or all of the activities of an internal audit function may also be outsourced to a third-party service provider. Neither the title of the function nor whether it is performed by the service organization or a third-party service provider is the sole determinant of whether or not the service auditor can use the work of internal auditors. Rather, it is the nature of the activities, the extent to which the internal audit function's organizational status and relevant policies and procedures support the objectivity of the internal auditors, competence of the internal auditors, and systematic and disciplined approach of the function that are relevant. References to using the work of the internal audit function include relevant activities of other functions or third-party providers that have these characteristics.

3.118 The objectivity and competence of internal auditors are important in determining whether to use their work and, if so, the nature and extent of the use of their work. However, a high degree of objectivity cannot compensate for a low degree of competence, nor can a high degree of competence compensate for a low degree of objectivity. Additionally, neither a high level of competence nor strong support for the objectivity of the internal auditors compensates for the lack of a systematic and disciplined approach when using the work of the internal audit function.

3.119 Based on an evaluation of the factors discussed in paragraphs 3.112–.118, in some circumstances the service auditor may determine that the risks of using the work of the internal audit function to obtain evidence or using internal auditors to provide direct assistance are too significant and the service auditor may decide not to use any of their work.

3.120 Because the service auditor has sole responsibility for the opinion expressed, the service auditor makes all significant judgments in the examination engagement, including when using the work of the internal audit function in obtaining evidence. As indicated in paragraph .43 of AT-C section 205, to prevent undue use of the internal audit function in obtaining evidence, the service auditor should plan to use less of the work of the function and perform more of the work directly:

    a. The more judgment is involved in

        i. planning and performing relevant procedures or

        ii. evaluating the evidence obtained

    b. the higher the assessed risk of material misstatement;

    c. the less the internal audit function's organizational status and relevant policies and procedures adequately support the objectivity of the internal auditors; and

    d. the lower the level of competence of the internal audit function.

3.121 The service auditor's sole responsibility for the opinion expressed is not reduced by the practitioner's use of the work of internal auditors. The service auditor, therefore, may not solely use tests performed by members of the internal audit function to support the service auditor's opinion on the operating effectiveness of controls.

3.122 The service auditor's use of the work of the internal audit function in a type 1 engagement generally would be more limited than it would be in a type 2 engagement because a type 1 engagement does not include tests of the operating effectiveness of controls and, therefore, there is less of an opportunity to use the work of the internal audit function in a type 1 engagement.

Coordinating Procedures With the Internal Audit Function

3.123 A practitioner planning to use the work of the internal audit function to obtain evidence may find it effective and efficient to discuss the planned use of the work with the internal audit function as a basis for coordinating activities.

3.124 In discussing the planned use of the work of the internal audit function in obtaining evidence, it may be useful to address the following as a basis for coordinating the respective activities:

- The timing of such work
- The nature of the work performed
- The extent of coverage
- Proposed methods of item selection and sample sizes
- Documentation of the work performed
- Review and reporting procedures

3.125 Coordination between the service auditor and the internal audit function is effective when, for example,

- discussions take place at appropriate intervals throughout the period.
- the service auditor informs the internal audit function of significant matters that may affect the function.
- the service auditor is advised of, and has access to, relevant reports of the internal audit function and is informed of any significant matters that come to the attention of the function when such matters may affect the work of the service auditor so that the service auditor is able to consider the implications of such matters for the service auditor's engagement.

3.126 Although the service auditor is not precluded from using work that the internal audit function has already performed, coordination of activities between the service auditor and internal audit function is likely to be most effective when appropriate interaction occurs before the internal audit function performs the work.

3.127 Communication with the internal audit function or the internal auditor, when using direct assistance, throughout the engagement may provide opportunities for internal auditors to bring up matters that may affect the work of the service auditor. The service auditor is then able to take such information into account in the service auditor's identification and assessment of risks of material misstatement and determine any potential impact to the nature, timing, or extent of testing.

Using the Work of an Other Practitioner

3.128 In certain circumstances, a service auditor may plan to use of the work of an other practitioner. Paragraph .31 of AT-C section 105 indicates that when the service auditor expects to use the work of an other practitioner, the practitioner has the following reporting options:

a. Assuming responsibility for the work of the other practitioner

b. Making reference to the other practitioner in the practitioner's report

3.129 Paragraph .31 of AT-C section 105 indicates that when a service auditor expects to use the work of an other practitioner, the service auditor should

a. obtain an understanding of whether the other practitioner understands and will comply with the ethical requirements that are relevant to the engagement and, in particular, is independent. (Similar to the service auditor, the other practitioner should be independent of both the service organization and the subservice organization.)

b. obtain an understanding of the other practitioner's professional competence. (The service auditor may make inquiries about the other practitioner to the other practitioner's professional organization or other practitioners, inquire about whether the other practitioner is subject to regulatory oversight, and read any publicly available regulatory reports, including reviews or inspections of the other practitioner's working papers.

c. communicate clearly with the other practitioner about the scope and timing of the other practitioner's work and findings. (Such communication enables the service auditor to plan the nature, timing, and extent of any procedures that relate to the work of the other practitioner, including the involvement of the service auditor in the work of the other practitioner. Due to complexities involved in the planning of the engagement and obtaining agreement between all parties, using the work of an other practitioner is most likely to be successful when these matters are addressed early in engagement planning.)

d. if assuming responsibility for the work of the other practitioner, be involved in the work of the other practitioner.

e. evaluate whether the other practitioner's work is adequate for the practitioner's purposes. (Upon completion of the other practitioner's work, the service auditor should obtain an understanding of the results of the other practitioner's work and findings associated with that work. The service auditor may obtain such an understanding through review of the report of the results of the other practitioner's procedures, discussions with the other practitioner, and inspection of the other practitioner's working papers.)

f. determine whether to make reference to the other practitioner in the practitioner's report. (As stated in paragraph 3.130, the service auditor ordinarily would not choose to refer to the other practitioner in the report because doing so would not result in a report that would be useful to user entities and their auditors.)

3.130   In applying paragraph .31 of AT-C section 105 to a service auditor's engagement, consider a situation in which management of a service organization wishes to engage a service auditor to perform a type 2 engagement under AT-C section 320 that includes the service organization and its subservice organization. The service auditor determines that the subservice organization has already engaged another service auditor (a subservice auditor) to perform a type 2 SOC 2® engagement[9] for the same period to be covered by the AT-C section 320 engagement and that addresses the services provided to the service organization and relevant controls. The following are some options for the service organization and service auditor:

- The service organization may carve out the subservice organization, in which case user auditors will need to obtain the type 2 SOC 2® report from the subservice organization.

- The service organization may request an inclusive type 2 SOC 1® report in which the service auditor performs all the work and does not use the work of the subservice auditor, other than to consider whether the subservice auditor's type 2 SOC 2® report provides evidence that relevant controls at the subservice organization are not suitably designed or operating effectively. (However the subservice auditor's type 2 SOC 2® report, if covering the same period as the service auditor's inclusive type 2 SOC 1® report, is unlikely to be available in time for use by the service auditor.)

- The service auditor may use the work of the subservice auditor and assume responsibility for that work. In this scenario, the service auditor would need to comply with the requirements in paragraph .31 of AT-C section 105. The description would include those aspects of the subservice organization's system that are relevant to user entities' internal control over financial reporting, and the description of tests of controls and results would include the tests performed by the subservice auditor and the results, without attributing the tests to the subservice auditor.

- The service auditor may use the work of the subservice auditor and make reference to the subservice auditor. In this scenario, the service auditor would need to comply with the requirements in paragraph .31 of AT-C section 105. The service organization's description would not include those aspects of the subservice organization's system that are relevant to user entities' internal control over financial reporting, and the description of tests of controls and results would not include the tests performed by the subservice auditor and the results. User auditors would need to obtain the type 2 SOC 2® report from the subservice organization. Consequently, the user auditors are not in a materially different position than they would be if the subservice organization were carved out. For that reason, inclusive reports in which the service auditor

---

[9] A SOC 2® engagement is performed under AT-C section 205, *Examination Engagements* (AICPA, *Professional Standards*), and addresses reporting on controls at a service organization relevant to security, availability, processing integrity, confidentiality, or privacy.

makes reference to an other practitioner are unlikely to be justified from a cost-benefit perspective.

3.131 The service auditor would not be able to use the report of the subservice auditor alone because that option would not satisfy the requirements in paragraph .31 of AT-C section 105, for example, the requirement to be involved in the work of the other practitioner.

———————————————

Chapter 4

Performing a Service Auditor's Engagement Under AT-C Section 320

In performing a service auditor's engagement, both the service organization and the service auditor have specific responsibilities. This chapter discusses responsibilities of the service auditor, matters the service auditor considers, and procedures the service auditor performs to test the fairness of the presentation of management's description of the service organization's system and the suitability of the design and operating effectiveness of the controls included in management's description of the service organization's system. This guide may not address all of the requirements and application guidance relevant to a service auditor's engagement and therefore should be read in conjunction with the following sections in AICPA *Professional Standards*: AT-C section 105, *Concepts Common to All Attestation Engagements*, AT-C section 205, *Examination Engagements*, and AT-C section 320, *Reporting on an Examination of Controls at a Service Organization Relevant to User Entities' Internal Control Over Financial Reporting* (AICPA, *Professional Standards*).

Responding to Assessed Risk and Obtaining Evidence

4.01 Paragraph .19 of AT-C section 205 requires the service auditor to obtain sufficient appropriate audit evidence to reduce attestation risk to an acceptably low level. Such evidence enables the service auditor to obtain reasonable assurance and to draw reasonable conclusions on which to base the service auditor's opinion. Paragraph .20 of AT-C section 320 requires the service auditor to design and implement overall responses to address the assessed risks of material misstatement for the subject matter.

4.02 The service auditor is responsible for determining the nature (types of test performed), timing (when the controls are tested), and extent (the number of testing procedures performed or size of the sample) of testing necessary to provide sufficient appropriate evidence that the controls were operating effectively throughout the period covered by the report.

4.03 Overall responses by the service auditor to address the risks of material misstatement of the subject matter may include the following:

- Emphasizing to the engagement team the need to maintain professional skepticism

- Assigning more-experienced staff or those with specialized skills or using specialists

- Providing more supervision

- Incorporating additional elements of unpredictability in the selection of further procedures to be performed

- Making changes to the nature, timing, or extent of procedures, for example, performing procedures at period-end instead of at an interim date or modifying the nature of the procedures to obtain more persuasive evidence

Evaluating Whether Management's Description of the Service Organization's System Is Fairly Presented

4.04 Paragraph .15 of AT-C section 320 identifies the attributes of suitable criteria for evaluating whether management's description of the service organization's system is fairly presented. Those criteria include, at a minimum,

- a. whether management's description of the service organization's system presents how the service organization's system was designed and implemented, including the following information about the service organization's system, if applicable:

  - i. The types of services provided including, as appropriate, the classes of transactions processed.

  - ii. The procedures, within both automated and manual systems, by which services are provided, including, as appropriate, procedures by which transactions are initiated, authorized, recorded, processed, corrected as necessary, and transferred to the reports and other information prepared for user entities.

  - iii. The information used in the performance of the procedures, including, if applicable, related accounting records, whether electronic or manual, and supporting information involved in initiating, authorizing, recording, processing, and reporting transactions. This includes the correction of incorrect information and how information is transferred to the reports and other information prepared for user entities.

  - iv. How the service organization's system captures and addresses significant events and conditions other than transactions.

  - v. The process used to prepare reports and other information for user entities.

  - vi. Services performed by a subservice organization, if any, including whether the carve-out method or the inclusive method has been used in relation to them.

  - vii. The specified control objectives and controls designed to achieve those objectives, including, as applicable, complementary user entity controls and complementary subservice organization controls assumed in the design of the service organization's controls.

  - viii. Other aspects of the service organization's control environment, risk assessment process, information and communications (including the related business processes), control activities, and monitoring activities that are relevant to the services provided.

    b. in the case of a type 2 report, whether management's description of the service organization's system includes relevant details of changes to the service organization's system during the period covered by the description.

    c. whether management's description of the service organization's system does not omit or distort information relevant to the service organization's system, while acknowledging that management's description of the service organization's system is prepared to meet the common needs of a broad range of user entities and their auditors, and may not, therefore, include every aspect of the service organization's system that each individual user entity may consider important in its own particular environment.

4.05 Paragraphs .A37–.A40 of AT-C section 320 provide guidance to the service auditor in determining whether the description of the service organization's system is fairly presented. Some of this guidance is discussed in more detail in paragraphs 4.06–.55 of this guide.

4.06 Paragraph .25 of AT-C section 320 requires the service auditor to obtain and read management's description of the service organization's system and to evaluate whether those aspects of the description that are included in the scope of the engagement are presented fairly, in all material respects, based on the criteria in management's assertion, including whether

    a. the control objectives stated in management's description of the service organization's system are reasonable in the circumstances.

    b. controls identified in management's description of the service organization's system were implemented (that is, actually placed in operation).

    c. complementary user entity controls and complementary subservice organization controls, if any, are adequately described.

    d. the services performed by a subservice organization, if any, are adequately described, including whether the carve-out method or the inclusive method has been used in relation to them.

4.07 The service auditor should determine through inquiries made in combination with other procedures whether the service organization's system has been implemented.

4.08 Paragraph .A37 of AT-C section 320 states that considering the following questions may assist the service auditor in determining whether management's description of the service organization's system is fairly presented, in all material respects, based on the criteria in management's assertion:

    ● Is the description prepared at a level of detail that could reasonably be expected to provide a broad range of user auditors with sufficient information to obtain an understanding of internal control in accordance with AU-C section 402, *Audit Considerations Relating to an Entity Using a Service Organization* (AICPA, *Professional Standards*)? The description need not address every aspect of the service organization's processing or the services provided to user entities and need not be so detailed that it would potentially enable a reader to compromise security or other controls at the service organization.

- Is the description prepared in a manner that does not omit or distort information that might affect the decisions of a broad range of user auditors; for example, does the description contain any significant omissions or inaccuracies regarding processing of which the service auditor is aware?

- Does the description include relevant details of changes to the service organization's system during the period covered by the description when the description covers a period of time?

- Have the controls identified in the description actually been implemented?

- If the inclusive method has been used, does the description separately identify controls at the service organization and controls at the subservice organization? Does the description include activities at the service organization that monitor the effectiveness of controls at the subservice organization?

- Are complementary user entity controls, if any, adequately described? In most cases, the control objectives stated in the description are worded so that they are capable of being achieved through the effective operation of controls implemented by the service organization alone. In some cases, however, the control objectives stated in the description cannot be achieved by the service organization alone because their achievement requires that particular controls be implemented by user entities. For example, to achieve specified control objectives, a user entity may need to review the completeness and accuracy of the input it provides to the service organization before submitting it to the service organization, or review the completeness and accuracy of reports the user entity receives from the service organization subsequent to processing. When the description does include complementary user entity controls, the description separately identifies those controls along with the specific control objectives that cannot be achieved by the service organization alone.

- If the carve-out method has been used, does the description identify the functions that are performed by the subservice organization? (When using the carve-out method, the description does not include the detailed processing or controls at the subservice organization.) Does the description include activities at the service organization that monitor the effectiveness of controls at the subservice organization as well as complementary subservice organization controls?

4.09 Comparing the service auditor's understanding of the services included in the scope of the engagement to the description of the service organization's system is an important process in determining whether the description is fairly presented.

4.10 As stated in paragraph .A38 of AT-C section 320, procedures the service auditor may perform to evaluate whether the description of the service organization's system is fairly presented typically include a combination of the following:

- Considering the nature of the user entities and how the services provided by the service organization are likely to affect them, for example, the predominant types of user entities, and whether the user entities are regulated

- Reading contracts with user entities to gain an understanding of the service organization's contractual obligations
- Observing the procedures performed by service organization personnel
- Reviewing the service organization's policy and procedure manuals and other documentation of the system, for example, flowcharts and narratives
- Performing walkthroughs of transactions through the service organization's system

4.11   The description is not fairly presented if it states or implies that controls are being performed when they are not being performed or if it inadvertently or intentionally omits relevant controls performed by the service organization that are not suitably designed or operating effectively. Paragraph 5.49 of this guide presents an example of a separate paragraph that would be added to the service auditor's report when the description includes controls that have not been implemented.

4.12   Paragraph .25*bi* of AT-C section 105 indicates that one of the preconditions for accepting an attestation engagement is that the subject matter is appropriate. Paragraph .A37*a* of AT-C section 105 indicates that an appropriate subject matter is identifiable and capable of consistent measurement or evaluation against the criteria. For that reason, the description of the service organization's system should not contain subjective statements that are not measureable. For example, describing a service organization as being "the world's best" or "the most respected in the industry" is subjective and, therefore, would not be appropriate for inclusion in the description of the service organization's system. Paragraph 5.50 of this guide presents an example of a separate paragraph that would be added to the service auditor's report when the description contains information that is not measureable and management will not revise the description.

4.13   One aspect of determining whether the description omits information that may affect user entities' internal control over financial reporting involves determining whether the description addresses all of the major aspects of the processing within the scope of the engagement that may be relevant to user auditors in assessing the risks of material misstatement of user entities' financial statements. Paragraph 5.52 of this guide presents an example of a separate paragraph that would be added to the service auditor's report when the description omits information that may be relevant to user entities' internal control over financial reporting.

4.14   A service organization may have controls that it considers to be outside the boundaries of the system, such as controls related to the conversion of new user entities to the service organization's systems. To avoid misunderstanding by readers of the description, the description should clearly delineate the boundaries of the system that is included in the scope of the engagement.

4.15   Paragraph .29 of AT-C section 320 states that, in a type 2 engagement, the service auditor should obtain an understanding of changes in the service organization's system that were implemented during the period covered by the service auditor's report. If the service auditor believes the changes would be considered significant by user entities and their auditors, the service auditor should determine whether those changes are included in the description of the service organization's system. A description of such changes would include a description of the controls before and after the change and an indication of when the controls changed. If management has not included such changes in the description of the service organization's system, the service auditor generally requests that management amend the description to include this information. If management will not include this information in the description, the service auditor should describe the changes in the service auditor's report and determine the effect on the service auditor's report. Paragraph 5.54 of this guide presents an example of a separate paragraph that would be added to the service auditor's report when the description omits changes to the service organization's controls.

4.16 When auditing the financial statements of an entity that uses a service organization (user entity), paragraph .09*a* of AU-C section 402 requires the auditor to obtain an understanding of how the user entity uses the services of a service organization in the user entity's operations, including the nature of the services provided by the service organization and the significance of those services to the user entity and their effect on the user entity's internal control relevant to the audit. Part of that understanding would include the types of information provided by the service organization to the user entity (such as individual reports or a reporting package) and the significance of such information to the user entity's internal control. The criterion for the description of a service organization's system in paragraph .15*av* of AT-C section 320 requires the description to include the process used to prepare reports and other information for user entities. For that reason, when the service auditor is evaluating the fairness of the presentation of the description of the service organization' system, the description would be expected to include a list of the reports and reporting packages provided to user entities. If the description does not include such a list, the service auditor should discuss the matter with management and recommend that such a list be added to the description.

Materiality Related to the Fair Presentation of the Description of the Service Organization's System

4.17 Paragraph .19 of AT-C section 320 indicates that the service auditor's consideration of materiality should include the fair presentation of the description of the service organization's system. The concept of materiality in the context of the fair presentation of the description relates to the information being reported on, not the financial statements of user entities. Materiality in this context primarily relates to qualitative factors, such as whether significant aspects of the processing have been included in the description or whether relevant information has been omitted or distorted. As outlined in paragraph .A28 of AT-C section 320, the concept of materiality takes into account the fact that the service auditor's report provides information about the service organization's system to meet the common information needs of a broad range of user entities and their auditors who have an understanding of the manner in which the system is being used by a particular user entity for financial reporting. Similarly, this concept extends to a service auditor's report for a single user entity. Materiality also applies with respect to the subservice organization when the inclusive method is used. In other words, materiality is considered in the context of the fair presentation of the service organization's description of its system for both the service organization and subservice organization.

4.18 The following are some examples related to materiality with respect to the fair presentation of the description of the service organization's system.

Example 1. Example Service Organization uses a subservice organization to perform all its back-office functions and elects to use the carve-out method of presentation. Management's description of the service organization's system includes information about the nature of the services provided by the subservice organization and describes the monitoring the service organization performs and other controls the service organization implements with respect to the processing performed by the subservice organization. The description includes such information because it is likely to be relevant to user entities' internal control over financial reporting and, therefore, would be considered material to management's description of the service organization's system.

Example 2. Example Service Organization is responsible for implementing general IT controls. The service organization's application controls cannot function without the underlying general IT controls; therefore, the general IT controls would be considered material to the description of the service organization's system and would be included in Example Service Organization's description of its system.

Example 3. Example Service Organization has multiple applications that enable management of the service organization to compare actual operating statistics with requirements in service level agreements with user entities. These applications do not process user entity transactions. Management may elect to exclude these applications from the description of Example Service Organization's system because they are not likely to be relevant to user entities' internal control over financial reporting and, therefore, are not material to the description.

4.19 Paragraph .17 of AT-C section 205 indicates that the service auditor should reconsider materiality if the practitioner becomes aware of information during the engagement that would have caused the service auditor to have initially determined a different materiality.

Evaluating Whether Control Objectives Are Reasonable in the Circumstances

4.20 In evaluating whether management's description of the service organization's system is fairly presented, paragraph .25*a* of AT-C section 320 requires the service auditor to determine whether the control objectives stated in management's description of the service organization's system are reasonable in the circumstances. Paragraphs 3.70–.76 and paragraphs 4.20–.33 of this guide discuss control objectives that are reasonable in the circumstances.

Relevance to User Entities' Internal Control Over Financial Reporting

4.21 Paragraph .04 of AT-C section 320 states that the focus of AT-C section 320 is on controls at service organizations likely to be relevant to user entities' internal control over financial reporting. Control objectives that relate to controls other than those that are likely to be relevant to user entities' internal control over financial reporting are not reasonable in the circumstances. For example, the control objective "Controls provide reasonable assurance that privacy commitments are communicated and met" would not be reasonable in the circumstances because a service organization's controls over the privacy of user entities' information are beyond the scope of an examination of a service organization's controls that are likely to be relevant to user entities' internal control over financial reporting.

4.22 As indicated in paragraph .A1 of AT-C section 320, controls related to a service organization's operations and compliance objectives may be relevant to a user entity's internal control over financial reporting. Such controls may pertain to assertions about presentation and disclosure relating to account balances, classes of transactions or disclosures, or may pertain to evidence that the user auditor evaluates or uses in applying auditing procedures. For example, a payroll processing service organization's controls related to the timely remittance of payroll deductions to government authorities may be relevant to a user entity because late remittances could incur interest and penalties that would result in a liability for the user entity. Similarly, a service organization's controls over the acceptability of investment transactions from a regulatory perspective may be considered relevant to a user entity's presentation and disclosure of transactions and account balances in its financial statements.

Represent Control Objectives That Service Organization's Controls Are Designed to Achieve

4.23 Another factor that affects the relevance of control objectives is whether they represent control objectives that the service organization's controls are designed to achieve. For example, a fund accounting agent that is not responsible for valuing securities ordinarily would not have a control objective stating the following:

> Controls provide reasonable assurance that portfolio securities are accurately valued.

Instead, to more accurately reflect what the controls are designed to achieve, the control objective may be revised to state the following:

> Controls provide reasonable assurance that portfolio securities are valued using prices obtained from sources authorized by the customer.

Relate to Types of Assertions Commonly Embodied in the Broad Range of User Entities' Financial Statements

4.24 Paragraph .A39 of AT-C section 320 indicates that control objectives that are reasonable in the circumstances relate to the types of assertions commonly embodied in the broad range of user entities' financial statements to which controls at the service organization could reasonably be expected to relate (for example, assertions about existence and accuracy that are affected by access controls that prevent or detect unauthorized access to the system). In evaluating whether the control objectives relate to the types of assertions commonly embodied in the broad range of user entities' financial statements, the service auditor should obtain an understanding of the services provided by the service organization, in combination with obtaining a high-level understanding of the components of the financial statements of user entities. For example, for a service organization that provides investment advisory and processing services to mutual funds, the service auditor could obtain and read a set of mutual fund financial statements and the contract between a mutual fund and the service organization to understand the processing performed by the service organization. In evaluating whether the control objectives relate to the assertions in the user entities' financial statements, the service auditor would compare the control objectives included in the description of the system to the assertions embedded in the financial statements of the mutual fund user entity.

4.25 As noted in paragraph .A39 of AT-C section 320, although the service auditor ordinarily will not be able to determine how controls at a service organization specifically relate to the assertions embodied in individual user entities' financial statements, matters such as the following are relevant when identifying the types of assertions to which those controls are likely to relate:

- The types of services provided by the service organization, including the classes of transactions processed
- The contents of reports and other information prepared for user entities
- The information used in the performance of procedures
- The types of significant events other than transactions that occur in providing the services
- Services performed by a subservice organization, if any
- The responsibility of the service organization to implement controls, including responsibilities established in contracts and agreements with user entities
- The risks to a user entity's internal control over financial reporting arising from information technology used or provided by the service organization

4.26 In evaluating whether a service organization's control objectives address the common financial statement assertions in user entities' financial statements, the service auditor may refer to

- appendix D, "Illustrative Control Objectives for Various Types of Service Organizations," of this guide;
- column 1 of table 4-1, "Types of Financial Statement Assertions, Related Service Organization Control Objectives, and Risks That Threaten the Achievement of the Control Objectives," of this guide;
- column 1 of table 4-2, "Types of Financial Statement Assertions About Account Balances at the Period End, Related Service Organization Control Objectives, and Risks That Threaten the Achievement of the Control Objectives," of this guide; and
- other sources, such as AICPA Audit and Accounting Guides for specialized industries, industry audit guides, and industry standards.

Completeness

4.27 Paragraph .A39 of AT-C section 320 also indicates that control objectives that are reasonable in the circumstances are complete. Although a complete set of control objectives can provide a broad range of user auditors with a framework to assess the effect of controls at the service organization on assertions commonly embodied in user entities' financial statements, the service auditor ordinarily will not be able to determine how controls at a service organization specifically relate to the assertions embodied in individual user entities' financial statements and cannot, therefore, determine whether control objectives are complete from the viewpoint of individual user entities or user auditors.

Control Objectives Specified by Law, Regulation, or an Outside Party

4.28 Although control objectives are usually specified by the service organization, they may be specified by law or regulation or by an outside party, such as a user entity or a user group. Paragraph .A39 of AT-C section 320 states that if the control objectives are specified by an outside party, including control objectives specified by law or regulation, the outside party is responsible for their completeness and reasonableness.

4.29 However, even when the control objectives are specified by an outside party, the service auditor still needs to exercise professional judgment in evaluating the completeness and reasonableness of the control objectives in the circumstances. For example, if an outside party specifies control objectives that only address application controls but the proper functioning of IT general controls is necessary for the application controls to operate effectively, the service organization would be expected to include the relevant IT general controls in its description of the service organization's system as they relate to the specified control objectives. Paragraph 5.60 of this guide presents an example of a paragraph that would be added to the service auditor's report when the service organization's control objectives are established by an outside party but that set of control objectives omits control objectives that the service auditor believes are necessary to achieve the control objectives established by the outside party. An example of such an omission is a set of control objectives that does not address the authorization, testing, documentation, and implementation of changes to existing applications.

Control Objectives Have Attributes of Suitable Criteria

4.30 As discussed in paragraph 3.74 of this guide, control objectives that are reasonable in the circumstances also have the attributes of objectivity and measurability.

Control Objectives Not Relevant to User Entities' Internal Control

4.31 A service organization may wish to include control objectives in its description that are not relevant to user entities' internal control over financial reporting, such as control objectives that address the privacy or confidentiality of information processed by a system, the availability of a system, the service organization's compliance with specified requirements of laws or regulations, or the efficiency of the service organization's operations. Control objectives that are not relevant to user entities' internal control over financial reporting would be considered "other information." The service auditor's responsibility for such other information is discussed in paragraph .57 of AT-C section 205. One option in these circumstances is for the service auditor to ask the service organization to remove these control objectives from the description and suggest that management of the service organization engage a practitioner to report on those control objectives separately under AT-C section 205. If the control objectives are relevant to the security, availability, processing integrity, confidentiality, or privacy of a system, the practitioner may suggest that the entity consider undergoing a SOC 2® engagement as described in table 1-1 and in appendix E, "Comparison of SOC 1®, SOC 2®, and SOC 3® Engagements and Related Reports," of this guide.

4.32 Control objectives that are not likely to be relevant to user entities' internal control over financial reporting may be included in a separate section of the type 1 or type 2 report that is not covered by the service auditor's report, such as a section entitled "Other Information Provided by the Service Organization." An example of such a control objective is one that addresses the service organization's business continuity and contingency planning. Such information generally is of interest to management of the user entities. However, because plans are not controls, a service organization would not ordinarily include in its description a unique control objective that addresses the adequacy of business continuity or contingency planning. Including such information in a separate section of the type 1 or type 2 report provides the means for service organization management to communicate its plans related to business continuity and contingency planning. Reporting guidance for such situations is presented in paragraph 5.57 of this guide.

After Engagement Has Been Accepted, Service Auditor Determines Control Objectives Are Not Reasonable in the Circumstances

4.33 In engagements other than those in which the control objectives are specified by law, regulation, or an outside party, if the service auditor determines after the engagement has been accepted that the control objectives are not reasonable in the circumstances because they do not have the attributes specified in paragraph .A39 of AT-C section 320 (relevance and completeness) as well as the additional attributes of suitable criteria identified in paragraph .A42 of AT-C section 105 (objectivity and measurability), the service auditor should discuss this matter with the appropriate party (usually management of the service organization). If management does not revise the control objectives to address the service auditor's concerns, the service auditor should determine whether

- the matter can be resolved,

- it is appropriate to continue with the engagement, and

- if the matter cannot be resolved but it is still appropriate to continue with the engagement, whether, and if so how, to communicate the matter in the service auditor's report.

Paragraphs 5.57–.63 of this guide present examples of a separate paragraph that would be added to the service auditor's report to describe the reason for the modification of the opinion when the control objectives are not reasonable in the circumstances.

Implementation of Service Organization Controls

4.34 Paragraph .25*b* of AT-C section 320 requires the service auditor to determine whether the controls identified in management's description of the service organization's system were implemented (that is, whether the controls exist and have been placed in operation).

4.35 Paragraph .26 of AT-C section 320 states that the service auditor should determine through inquiries made in combination with other procedures whether the service organization's system has been implemented (inquiry alone is not sufficient). Such other procedures may include

- observation,

- inspection of records and other documentation of the manner in which the service organization's system operates and controls are applied, and

- reperformance of the manner in which transactions are processed through the system and controls are applied.

4.36 Paragraph .A40 of AT-C section 320 also indicates that the procedures the service auditor performs to determine whether the system described by the service organization has been implemented may be similar to, and performed in conjunction with, procedures to obtain an understanding of the system. For example, when performing a walkthrough to verify the service auditor's understanding of the design of controls, the service auditor may also determine whether controls have been implemented. Performing a walkthrough entails asking relevant members of the service organization's management and staff to describe and demonstrate their actions in performing a procedure. A walkthrough generally includes tracing one or more transactions from initiation through how information is transferred to the reports and other information prepared for user entities, including the relevant information systems. Ordinarily, a service auditor will also obtain documentary evidence of the performance of controls or observe the controls being performed during the walkthrough. It may also be helpful to use flowcharts, questionnaires, or data flow diagrams to facilitate understanding the design of the controls.

4.37 An appropriately performed walkthrough provides an opportunity to verify the service auditor's understanding of the flow of transactions and the design of the controls. Probing questions, combined with other walkthrough procedures, enable the service auditor to gain a sufficient understanding of the processes and to determine whether procedures are actually performed as stated in the description of the service organization's system.

4.38 The description of the service organization's system should include only controls that have been implemented. If the service auditor determines that certain controls identified in management's description have not been implemented, the service auditor may ask management of the service organization to remove those controls from the description. In turn, the service auditor should consider only controls that have been implemented when assessing the suitability of the design and operating effectiveness of controls. If management decides not to remove controls that have not been implemented from the description, the service auditor should consider the effect of the misstatement on the service auditor's conclusion regarding the fair presentation of the description. Paragraph 5.49 of this guide presents an example of a separate paragraph that would be added to the service auditor's report when the description includes controls that have not been implemented. In evaluating the suitability of the design and operating effectiveness of the controls, the service auditor should consider whether the failure to implement certain controls results in controls not being suitably designed.

4.39 The fact that controls are implemented does not imply that they are suitably designed or operating with sufficient effectiveness to achieve the control objectives. The procedures the service auditor performs to assess the suitability of design and operating effectiveness of controls are discussed in paragraphs 4.56–.77 of this guide.

Complementary User Entity Controls

4.40 In many cases the control objectives stated in the description of the service organization's system cannot be achieved by the service organization without the implementation by the user entities of specific controls that are necessary to achieve the control objectives (complementary user entity controls). In evaluating the description, paragraph .25c of AT-C section 320 requires the service auditor to read the description and evaluate whether complementary user entity controls and complementary subservice organization controls, if any, are adequately described. To evaluate whether complementary user entity controls included in the description are adequately described, the service auditor may read contracts with user entities or perform other procedures to gain an understanding of the user entities' responsibilities and whether those responsibilities are appropriately described in management's description of the service organization's system. Complementary subservice organization controls are discussed in paragraph 4.51.

4.41 For example, a service organization that provides payroll services to user entities and electronically receives payroll data from user entities would include the following control objective in its description:

> Controls provide reasonable assurance that input to the payroll application is authorized.

This control objective could not be achieved without the implementation of input controls at the user entities because transaction initiation and authorization rests with them. The service organization can only be responsible for determining that input transactions are received from authorized sources as established by the user entities. Accordingly, the description would include a complementary user entity control consideration, such as the following:

> Controls are implemented by user entities to provide reasonable assurance that input to the payroll application is authorized.

Alternatively, the control objective could be modified so that it could be achieved without a complementary user entity control, such as the following:

> Controls provide reasonable assurance that input is received from authorized sources.

4.42 Paragraph 5.65 of this guide presents an example of a separate paragraph that would be added to the service auditor's report when complementary user entity controls are necessary for one or more control objectives to be achieved but the description of the service organization's system omits such complementary user entity control considerations.

Subservice Organizations

4.43 Paragraph .A37 of AT-C section 320 includes questions the service auditor may consider in determining whether the description of the service organization's system for a service organization that uses a subservice organization is fairly presented. Information in service level agreements and contracts between the service organization and the subservice organization may assist the service auditor in determining whether relevant controls at a subservice organization are appropriately described.

4.44 Paragraph .11 of AT-C section 320 indicates that if the service organization has used the inclusive method of presentation, the service auditor should apply the requirements in AT-C sections 105, 205, and 320 to the services provided by the subservice organization. The definition of *inclusive method* in paragraph .08 of AT-C section 320 indicates that, when the inclusive method is used, management's description of the service organization's system includes a description of the nature of the services provided by the subservice organization as well as the subservice organization's relevant control objectives and related controls. Accordingly, the service auditor should determine whether the description of the service organization's system includes that information.

4.45 If the description uses the inclusive method, the fifth bullet of paragraph .A37 of AT-C section 320 asks the service auditor to consider whether the description of the service organization's system separately identifies controls at the service organization and controls at the subservice organization. AT-C section 320 does not prescribe how the description should be modified to differentiate between aspects of the description that address the service organization and aspects that address the subservice organization; however, examples 1–2 of appendix B, "Illustrative Type 2 Reports—Inclusive Method, Including Illustrative Management Representation Letters," of this guide illustrates one method of doing so.

4.46 The definition of the *carve-out method* in paragraph .08 of AT-C section 320 indicates that, if the carve-out method is used, management's description of the service organization's system identifies the nature of the services performed by the subservice organization and excludes from the description and from the scope of the service auditor's engagement the subservice organization's relevant control objectives and related controls. Accordingly, if the service organization has used the carve-out method of presentation, the service auditor should determine whether the description identifies the nature of the services performed by the subservice organization.

4.47 If the carve-out method is used, paragraph .A27 of AT-C section 320 indicates that the description of the service organization's system and the scope of the service auditor's engagement include controls at the service organization that monitor the effectiveness of controls at the subservice organization, which may include some combination of ongoing monitoring to determine that potential issues are identified timely and separate evaluations to determine that the effectiveness of internal control is maintained over time. Examples of monitoring controls include reviewing and reconciling output reports, holding periodic discussions with the subservice organization, making regular site visits to the subservice organization, testing controls at the subservice organization by members of the service organization's internal audit function, reviewing type 1 or type 2 reports on the subservice organization's system prepared pursuant to AT-C section 320 or AT-C section 205, and monitoring external communications, such as customer complaints relevant to the services provided by the subservice organization.

4.48 When the carve-out method is used and the subservice organization has provided a type 1 or type 2 report to user entities, the service auditor should determine whether the service organization has included and addressed relevant complementary user entity control considerations described in the subservice organization's type 1 or type 2 report or specified in the contract or service level agreement between the service organization and the subservice organization.

4.49 A service organization may use multiple subservice organizations and may prepare its description using the carve-out method of presentation for one or more subservice organizations and the inclusive method of presentation for others. The service auditor should determine whether the guidance concerning the inclusive method of presentation has been applied to all the subservice organizations for which the inclusive method is used and that the guidance concerning the carve-out method has been applied to all the subservice organizations for which the carve-out method has been used.

4.50 Paragraph 5.67 of this guide addresses report modifications when the service organization does not disclose that it uses subservice organizations to perform functions that are likely to be relevant to user entities' internal control over financial reporting.

Complementary Subservice Organization Controls

4.51 In some cases, the control objectives stated in the description cannot be achieved by the service organization alone because their achievement requires that particular controls be implemented by subservice organizations. Controls that need to be implemented by subservice organizations are referred to as *complementary subservice organization controls* and are defined in paragraph .08 of AT-C section 320 as "controls that management of the service organization assumes, in the design of the service organization's system, will be implemented by the subservice organizations and are necessary to achieve the control objectives stated in management's description of the service organization's system." Complementary user entity controls are discussed in paragraph 4.40 of this guide.

4.52 Paragraph .25c of AT-C section 320 requires the service auditor to read the description and evaluate whether complementary user entity controls and complementary subservice organization controls, if any, are adequately described. To evaluate whether complementary subservice organization controls included in the description are adequately described, the service auditor may read contracts with subservice organizations, user and technical manuals provided by the subservice organization, and perform other relevant procedures to gain an understanding of the subservice organization's responsibilities and whether those responsibilities are appropriately described in management's description of the service organization's system.

4.53 For example, if a service organization uses an application hosting subservice organization to manage all of its information technology systems, controls at the application hosting subservice organization are likely to be necessary for the service organization's application controls to operate effectively. Accordingly, the description would include a complementary subservice organization control consideration, such as the following:

> Controls provide reasonable assurance that changes to application programs and related data management systems are authorized, tested, documented, approved, and implemented to result in the complete, accurate, and timely processing and reporting of transactions and balances.

4.54 In another scenario, a service organization that is responsible for processing medical, vision, and dental insurance claims outsources the processing of a specific type of claim, for example those related to dental insurance, to a subservice organization. In this scenario, the service organization may have a control objective that states:

> Controls provide reasonable assurance that medical, vision, and dental claims are processed completely and accurately.

Due to the outsourcing of the dental claims processing, management would need to specify complementary subservice organization controls in its description, such as the following:

> For Control Objective X, service organization management assumes that the subservice organization has implemented controls that address the completeness and accuracy of dental claims processing, such as the following:
>
> - Data input checks to help ensure the accuracy of input
> - Secondary review of dental claim data entered into the XYZ system for accuracy
> - Reconciliation of dental claims received to claims input into the XYZ system to help ensure completeness
> - Segregation of duties controls to help ensure that claims data is reviewed by an individual separate from the individual processing the claim

4.55 Paragraph 5.66 of this guide presents an example of a separate paragraph that would be added to the service auditor's report when complementary subservice organization controls are necessary for one or more control objectives to be achieved but the service organization fails to include such complementary subservice organization control considerations in its description of the service organization's system.

Obtaining and Evaluating Evidence Regarding the Suitability of the Design of Controls

4.56 Paragraph .10*bv* of AT-C section 320 indicates that one of the preconditions for engagement acceptance or continuance is that management of the service organization agree to the terms of the engagement by acknowledging and accepting its responsibility for identifying the risks that threaten the achievement of the control objectives stated in the description and designing, implementing, and documenting controls that are suitably designed and operating effectively to provide reasonable assurance that the control objectives stated in the description of the service organization's system will be achieved.

4.57 Paragraph .16 of AT-C section 320 indicates that the minimum attributes of suitable criteria for evaluating whether controls are suitably designed include whether

a. the risks that threaten the achievement of the control objectives stated in management's description of the service organization's system have been identified by management.

b. the controls identified in management's description of the service organization's system would, if operating effectively, provide reasonable assurance that those risks would not prevent the control objectives stated in the description from being achieved.

4.58 Paragraph .27 of AT-C section 320 requires the service auditor to assess whether the controls that management identified in its description of the service organization's system as the controls that achieve the related control objectives are suitably designed to achieve the related control objectives by

   a. obtaining an understanding of management's process for identifying and evaluating the risks that threaten the achievement of the control objectives and assessing the completeness and accuracy of management's identification of those risks;

   b. evaluating the linkage of the controls identified in management's description of the service organization's system with those risks, including risks arising from each of the described classes of transactions and risks that IT poses to the user entity's internal control over financial reporting; and

   c. determining that the controls have been implemented.

If the inclusive method has been used, this requirement is also applicable to controls at the subservice organization.

4.59 Management of a service organization is responsible for designing and implementing controls that achieve the related control objectives, identifying the risks that threaten the achievement of those control objectives, and evaluating the linkage of the controls to the risks that threaten the achievement of the related control objectives. In many cases, the service auditor may be able to obtain management's documentation of its identification of risks and evaluation of the linkage of controls to those risks, which may be helpful in evaluating the completeness of management's identification of risks and the effectiveness of the controls in mitigating those risks.

4.60 Paragraph .19 of AT-C section 320 indicates that the service auditor's consideration of materiality should include the suitability of the design of controls to achieve the related control objectives. Paragraph .A29 of AT-C section 320 states, in part, that the service auditor's consideration of materiality with respect to the design of controls primarily includes the consideration of qualitative factors, for example, whether the controls have the ability as designed to provide reasonable assurance that the control objectives stated in management's description of the service organization's system would be achieved. Paragraph .17 of AT-C section 205 indicates that the service auditor should reconsider materiality if the practitioner becomes aware of information during the engagement that would have caused the service auditor to have initially determined a different materiality.

4.61 Paragraph .A17 of AT-C section 320 elaborates on the relationship between control objectives, risks, and controls.

   .A17 Control objectives relate to risks that controls seek to mitigate. For example, the risk that a transaction is recorded at the wrong amount or in the wrong period can be expressed as a control objective that transactions are recorded at the correct amount and in the correct period. Management is responsible for identifying the risks that threaten achievement of the control objectives stated in management's description of the service organization's system. A service organization's controls may be designed with the assumption that user entities will have implemented complementary user entity controls or that subservice organizations will have implemented complementary subservice organization controls that are necessary to achieve the control objectives. The risks that management identifies also include the risk that such controls were not implemented by user entities or subservice organizations or that those controls were not operating effectively. Management may have a formal or informal process for identifying relevant risks. A formal process may include estimating the significance of identified risks, assessing the likelihood of their occurrence, and deciding about actions to address them. However, because control objectives relate to risks that controls seek to mitigate, thoughtful identification by management of control objectives when designing, implementing, and documenting the service organization's system may itself comprise an informal process for identifying relevant risks.

Types of Assertions in User Entities' Financial Statements

4.62 A relevant matter in assessing the reasonableness of the control objectives, as discussed in the first bullet of paragraph .A39 of AT-C section 320, is whether the control objectives relate to the types of assertions commonly embodied in a broad range of user entity financial statements to which controls at the service organization could reasonably be expected to relate (for example, assertions about existence and accuracy that are affected by access controls that prevent or detect unauthorized access to the system). Table 4-1, "Types of Financial Statement Assertions About Classes of Transactions and Events During a Period, Related Service Organization Control Objectives, and Risks That Threaten the Achievement of the Control Objectives," and table 4-2, "Types of Assertions About Account Balances at the Period End, Related Service Organization Control Objectives, and Risks That Threaten the Achievement of the Control Objectives," present the types of assertions that may exist in a user entity's financial statements, illustrative service organization control objectives that relate to those types of assertions, and the risks that threaten the achievement of those control objectives. Because the control objectives in the table are illustrative, they would need to be tailored to the specific circumstances.

4.63 Table 4-1 presents the categories of assertions that may exist in a user entity's financial statements and that may be affected when the service provided by the service organization involves processing transactions and recording events for user entities.[1]

---

[1] If the services provided by the service organization include preparation of user entity financial statements, the following user entity assertions about presentation and disclosure may also be relevant:

- *Occurrence and rights and obligations.* Disclosed events, transactions, and other matters have occurred and pertain to the entity.
- *Completeness.* All disclosures that should have been included in the financial statements have been included.
- *Classification and understandability.* Financial information is appropriately presented and described and disclosures are clearly expressed.
- *Accuracy and valuation.* Financial and other information is disclosed fairly and at appropriate amounts.

Table 4-1

Types of Financial Statement Assertions[2] About Classes of Transactions and Events During a Period, Related Service Organization Control Objectives, and Risks That Threaten the Achievement of the Control Objectives

User Entity Financial Statement Assertions	Illustrative Service Organization Control Objectives Controls provide reasonable assurance that ...	Illustrative Risks[3] That Threaten the Achievement of the Control Objectives as They Relate to the User Entities' Financial Statements
Occurrence. Transactions and events that have been recorded have occurred and pertain to the entity.	• transactions are authorized and received only from authorized sources.[4] • transactions are validated[5] in a complete, accurate, and timely manner.[6]	Unauthorized transactions are entered and not detected. For example, manual transactions are not reviewed and approved by authorized individuals, or transactions are entered by unauthorized individuals. Invalid transactions are entered and not detected. For example, duplicate transactions are entered. Entered transactions are not validated against master data and other management authorization criteria. For example, automated transactions are not validated against master data, or transactions that do not correspond with master data are not rejected. Transactions are incorrectly attributed to the entity. Transactions are incorrectly processed so that invalid transactions are recorded, for example, recorded as a result of a logic error in the application.

(continued)

---

[2] Paragraph .A114 of AU-C section 315, *Understanding the Entity and Its Environment and Assessing the Risks of Material Misstatement* (AICPA, *Professional Standards*).

[3] The risks that threaten the achievement of the service organization's control objectives are dependent on the unique facts and circumstances of the service organization.

[4] Transaction data may be received in paper or electronic form or by telephone, for example, by a call center. The service organization may have separate control objectives for each method of receipt.

[5] Validation includes determining that the recorded transaction has occurred and pertains to the user entity. It also includes correcting invalid data and properly reentering corrected data.

[6] A timely manner also includes recording the transaction in the correct period.

Types of Financial Statement Assertions—*continued*

User Entity Financial Statement Assertions	Illustrative Service Organization Control Objectives Controls provide reasonable assurance that ...	Illustrative Risks That Threaten the Achievement of the Control Objectives as They Relate to the User Entities' Financial Statements
		Transaction reports provided to user entities inappropriately accumulate transactions. For example, transaction reports include invalid transactions or information that is inconsistent with the transaction detail maintained by the service organization.
		Master data are inaccurate or incomplete.
		Unauthorized or invalid transactions are entered as a result of compromises in IT general controls.
		Physical media needed to process a transaction are not properly controlled. For example, blank checks are stolen and improper; unauthorized checks are issued.
Completeness. All transactions and events that should have been recorded have been recorded.	• transactions are entered, processed, recorded, and reported in a complete manner.	All authorized and valid transactions are not recorded. For example, transactions are incorrectly rejected, are not properly reentered, are not entered on a timely basis, or are recorded in the accounts of the wrong entity.
		Applications incorrectly process transactions so that all authorized and valid transactions are not recorded. For example, all transactions are not processed, processing is incomplete, or programming logic is incorrect
		Transaction reports provided to user entities inappropriately accumulate valid and authorized transactions. For example, valid transactions are excluded, or reported information is inconsistent with transaction detail maintained by the service organization.

Types of Financial Statement Assertions—*continued*

User Entity Financial Statement Assertions	Illustrative Service Organization Control Objectives Controls provide reasonable assurance that ...	Illustrative Risks That Threaten the Achievement of the Control Objectives as They Relate to the User Entities' Financial Statements
		Authorized and valid transactions are not recorded or reported as a result of compromises in IT general controls.
Accuracy. Amounts and other data relating to recorded transactions and events have been recorded appropriately.	• transactions are entered, processed, recorded, and reported in an accurate manner.	Inaccurate or incomplete amounts or other relevant transaction data are entered and not detected. For example, expected transaction data is missing, does not match expected field values, or does not fall within predetermined limits. Master data are inaccurate or incomplete. Applications process transactions incorrectly, so that transactions contain inaccurate amounts or inaccuracies in other relevant transaction data. For example, a logic error in the application results in incorrect programmed calculations. Transaction reports provided to user entities inappropriately accumulate transactions. For example, reports include transactions containing inaccurate amounts or inaccuracies in other relevant data. Inaccurate or incomplete amounts or other relevant data are recorded or reported as a result of compromises in IT general controls.
Cutoff. Transactions and events have been recorded in the correct accounting period.	• transactions are entered, processed, recorded, and reported in a timely manner.[7]	The incorrect period is entered for the transaction or the period is omitted and is not detected. Applications process transactions incorrectly so that transactions are recorded or reported in an incorrect period, for example, as a result of a logic error in the application.

(continued)

---

[7] Ibid.

Types of Financial Statement Assertions—*continued*

User Entity Financial Statement Assertions	Illustrative Service Organization Control Objectives Controls provide reasonable assurance that ...	Illustrative Risks That Threaten the Achievement of the Control Objectives as They Relate to the User Entities' Financial Statements
		Transactions are recorded or reported in the wrong period as a result of compromises in IT general controls.
		Entered transactions are not validated in a timely manner.
Classification. Transactions and events have been recorded in the proper accounts.	• transactions are recorded and reported in the proper accounts. *Note*: Entering, processing, recording, and reporting transactions in a complete, accurate, and timely manner includes appropriate classification to facilitate proper reporting by the user entity.	An incorrect account is entered for a transaction and is not detected. Applications process transactions incorrectly, so that transactions are recorded in the wrong account, for example, as a result of a logic error in the application. Transaction reports provided to user entities inappropriately accumulate transactions, resulting in transactions being reported in the wrong accounts. Transactions are classified in the wrong accounts as a result of compromises in IT general controls.

4.64 Table 4-2 presents the categories of assertions that may exist in a user entity's financial statements and that may be affected when the service provided by the service organization involves maintaining balances for user entities, including detail trial balances or general ledgers.[8]

---

[8] If the services provided by the service organization include preparing user entity financial statements, the following user entity assertions about presentation and disclosure may also be relevant:

- *Occurrence and rights and obligations.* Disclosed events and transactions have occurred and pertain to the entity.
- *Completeness.* All disclosures that should have been included in the financial statements have been included.
- *Classification and understandability.* Financial information is appropriately presented and described and disclosures are clearly expressed.
- *Accuracy and valuation.* Financial and other information are disclosed fairly and at appropriate amounts.

Table 4-2

Types of Financial Statement Assertions About Account Balances at the Period End, Related Service Organization Control Objectives, and Risks That Threaten the Achievement of the Control Objectives

User Entity Financial Statement Assertions	Illustrative Service Organization Control Objectives Controls provide reasonable assurance that . . .	Illustrative Risks That Threaten the Achievement of the Control Objectives as They Relate to the User Entities' Financial Statements
Existence. Assets, liabilities, and equity interests exist.	• balances represent valid asset, liability, and equity interest balances and are classified properly.	Invalid transactions are recorded or reported in the account balance. Recorded or reported balances include valid transactions that should be recorded in another account. Balances do not reconcile to subsidiary detail, for example, because reconciliations are not performed or are not properly performed. Proper adjustments for reconciling items are not recorded or are not recorded in a timely manner. Recorded adjustments to account balances are not authorized and approved. Master data are inaccurate or incomplete. Unauthorized or invalid transactions are recorded in account balances as a result of compromises in IT general controls.
Rights and obligations. The entity holds or controls the rights to assets, and liabilities are the obligations of the entity.	• asset and liability balances relate to rights or obligations of the user entity.	User entity asset or liability balances include balances that are not rights and obligations of the user entity; for example, the balances pertain to another entity.

(continued)

Types of Financial Statement Assertions—*continued*

User Entity Financial Statement Assertions	Illustrative Service Organization Control Objectives Controls provide reasonable assurance that . . .	Illustrative Risks That Threaten the Achievement of the Control Objectives as They Relate to the User Entities' Financial Statements
		Master data are inaccurate or incomplete.
		User entity assets or liabilities are improperly recorded as a result of compromises in IT general controls.
Completeness. All assets, liabilities, and equity interests that should have been recorded have been recorded.	• balances represent all asset, liability, and equity interest balances that should have been recorded.	Recorded or reported balances do not include all valid transactions; for example, account numbers are invalid, or transactions are incorrectly recorded in another account.
		Balances do not reconcile to subsidiary detail, for example, because reconciliations are not performed or are not properly performed.
		Proper adjustments for reconciling items are not recorded or are not recorded in a timely manner.
		Not all authorized or approved adjustments to account balances are recorded.
		Master data are inaccurate or incomplete.
		Not all valid transactions are recorded or reported in account balances as a result of compromises in IT general controls.

Types of Financial Statement Assertions—*continued*

User Entity Financial Statement Assertions	*Illustrative Service Organization Control Objectives* Controls provide reasonable assurance that . . .	*Illustrative Risks That Threaten the Achievement of the Control Objectives as They Relate to the User Entities' Financial Statements*
Valuation and allocation. Assets, liabilities, and equity interests are included in the financial statements at appropriate amounts, and any resulting valuation or allocation adjustments are appropriately recorded.	• asset, liability, and equity interest balances are reported at accurate amounts.	Balances are recorded or reported at inaccurate amounts. Amounts for valid transactions are not properly or completely summarized in the recorded or reported account balance. Valuation or allocation calculations are not properly performed. Valuation or allocation adjustments are not recorded or reported accurately and in a timely manner. Balances do not reconcile to subsidiary detail, for example, because reconciliations are not performed or are not properly performed. Proper adjustments for reconciling items are not recorded or are not recorded in a timely manner. Adjustments to recorded account balances are not authorized or approved. Authorized and approved adjustments to account balances are not recorded. Master data are inaccurate or incomplete. Balances and underlying transactions are not properly valued or allocated as a result of compromises in IT general controls.

IT General Control Objectives and Related Risks

4.65 In addition, the control objectives would include IT general control objectives that are necessary to achieve the application control objectives (related to classes of transactions and events as well as account balances) and are therefore likely to be relevant to controls over financial reporting at user entities. IT general controls are assessed in relation to their effect on applications and data that are likely to be relevant to financial reporting at user entities. IT general control objectives and related controls are typically reported separately from application controls. Table 4-3, "IT General Control Objectives and Risks That Threaten the Achievement of the Control Objectives," presents illustrative IT general control objectives and the risks that threaten their achievement.

Table 4-3

IT General Control Objectives and Risks That Threaten the Achievement of the Control Objectives

	Illustrative Service Organization IT General Control Objectives Controls provide reasonable assurance that . . .	*Illustrative Risks That Threaten the Achievement of the IT General Control Objectives*
Information Security	• logical access[9] to programs, data, and computer resources[10] relevant to user entities' internal control over financial reporting is restricted to authorized and appropriate users and such users are restricted to	Unauthorized users gain access to and modify data or applications. Authorized users make unauthorized or inappropriate use of or modification to applications or application data. Segregation of duties is not effective or is not enforced by logical access security measures.

[9] In assessing the logical access controls over programs, data, and computer resources, the service organization considers

- logical access controls that may affect the user entities' financial statements. Generally, this would begin with the access controls directly over the application. If the effectiveness of application-level security is dependent on the effectiveness of network and operating system controls, these are also considered. Controls over direct access to the databases or data files and tables are considered as well.

- the configuration and administration of security tools and techniques, and monitoring controls designed to identify and respond to security violations in a timely manner.

[10] Computer resources include, but are not limited to, computer equipment, network equipment, storage media, and other hardware supporting the services provided by the service organization.

IT General Control Objectives and Risks That Threaten the Achievement of the Control Objectives—*continued*

	Illustrative Service Organization IT General Control Objectives Controls provide reasonable assurance that . . .	*Illustrative Risks That Threaten the Achievement of the IT General Control Objectives*
	performing authorized and appropriate actions.[11]	Logical access security measures are bypassed through physical access to sensitive system resources, resulting in unauthorized access and changes to data or applications.
	• physical access to computer and other resources[12] relevant to user entities' internal control over financial reporting is restricted to authorized and appropriate personnel.	Physical media is taken or copied. Unauthorized use is made of system resources. Unauthorized physical access is not detected.
Change Management	• changes to application programs and related data management systems[13] are authorized, tested, documented, approved, and implemented to result in the	Authorized changes are not entered or are not entered accurately. Application specifications are inconsistent with management needs, intent, or requirements. Application change process is not initiated when business rules, calculations, or processes change.

(continued)

---

[11] Many service organizations have features enabling customers to directly access programs and data. In assessing the logical access controls over programs and data, the service organization considers controls over security related to service organization personnel, the service organization's customers, and the customers' clients, as applicable, as well as the likely effect of these controls on user entities' financial statements.

[12] Other resources include, but are not limited to, buildings, vaults, and negotiable instruments.

[13] Data management systems include database management systems, specialized data transport, or communications software (often called middleware), data warehouse software, and data extraction or reporting software. Controls over data management systems may enhance user authentication or authorization, the availability of system privileges, data access privileges, application processing hosted within the data management systems, and segregation of duties.

IT General Control Objectives and Risks That Threaten the Achievement of the Control Objectives—*continued*

	Illustrative Service Organization IT General Control Objectives Controls provide reasonable assurance that . . .	*Illustrative Risks That Threaten the Achievement of the IT General Control Objectives*
	complete, accurate, and timely[14] processing and reporting of transactions and balances relevant to user entities' internal control over financial reporting.[15]	Application logic does not function properly or as specified. Unauthorized changes are made to production applications. Application changes are not approved. Application configuration changes made to the system are not authorized or authorized changes are not made. Authorized application configuration changes are not entered accurately in the system. Application configuration changes are implemented before or after the appropriate time.
	• network infrastructure[16] is configured as authorized to (1) support the effective functioning of application controls to result in valid, complete, accurate, and	Unauthorized changes are made to application configurations. Unauthorized changes are made to infrastructure and infrastructure configurations. Infrastructure and infrastructure configurations do not

[14] Timeliness may be relevant in particular situations, for example, when emergency changes are needed or when changes that would likely affect the user entities' information systems are being implemented to meet contractual requirements. Controls for emergency changes typically will be different from those for planned changes.

[15] This control objective is quite broad and should be tailored to the service organization's environment. For example, if the service organization has different controls for developing new applications or for making changes to applications or databases, it might be clearer to have separate control objectives for each of these.

[16] Network infrastructure includes all of the hardware, software, operating systems, and communication components within which the applications and related data management systems operate.

IT General Control Objectives and Risks That Threaten the Achievement of the Control Objectives—*continued*

	Illustrative Service Organization IT General Control Objectives Controls provide reasonable assurance that . . .	*Illustrative Risks That Threaten the Achievement of the IT General Control Objectives*
	timely[17] processing and reporting of transactions and balances relevant to user entities' financial reporting; (2) protect data relevant to user entities' financial reporting from unauthorized changes;[18] and (3) support user entities' internal control over financial reporting.	support the proper functioning of application processing, logical security, or availability of data and files, resulting in unauthorized access to applications or data. Network infrastructure is not updated on a timely basis to protect against known vulnerabilities. Emergency configuration changes are not authorized or appropriate. Unauthorized changes to infrastructure are not detected.
Computer Operations	• application and system processing[19] relevant to user entities' internal control over financial reporting are authorized and	Programs are not executed in the correct order. Programs are not executed within scheduled timeframes. Programs do not execute completely.

(continued)

---

[17] Timeliness may be relevant in particular situations, for example, when emergency changes are needed or when changes are being implemented to meet contractual requirements.

[18] Program change controls over network infrastructure include, as appropriate, the authorization, testing, documentation, approval, and implementation of changes to network infrastructure. In assessing change management, the service organization considers the configuration and administration of the security tools and techniques, and monitoring controls designed to identify exceptions to authorized network infrastructure, applications, and data management systems (for example, database structures) and act upon them in a timely manner. If the service organization has different controls for new implementations or making changes to the infrastructure, applications, or data management systems, it might be clearer to have separate control objectives that address the controls over each type of infrastructure. There may also be separate control objectives for controls over new implementations and controls over changes to existing resources.

[19] The processing in this control objective refers to the batch processing of data. It typically does not include the scheduling of file backups. Should the service organization have significant online, real-time processing, it may tailor this control objective or add a new control objective to address controls over the identification, tracking, recording, and resolution of problems and errors in a complete, accurate, and timely manner.

IT General Control Objectives and Risks That Threaten the Achievement of the Control Objectives—*continued*

	Illustrative Service Organization IT General Control Objectives Controls provide reasonable assurance that . . .	*Illustrative Risks That Threaten the Achievement of the IT General Control Objectives*
	executed in a complete, accurate, and timely manner, and deviations, problems, and errors that may affect user entities' internal control over financial reporting are identified, tracked, recorded, and resolved in a complete, accurate, and timely manner.	Abnormally ended programs corrupt the data they were processing. Restarted programs result in incomplete processing or duplicate processing of data. Processing problems and errors are not detected or are not detected in a timely manner. Processing problems are not appropriately resolved in a timely manner. Controls are overridden. Emergency access privileges are misused.
	• data transmissions between the service organization and its user entities and other outside entities that affect user entities' internal control over financial reporting are from authorized sources and are complete, accurate, secure, and timely.[20] • data relevant to user entities' financial reporting is backed up regularly and available for restoration in the event of processing errors or unexpected processing interruptions.	Data transmissions do not occur in a timely manner. Data transmissions are not received. Data transmissions are incomplete. Data transmissions are not accurate. Data is transmitted more than once. Data is corrupted or lost and is not recoverable.

[20] This control objective may also be presented as part of logical access security or as part of the business operations related to data input or reporting.

4.66 The service organization's control objectives may also include other conditions that affect the effectiveness of application controls (related to classes of transactions, events, or account balances). For example, the effectiveness of application controls generally depends on the reliability of master data. Master data is the key information that is relatively constant and referenced or shared between multiple functions or applications (for example, a customer master record, which contains the customer number, shipping address, billing address, key contact information, and payment terms). Consequently, an additional control objective that may be necessary is "Controls provide reasonable assurance that master data is valid, authorized, and established and maintained in a complete, accurate, and timely manner." The following are examples of risks that threaten the achievement of the master data control objective:

- Unauthorized or invalid master data records are created.
- Master data records contain incomplete or incorrect data.
- Not all authorized master data records are included in the master files.
- Unauthorized changes are made to master data.
- Authorized changes to master data are not made or are not made on a timely basis.
- Unauthorized, invalid, or incorrect master data files are not detected and corrected on a timely basis.
- Unauthorized, invalid, or incorrect master data exists as a result of compromises in IT general controls.

4.67 Paragraph .A41 of AT-C section 320 indicates that the risks that threaten the achievement of the control objectives stated in management's description of the service organization's system also encompass the risks of fraud and unintentional acts that threaten the achievement of the control objectives. Risks related to fraud may include management override of controls at the service organization; misappropriation of user entity assets by service organization personnel; creation, by service organization personnel, of false or misleading documents or records of user entity transactions processed by the service organization; and fraud by parties outside the service organization, for example, vendors and user entities. The description of the service organization's system would be expected to address control objectives that may have a higher risk of being subjected to fraud and unintentional acts.

Linking Controls to Risks

4.68 With management of the service organization having identified the risks that threaten the achievement of the control objectives, the service auditor should evaluate whether the controls at the service organization are suitably designed to address the risks. Paragraph .A42 of AT-C section 320 indicates that from the viewpoint of the service auditor, a control is suitably designed if individually, or in combination with other controls, it would, when complied with satisfactorily, provide reasonable assurance that the control objective(s) stated in the description of the service organization's system are achieved.

4.69 In assessing the suitability of the design of the controls included in management's description, paragraph .27*b* of AT-C section 320 also requires the service auditor to evaluate the linkage of those controls with the risks that threaten the achievement of the related control objectives. In doing so, the service auditor determines whether a control on its own or in combination with other controls, including aspects of the control environment, risk assessment, and monitoring, prevents, or detects and corrects, errors that could result in the nonachievement of the specified control objective.

4.70 The service organization may have different controls in place to address each of the risks associated with the control objective; therefore, multiple controls may be needed in order for the service auditor to conclude on the design of controls relating to each of the risks associated with the control objective. When a control objective is subject to multiple risks (for example, risks related to the authorization, accuracy, completeness, and timeliness of transaction processing), the service auditor would need to link the applicable controls to each of the risks associated with the control objective. In addition, the service organization's processing may take different forms depending on how information is received from user entities. For example, transactions may be received by mail, phone, fax, voice response unit, or Internet. One or more controls may be designed to achieve the control objectives that support the way transactions are received.

Multiple Controls Address the Same Control Objective

4.71 Paragraph .A44 of AT-C section 320 states that controls may consist of a number of activities directed at the achievement of various control objectives. Consequently, if the service auditor evaluates certain activities as being ineffective in achieving a particular control objective, the existence of other activities may enable the service auditor to conclude that controls related to the control objective are suitably designed to achieve the control objective. Alternatively, other controls that would enable the control objective to be achieved may not exist at the service organization and the control objective would not be achieved.

Information Needed to Evaluate Design of Control

4.72 In order for the service auditor to evaluate the suitability of the design of a control, the description of the control would need to include the following information:

- The frequency or timing of the occurrence or performance of the control, by stating, for example: "Management reviews error reports monthly." or "The custodian specialist reviews reconciling items on a daily basis."

- The party responsible for conducting the activity, by stating, for example: "The Director of Trading reviews . . ." or "The accounting associate compares . . ."

- The specific activity being performed by the individual performing the control, by stating, for example: "Custodian cash positions are compared to the cash positions in the accounting system." or "On a daily basis, the accounting manager reviews outstanding receivables that exceed $10,000 and signs off as evidence of review."

- The source of the information to which the control is applied, by stating, for example: "The custody clerk researches and resolves exceptions listed in the daily exception report."

Effect of Other Components of Internal Control on Design of Controls

4.73 The service auditor may determine that aspects of the service organization's control environment, risk assessment, information and communications, and monitoring are necessary for controls to be suitably designed to achieve the control objectives. The service auditor may conclude that controls are not suitably designed to achieve certain control objectives because of deficiencies in one or more of these components of the service organization's internal control. Paragraphs 4.87–.88 of this guide address how a service organization's control environment, risk assessment, information system, and monitoring may affect the operating effectiveness of a service organization's controls and the service auditor's tests of controls.

Control Necessary to Achieve Control Objective Is Missing

4.74 The service auditor may conclude that there are no controls in place to support one or more elements of a control objective. For example, a service organization may include the following control objective in management's description of the service organization's system: "Controls provide reasonable assurance that user entity transactions are initially recorded completely, accurately, and in a timely manner." User entities may submit transaction processing requests by telephone or electronically. The service organization has identified in its description of the service organization's system controls that address the processing of electronic transaction requests received from user entities, but it has not identified controls that address transaction requests received via telephone. In this scenario, the service auditor would conclude that controls were not suitably designed to process transaction requests received via telephone.

Difference Between Deficiency in Design and Deficiency in Operating Effectiveness

4.75 A deficiency in the *design* of a control occurs when a control necessary to meet the control objective is missing or an existing control is not properly designed so that, even if the control operates as designed, the related control objective would not be met. A deficiency in the *operation* of a control exists when a properly designed control does not operate as designed or when the person performing the control does not possess the necessary authority or competence to perform the control effectively.[21] A service organization may be able to correct a deficiency in the operation of a control, for example, by designating a more qualified individual to perform the control. However, if the design of the control is deficient, it will not be effective no matter who performs the control.

4.76 After performing the procedures and considering the matters described in paragraphs 4.56–.75, the service auditor should assess whether the controls that management identified in its description of the service organization's system as the controls that achieve the control objectives were suitably designed to achieve those control objectives.

4.77 Paragraphs 5.68–.70 of this guide present examples of a separate paragraph that would be added to the service auditor's report when the service

---

[21] From the definition of *deficiency in internal control* in the AU-C glossary in the introduction to the AU-C section of AICPA *Professional Standards*.

auditor determines that controls are not suitably designed to achieve one or more control objectives or the service auditor is unable to obtain sufficient appropriate evidence that controls were suitably designed to achieve a specified control objective.

Obtaining and Evaluating Evidence Regarding the Operating Effectiveness of Controls in a Type 2 Engagement

4.78 Paragraph .A46 of AT-C section 320 states that from the viewpoint of the service auditor, a control is operating effectively if, individually or in combination with other controls, it provides reasonable assurance that the control objectives stated in management's description of the service organization's system are achieved. The objective of tests of controls is to evaluate how controls were applied, the consistency with which they were applied, and by whom or in what manner they were applied. When a service organization uses the inclusive method, the service auditor should evaluate the operating effectiveness of controls at both the service organization and the subservice organization.

Materiality With Respect to Operating Effectiveness of Controls

4.79 Paragraph .19 of AT-C section 320 states that the service auditor's consideration of materiality should include the operating effectiveness of controls to achieve the related control objectives stated in the description. Paragraph .A29 of AT-C section 320 states that materiality with respect to the operating effectiveness of controls includes the consideration of both quantitative factors, such as the tolerable rate of deviation (the maximum rate of deviations in the operation of the prescribed control that the service auditor is willing to accept without concluding that the control did not operate effectively during some or all of the period) and observed rate of deviation, as well as qualitative factors, such as the nature and cause of any observed deviations. Paragraph .17 of AT-C section 205 indicates that the service auditor should reconsider materiality if the practitioner becomes aware of information during the engagement that would have caused the service auditor to have initially determined a different materiality.

Determining Which Controls to Test

4.80 Paragraph .28 of AT-C section 320 indicates that, when performing a type 2 engagement, the service auditor should test those controls that management has identified in its description of the service organization's system as the controls that achieve the control objectives and should assess the operating effectiveness of those controls throughout the period.

4.81 The service auditor may conclude that all or only a portion of the controls identified by management are necessary to achieve a given control objective. If the service auditor determines that certain controls are not necessary to achieve a control objective, management may remove those controls from the description of the service organization's system or, if management of the service organization prefers to include the controls in the description of the service organization's system, the service auditor may indicate in the report that no testing was performed on them so that user entities are clear about which controls were tested and which controls were not tested. If management chooses not to remove controls from the description, the service auditor is still responsible for determining that the controls that were not tested were fairly presented and implemented.

4.82 When performing a type 2 engagement, paragraph .15*b* of AT-C section 320 indicates that one of the criteria for evaluating the fairness of the presentation of the description of the service organization's system is that the description include relevant details of changes to the service organization's system. Paragraph .29 of AT-C section 320 requires the service auditor to obtain an understanding of such changes. If the service auditor believes the changes would be considered significant by user entities and their auditors, the service auditor should determine whether information about those changes is included in management's description of the service organization's system and whether superseded controls are relevant to the achievement of one or more control objectives. If so, the service auditor should, if possible, test the superseded controls before the change. If the service organization has used the inclusive method, the service auditor should consider changes to controls at both the service organization and the subservice organization. Paragraph 5.54 of this guide presents an example of a separate paragraph that would be added to the service auditor's report when information about such changes is omitted from management's description of the service organization's system.

4.83 Although one control related to a given control objective may not be suitably designed to achieve that control objective, other controls may be suitably designed to achieve that control objective. The service auditor should test the controls that are suitably designed, identify the controls that were tested in the description of tests of controls and results, and determine the effect on the service auditor's report.

4.84 If design deficiencies in controls intended to achieve a given control objective are pervasive, the service auditor generally would not test the operating effectiveness of the controls related to that control objective.

Options for Presenting Tests of the Operating Effectiveness of Controls for Controls That Were Subsequently Deemed Not Suitably Designed

4.85 Ordinarily, a service auditor would not test the operating effectiveness of a control that is not suitably designed, but a service auditor may not detect a design deficiency in a control when evaluating the design of controls and then later identify the design deficiency when testing the operating effectiveness of controls. Should the service auditor include, in the description of tests of controls and results, tests of the operating effectiveness of controls that were determined to be not suitably designed when the service auditor tested the operating effectiveness of those controls?

The following are some possible alternatives:

- If the service auditor's opinion is modified because controls were not suitably designed to achieve the related control objective, include the information about those tests of controls and results in the description of tests of controls and results and also indicate that the control objective was not achieved because the controls were not suitably designed.

- If the service auditor's opinion is modified because the controls were not suitably designed to achieve the related control objective, management may wish to include the information about the tests of those controls and results in the section of the type 2 report that addresses other information. (Placement in the other information section would be an appropriate option because the service auditor has concluded that a design deficiency exists that precludes achieving the control objective, and as a result, the service auditor is not expressing an opinion on the tests of operating effectiveness.)

- If a design deficiency exists but the control objective was achieved because other controls have been implemented that address one or more elements of the control objective, include the information about the tests of controls and results in the description of tests of controls and results, and place an asterisk next to that information with a footnote describing the design deficiency.

4.86 Paragraphs 5.71–.74 of this guide contain an example of a separate paragraph that would be added to the service auditor's report for each of the following situations:

- Controls were not operating effectively.

- A scope limitation related to the operating effectiveness of controls exists.

- The service auditor wishes to communicate other matters related to the operating effectiveness of controls.

Designing and Performing Tests of Controls

4.87 The service organization's control environment, risk assessment, information and communications, and monitoring components of internal control related to the service provided to user entities may enhance or mitigate the effectiveness of specific controls. If the service auditor determines that aspects of these components of the service organization's internal control undermine or do not support the effectiveness of controls, the service auditor should design and perform further procedures whose nature, timing, and extent are based on, and responsive to, the assessed risks of material misstatement resulting from the less effective aspects of these components of internal control. In some situations, the service auditor may conclude that controls are not operating effectively to achieve certain control objectives because of deficiencies in these components of internal control. Paragraph 4.73 of this guide addresses the effect of the service organization's control environment, risk assessment, information system, and monitoring on the suitability of the design of controls.

4.88 An example of the effect of these components of the service organization's internal control on other controls is illustrated at Example Service Organization, where management determines bonuses based on zero processing errors. In this environment, service organization personnel may be tempted to suppress errors in order to receive bonuses. The service auditor may substantially increase the extent of testing performed, perhaps even testing the entire population, to determine whether controls are operating effectively to achieve the control objective.

Nature of Tests of Controls

4.89 The nature and objectives of tests to evaluate the operating effectiveness of controls are different from those performed to evaluate the suitability of the design of controls. Paragraph .31 of AT-C section 320 states that, when designing and performing tests of controls, the service auditor should

    a. perform other procedures such as inspection (for example, of documents, reports, or electronic files), observation (for example, of the application of the control), or reperformance in combination with inquiry to obtain evidence about

        i. how the control was applied,

        ii. the consistency with which the control was applied, and

        iii. by whom or by what means the control was applied.

    b. determine whether the controls to be tested depend on other controls, and if so, whether it is necessary to obtain evidence supporting the operating effectiveness of those other controls.

    c. determine an effective method for selecting the items to be tested to meet the objectives of the procedure.

4.90 Inquiry alone does not provide sufficient appropriate evidence of the operating effectiveness of controls. Some tests of controls provide more convincing evidence of the operating effectiveness of controls than others. Performing inquiry combined with inspection or reperformance ordinarily provides more convincing evidence than performing inquiry and observation. For example, a service auditor may inquire about and observe a service organization's physical building security during the initial walkthroughs. Because an observation is pertinent only at the point in time at which it is made, the service auditor would supplement the observation with other procedures to obtain sufficient appropriate evidence regarding the operating effectiveness of the control. For example the service auditor may inspect the video tapes that monitor the entrance of the facility, select a sample of individuals who enter the building, and determine whether the names of those individuals are included on the service organization's list of individuals authorized to access the building during that period.

4.91 The type of control being tested may affect the nature, timing, and extent of the testing performed by the service auditor. For example, for some controls, operating effectiveness is evidenced by documentation. In such circumstances, the service auditor may decide to inspect the documentation. Other controls may not leave evidence of their operation that can be tested at a later date, and accordingly, the service auditor may need to test the operating effectiveness of such controls at various times throughout the period.

4.92 There may be instances in which evidence that would have demonstrated the operating effectiveness of the controls has been lost, misplaced, or inadvertently deleted by the service organization. In such instances, the service auditor evaluates the type of evidence available and whether the effectiveness of the control can be tested through other procedures, such as observation, that would provide sufficient evidence of the operating effectiveness of the control throughout the period. However, depending on the control activity and its significance to meeting the control objective, tests such as observation may not alone provide sufficient evidence.

Evaluating the Reliability of Information Produced by the Service Organization

4.93 Paragraph .35 of AT-C section 205 and paragraph .30 of AT-C section 320 indicate that when the service auditor uses information produced by the service organization, the service auditor should evaluate whether the information is sufficiently reliable for the service auditor's purposes; this includes obtaining evidence about the accuracy and completeness of the information and evaluating whether the information is sufficiently precise and detailed. The reliability of information depends on the nature and source of the information and the circumstances under which it is obtained. The following are three types of information produced by a service organization that the service auditor may use in an engagement performed under AT-C section 320:

1. Information provided by the service organization in response to ad hoc requests from the service auditor, for example, a request for a population list, such as a population of application changes that the service auditor uses to select a sample of items for testing

2. Information used in the execution of a control, for example, a user access list used by service organization personnel in an access review control

3. Information prepared for user entities, for example, a reporting package provided to user entities, system-generated reports, an invoice, or a payroll file reflecting the results of processing a payroll

4.94 The service auditor may identify information produced by the service organization during the service auditor's evaluation of the fairness of the presentation of management's description of the service organization's system or during the evaluation of the design, implementation, or operating effectiveness of the controls included in the description.

4.95 Information produced by the service organization may be produced

- manually or generated by a system.
- one time (for example, a population list provided to the service auditor for use in selecting a sample of items to be tested) or may be produced on a recurring basis (for example, a manually prepared exception report prepared on a weekly basis).

4.96 When evaluating the fairness of the presentation of management's description of the service organization's system, the service auditor should identify the types of information included in the description that may be subject to reliability testing by the service auditor and how such information is provided to the service auditor in response to the service auditor's ad hoc requests, used in the execution of controls, or prepared for user entities.

4.97 Questions that are relevant when assessing the reliability of the information produced by the service organization may include the following:

- Where is the information produced or generated? For example, is it generated from the service organization's applications or systems, from manually produced reports, or from third-party vendors outside the service organization?
- How is the information used by the service organization and how will it be used by user entities?
- What effect could the information have on user entities?

- Is the information stored in a controlled information technology environment or an ad hoc reporting database or data warehouse?

- Is the information highly structured and complex or relatively straightforward?

- Does the information originate from a system already subject to the service auditor's procedures or a system beyond the scope of the service auditor's examination?

- What is the basis for the service organization's comfort with the reliability of the information?

- Were any classes or ranges of data excluded from the information provided by the service organization? If so, were those exclusions appropriate?

4.98 Determining the nature and extent of evidence needed to assess the reliability of information produced by the service organization is a matter of professional judgment. The service auditor may obtain evidence about the reliability of such information when testing controls or may develop specific procedures that address this information. The more important the information or the control, the more persuasive the evidence about the reliability of the information should be. Because a type 2 report covers a period of time, the service auditor should evaluate the reliability of the information produced by the service organization throughout the period of time.

4.99 The following are matters that are relevant when assessing the reliability of information used in the execution of a control:

- The risk that one or more control objectives would not be achieved if the information produced by the service organization is not reliable

- The degree to which the effectiveness of the control depends on the reliability of the information

- The degree to which the reliability of the information produced depends on other controls, for example, IT general controls.

4.100 The following are examples of procedures the service auditor may perform when evaluating the reliability of various types of information produced by the service organization:

Example 1: Information provided by the service organization to the service auditor in response to an ad hoc request from the service auditor

The service organization provides the service auditor with a system-generated list of new accounts set up during the period. In evaluating the accuracy and completeness of the list of new accounts set up during the period, the service auditor may

    a. observe the generation of the list of new accounts set up during the period, confirm that the correct source was queried and that the date range and type of account parameters were accurately entered, and determine whether any exclusions are listed,

    b. inspect the list for any new accounts with a "created on date" that is outside the date range specified, and

    c. test the IT general controls supporting the system.

Example 2: Information used in the execution of a control

The description of the service organization's system states that a list of terminated employees is automatically produced by the Human Resources Management System (HRMS) application on a weekly basis and that access to supporting business applications by terminated employees is removed on the date of termination. In evaluating the accuracy and completeness of the termination report, the service auditor may

    a. observe the human resources manager enter the date range and termination parameter into the reporting tool within the production environment of the HRMS application,

    b. inspect the report for any termination dates outside the date range specified, and

    c. test the IT general controls supporting the HRMS.

Example 3: Information used in the execution of a control

The description of the service organization's system states that for each bank account, the general ledger system automatically reconciles the cash account monthly and generates a report of aged reconciling items. The aged reconciling items are researched and resolved by the accounting clerk. The supervisor reviews the month-end reconciliation and aged reconciling items and forwards the schedule of aged reconciling items to senior management for review. In evaluating the accuracy and completeness of the report of aged reconciling items, the service auditor may

    a. validate the population list of all bank accounts reconciled to the general ledger,

    b. reperform the month-end bank reconciliation to identify reconciling items and their aging according to documented policy requirements, and

    c. compare the reconciling items and their aging to the schedule sent to senior management for review.

Example 4: Information prepared for user entities

The description of the service organization's system states that mutual fund 12b-1 fees are automatically calculated by the system, charged to client accounts, and completely and accurately reported on statements provided to mutual fund user entities. In evaluating the accuracy and completeness of this information, the service auditor may

    a. reperform, in a test environment that mirrors production, the automated calculation of 12b-1 fees charged to a client's account for a transaction,

    b. determine whether the 12b-1 charged to the client's account agrees with the recalculated fee in item (*a*) and is completely and accurately reported on the statement prepared for the user entities of the mutual fund, and

    c. test the IT general controls supporting system.

Timing of Tests of Controls

4.101   The following are factors that are relevant to the service auditor's determination of the timing of tests of controls:

- When the information will be available and when it will no longer be available. For example,

    — electronic files may be overwritten after a period of time,

    — procedures may occur only at certain times during the period, and

    — certain test procedures may need to be performed after the end of the period, such as reviewing the reconciliations of general ledger balances to external statements that are generated after the end of the period.

- The significance of the control being tested.

4.102   The service auditor may perform tests of controls at interim dates, at the end of the period, or after the end of the period if the tests relate to controls that were in operation during the period but do not leave evidence until after the end of the period. Performing procedures at an interim date may assist the service auditor in identifying, at an early stage of the examination, any potential deficiencies in the design or operating effectiveness of controls and, consequently, provides an opportunity for the service organization to resolve identified deficiencies prior to the end of the period, regardless of the service auditor's determination about whether they affect the service auditor's report. When the service auditor performs tests of the operating effectiveness of controls at an interim period, the service auditor should determine the extent of additional testing necessary for the remaining period.

Extent of Tests of Controls

4.103   The *extent* of the service auditor's testing refers to the size of the sample tested or the number of observations of a control activity. The extent of testing is based on the service auditor's professional judgment after considering the tolerable rate of deviation; the expected rate of deviation; the frequency with which the control operates; the length of the testing period; the significance of the control to preventing, or detecting and correcting, errors; and whether other controls support the achievement of the control objective.

4.104   The service auditor should test the operating effectiveness of the controls in effect throughout the period covered by the report and determine whether the control has occurred a sufficient number of times to be assessed as operating effectively. For example, if the control operated daily, the service auditor would test the operation of the control for a sufficient number of days throughout the period covered by the report to determine whether the control operated effectively throughout the entire period of the report. The shorter the test period, the more likely the service auditor will be unable to perform sufficient testing and obtain sufficient appropriate evidence to express an opinion on the operating effectiveness of controls.

4.105   Paragraph .A48 of AT-C section 320 indicates that evidence about the satisfactory operation of controls in prior periods does not provide evidence of the operating effectiveness of controls during the current period. The service auditor expresses an opinion on the effectiveness of controls throughout each period; therefore, sufficient appropriate evidence about the operating effectiveness of controls throughout the current period is required for the service auditor to express that opinion for the current period.

4.106 Paragraph .A48 of AT-C section 320 also states that knowledge of modifications to the service auditor's report or deviations observed in prior engagements may be considered in assessing risk and may lead the service auditor to increase the extent of testing in the current period. For example, the service auditor's report on Example Service Organization's ABC System for the prior year was qualified due to deficiencies in the operating effectiveness of controls related to the accuracy of distribution transactions. In the current year, the service auditor learns that service organization management has made changes to controls to address the deficiencies. Knowing of the qualification in the prior year and the changes made to the controls, the service auditor may decide to increase the number of items to be tested in the current examination period because observed prior-year deviations increase the risk that the controls did not operate effectively in the current period.

Superseded Controls

4.107 If (a) the service organization makes changes to controls during the period, (b) the superseded controls are relevant to the achievement of the control objectives stated in the description, and (c) the service auditor believes the changes would be considered significant by user entities and their auditors, the service auditor should, if possible, test the superseded controls before the change. For example, during the period June 1, 20X0, to May 31, 20X1, Example Service Organization decided to automate a control that was previously performed manually. The service organization automated the control on December 15, 20X0. The service auditor tests the manual control for the period from June 1, 20X0, to December 14, 20X0, considering the nature and frequency of the performance of the control, and then tests the automated control for the period from December 15, 20X0, to May 31, 20X1, again giving consideration to the nature and frequency of the performance of the control.

4.108 If (a) the service auditor is unable to test the superseded control (for example, because the control does not leave evidence of its operation after a period of time or the service auditor was engaged after the control was superseded), (b) the control would be considered significant by user entities and their auditors (the control is necessary to achieve the control objectives), and (c) the control is relevant to the achievement of the control objectives stated in the description, a scope limitation exists and the service auditor should modify the service auditor's opinion. (See the relevant paragraphs within paragraphs .68–.84 of AT-C section 205 for reporting requirements when the service auditor is unable to obtain sufficient appropriate evidence.) Paragraph 5.72 of this guide presents an example of a separate paragraph that would be added to the service auditor's report when a scope limitation related to the operating effectiveness of controls exists.

4.109 If a control objective is composed of several elements (for example, "Controls provide reasonable assurance that transactions are authorized and entered into the order capture system completely, accurately, and on a timely basis"), the service auditor would need to link the applicable controls to each of the elements (authorization, completeness, accuracy, and timeliness) included in the control objective. The service auditor may determine that a deficiency exists in the design of the control that addresses the timeliness with which transactions are entered but that controls related to authorization, completeness, and accuracy are suitably designed. Because information about the design of controls related to authorization, completeness, and accuracy could be relevant to user entities, and those controls are suitably designed, the service auditor would test the operating effectiveness of those controls and would determine what effect the control that is not suitably designed will have on the service auditor's report.

4.110 If a control objective is composed of several elements and one of the elements is not achieved, the service auditor may

- conclude that the element of the control objective that is not achieved prevents the entire control objective from being achieved.

- suggest to management that the element of the control objective that was not achieved be disaggregated from the multiple-element control objective and be presented as a separate control objective. The service auditor would determine what effect the control that is not suitably designed and the disaggregated control objective will have on the service auditor's report.

Selecting Items to Be Tested

4.111 Paragraph .31 of AT-C section 205 indicates that when the service auditor uses sampling to select the items to be tested, the service auditor should, when designing the sample, consider the purpose of the procedure and the characteristics of the population from which the sample will be drawn. Sampling involves

a. determining a sample size sufficient to reduce sampling risk to an acceptably low level.

b. selecting items for the sample in such a way that the practitioner can reasonably expect the sample to be representative of the relevant population and likely to provide the practitioner with a reasonable basis for conclusions about the population.

c. treating a selected item to which the practitioner is unable to apply the designed procedures or suitable alternative procedures as a deviation from the prescribed control in the case of tests of controls.

d. investigating the nature and cause of deviations[22] or misstatements identified and evaluating their possible effect on the purpose of the procedure and on other areas of the engagement.

e. evaluating the results of the sample, including sampling risk, and projecting misstatements found in the sample to the population.

f. evaluating whether the use of sampling has provided an appropriate basis for evaluating conclusions about the population that has been tested.

The AICPA Audit Guide *Audit Sampling* provides guidance that may be useful to a service auditor who has decided to use sampling in performing a service auditor's engagement.

4.112 Automated application controls generally are tested only once or a few times if effective IT general controls are present.

---

[22] The term *deviations* refers to instances in which tests of controls indicate that the control was not operating effectively to achieve the related control objective.

Using the Work of Internal Auditors

4.113 Paragraph .40 of AT-C section 205 states, "When using the work of the internal audit function, the practitioner should perform sufficient procedures on the body of work of the internal audit function as a whole that the practitioner plans to use to determine its adequacy for the purpose of the examination engagement, including reperforming some of the body of work of the internal audit function that the practitioner intends to use in obtaining evidence."

4.114 Factors that are relevant in determining the nature, timing, and extent of the service auditor's procedures on specific work of the internal audit function include the service auditor's assessment of the significance of that work to the service auditor's conclusions (for example, the significance of the risks that the controls tend to mitigate), the service auditor's evaluation of the internal audit function, and the evaluation of the specific work of the internal audit function. In addition to reperformance (examining some of the items already examined by the internal audit function or sufficient other similar items not actually examined by the internal audit function), such other procedures may involve a combination of inquiry, observation, or examination to enable the service auditor to evaluate the specific work of the internal audit function.

4.115 It is the service auditor's responsibility to make all significant judgments in the examination engagement, including when using the work of the internal audit function in obtaining evidence. Such judgments include, but are not limited to, the following:

- Assessing the risks of material misstatement
- Evaluating the sufficiency of tests performed
- Evaluating significant estimates
- Evaluating the adequacy of the description of the service organization's system and other matters affecting the service auditor's report

4.116 Relevant factors in determining whether to use the work of the internal audit function to obtain evidence about the operating effectiveness of controls include the pervasiveness of the control and the potential for management override of the control. As the significance of these factors increases, so does the need for the service auditor, rather than the internal audit function, to perform the tests, and conversely, as these factors decrease in significance, the need for the service auditor to perform the tests decreases.

4.117 Paragraph .35 of AT-C section 205 indicates that when the service auditor uses information produced by the service organization, the service auditor should evaluate whether the information is sufficiently reliable for the practitioner's purposes, including, as necessary, the following:

a. Obtaining evidence about the accuracy and completeness of the information

b. Evaluating whether the information is sufficiently precise and detailed for the practitioner's purposes

Paragraph 4.100 of this guide includes examples of procedures the service auditor may perform when evaluating the reliability of various types of information produced by the service organization.

4.118 The responsibility to report on management's description of the service organization's system and the suitability of the design and operating effectiveness of controls rests solely with the service auditor and cannot be shared with the internal audit function. Therefore, the judgments about the significance of deficiencies in the design or operating effectiveness of controls, the sufficiency of tests performed, the evaluation of identified deficiencies, and other matters that affect the service auditor's report are those of the service auditor. In making judgments about the extent of the effect of the work of the internal audit function on the service auditor's procedures, the service auditor may determine, based on the risk associated with the controls and the significance of the judgments relating to them, that the service auditor will perform the work relating to some or all of the controls rather than using the work performed by the internal audit function.

Direct Assistance

4.119 Paragraph .42 of AT-C section 205 states, "When using internal auditors to provide direct assistance to the practitioner, the practitioner should direct, supervise, and review the work of the internal auditors." As part of directing and supervising internal auditors, examples of matters that the service auditor would ordinarily communicate to the internal auditors include the following:

- Their responsibilities

- The objectives of the procedures they are to perform

- Matters that may affect the nature, timing, and extent of examination procedures, including any potential issues

- Instructions to bring any issues identified during the examination to the attention of the service auditor

4.120 The service auditor's review of the work of internal auditors would include testing some of the work performed by the internal auditors.

4.121 Paragraph .44 of AT-C section 205 requires the service auditor, before the conclusion of the engagement, to evaluate whether the use of the work of the internal audit function or the use of internal auditors to provide direct assistance results in the practitioner still being sufficiently involved in the examination given the practitioner's sole responsibility for the opinion expressed.

Revision of Risk Assessment

4.122 Paragraph .34 of AT-C section 205 states that the service auditor's assessment of the risks of material misstatement may change during the course of the engagement as additional evidence is obtained. In circumstances in which the service auditor obtains evidence from performing further procedures, or if new information is obtained, either of which is inconsistent with the evidence on which the practitioner originally based the assessment, the service auditor should revise the assessment and modify the planned procedures accordingly. The modified procedures may include asking the service organization to examine the matter identified by the service auditor and to make adjustments to the subject matter if appropriate, for example, revisions to the description of the service organization's system.

Evaluating the Results of Procedures

4.123 Sufficient appropriate evidence is necessary to support the service auditor's opinion and report. Such evidence is cumulative in nature and may come from sources inside or outside the service organization. Evidence comprises both information that supports and corroborates aspects of the subject matter and any information that contradicts aspects of the subject matter. In addition, in some cases, the absence of information (for example, refusal by the responsible party to provide a requested representation) should be considered by the practitioner and, therefore, also constitutes evidence.

4.124 The service auditor should evaluate the sufficiency and appropriateness of the evidence obtained in the context of the engagement and, if necessary, attempt to obtain further evidence.

4.125 As discussed in paragraphs .46–.47 of AT-C section 205, if the service auditor is unable to obtain necessary further evidence, the service auditor should consider the implications for the service auditor's opinion related to the service auditor's inability to obtain sufficient appropriate evidence. Such implications are discussed in paragraphs .68–.84 of AT-C section 205 and paragraphs 4.175, 5.40–.42, 5.70, 5.72, and 5.75 of this guide.

4.126 As discussed in paragraph .59 of AT-C section 205, the service auditor should form an opinion on the fairness of the presentation of the description and the suitability of the design and operating effectiveness of the controls, based on the service auditor's conclusion regarding (*a*) whether uncorrected misstatements are material, individually or in the aggregate, and (*b*) the sufficiency and appropriateness of the evidence obtained.

Evaluating Misstatements—General

4.127 As discussed in paragraph .45 of AT-C section 205, the service auditor should accumulate misstatements identified during the engagement other than those that are clearly trivial. Paragraph .10 of AT-C section 105 defines the term *misstatement* as

> A difference between the measurement or evaluation of the subject matter by the responsible party and the proper measurement or evaluation of the subject matter based on the criteria. Misstatements can be intentional or unintentional, qualitative or quantitative, and include omissions. In certain engagements, a misstatement may be referred to as a *deviation, exception,* or *instance of noncompliance.*

In this guide

- the term *misstatement* is used to refer to an error or omission in the description of the service organization's system and may be used in the generic sense to refer to a deficiency in the design of a control or a deficiency in the operating effectiveness of a control

- the term *deviation* or *exception* is used to refer to an instance in which a test of controls indicates that the control was not operating effectively to achieve the related control objective.

- the term *deficiency in the design of a control* is used when (a) a control necessary to achieve the control objective is missing or (b) an existing control is not properly designed so that, even if the control operates as designed, the control objective would not be achieved.

- the term *deficiency in the operating effectiveness of a control*[23] is used when a properly designed control does not operate as designed or when the person performing the control does not possess the necessary authority or competence to perform the control effectively.

4.128 The service auditor should accumulate misstatements related to each of the three opinions: the fairness of the presentation of the description, the suitability of the design of the controls to achieve the related control objectives, and the operating effectiveness of the controls to achieve the related control objectives. Misstatements in an individual component of the service auditor's opinion (for example, the opinion on management's description of the service organization's system) may affect the other components of the opinion (the opinion on the suitability of the design or operating effectiveness of controls). For example,

- if the description of the service organization's system includes controls that have not been implemented, the opinion on the description of the service organization's system will be affected and the opinion on the suitability of the design and operating effectiveness of the controls may be affected because controls that are needed to achieve the related control objectives have not been implemented.
- if the description of the service organization's system includes controls that are not suitably designed, the deficiency in the design of the controls would also affect the operating effectiveness of the controls because, even if the controls operate as designed, the control objective would not be achieved due to the deficiency in the design of the controls.

Evaluating Misstatements in the Description of the Service Organization's System

4.129 In evaluating the fairness of the presentation of management's description of the service organization's system, the service auditor should accumulate instances in which the description of the service organization's system is misstated. The following are examples of misstatements with respect to the fair presentation of the description:

- Inclusion of inappropriate information, for example, controls that have not been implemented; information that is not measureable; and control objective(s) that are incomplete, not relevant to user entities' internal control over financial reporting, or not measureable
- Omission of necessary information, for example, omission of information about relevant subsequent events or changes to controls,

---

[23] The terms *deficiency in the design of a control* and *deficiency in the operating effectiveness of a control* are adapted from paragraph .07 of AU-C section 265, *Communicating Internal Control Related Matters Identified in an Audit* (AICPA, *Professional Standards*), which states, "A deficiency in internal control exists when the design or operation of a control does not allow management or employees, in the normal course of performing their assigned functions, to prevent, or detect and correct, misstatements on a timely basis. A deficiency in *design* exists when (*a*) a control necessary to meet the control objective is missing, or (*b*) an existing control is not properly designed so that, even if the control operates as designed, the control objective would not be met. A deficiency in *operation* exists when a properly designed control does not operate as designed or when the person performing the control does not possess the necessary authority or competence to perform the control effectively."

relevant control objective(s), complementary user entity controls, or complementary subservice organization controls

- Changes without reasonable justification, for example, revision of a control objective during the engagement without reasonable justification, or changes from the inclusive method to the carve-out method without reasonable justification

- Misstatements of fact

If the service auditor determines that the effects of identified misstatements, individually or in the aggregate, are material with respect to the fair presentation of the description, based on a consideration of materiality as discussed in paragraphs 4.17–.19, the service auditor should modify the opinion on the description, as discussed in paragraphs 5.35–.67.

Evaluating Deficiencies in the Suitability of the Design of Controls

4.130 In evaluating the suitability of the design of controls, the service auditor should accumulate instances in which controls were not suitably designed to achieve the related control objectives, which are considered misstatements in an engagement performed under AT-C section 320 and also may be referred to as deficiencies in the design of controls as defined in paragraph 4.127. For each control objective, the service auditor should consider whether controls are suitably designed to achieve the related control objective. Generally, if controls are not suitably designed to achieve one or more control objectives, such misstatement is considered material.

4.131 If the service auditor determines that the effects of identified deficiencies in the suitability of the design of controls, individually or in the aggregate, are material, based on a consideration of materiality as discussed in paragraph 4.60, the service auditor should modify the opinion on the suitability of the design of controls, as discussed in paragraphs 5.35–.47 and 5.68–.70 of this guide.

Evaluating Deviations in the Results of Tests of Controls (Deficiencies in the Operating Effectiveness of Controls)

4.132 In evaluating the results of tests of controls and the significance of deviations noted, the service auditor should accumulate instances in which controls did not operate effectively, which are considered misstatements in an engagement performed under AT-C section 320 and also may be referred to as deficiencies in the operating effectiveness of controls, as defined in paragraph 4.127. The service auditor does this for the purpose of evaluating whether, individually or in the aggregate, such misstatements are material when forming the service auditor's opinion. The service auditor's evaluation of whether a control objective has been achieved includes consideration of whether other controls at the service organization that address the same control objective mitigate the effect of a control that is not operating effectively. Generally, if controls are not operating effectively to achieve one or more control objectives, such misstatement is considered material.

4.133 Paragraph .32 of AT-C section 320 requires the service auditor to investigate the nature and cause of any deviations identified and determine whether

    a. identified deviations are within the expected rate of deviation and are acceptable. If so, the testing that has been performed provides an appropriate basis for concluding that the control operated effectively throughout the specified period.

b. additional testing of the control or of other controls is necessary to reach a conclusion about whether the controls related to the control objectives stated in management's description of the service organization's system operated effectively throughout the specified period.

c. the testing that has been performed provides an appropriate basis for concluding that the control did not operate effectively throughout the specified period.

4.134 If, as a result of performing the procedures identified in paragraph 4.133, the service auditor becomes aware that any identified deviations have resulted from fraud by service organization personnel, the service auditor should assess the risk that management's description of the service organization's system is not fairly presented, the controls are not suitably designed, and, in a type 2 engagement, the controls are not operating effectively.

4.135 In addition, paragraph .33 of AT-C section 205 states that the practitioner should respond appropriately to fraud or suspected fraud and noncompliance or suspected noncompliance with laws or regulations affecting the subject matter that is identified during the engagement. Paragraph .A29 of AT-C section 205 indicates that in these circumstances (unless prohibited by law, regulation, or ethics standards), it may be appropriate for the service auditor to, for example,

- discuss the matter with the appropriate party(ies).
- request that the responsible party consult with an appropriately qualified third party, such as the entity's legal counsel or a regulator.
- consider the implications of the matter in relation to other aspects of the engagement, including the practitioner's risk assessment and the reliability of written representations from the responsible party.
- obtain legal advice about the consequences of different courses of action.
- communicate with third parties (for example, a regulator).
- withdraw from the engagement.

4.136 If the service auditor determines that the effects of identified deficiencies in the operating effectiveness of controls, individually or in the aggregate, are material, based on a consideration of materiality as discussed in paragraph 4.79, the auditor should modify the opinion on the operating effectiveness of the controls, as discussed in paragraphs 5.35–.47 and 5.71–.74.

Evaluating the Sufficiency and Appropriateness of Evidence

4.137 *Sufficient* appropriate evidence is primarily obtained from procedures performed during the course of the engagement. It may, however, also include information obtained from other sources, such as previous engagements (provided the service auditor has determined whether changes have occurred since the previous engagement that may affect its relevance to the current engagement) or a firm's quality control procedures for client acceptance and continuance. For example, the service auditor's experience in the prior period with rates of error in testing may be used in assessing the risks of material misstatement and determining the extent of testing. However, with respect to engagements performed under AT-C section 320, paragraph .28 of that section states that evidence obtained in prior engagements about the satisfactory operation of controls in prior periods does not provide a basis for a reduction in testing, even if it is supplemented with evidence obtained during the current period.

4.138   The sufficiency and appropriateness of evidence are interrelated. *Sufficiency of evidence* is the measure of the quantity of evidence. The quantity of the evidence needed is affected by the risks of material misstatement and also by the quality of such evidence.

4.139   *Appropriateness of evidence* is the measure of the quality of evidence, that is, its relevance and reliability in providing support for the service auditor's opinions. The reliability of evidence is influenced by its source and nature and is dependent on the individual circumstances under which it is obtained. Generalizations about the reliability of various kinds of evidence can be made; however, such generalizations are subject to important exceptions. Even when evidence is obtained from sources external to the responsible party, circumstances may exist that could affect its reliability. For example, evidence obtained from an independent external source may not be reliable if the source is not knowledgeable. Recognizing that exceptions may exist, the following generalizations about the reliability of evidence may be useful:

- Evidence is more reliable when it is obtained from independent sources outside the appropriate party(ies).
- Evidence that is generated internally is more reliable when the related controls are effective.
- Evidence obtained directly by the service auditor (for example, observation of the application of a control) is more reliable than evidence obtained indirectly or by inference (for example, inquiry about the application of a control).
- Evidence is more reliable when it exists in documentary form, whether paper, electronic, or other media (for example, a contemporaneously written record of a meeting is ordinarily more reliable than a subsequent oral representation of what was discussed).
- Evidence provided by original documents is more reliable than evidence provided by photocopies, facsimiles, or documents that have been filmed, digitized, or otherwise transformed into electronic form, the reliability of which may depend on the controls over their preparation and maintenance.

4.140   Evidence obtained from different sources or of a different nature ordinarily provides more assurance than evidence from items considered individually. In addition, obtaining evidence from different sources or of a different nature may indicate that an individual item of evidence is not reliable. For example, corroborating information obtained from a source independent of the responsible party may increase the assurance the service auditor obtains from a representation from the responsible party. Conversely, when evidence obtained from one source is inconsistent with that obtained from another, the service auditor should determine what additional procedures are necessary to resolve the inconsistency.

4.141   Whether sufficient appropriate evidence has been obtained on which to base the service auditor's opinion is a matter of professional judgment. The service auditor's professional judgment regarding what constitutes sufficient appropriate evidence is influenced by such factors as the following:

- The significance of a potential misstatement and the likelihood that it will have a material effect, individually or aggregated with other potential misstatements, on the subject matter or assertion
- The effectiveness of the responsible party's responses to address the known risks
- The experience gained during previous examination or review engagements with respect to similar potential misstatements
- The results of procedures performed, including whether such procedures identified specific misstatements
- The source and reliability of the available information
- The persuasiveness of the evidence
- The service auditor's understanding of the responsible party and its environment

4.142 An examination engagement is a cumulative and iterative process. As the service auditor performs planned procedures, the evidence obtained may cause the service auditor to change the nature, timing, or extent of other planned procedures. Information that differs significantly from the information on which the risk assessments and planned procedures were based may come to the service auditor's attention. For example,

- the extent of the misstatements that the service auditor detects is greater than expected. (This may alter the service auditor's professional judgment about the reliability of particular sources of information.)
- the service auditor may become aware of discrepancies in relevant information or conflicting or missing evidence.
- procedures performed toward the end of the engagement may indicate a previously unrecognized risk of material misstatement. In such circumstances, the service auditor may need to reevaluate the planned procedures.

Other Considerations When Evaluating Evidence

4.143 Paragraph .60 of AT-C section 205 states that the practitioner should evaluate, based on the evidence obtained, whether the presentation of the subject matter or assertion is misleading within the context of the engagement. In making that evaluation, the practitioner may consider whether additional disclosures are necessary to describe the subject matter, assertion, or criteria. Additional disclosures may, for example, include

- the measurement or evaluation methods used when the criteria allow for choice among methods;
- significant interpretations made in applying the criteria in the engagement circumstances;
- subsequent events, depending on their nature and significance; and
- whether there have been any changes in the measurement or evaluation methods used.

The service auditor is not required to determine whether the presentation discloses all matters related to the subject matter, assertion, or criteria or all matters intended users may consider in making decisions based on the presentation.

Controls Did Not Operate During the Period Covered by the Service Auditor's Report

4.144 In various circumstances, management's description of the service organization's system may include controls that ordinarily operate during the period covered by the service auditor's report but that did not operate during that period because the circumstances that warrant the operation of those controls did not occur during that period. Paragraphs 4.145–.150 of this guide include

- various scenarios in which the service auditor is unable to test controls because they did not operate during the period covered by the report.

- guidance regarding how those circumstances may affect management's assertion, the service auditor's description of tests of controls and results, and the service auditor' report.

Service Auditor Tests Other Controls Related to the Control Objective to Obtain Evidence About Whether the Control Objective Was Met

4.145 Even though a control did not operate during the period covered by the report, the service auditor may be able to obtain evidence about whether the control objective, or element of the control objective, was met. For example, consider a control that operates only when a new user is provided with logical access to a particular application, during a period in which there were no new users of the application. Other controls, such as controls related to the revocation of logical access for terminated employees and periodic access reviews, if operating during the period covered by the report, could be tested by the service auditor to provide evidence that the following control objective was met: "Logical access to programs, data, and computer resources is restricted to authorized and appropriate users and such users are restricted to performing authorized and appropriate actions." In these circumstances,

- the service organization would not need to modify its assertion.
- the service auditor would indicate in the service auditor's description of tests of controls and results
    - that the circumstance that warrants the operation of the control did not occur during the period covered by the report,
    - the reason why that circumstance did not occur, and that
    - therefore no testing was performed.
- the service auditor would not need to modify the scope or opinion paragraph of the service auditor's report.

Control Objective Consists of Multiple Elements; The Element of the Control Objective for Which Controls Did Not Operate During the Period Is Presented as a Separate Control Objective

4.146 As another example, consider the following control objective: "Controls provide reasonable assurance that changes to application programs and related data management systems are authorized, tested, documented, approved, and implemented to result in the complete, accurate, and timely processing and reporting of transactions and balances." If no changes were made to the application programs during the period covered by the report, but changes were made to the data management systems during that period, management may present the element of the control objective for which controls did not operate as a separate control objective. In doing so, the element of the control objective that addresses changes in application programs would be separated from the element of the control objective that addresses changes in data management systems, and the description of the service organization's system would clearly identify the controls that did not operate during the period. In these circumstances,

    a. management would disclose in its assertion that controls related to changes in application programs did not operate during the period covered by the report because the circumstances that warrant the operation of those controls did not occur during that period.

    b. the service auditor would indicate in the service auditor's description of tests of controls and results that controls related to changes in application programs did not operate during the period covered by the report because the circumstances that warrant the operation of those controls did not occur during the period covered by the report; therefore, the service auditor did not test the operating effectiveness of those controls.

    c. the service auditor would include the information in item (*b*) in the service auditor's report, either in the scope paragraph or in a separate paragraph. The opinion paragraph of the service auditor's report would not be modified.

Control Objective Consists of Multiple Elements; Service Organization Does Not Present as a Separate Control Objective the Element of the Control Objective for Which Controls Did Not Operate During the Period

4.147 If management of the service organization does not present as a separate control objective the element of the control objective for which controls did not operate during the period covered by the report, or based on the facts and circumstances, it is not prudent to separate the elements of the control objective,

    a. management would disclose in its assertion that controls related to the element of the control objective that addresses changes in application programs did not operate during the period covered by the report because the circumstances that warrant the operation of those controls did not occur during that period.

    b. the service auditor would indicate in the service auditor's description of tests of controls and results that controls related to the element of the control objective that addresses changes in application programs did not operate during the period covered by the report because the circumstances that warrant the operation of those controls did not occur during that period; therefore, the service auditor did not test the operating effectiveness of those controls.

c.   the service auditor would include the information in item (b) in the service auditor's report, either in the scope paragraph or in a separate paragraph. The opinion paragraph of the service auditor's report would not be modified.

4.148   The following is an example of a paragraph that would be included in the service auditor's report:

As noted in management's description, controls related to changes in application programs did not operate during the period January 1, 201X, to December 31, 201X, because the circumstances that warrant the operation of those controls did not occur during that period. Therefore, we did not test the operating effectiveness of controls related to the control objective "Controls provide reasonable assurance that changes to application programs and related data management systems are authorized, tested, documented, approved, and implemented to result in the complete, accurate and timely processing and reporting of transactions and balances," solely as they relate to changes in the application programs.

None of the Controls Related to a Control Objective Operated During the Period Covered by the Report

4.149   An additional situation may be encountered in which none of the controls related to an entire control objective operated during the period covered by the service auditor's report. An example would be a situation in which there were no new accounts during the period covered by the report, but the description of the service organization's system includes controls related to new account setups and also includes a related control objective. In these circumstances,

a.   management would disclose in its assertion that controls related to new account setups did not operate during the period covered by the report because the circumstances that warrant the operation of those controls did not occur during that period.

b.   the service auditor would indicate in the description of tests of controls and results that the circumstances that would warrant the operation of controls related to new account setups did not occur during the period covered by the report and, therefore, no testing was performed.

c.   the service auditor would include the information in item (b) in the service auditor's report, either in the scope paragraph or in a separate paragraph. The opinion paragraph of the service auditor's report would not be modified.

In this situation, management may also decide to remove the control objective and related controls from its description of the service organization's system and include them in a separate section of the type 2 report entitled "Other Information Provided by the Service Organization."

Paragraph 5.74 provides an example of a paragraph that may be added to the service auditor's report when controls did not operate during the examination period for an entire control objective. This example may be adapted and used in situations in which controls related to elements of a control objective did not operate during the examination period.

Extending or Modifying the Period

4.150 A service auditor may encounter situations in which management of a service organization requests that the period covered by an existing type 2 report be extended or modified. For example, the service auditor has previously reported on the period January 1, 20X1, to June 30, 20X1 (the original period), and management requests that the period be extended by three months to cover the period January 1, 20X1, to September 30, 20X1 (the extended period). In this case, six months of the extended period would have been tested, and three months of the extended period (new period) would not yet have been tested.

4.151 Generally, the scope of the description of the service organization's system for the new period would be unchanged from the scope for the original period; therefore, portions, if not all, of the prior description of the system, including control objectives, controls, complementary user entity control considerations, and the service auditor's relevant tests and results, would be relevant to the engagement covering the extended or modified period.

4.152 If the description of the service organization's system for the extended or modified period is consistent with that of the original period, relevant evidence about the operating effectiveness of controls consists of evidence obtained from tests of controls performed for the portion of the original period and evidence obtained from tests of controls performed for the extended or modified period.

4.153 Thus, for example, if the service auditor performed tests of the operating effectiveness of controls during the original period (January 1, 20X1, to June 30, 20X1) for a sample of 13 items that relate to the period April 1, 20X1, through June 30, 20X1, the tests of operating effectiveness performed on the sample of 13 items could be used as evidence for the modified period.

4.154 The service auditor should also obtain an understanding of any changes to the service organization's system that occurred during the new period, including changes to the services, control environment, controls, user entities, and personnel. Paragraphs 4.15, 4.82, and 4.107 of this guide discuss the service auditor's responsibilities for obtaining an understanding of and performing procedures that address changes in the service organization's system.

4.155 The service auditor may decide that it is necessary to perform additional tests for the portion of the modified or extended period included in the original period, and the results of those tests along with any additional information that the service auditor becomes aware of would be considered in forming a conclusion about the fairness of the presentation of the description of the system, the suitability of the design of the controls, or the operating effectiveness of the controls for the modified or extended period.

4.156 When forming the service auditor's opinion, conclusions reached during the original period are taken into consideration in addition to the results of tests performed and other evidence obtained related to the extended or modified period. In making a determination about the nature and extent of the additional evidence needed for the extended or modified period, the service auditor may consider the following:

- The overall control environment
- The significance of the assessed risks
- The specific controls that were tested during the portion of the original report period included in the extended or modified period and the nature and extent of the evidence obtained for that period
- The nature, timing, and extent of procedures performed for the portion of the original period included in the extended or modified period
- The length of the extended or modified period

4.157 If there have been major changes in the service organization's system, it may not be appropriate to perform an engagement for an extended or modified period. For example, if a service organization converted from one application processing system to another during the new period, and it made significant modifications to the controls, the service auditor may decide that communicating information about changes in controls may present challenges for user entities and, therefore, may decide that an engagement covering an extended or modified period is not appropriate.

Management's Written Representations for the Extended or Modified Period

4.158 Paragraphs 4.178–.190 contain information about the requirement for the service auditor to request written representations from management of the service organization. When the engagement covers a modified or extended period, the service auditor should obtain management's written representations in the form of a representation letter addressed to the service auditor and dated as of the same date as the service auditor's report that covers the entire extended or modified period (that is, the portion of the original period included in the modified or extended period plus the new period).

Deficiencies That Occur During the Original, Extended, or Modified Period

4.159 The service auditor assesses any deficiencies identified in the original period and corrected during the new period to determine their overall effect on, and whether disclosures are required in, the service auditor's report. Similarly, deficiencies noted in the extended or modified period are also evaluated to determine their effect on the service auditor's report.

4.160 Any deficiencies identified in the portion of the original period that is included in the extended or modified period should be included in the report on the extended or modified period, even if they were corrected during the extended or modified period. The service auditor should consider the status of any exceptions, deficiencies, or other matters noted in the portion of the original period that is also included in the extended or modified period, plus any exceptions, deficiencies, or other matters noted during the new period. For example, assume that the original report covered the period January 1, 20X1, to June 30, 20X1, and included a deficiency in operating effectiveness. Also assume that the deficiency was corrected on August 15, 20X1. For a report covering an examination period January 1 through September 30, the deficiency in operating effectiveness would be reported for the period from January 1 through September 30, 20X1. No reference to the original report is made in the extended or modified report.

4.161 For deficiencies reported in the original report that have not been corrected, the service auditor may evaluate the reasons that the deficiency has not been corrected and consider the effect on the engagement.

4.162 The service auditor may use evidence obtained for the original period that is included in the extended or modified period. Assume that the original period covered by the report is January 1, 20X1, to August 31, 20X1, and the modified period is April 1, 20X1, to December 31, 20X1. Five months of the modified period were tested and four months were untested. Twenty-five items were tested in the original period, of which 12 relate to the five months that were included in the modified period. There was 1 test exception noted for those 12 items. Thirteen additional items were tested for the modified period, and 1 exception was identified. The description of the results of tests would identify the total number of exceptions identified based on the total number of tests performed (for example, "Two exceptions were identified in a sample of 25 items selected for testing. The service auditor's conclusion on the achievement of the control objective would be based on an exception rate of 2 of 25.").

Other Matters Related to Performing the Engagement

Controls Designed by a Party Other Than Management of the Service Organization

4.163 In some cases, management of a service organization is asked to implement controls relevant to user entities' internal control over financial reporting that were designed by another party, for example, a user entity or former members of management of a recently acquired service organization. The members of management who would ordinarily provide the assertion (typically those directly responsible for the day-to-day operations of the service organization) may not be in a position to provide an assertion about the suitability of the design of such controls. In that case, other members of management, for example, members of corporate management, may be in a position to, and may agree to, provide such an assertion. Otherwise, the service auditor may not perform the engagement under AT-C section 320. In this situation, management of the service organization may be in a position to assert that the controls operated as described. If so, management may engage the service auditor or another practitioner to test whether the controls were operating as described in either an agreed-upon procedures engagement under AT-C section 215, *Agreed-Upon Procedures Engagements* (AICPA, *Professional Standards*), or an examination engagement under AT-C section 205.

Communicating Known and Suspected Fraud, Noncompliance With Laws or Regulations, Uncorrected Misstatements, and Deficiencies in the Design or Operating Effectiveness of Controls

4.164 Paragraph .85 of AT-C section 205 requires the service auditor to communicate to management of the service organization known and suspected fraud and noncompliance with laws or regulations and uncorrected misstatements, which in an engagement performed under AT-C section 320 would be misstatements in the fair presentation of the description, deficiencies in the suitability of the design of controls, and deficiencies in the operating effectiveness of controls.

Management Requests a Change in the Scope of the Engagement

4.165 Management of a service organization may request that the service auditor change the scope of the engagement after the terms of the engagement have been agreed to, for example, a request to change from a type 2 to a type 1 engagement or from an examination engagement to a consulting engagement. Paragraph .29 of AT-C section 105 indicates that the service auditor should not agree to a change in the terms of the engagement when no reasonable justification for the change exists. Paragraph .A21 of AT-C section 320 indicates that a request to change the scope of the engagement may not have a reasonable justification if, for example, the request is made

- to exclude certain control objectives at the service organization from the scope of the engagement because of the likelihood that the service auditor's opinion would be modified with respect to those control objectives.

- to prevent the disclosure of deviations identified at a subservice organization by requesting a change from the inclusive method to the carve-out method. (See paragraph 5.64 of this guide for an example of a separate paragraph that would be added to the service auditor's report when the service organization changes from the inclusive method to the carve-out method for a subservice organization without reasonable justification.)

4.166 Paragraph .A22 of AT-C section 320 indicates that a request to change the scope of the engagement may have a reasonable justification when, for example, the request is made because the service organization (a transfer agent), after providing the description of its system to the service auditor, decides that it would like to remove a control objective related to new fund setup because only one fund was set up during the reporting period, and management of the fund had performed its own testing. The service auditor concluded that the removal of the control objective related to new fund setup was reasonable in the circumstances because the objective was not relevant to a broad range of user entities during the examination period.

4.167 Paragraph .29 of AT-C section 105 indicates that if a change in the terms of the engagement is made, the service auditor should not disregard evidence that was obtained prior to the change.

Forming the Opinion

4.168 Paragraph .68 of AT-C section 205 states that the practitioner should modify the opinion when either of the following circumstances exist and, in the practitioner's professional judgment, the effect of the matter is or may be material:

a. The practitioner is unable to obtain sufficient appropriate evidence to conclude that the subject matter is in accordance with (or based on) the criteria, in all material respects.

    b. The practitioner concludes, based on evidence obtained, that the subject matter is not in accordance with (or based on) the criteria, in all material respects.

4.169 In addition, paragraph .69 of AT-C section 205 states that when the practitioner modifies the opinion, the practitioner should include a separate paragraph in the practitioner's report that provides a description of the matter(s) giving rise to the modification.

4.170 If a modified opinion is appropriate, the service auditor should determine whether to issue a qualified opinion, an adverse opinion, or a disclaimer of opinion. As indicated in paragraph .A103 of AT-C section 205, the decision regarding which type of modified opinion is appropriate depends upon the following:

    a. The nature of the matter giving rise to the modification (that is, whether the subject matter of the engagement is in accordance with [or based on] the criteria, in all material respects or, in the case of an inability to obtain sufficient appropriate evidence, may be materially misstated)

    b. The service auditor's professional judgment about the pervasiveness of the effects or possible effects of the matter on the subject matter of the engagement

4.171 When determining whether to modify the service auditor's opinion and the type of opinion to be issued, the service auditor should evaluate whether misstatements in the description of the service organization's system and deficiencies in the suitability of the design and operating effectiveness of the controls (throughout the specified period in a type 2 engagement and as of a specified date in a type 1 engagement) are material, individually or in the aggregate. Materiality is discussed in paragraphs 4.17–.19, 4.60, 4.79, and 5.03 of this guide. Paragraph .A15 of AT-C section 205 states that materiality is considered in the context of qualitative factors and, when applicable, quantitative factors. The following are examples of qualitative and quantitative factors:

Qualitative Factors

- The likelihood that misstatements in the description of the service organization's system or deficiencies in the suitability of the design or operating effectiveness of controls at the service organization will result in misstatements in the user entities' financial statements

- Whether user entities and user auditors could be misled if the service auditor's opinion or individual components of the opinion were not modified

Quantitative Factors

- The tolerable rate of deviations that the service auditor has established

- The magnitude of the misstatements that could occur in the user entities' financial statements as a result of misstatements in the description of the service organization's system or deficiencies in the suitability of the design or operating effectiveness of controls at the service organization

4.172   In applying paragraph .A105 of AT-C section 205, the term *pervasive* describes the effects or possible effects of the aggregate misstatements in management's description of the service organization's system or deficiencies in the suitability of the design or operating effectiveness of controls, if any, that are undetected due to an inability to obtain sufficient appropriate evidence. Pervasive effects or possible effects on the fairness of the presentation of the description, on the suitability of the design of controls, and on the operating effectiveness of controls are those that, in the practitioner's professional judgment,

    a.   are not confined to specific aspects of the description, or the design or operating effectiveness of controls;

    b.   if so confined, represent or could represent a substantial proportion of the description, or the design or operating effectiveness of controls; or

    c.   are fundamental to the intended users' understanding of the service organization's system, or the design and operating effectiveness of controls.

4.173   The following are examples of quantitative and qualitative factors that are relevant to the service auditor's consideration of whether identified misstatements in the description of the service organization's system or deficiencies in the design or operating effectiveness of the controls are pervasive:

- The extent of the description for which the service auditor is unable to obtain sufficient appropriate evidence (for example, if misstatements are not limited to specific areas of the description that can be clearly identified in the service auditor's report, the effect would likely be pervasive

- The number and significance of control objectives for which the service auditor is unable to obtain sufficient appropriate evidence about the design or operating effectiveness of controls (for example, if the deficiencies preclude the achievement of many or most of the control objectives, the effect would likely be pervasive)

- Whether providing an opinion on the portion of the description of the service organization's system or the design or operating effectiveness of controls for which sufficient appropriate evidence was obtained would be misleading in light of the aggregate effect of the misstatements in the description or deficiencies in the design or operating effectiveness of the controls

4.174   Table 4-4 identifies the type of modified opinion to be issued based on the nature of the matter giving rise to the modification and the service auditor's professional judgment about the materiality of the matter and the pervasiveness of its effects or possible effects on the fairness of the presentation of management's description of the service organization's system, the suitability of the design of the service organization's controls, and in the case of a type 2 report, the operating effectiveness of the service organization's controls.

Table 4-4

Factors to Consider When Determining the Type of Modified Opinion to Be Issued

Nature of Matter Giving Rise to the Modification	*Practitioner's Professional Judgment About the Pervasiveness of the Effects or Possible Effects on the Description, on the Suitability of the Design of Controls, and on the Operating Effectiveness of Controls*	
	Material but Not Pervasive	*Material and Pervasive*
Scope limitation. An inability to obtain sufficient appropriate evidence.	Qualified opinion	Disclaimer of opinion
Material misstatements. The description is materially misstated or the controls are not suitably designed or operating effectively to achieve one or more of the related control objectives stated in management's description of the service organization's system.	Qualified opinion	Adverse opinion

Documentation

4.175 Paragraphs .87–.89 of AT-C section 205 contain requirements for the service auditor to document the following:

- The nature, timing, and extent of the procedures performed to comply with the relevant AT-C sections and applicable legal and regulatory requirements, including

  - the identifying characteristics of the specific items or matters tested

  - who performed the work and the date such work was completed

  - the discussions with the responsible party or others about findings or issues that, in the service auditor's professional judgment, are significant, including the nature of the significant findings or issues discussed, and when and with whom the discussions took place

— the following matters related to management's written representations, if applicable:

- Management will not provide one or more of the requested written representations

- The service auditor concludes that there is sufficient doubt about the competence, integrity, ethical values, or diligence of those providing the written representations or that the written representations are otherwise not reliable

— who reviewed the engagement work performed and the date and extent of such review

- The results of the procedures performed and the evidence obtained

- If the service auditor has identified information that is inconsistent with the service auditor's final conclusion regarding a significant finding or issue, how the service auditor addressed the inconsistency

- If facts become known to the service auditor after the date of the report that, had they been known to the service auditor at that date, may have caused the service auditor to revise the report, and the service auditor performs new or additional procedures or draws new conclusions after the date of the service auditor's report,

— the circumstances encountered;

— the new or additional procedures performed, evidence obtained, and conclusions reached and their effect on the report; and

— when and by whom the resulting changes to the documentation were made and reviewed

4.176 The service auditor should assemble the engagement documentation in an engagement file and complete the administrative process of assembling the final engagement file no later than 60 days following the service auditor's report release date. After the documentation completion date, the service auditor should not delete or discard documentation of any nature before the end of its retention period. If the service auditor finds it necessary to amend existing documentation or add new engagement documentation after the documentation completion date, the service auditor should, regardless of the nature of the amendments or additions, document the specific reasons for making the amendments or additions and when and by whom they were made and reviewed.

Completing the Engagement

4.177 Procedures that are usually performed toward the end of a service auditor's engagement include the following:

- Obtaining representations from management of the service organization

- Inquiring about subsequent events and evaluating the need for disclosure of such events, for example, inquiries about information contained in relevant reports issued during the subsequent period by internal auditors, other practitioners, or regulatory agencies or obtained through other professional engagements for that service organization

If the service auditor wishes to do so, the service auditor may provide recommendations to management of the service organization, generally related to controls that affect user entities' internal control over financial reporting, as discussed in paragraph 5.94 of this guide.

Requesting Written Representations

4.178 Paragraph .38 of AT-C section 320 requires the service auditor to request from management the written representations required by paragraph .50 of AT-C section 205 as well as those required by paragraph .36 of AT-C section 320. Although paragraph .38 indicates that the request should be made to management, paragraph .09 of AT-C section 320 indicates that the service auditor should determine the appropriate person(s) within the service organization's management or governance structure with whom to interact, including considering which person(s) has the appropriate responsibilities for and knowledge of the matters concerned. In addition, paragraph .A54 of AT-C section 320 states that, in certain circumstances, the service auditor may obtain written representations from parties in addition to management of the service organization, such as those charged with governance.

4.179 In some cases, the party making the assertion may be indirectly responsible for and knowledgeable about specified matters covered in the representations. For example, the CEO of the service organization may be knowledgeable about certain matters through personal experience and about other matters through employees who report to the CEO. The service auditor may request that individuals who are directly or indirectly responsible for and knowledgeable about matters covered in the written representations provide their own representations.

4.180 Paragraph .37 of AT-C section 320 indicates that if the service organization uses a subservice organization, and management's description of the service organization's system uses the inclusive method, the service auditor should also request the written representations identified in paragraph .50 of AT-C section 205 and paragraph .36 of AT-C section 320 from management of the subservice organization.

4.181 Paragraph .A57 of AT-C section 320 states that, if the service auditor is unable to obtain written representations regarding relevant control objectives and related controls at the subservice organization, management of the service organization may be able to use the carve-out method.

4.182 Paragraph .A56 of AT-C section 320 states that the service auditor may consider it necessary to request written representations other than those included in paragraph .36 of AT-C section 320. This would be determined based on the facts and circumstances of the particular engagement. For example, if changes to the service organization's controls have occurred during the period covered by the service auditor's report, there might be a need to request representations that address the period before the change and the period after the change.

4.183 The written representations required by paragraph .50 of AT-C section 205 are identified in items (a)–(i) of the following list, and the written representations required by paragraph .36 of AT-C section 320 are identified in items (j)–(k). (Illustrative representation letters that have been tailored to a service auditor's engagement are included in appendix B, "Illustrative Type 2 Reports–Inclusive Method, Including Illustrative Management Representation Letters," and appendix C, "Illustrative Management Representation Letters," of this guide.) Paragraph .50 of AT-C section 205 states that the representations should

    a. include the responsible party's assertion about the subject matter based on the criteria.

    b. state that all relevant matters are reflected in the measurement or evaluation of the subject matter or assertion.

    c. state that all known matters contradicting the subject matter or assertion and any communication from regulatory agencies or others affecting the subject matter or assertion have been disclosed to the practitioner, including communications received between the end of the period addressed in the written assertion and the date of the practitioner's report.

    d. acknowledge responsibility for

        i. the subject matter and the assertion;

        ii. selecting the criteria, when applicable; and

        iii. determining that such criteria are appropriate for the responsible party's purposes.

    e. state that any known events subsequent to the period (or point in time) of the subject matter being reported on that would have a material effect on the subject matter or assertion have been disclosed to the practitioner.

    f. state that the responsible party has provided the service auditor with all relevant information and access.

    g. if applicable, state that the responsible party believes the effects of uncorrected misstatements are immaterial, individually and in the aggregate, to the subject matter.

    h. if applicable, state that significant assumptions used in making any material estimates are reasonable.

    i. state that the responsible party has disclosed to the practitioner

        i. all deficiencies in internal control relevant to the engagement of which the responsible party is aware;

        ii. its knowledge of any actual, suspected, or alleged fraud or noncompliance with laws or regulations affecting the subject matter; and

        iii. other matters as the practitioner deems appropriate.

4.184 Paragraph .36 of AT-C section 320 requires the practitioner to request additional representations in an engagement performed under AT-C section 320. Those representations are that management has disclosed any of the following of which it is aware:

    a. Instances of noncompliance with laws and regulations or uncorrected misstatements attributable to the service organization that may affect one or more user entities *b.* Knowledge of any actual, suspected, or alleged fraud by management or the service organization's employees that could adversely affect the fairness of the presentation of management's description of the service organization's system or the completeness or achievement of the control objectives stated in the description

4.185 Paragraph .A55 of AT-C section 320 clarifies that the written representations required by paragraph .36 of that section are separate from and in addition to the assertion that accompanies management's description of the service organization's system.

4.186 Paragraph .54 of AT-C section 205 states, in part, that the written representations should be as of the date of the service auditor's report.

4.187 Paragraph .55 of AT-C section 205 indicates that if management does not provide one or more of the requested representations, or the practitioner concludes that there is sufficient doubt about the competence, integrity, ethical values, or diligence of those providing the written representations, or the practitioner concludes that the written representations are otherwise not reliable, the practitioner should

    a. discuss the matter with the appropriate party;

    b. reevaluate the integrity of those from whom the representations were requested or received and evaluate the effect that this may have on the reliability of representations and evidence in general; and

    c. if any of the matters are not resolved to the practitioner's satisfaction, take appropriate action.

4.188 Paragraph .A64 of AT-C section 205 further indicates that the refusal to furnish such evidence in the form of written representations constitutes a limitation on the scope of the examination sufficient to preclude an unmodified opinion and may be sufficient to cause the practitioner to withdraw from the engagement. Paragraph 5.42 of this guide contains an illustrative type 2 report disclaiming an opinion because management will not provide one or more of the written representations requested by the service auditor.

4.189 Because management's written representations are an important consideration when forming the service auditor's opinion, the service auditor would not ordinarily be able to issue the report until the service auditor had received the representation letter. Illustrative representation letters for a service auditor's engagement are presented in appendixes B and C of this guide.

Engaging Party Is Not the Responsible Party

4.190 Paragraph .51 of AT-C section 205 provides the option of obtaining oral (rather than written) representations from the responsible party in an examination engagement in which the engaging party is not the responsible party and the responsible party refuses to provide the required written representations. For example, an industry group representing user entities of a particular service organization may engage a service auditor to perform a type 2 engagement at that service organization. In this scenario, the engaging party is not the responsible party. It should be noted, however, that paragraph .38 of AT-C section 320 states that the practitioner should request the written representations required by paragraph .50 of AT-C section 205 and paragraph .36 of AT-C section 320 even if the engaging party is not the responsible party. The alternative provided in paragraph .51 of AT-C section 205 of obtaining oral representations is not permitted in an engagement performed under AT-C section 320.

Representations From the Engaging Party When Not the Responsible Party

4.191 When the engaging party is not the responsible party, paragraph .52 of AT-C section 205 requires the practitioner to request written representations from the engaging party, in addition to those requested from the responsible party, in the form of a letter addressed to the practitioner. Those representations should

- a. acknowledge that the responsible party is responsible for the subject matter and assertion.
- b. acknowledge the engaging party's responsibility for selecting the criteria, when applicable.
- c. acknowledge the engaging party's responsibility for determining that such criteria are appropriate for its purposes.
- d. state that the engaging party is not aware of any material misstatements in the subject matter or assertion.
- e. state that the engaging party has disclosed to the practitioner all known events subsequent to the period (or point in time) of the subject matter being reported on that would have a material effect on the subject matter or assertion.
- f. address other matters as the practitioner deems appropriate.

Subsequent Events Up to the Date of the Service Auditor's Report

4.192 Paragraph .48 of AT-C section 205 requires the service auditor to

- inquire whether management, and if different, the engaging party, is aware of any events subsequent to the period (or point in time) covered by the examination engagement up to the date of the service auditor's report that could have a significant effect on the subject matter or management's assertion and
- apply other appropriate procedures to obtain evidence regarding such events.

4.193 Based on the requirements in paragraph .48 of AT-C section 205 and paragraph .35 of AT-C section 320 and the application guidance in paragraph .A56 of AT-C section 205, if the service auditor becomes aware, through inquiry or otherwise, of such an event, or any other event that is of such a nature and significance that its disclosure is necessary to prevent users of the report from being misled, and information about that event is not adequately disclosed by management in its description of the service organization's system, the service auditor should take appropriate actions. Ordinarily, the service auditor would request that management amend the description to include the necessary disclosure. If management refuses to amend the description, appropriate actions that the service auditor may take include disclosing the event in the service auditor's report and modifying the service auditor's opinion or withdrawing from the engagement. Paragraph 5.53 of this guide presents an example of a separate paragraph that would be added to the service auditor's report when the description omits information about a subsequent event that is of such a nature and significance that its disclosure is necessary to prevent users of a type 1 or type 2 report from being misled.

4.194 The following are examples of subsequent events that could affect management's assertion or management's description of the service organization's system:

- A defalcation occurred at the service organization.

- After the period covered by the service auditor's report, it was discovered that the signatures on a number of non-automated trade execution instructions submitted during the examination period that appeared to be authenticated by signature verification had been forged.

- After the period covered by the service auditor's report, management discovered that during the last quarter of the period covered by the service auditor's report the IT security director had provided all of the programmers with access to the production data files, enabling them to modify data.

4.195 Situations may exist in which the event that is discovered subsequent to the period covered by management's description of the service organization's system up to the date of the service auditor's report would likely have no effect on the subject matter or management's assertion because the underlying situation did not occur or exist until after the period covered by management's description of the service organization's system; however, the matter may be sufficiently important for disclosure by management in its description and potentially by the service auditor in a separate paragraph of the service auditor's report. The following are examples of such subsequent events:

- The service organization was acquired by another entity.

- The service organization experienced a significant operating disruption or other extraordinary event such as an event caused by weather or other natural disasters.

- A data center hosting service organization that provides applications and technology that enable user entities to process financial transactions made significant changes to its information system, such as a system conversion or significant outsourcing of operations.

4.196 The service organization may wish to disclose such events in a separate section of the type 1 or type 2 report entitled, for example, "Other Information Provided by the Service Organization," as described in paragraphs 5.23–.34 of this guide.

Management's Responsibilities During Engagement Completion

4.197 The responsibilities of management of the service organization toward the end of the engagement include

- modifying the description of the service organization's system, if appropriate (paragraphs 4.04–.55 address the evaluation of management's description of the service organization's system and identify a number of situations in which the service auditor would recommend that management of the service organization modify the description of the service organization's system.);

- modifying management's written assertion, if appropriate;
- providing written representations;
- informing the service auditor of subsequent events; and
- distributing the report to appropriate parties.

Chapter 5

Reporting

> This chapter discusses the elements of a service auditor's report and the responsibilities of the service auditor and matters the service auditor considers when reporting on a service auditor's engagement. This chapter principally focuses on type 2 reports. This guide may not address all of the requirements and application guidance relevant to a service auditor's engagement and therefore should be read in conjunction with the following sections in AICPA *Professional Standards*: AT-C section 105, *Concepts Common to All Attestation Engagements*, AT-C section 205, *Examination Engagements*, and AT-C section 320, *Reporting on an Examination of Controls at a Service Organization Relevant to User Entities' Internal Control Over Financial Reporting* (AICPA, *Professional Standards*).

5.01 The service auditor's responsibilities for reporting on the engagement include preparing

- a written description of the tests of controls performed by the service auditor and the results of those tests and
- the service auditor's report, including all of the report elements for a type 2 report identified in paragraph .40 of AT-C section 320 (and paragraph .41 for a type 1 report), and modifying the report if the service auditor determines it is appropriate to do so.

Describing Tests of Controls and Results

5.02 Paragraph .40*k* of AT-C section 320 states that a service auditor's type 2 report should contain a reference to a description of the service auditor's tests of controls and the results thereof. The description should identify the controls that were tested, whether the items tested represent all or a selection of the items in the population, and the nature of the tests performed in sufficient detail to enable user auditors to determine the effect of such tests on their risk assessments and to respond to assessed risk. Table 5-1, "Information to Be Included When Describing Tests of Controls and Results," summarizes the information to be included when describing the service auditor's tests of controls and results.

Table 5-1

Information to Be Included When Describing Tests of Controls and Results

Information to Be Described	If No Deviations[1] Were Identified	If Deviations Were Identified
The controls that were tested	Required	Required
Whether the items tested represent all or a selection of the items in the population	Required	Required
The nature of the tests performed in sufficient detail to enable user auditors to determine the effect of such tests on their risk assessments	Required	Required
The number of items tested	Not required	Required
The number and nature of the deviations	N/A	Required
Causative factors (for identified deviations)	N/A	Optional

5.03 The concept of materiality is not applied when reporting the results of tests of controls for which deviations have been identified because the service auditor does not have the ability to determine whether a deviation will have significance to a particular user entity or user auditor beyond whether it prevents a control from operating effectively. Consequently, the service auditor's description of tests of controls and results includes all deviations. If the service auditor has not identified any deviations, the service auditor may document those results with a phrase such as "No exceptions noted" or "No deviations noted." Appendix A, "Illustrative Type 2 Reports," and appendix B, "Illustrative Type 2 Reports—Inclusive Method, Including Illustrative Management Representation Letters," of this guide contain a number of examples of descriptions of tests of controls in which no deviations have been identified.

5.04 The description of tests of controls need not be a duplication of the service auditor's detailed audit program, which might make the report too voluminous for user auditors and provide more than the required level of detail. The description is intended to provide the user auditors with sufficient detail about the nature and extent of the service auditor's procedures to enable them to obtain evidence about the operating effectiveness of the service organization's controls. In table 5-2, "Relevant Information When Describing Tests of Controls," the first column identifies in greater detail the information to be included in the service auditor's description of tests of controls and results, and the second column provides an example of each item in the first column.

---

[1] In this guide, the term *deviation* or *exception* refers to an instance in which a test of controls indicates that the control was not operating effectively to achieve the related control objective.

©2017, AICPA

Table 5-2

Relevant Information When Describing Tests of Controls

Relevant Information When Describing a Test of Controls	Example
The nature of the tests performed (generally inquiry, observation, inspection, or reperformance)	*Observed* the existence of signage in the facility lobby directing personnel to contact the Ethics Help Line to report ...
The document or electronic file to which the practitioner referred to obtain evidence	Inspected the *Information Security Office Charter* to determine whether • the roles and responsibilities of members of Security Office are defined. • the reporting relationship of the chief information security officer to entity leadership is defined. • ...
The extent of testing, for example, the size of the sample tested or the number of observations of a control activity	Selected *a sample of requests for access to the system made during the months of March, June, September, and December 20XX* to determine whether access was granted or denied based on the entity's access criteria.
The title and role of the service organization personnel to whom inquiries were directed	Inquired of *the data center security officer* responsible for ensuring that all visitors are signed in based on government-issued credentials and escorted throughout the facility, regarding procedures for visitors ...
The documents, files, or other sources from which the tested items were selected	Inspected a sample of terminated employees *from a list generated by the human resources system* and compared the termination date per the listing to the access card deactivation dates for each terminated employee per the access system ...
Any testing performed on underlying electronic audit evidence (for example, system-generated reports)	Obtained one daily termination report that was automatically generated from the human resources management system and emailed to the facilities manager. Obtained the system script used to generate and email the report to determine if terminations are appropriately included in the report and the list is automatically routed to the facilities manager after generation ...

5.05   In describing the extent of the testing, the service auditor should indicate whether items tested represent all or a selection of the items in the population. The service auditor is not required to indicate the size of the sample unless deviations have been identified during testing. If deviations have been identified, the service auditor should include the number of items tested and the number and nature of the deviations identified, even if, on the basis of tests performed, the service auditor concludes that the control objectives were achieved.

5.06   If deviations in tests of controls have been identified, it may be helpful to users of the report for management to disclose, to the extent known, the causative factors for the deviations, the controls that mitigate the effect of the deviations, corrective actions taken, and other qualitative factors that would assist users in understanding the effect of the deviations. Such information may be presented in management's description of the service organization's system or in a separate section of the type 2 report entitled "Other Information Provided by the Service Organization." Information in this section is not covered by the service auditor's report. If management's responses to deviations in tests of controls are included in the description of the service organization's system, such responses are usually included along with the description of the applicable control and related control objective. If that is the case, the service auditor should determine through inquiries in combination with other procedures whether there is evidence supporting the action described by management in its response. If the response includes forward-looking information, such as future plans to implement controls or to address deviations, such information should be included in the section "Other Information Provided by the Service Organization." Paragraphs 5.23–.34 of this guide address other information that is not covered by the service auditor's report.

5.07   The following example illustrates the documentation of tests of controls for which deviations have been identified. It is assumed that in each situation other relevant controls and tests of controls would also be described.

Control Objective

Controls provide reasonable assurance that trades are authorized, processed, and recorded in a complete, accurate, and timely manner.

Example Service Organization's Controls

Trades are initiated only upon receipt of a trade authorization form signed by an employee of the user entity who has been specifically designated by the user entity to authorize trades. Trade authorization forms that are received are validated as bearing the name of a designated user entity employee.

Service Auditor's Tests of Controls

Inquired of the trading desk clerks about the procedures performed upon receipt of trade authorizations. For a sample of trades selected from the trade register for the period, inspected a sample of trade authorizations for the signatures of authorized user entity employees, comparing the signature on the trade authorization to a list of designated employees authorized to initiate trades for the user entity.

Results of Tests of Controls

1. One of the n trade authorizations[2] sampled was missing the signature of an authorized user entity employee.

Management's Response

Management informed us that, after this exception was brought to their attention, management contacted the user entity and was told that the user entity's records indicate that an authorized employee of the user entity forgot to sign the trade authorization and called the service organization on the same day to authorize the trade. Management subsequently requested and received written confirmation from the user entity that the employee in question was authorized to, and did, approve the trade by telephone on the date the trade was submitted. Management provided us with that written confirmation ...

Results of Tests of Controls

2. One of the n trade authorizations sampled was signed, but the name of the individual who signed it was not on the list of authorized employees at the time.

Management's Response

After this exception was brought to management's attention, management informed us that it had contacted the user entity and was told that the individual who signed the trade authorization was an authorized employee on the date the trade was submitted. However, the list of authorized employees had not been updated by the user entity in a timely manner. Management requested and received written confirmation from the user entity that the signature in question was that of an employee authorized to approve trades on the date the trade was submitted, and they provided us with that confirmation.

No other exceptions were noted.

Describing Tests of Controls and Results When Using the Internal Audit Function

5.08 If the work of the internal audit function has been used, the service auditor should not make reference to that work in the service auditor's opinion. Notwithstanding its degree of autonomy and objectivity, the internal audit function is not independent of the service organization. The service auditor has sole responsibility for the opinion expressed in the service auditor's report, and that responsibility is not reduced by the service auditor's use of the work of the internal audit function.

5.09 Paragraph .40kv of AT-C section 320 indicates that, if the work of the internal function has been used in tests of controls to obtain evidence, the part of the service auditor's report that describes the service auditor's tests of controls and results should include a description of the internal auditor's work and of the service auditor's procedures with respect to that work. Paragraph .A65 of AT-C section 320 states that the work of the internal audit function referred to in paragraph .40kv does not include tests of controls performed by internal auditors as part of direct assistance. Such tests are designed by the service auditor and performed under the direction, supervision, and review of the service auditor and, therefore, receive the same scrutiny by the service auditor as if

---

[2] The letter n is used to represent the size of the sample.

they were performed by the engagement team. Accordingly, the description of tests of controls and results need not distinguish between the tests performed by members of the internal audit function as part of direct assistance and the tests performed by the service auditor.

5.10 Paragraph .A66 of AT-C section 320 emphasizes the points made in paragraphs 5.08–.09 by stating, "Other than the description of the work of the internal auditors referred to in paragraph .40*kv*, the service auditor's report does not make any reference to the use of the work of the internal audit function to obtain evidence or to the use of internal auditors to provide direct assistance."

5.11 Paragraph .A64 of AT-C section 320 states that when the work of the internal audit function has been used in performing tests of controls to obtain evidence, the service auditor's description of that work and of the service auditor's procedures with respect to that work may be presented in a number of ways, for example, by including introductory material in the description of tests of controls indicating that certain work of the internal audit function was used in performing tests of controls and describing the service auditor's procedures with respect to that work or by attributing individual tests to the internal audit function and describing the service auditor's procedures with respect that work.

5.12 The following are examples of introductory material that may be included in the description of tests of controls and results to inform users of the service auditor's report that the service auditor has used the work of the internal audit function to obtain evidence regarding the operating effectiveness of controls:

> *Example 1.* Throughout the examination period, members of XYZ Service Organization's internal audit function performed tests of controls related to the control objectives that address withdrawals, corporate actions, and dividends. Members of the internal audit function observed the control being performed, inspected documentation of and reperformed the control activities, and did not identify any deviations in testing. We reperformed selected tests that had been performed by members of the internal audit function and found no exceptions.

> *Example 2.* Members of XYZ Service Organization's internal audit function performed tests of controls for the following control objectives:

> - Controls provide reasonable assurance that withdrawals are authorized and processed in a complete, accurate, and timely manner.
> - Controls provide reasonable assurance that corporate actions are processed and recorded in a complete, accurate, and timely manner.
> - Controls provide reasonable assurance that dividends are processed and recorded in a complete, accurate, and timely manner.

> The tests performed by members of the internal audit function included inquiry of relevant parties who performed the control activities, observation of the control being performed at different times during the examination period, and inspection of the documentation for a sample of transactions. No deviations were noted by members of the internal audit function. We tested the work of members of the internal audit function through a combination of independent testing and reperformance and noted no exceptions.

5.13 The following are examples of descriptions of tests of controls and results that identify the tests performed by the internal audit function and attribute that work to them.

Example 1. When withdrawal requests are received, the processing clerk compares the name of the individual requesting the withdrawal to a client-provided list of individuals authorized to make such requests. The processing clerk who performs this control initials the request form to indicate that the comparison has been performed. Requests from individuals whose names are not on the client-provided list are rejected and sent back to the client.

Tests Performed by the Internal Audit Function

- Inquired of the processing clerk responsible for performing the control regarding the procedures performed when a withdrawal request is received.
- Observed the employee performing the control on multiple occasions throughout the examination period.
- For a sample of withdrawals made during the examination period that were selected from the payments register, compared the name on the withdrawal request to the client-provided list of individuals authorized to make such requests, and determined that the request had been initialed by the processing clerk.

Tests Performed by the Service Auditor

- Inquired of the processing clerk responsible for performing the control regarding the procedures performed when a withdrawal request is received.
- For a sample of items tested by members of the internal audit function, reperformed the test.
- For an additional sample of withdrawals made during the examination period that were selected from the payments register, compared the name on the withdrawal request to the client-provided list of employees authorized to make such requests, and determined that the request had been initialed by the processing clerk.

Results of Tests

No exceptions noted.

Example 2. When withdrawal requests are received, the processing clerk compares the name of the individual requesting the withdrawal to a client-provided list of employees authorized to make such requests. The clerk performing this control initials the request form or electronic request to indicate that the comparison has been performed. Requests from individuals who are not on the client-provided list are rejected and sent back to the client.

Tests Performed

- Members of the internal audit function inquired of the clerk responsible for performing the control regarding the procedures followed when withdrawal requests are received.

- Members of the internal audit function made multiple observations throughout the examination period of the clerk performing the control.

- For a sample of withdrawals during the examination period that were selected from the payments register, the members of the internal audit function and the service auditor compared the name on the withdrawal request form or electronic request to the client-provided list of individuals authorized to make such requests and determined that the request had been initialed by the processing clerk.

- The service auditor reperformed the testing for a sample of items tested by members of the internal audit function.

Results of Tests

No exceptions noted.

Describing Tests of the Reliability of Information Produced by the Service Organization

5.14   When the service auditor performs procedures to assess the reliability of information produced by the service organization, the service auditor's description of tests of controls and results may include a description of the procedures the service auditor performed to test the reliability of the information. The service auditor may

- provide this information in summary form in the description of tests of controls and results or

- identify the individual procedures performed on a control-by-control basis.

5.15   The following is an example of introductory material in summary form that may be included in the description of tests of controls and results to inform users of the service auditor's report that the service auditor has performed procedures that address the reliability of information provided to the service auditor in response to an ad hoc request for information used in the performance of a control:

> Observation and inspection procedures were performed as it relates to [system-generated reports, queries, and listings] to assess the accuracy and completeness (reliability) of the information used in our tests of controls.

5.16   When the service auditor performs procedures to assess the reliability of information prepared for user entities, the procedures performed by the service auditor would be included in the description of the tests of the applicable control and results of the tests. The following are some examples of language that may be used to inform users of the service auditor's report of the specific procedures the service auditor performed to address the reliability of information used in the performance of a control:

> Obtained a daily termination report that was produced automatically by the Human Resources Management System and provided to the facilities manager during the specified period. Inspected the query used to generate the daily termination report used in the execution of the control to determine whether terminations are appropriately included in the report provided to the facilities manager.

For reports that include loans processed with a balance greater than or equal to $50,000, inspected the query used to generate the report to determine whether such loans were appropriately included in the report.

Preparing the Service Auditor's Report

Elements of the Service Auditor's Report

5.17 Paragraph .40 of AT-C section 320 identifies the elements that should be included in a type 2 report, and paragraph .41 of AT-C section 320 identifies the elements that should be included in a type 1 report.

5.18 Table 5-3, "Elements of a Service Auditor's Report," identifies where each required element of a type 2 report included in paragraph .40 of AT-C section 320 is illustrated in this guide, primarily referencing appendix A, which contains illustrative type 2 reports. The table also identifies the related item for a type 1 report if the requirement for a type 1 report in paragraph .41 of AT-C section 320 differs from the requirement for a type 2 report. A service auditor's type 2 report should contain all of the elements identified in paragraph .40 of AT-C section 320 and a service auditor's type 1 report should contain all of the elements identified in paragraph .41 of AT-C section 320.

Table 5-3

Elements of a Service Auditor's Report

Paragraph in AT-C Section 320 That Contains the Requirement	Illustration of the Required Element in This Guide	Required Element and Additional Comments
.40a*	appendix A, example 1	A title that includes the word *independent*.
.40b*	appendix A, example 1	An appropriate addressee as required by the circumstances of the engagement. (In most cases, the service auditor is engaged by the service organization and would address the service auditor's report to management of the service organization. However, the service auditor may be engaged by one or more user entities or the board of directors of the service organization and, in such cases, would address and provide the report to the party that engaged the service auditor.)
.40c*	appendix A, example 1	Identification of the following:

(continued)

Elements of a Service Auditor's Report—*continued*

Paragraph in AT-C Section 320 That Contains the Requirement	Illustration of the Required Element in This Guide	Required Element and Additional Comments
.40ci*	appendix A, example 1	• Management's description of the service organization's system, the function performed by the system, and the period to which the description relates.
.40cii***	appendix A, example 1	• The criteria against which the fairness of the presentation of the description and the suitability of the design and operating effectiveness of the controls to achieve the related control objectives stated in the description were evaluated. (The criteria are identified in management's assertion and incorporated by reference in the service auditor's report.)
.41cii**	not illustrated	• The criteria against which the fairness of the presentation of the description and the suitability of the design of the controls to achieve the related control objectives stated in the description were evaluated. (The criteria are identified in management's assertion and incorporated by reference in the service auditor's report.)
.40ciii*	appendix A, example 1 and paragraphs 5.24, 5.34, and 5.55–.56	• Any information included in a document containing the service auditor's report that is not covered by the service auditor's report.
.40civ*	appendix A, example 2 (carve out) appendix B, example 1 (inclusive)	• Any services performed by a subservice organization and whether the carve-out method or the inclusive method was used in relation to them. Depending on which method is used, the following should be included:
.40civ(1)*	appendix A, example 2	— If the carve-out method was used, a statement indicating that

Elements of a Service Auditor's Report—*continued*

Paragraph in AT-C Section 320 That Contains the Requirement	Illustration of the Required Element in This Guide	Required Element and Additional Comments
.40civ(1)(a)*	appendix A, example 2	• management's description of the service organization's system excludes the control objectives and related controls of the relevant subservice organizations.
.40civ(1)(b)*	appendix A, example 2	• certain control objectives specified by the service organization can be achieved only if complementary subservice organization controls assumed in the design of the service organization's controls are suitably designed and operating effectively.
.40civ(1)(c)*	appendix A, example 2	• the service auditor's procedures do not extend to such complementary subservice organization controls.
.40civ(2)*	appendix B, example 1	— If the inclusive method was used, a statement that management's description of the service organization's system includes the subservice organization's specified control objectives and related controls, and that the service auditor's procedures included procedures related to the subservice organization.
.40d*	appendix A, example 1	A statement that the controls and control objectives included in the description are those that management believes are likely to be relevant to user entities' internal control over financial reporting, and the description does not include those aspects of the system that are not likely to be relevant to user entities' internal control over financial reporting.

(continued)

AAG-ASO 5.18

Elements of a Service Auditor's Report—*continued*

Paragraph in AT-C Section 320 That Contains the Requirement	Illustration of the Required Element in This Guide	Required Element and Additional Comments
.40e*	appendix A, example 1	If management's description of the service organization's system refers to the need for complementary user entity controls, a statement that the service auditor has not evaluated the suitability of the design or operating effectiveness of complementary user entity controls, and that the control objectives stated in the description can be achieved only if complementary user entity controls are suitably designed and operating effectively, along with the controls at the service organization.
.40f*	appendix A, example 1	A reference to management's assertion and a statement that management is responsible for
.40fi*	appendix A, example 1	• preparing the description of the service organization's system and the assertion, including the completeness, accuracy, and method of presentation of the description and assertion. Paragraph .A18 states that the service organization's assertion may be attached to the description of the service organization's system or may be included in the description if clearly segregated from the description, for example, through the use of headings.
.40fii*	appendix A, example 1	• providing the services covered by the description of the service organization's system.
.40fiii*	appendix A, example 1	• specifying the control objectives and stating them in the description of the service organization's system.
.40fiv*	appendix A, example 1	• identifying the risks that threaten the achievement of the control objectives.
.40fv*	appendix A, example 1	• selecting the criteria.

Elements of a Service Auditor's Report—*continued*

Paragraph in AT-C Section 320 That Contains the Requirement	Illustration of the Required Element in This Guide	Required Element and Additional Comments
.40*f*vi*	appendix A, example 1	• designing, implementing, and documenting controls that are suitably designed and operating effectively to achieve the related control objectives stated in the description of the service organization's system.
.40*g**	appendix A, example 1	A statement that the service auditor is responsible for expressing an opinion on the fairness of the presentation of management's description of the service organization's system and on the suitability of the design and operating effectiveness of the controls to achieve the related control objectives stated in the description based on the service auditor's examination.
.41*g***	not illustrated	A statement that the service auditor is responsible for expressing an opinion on the fairness of the presentation of management's description of the service organization's system and on the suitability of the design of the controls to achieve the related control objectives stated in the description based on the service auditor's examination.
.40*h**	appendix A, example 1	A statement that
.40*h*i*	appendix A, example 1	• the examination was conducted in accordance with attestation standards established by the American Institute of Certified Public Accountants.
.40*h*ii*	appendix A, example 1	• those standards require that the service auditor plan and perform the examination to obtain reasonable assurance about whether, in all material respects, based on the criteria in management's assertion, management's description of the service organization's system is fairly presented and the controls are suitably designed and operating effectively throughout the specified period to achieve the related control objectives.

(continued)

Elements of a Service Auditor's Report—*continued*

Paragraph in AT-C Section 320 That Contains the Requirement	Illustration of the Required Element in This Guide	Required Element and Additional Comments
.41*h*ii**	not illustrated	• those standards require that the service auditor plan and perform the examination to obtain reasonable assurance about whether, in all material respects, based on the criteria in management's assertion, management's description of the service organization's system is fairly presented, and the controls are suitably designed as of the specified date to achieve the related control objectives.
.40*h*iii*	appendix A, example 1	• the service auditor believes the evidence obtained is sufficient and appropriate to provide a reasonable basis for the service auditor's opinion.
.40*i****	appendix A, example 1	A statement that an examination of management's description of a service organization's system and the suitability of the design and operating effectiveness of the service organization's controls to achieve the related control objectives stated in the description involves
.41*i***	not illustrated	A statement that an examination of management's description of a service organization's system and the suitability of the design of the service organization's controls to achieve the related control objectives stated in the description involves
.40*ii****	appendix A, example 1	• performing procedures to obtain evidence about the fairness of the presentation of the description and the suitability of the design and operating effectiveness of the controls to achieve the related control objectives stated in the description based on the criteria in management's assertion.
.41*ii***	not illustrated	• performing procedures to obtain evidence about the fairness of the presentation of the description and the suitability of the design of the controls to achieve the related control objectives stated in the description based on the criteria in management's assertion.

Elements of a Service Auditor's Report—*continued*

Paragraph in AT-C Section 320 That Contains the Requirement	Illustration of the Required Element in This Guide	Required Element and Additional Comments
.40*i*ii***	appendix A, example 1	• assessing the risks that management's description of the service organization's system is not fairly presented and that the controls were not suitably designed or operating effectively to achieve the related control objectives.
.41*i*ii**	not illustrated	• assessing the risks that management's description of the service organization's system is not fairly presented and that the controls were not suitably designed to achieve the related control objectives.
.40*i*iii***	appendix A, example 1	• testing the operating effectiveness of those controls that management considers necessary to provide reasonable assurance that the related control objectives stated in management's description of the service organization's system were achieved.
.40*i*iv*	appendix A, example 1	• evaluating the overall presentation of management's description of the service organization's system, suitability of the control objectives stated in the description, and suitability of the criteria specified by the service organization in its assertion.
.40*j**	appendix A, example 1	A description of the inherent limitations of controls, including that projecting to the future any evaluation of the fairness of the presentation of management's description of the service organization's system or conclusions about the suitability of the design or operating effectiveness of the controls to achieve the related control objectives is subject to the risk that controls at a service organization may become ineffective.
.41*k**	not illustrated	A statement that the service auditor has not performed any procedures regarding the operating effectiveness of controls and, therefore, expresses no opinion thereon.
.40*k***	appendix A, example 1	A reference to a description of the service auditor's tests of controls and the results thereof that includes

(continued)

Elements of a Service Auditor's Report—*continued*

Paragraph in AT-C Section 320 That Contains the Requirement	Illustration of the Required Element in This Guide	Required Element and Additional Comments
.40*k*i***	appendix A, example 1	• an identification of the controls that were tested.
.40*k*ii***	appendix A, example 1	• whether the items tested represent all or a selection of the items in the population.
.40*k*iii***	appendix A, example 1	• the nature of the tests in sufficient detail to enable user auditors to determine the effect of such tests on their risk assessments.
.40*k*iv***	paragraphs 5.02 and 5.07	• any identified deviations in the operation of controls included in the description, the extent of testing performed by the service auditor that led to the identification of deviations (including the number of items tested), and the number and nature of the deviations noted (even if, on the basis of tests performed, the service auditor concludes that the related control objective was achieved).
.40*k*v***	paragraphs 5.12–.13	• if the work of the internal audit function has been used in tests of controls to obtain evidence, a description of the internal auditor's work and of the service auditor's procedures with respect to that work.
.40*l**	appendix A, example 1	The service auditor's opinion on whether, in all material respects, based on the criteria described in management's assertion,
.40*l*i*	appendix A, example 1	• management's description of the service organization's system fairly presents the service organization's system that was designed and implemented throughout the specified period.
.40*l*ii*	appendix A, example 1	• the controls related to the control objectives stated in management's description of the service organization's system were suitably designed to provide reasonable assurance that the control objectives would be achieved if the controls operated effectively throughout the specified period.

Elements of a Service Auditor's Report—*continued*

Paragraph in AT-C Section 320 That Contains the Requirement	Illustration of the Required Element in This Guide	Required Element and Additional Comments
.40*l*iii***	appendix A, example 1	• the controls operated effectively to provide reasonable assurance that the control objectives stated in management's description of the service organization's system were achieved throughout the specified period.
.40*l*iv*	appendix A, example 1	• if the application of complementary user entity controls is necessary to achieve the related control objectives stated in management's description of the service organization's system, a statement to that effect.
.40*l*v*	appendix A, example 2	• if the application of complementary subservice organization controls is necessary to achieve the related control objectives stated in management's description of the service organization's system, a statement to that effect.
.40*m**	appendix A, example 1	An alert, in a separate paragraph, that restricts the use of the report. The alert should
.40*m*i*	appendix A, example 1	• state that the report, including the description of tests of controls and results thereof, is intended solely for the information and use of management of the service organization, user entities of the service organization's system during some or all of the period covered by the report, and the auditors who audit and report on such user entities' financial statements or internal control over financial reporting. (Paragraph .A70 of AT-C section 320 states that a user entity is also considered a user entity of the service organization's subservice organization if controls at subservice organizations are relevant to internal control over financial reporting of the user entity. In such case, the user entity is referred to as an indirect or downstream user entity of the subservice organization. Consequently, an indirect or downstream user entity may be included in the group to whom use of the service auditor's report is restricted if controls at the service organization are relevant to internal control over financial reporting of such indirect or downstream user entity.)

(continued)

Elements of a Service Auditor's Report—*continued*

Paragraph in AT-C Section 320 That Contains the Requirement	Illustration of the Required Element in This Guide	Required Element and Additional Comments
.40*m*ii*	appendix A, example 1	• state that the report is not intended to be, and should not be, used by anyone other than the specified parties.
.40*n**	appendix A, example 1	The manual or printed signature of the service auditor's firm.
.40*o**	appendix A, example 1	The city and state where the service auditor practices.
.40*p**	appendix A, example 1	The date of the report. (The report should be dated no earlier than the date on which the service auditor has obtained sufficient appropriate evidence on which to base the service auditor's opinion, including evidence that
.40*p*i*	appendix A, example 1	• management's description of the service organization's system has been prepared,
.40*p*ii*	appendix A, example 1	• management has provided a written assertion, and
.40*p*iii*	appendix A, example 1	• the attestation documentation has been reviewed.)

* indicates requirements that are applicable to both type 1 and type 2 reports.
** indicates requirements that are applicable only to a type 1 report.
*** indicates requirements that are applicable only to a type 2 report.

Report and Assertion When Service Organization Uses the Carve-Out Method

5.19   When a service organization uses a subservice organization, paragraphs .40*c*iv and .41*c*iv of AT-C section 320 require the service auditor's report to identify any services performed by the subservice organization and whether the carve-out method or inclusive method was used in relation to them. If the carve-out method was used, paragraphs .40*c*iv(1) and .41*c*iv(1) of AT-C section 320 require that the service auditor's report include a statement indicating that

- management's description of the service organization's system excludes the control objectives and related controls at relevant subservice organizations,

- certain control objectives specified by the service organization can be achieved only if complementary subservice organization controls assumed in the design of the service organization's controls are suitably designed and operating effectively, and

- the service auditor's procedures do not extend to such complementary subservice organization controls.

Because the application of complementary subservice organization controls is necessary to achieve the related control objectives, paragraphs .40*l*v and .41*l*iv of AT-C section 320 require that the service auditor's opinion include a statement to that effect. This would be accomplished by modifying subparagraphs (*b*) and (*c*) of the opinion paragraph, as illustrated in paragraph 5.20, to indicate that the achievement of the service organization's control objectives is dependent on the suitability of the design and operating effectiveness of complementary subservice organization controls.

5.20 The following are illustrative scope and opinion paragraphs of a type 2 report for a service organization that uses the carve-out method to present a subservice organization. Because complementary user entity controls are commonly required by service organizations, the illustrative paragraphs also include language related to complementary user entity controls. New language is shown in boldface italics:

Scope

We have examined XYZ Service Organization's description of its [*type or name of*] system entitled "XYZ Service Organization's Description of Its [*type or name of*] System" for processing user entities' transactions [*or identification of the function performed by the system*] throughout the period [*date*] to [*date*] (description) and the suitability of the design and operating effectiveness of the controls included in the description to achieve the related control objectives stated in the description, based on the criteria identified in "XYZ Service Organization's Assertion" (assertion). The controls and control objectives included in the description are those that management of XYZ Service Organization believes are likely to be relevant to user entities' internal control over financial reporting, and the description does not include those aspects of the [*type or name of*] system that are not likely to be relevant to user entities' internal control over financial reporting.

XYZ Service Organization uses a subservice organization to [identify the function or service provided by the subservice organization]. The description includes only the control objectives and related controls of XYZ Service Organization and excludes the control objectives and related controls of the subservice organization. The description also indicates that certain control objectives specified by XYZ Service Organization can be achieved only if complementary subservice organization controls assumed in the design of XYZ Service Organization's controls are suitably designed and operating effectively, along with related controls at XYZ Service Organization. Our examination did not extend to controls of the subservice organization and we have not evaluated the suitability of the design or operating effectiveness of such complementary subservice organization controls.

The description indicates that certain control objectives specified in the description can be achieved only if complementary user entity controls assumed in the design of XYZ Service Organization's controls are suitably designed and operating effectively, along with related controls at the service organization. Our examination did not extend to such complementary user entity controls and we have not evaluated the suitability of the design or operating effectiveness of such complementary user entity controls.

Opinion

In our opinion, in all material respects, based on the criteria described in XYZ Service Organization's assertion,

> *Item (a) of the opinion paragraph related to the fairness of the presentation of the description of the service organization's system is unchanged.*

>> b. the controls related to the control objectives stated in the description were suitably designed to provide reasonable assurance that the control objectives would be achieved if the controls operated effectively throughout the period [*date*] to [*date*] **and subservice organizations and user entities applied the complementary controls assumed in the design of XYZ Service Organization's controls throughout the period [*date*] to [*date*].**

>> c. the controls operated effectively to provide reasonable assurance that the control objectives stated in the description were achieved throughout the period [*date*] to [*date*] **if complementary subservice organization and user entity controls assumed in the design of XYZ Service Organization's controls operated effectively throughout the period [date] to [date].**

5.21 In addition, management would modify its assertion to reflect the modifications to the service auditor's report discussed in paragraph 5.19 of this guide. An example of such an assertion is illustrated in paragraphs 5.96–.97 of this guide and in the illustrative assertions in appendixes A and B.

Report When Assuming Responsibility for Work of An Other Practitioner

5.22 When the service auditor assumes responsibility for the work of another practitioner, the service auditor does not refer to the other practitioner in the service auditor's report. The description of the subservice organization's system and the description of tests of controls and results prepared by the other practitioner would be included in the service auditor's inclusive type 2 report, which would make the report useful to user entities and their auditors.

Other Information That Is Not Covered by the Service Auditor's Report

5.23 Management may wish to include, either in the description of the service organization's system, in a separate section of the type 1 or type 2 report, or in an attachment to the description, other information that is not covered by the service auditor's report.

5.24 Paragraphs .40*c*iii and .41*c*iii of AT-C section 320 require that the service auditor's report identify any information included in a document containing the service auditor's report that is not covered by the service auditor's report. Typically, this would be information the service organization wishes to communicate to user entities that is beyond the scope of the engagement. Such information may be prepared by the service organization or by another party. Examples of such information include the following:

- Future plans for new systems or system conversions

- Other services provided by the service organization that are not included in the scope of the engagement

- Qualitative information, such as marketing claims, that may not be measurable

- Information related to the privacy of personally identifiable or medical information

- Information that would not be considered relevant to user entities' internal control over financial reporting, such as information about the service organization's business continuity plans

- Responses from management regarding deviations in tests of controls, such as information about causative factors for deviations identified in the service auditor's tests of controls, the controls that mitigate the effect of the deviations, corrective actions taken, and expected future plans to correct controls

- A report comparing the service organization's performance to its commitments to user entities per service level agreements, or a newsletter containing information about events at the service organization

- A description of a subsequent event that does not affect the functions and processing performed by the service organization during the period covered by the service auditor's report but may be of interest to user entities

5.25 Generally, such other information may be presented in a section of the type 2 or type 1 report entitled "Other Information Provided by the Service Organization." Information in this section is not covered by the service auditor's report; however, the service auditor is required to perform the procedures outlined in paragraph 5.29 of this guide on the other information.

5.26 Paragraph 5.34 of this guide presents an example of a separate paragraph that would be added to the service auditor's report to identify information that (a) is not covered by the service auditor's report and (b) is appropriately segregated and identified as such.

5.27 Paragraph 5.55 of this guide presents an example of a separate paragraph that would be added to the service auditor's report when information that is not covered by the service auditor's report is not appropriately segregated and identified as such.

5.28 If management wishes to include in the description of the service organization's system its responses to deviations in tests of controls (rather than to include the responses in the section of the type 2 report containing information that is not covered by the service auditor's report), such responses are usually included along with the description of the applicable control and related control objective. In that case, the service auditor should determine through inquiries in combination with other procedures whether there is evidence supporting the action described by management in its response.

5.29 Paragraph .57 of AT-C section 205 indicates that if, prior to or after the release of the service auditor's report, the service auditor is willing to permit the inclusion of the service auditor's report in a document that contains the description of the service organization's system or management's assertion and other information, the service auditor should read the other information to identify

 a. material inconsistencies with management's description of the service organization's system, management's assertion, or the service auditor's report.

 b. a material misstatement of fact in the other information, the description of the service organization's system, management's assertion, or the service auditor's report. (Other information may bring to light a material misstatement of fact in the description, assertion, or service auditor's report that the service auditor did not identify when evaluating the fairness of the presentation of the description or the suitability of the design or operating effectiveness of the controls.)

5.30 Paragraph .57 of AT-C section 205 indicates that if a material misstatement of fact or a material inconsistency exists (as described in paragraph 5.29 of this guide), the service auditor should discuss the matter with management of the service organization. The service auditor would ordinarily request that management correct or delete the other information.

5.31 If management refuses to correct or delete the other information containing a material inconsistency or a material misstatement of fact, paragraph .A67 of AT-C section 205 identifies the following examples of further actions the service auditor may take:

- Requesting the appropriate party(ies) consult with a qualified third party, such as the appropriate party(ies)'s legal counsel
- Obtaining legal advice about the consequences of different courses of action
- If required or permissible, communicating with third parties (for example, a regulator)
- Describing the material inconsistency in the practitioner's report
- Withdrawing from the engagement, when withdrawal is possible under applicable laws and regulations

5.32 Paragraph 5.56 of this guide presents an example of a separate paragraph that would be added to the service auditor's report when the description includes other information that is materially inconsistent with the information in the description of the service organization's system and management refuses to correct it or remove it from the description.

5.33 Paragraph .A3 of AT-C section 320 indicates, in part, that AT-C section 320 is not intended to permit reports issued under AT-C section 320 to include in the description of the service organization's system aspects of their services not likely to be relevant to user entities' internal control over financial reporting. Depending on the content of the other information included in the description, and the service auditor's professional judgment, the service auditor may determine that the other information is not likely to be relevant to user entities' internal control over financial reporting and is therefore materially inconsistent with the description.

5.34 The following is an example of a separate paragraph that would be added to the service auditor's report to identify other information provided by the service organization and to disclaim an opinion on it:

> The information about XYZ Service Organization's inventory application in section 5, "Other Information Provided by XYZ Service Organization," is presented by management of XYZ Service Organization to provide additional information and is not a part of XYZ Service Organization's description of its payroll system made available to user entities during the period June 1, 20X0, to May 31, 20X1. Information about XYZ Service Organization's inventory application has not been subjected to the procedures applied in the examination of the description of the payroll system and of the suitability of the design and operating effectiveness of controls to achieve the related control objectives stated in the description of the payroll system and, accordingly, we express no opinion on it.

Modifications to the Service Auditor's Report

5.35 Paragraph .68 of AT-C section 205 requires the service auditor to modify the opinion when either of the following circumstances exist and, in the service auditor's professional judgment, the effect of the matter is or may be material:

> *a.* The service auditor is unable to obtain sufficient appropriate evidence to conclude that the subject matter is in accordance with (or based on) the criteria, in all material respects.
>
> *b.* The service auditor concludes, based on evidence obtained, that the subject matter is not in accordance with (or based on) the criteria, in all material respects.

Paragraph .69 of AT-C section 205 indicates that when the service auditor modifies the opinion, the service auditor should include a separate paragraph in the service auditor's report that provides a description of the matter(s) giving rise to the modification.

5.36 In applying paragraphs .68–.69 of AT-C section 205 to an engagement performed under AT-C section 320, the service auditor's opinion should be modified and the service auditor's report should include a description of the matter(s) giving rise to the modification if the service auditor concludes that

> *a.* management's description of the service organization's system is not fairly presented, in all material respects;
>
> *b.* the controls are not suitably designed to provide reasonable assurance that the control objectives stated in management's description of the service organization's system would be achieved if the controls operated effectively, in all material respects;
>
> *c.* in the case of a type 2 report, the controls did not operate effectively throughout the specified period to achieve the related control objectives stated in management's description of the service organization's system, in all material respects; or
>
> *d.* the service auditor is unable to obtain sufficient, appropriate evidence.

The objective of including a description of each of the matters giving rise to the modification is to enable report users to develop their own assessments of the effect of deviations on user entities' internal control over financial reporting. Paragraphs 5.44 and 5.49–.74 of this guide contain examples of a separate paragraph that describes the matters giving rise to a modification, and paragraph 5.42 of this guide contains a service auditor's report in which the service auditor disclaims an opinion.

Qualified Opinion

5.37 Generally, the service auditor expresses a qualified opinion if the misstatements in management's description of the service organization's system or deficiencies in the suitability of the design or operating effectiveness of the controls are limited to one or more, but not all, aspects of the description of the service organization's system or control objectives and do not affect the service auditor's opinion on other aspects of the description of the service organization's system or other control objectives.

5.38 When the service auditor has determined that a qualified opinion is appropriate, in addition to adding a separate paragraph to the service auditor's report describing the matter(s) giving rise to the modification, the service auditor should modify the opinion paragraph of the service auditor's report as follows. New language is shown in boldface italics:

> In our opinion, ***except for the matter referred to in the preceding paragraph,*** in all material respects, based on the criteria described in [*service organization's*] assertion in section 2, ...

5.39 Generally, the service auditor expresses an adverse opinion if the misstatements in management's description of the service organization's system or deficiencies in the suitability of the design or operating effectiveness of the controls are material and pervasive throughout the description or across all or most of the control objectives.

Disclaimer of Opinion

5.40 Paragraph .74 of AT-C section 205 indicates that the service auditor should disclaim an opinion when the service auditor is unable to obtain sufficient appropriate evidence on which to base the opinion, and the service auditor concludes that the possible effects on the subject matter of undetected misstatements, if any, could be both material and pervasive. In those circumstances, the service auditor's opinion should be modified and the service auditor's report should include a separate paragraph containing a clear description of the matter(s) giving rise to the modification. In a disclaimer of opinion, that paragraph describes the respects in which the examination did not comply with the attestation standards. If the service auditor plans to disclaim an opinion and the limited procedures performed by the service auditor cause the service auditor to conclude that the subject matter is materially misstated (certain aspects of management's description of the service organization's system are not fairly presented, certain controls are not suitably designed, or certain controls did not operate effectively), the service auditor should include in the service auditor's report a clear description of the matter(s) that causes the subject matter to be materially misstated.

5.41 When disclaiming an opinion

- the first sentence of the service auditor's report is revised to state, "We were engaged to examine" rather than "We have examined."

- the standards under which the service auditor conducts an examination are identified at the end of the third sentence of the first paragraph of the report, rather than in a separate sentence in the second paragraph of the report.

- the report omits statements

  — indicating what those standards require of the practitioner.

  — indicating that the practitioner believes the evidence obtained is sufficient and appropriate to provide a reasonable basis for the service auditor's opinion.

  — describing the nature of an examination engagement.

5.42 The following is an illustrative service auditor's report in which the service auditor disclaims an opinion because of a scope limitation (management refuses to provide one or more written representations.)

[*Appropriate Addressee*]

We were engaged to examine XYZ Company's description of its medical claims processing system entitled "XYZ Company's Description of its Medical Claims Processing System" for processing medical claims throughout the period [*date*] to [*date*] (description) and the suitability of the design and operating effectiveness of the controls included in the description to achieve the related control objectives stated in the description, based on the criteria identified in "XYZ Service Organization's Assertion" (assertion). XYZ Company's management is responsible for the fairness of the presentation of the description and the suitability of the design and operating effectiveness of the controls included in the description. Our responsibility is to express an opinion on the fairness of the presentation of the description and the suitability of the design and operating effectiveness of the controls included in the description, based on conducting the examination in accordance with attestation standards established by the American Institute of Certified Public Accountants.

Attestation standards established by the American Institute of Certified Public Accountants require that we request certain written representations from management, including a representation that all relevant matters are reflected in the measurement or evaluation of the fairness of the presentation of the description of the service organization's system and the suitability of design and operating effectiveness of controls. We requested that management provide us with such a representation but management refused to do so.

Because of the limitation on the scope of our examination discussed in the preceding paragraph, the scope of our work was not sufficient to enable us to express, and we do not express, an opinion on whether XYZ Company's description of its medical claims processing system throughout the period [*date*] to [*date*] is fairly presented or on whether the controls included in the description were suitability designed and operating effectively to achieve the related control objectives stated in the description, based on the criteria identified in XYZ Company's assertion, in all material respects.

Management Will Not Provide a Written Assertion but Law or Regulation Does Not Permit Service Auditor to Withdraw From Engagement

5.43 Ordinarily, if management refuses to provide a written assertion, the service auditor is required to withdraw from the engagement. However, if the service auditor is required by law or regulation to accept or continue an engagement to report on controls at a service organization and management refuses to provide a written assertion, the service auditor may conduct the engagement and, ultimately, should disclaim an opinion.

5.44 The following is an example of a separate paragraph that would be added to the service auditor's report to describe the respects in which the examination did not comply with attestation standards applicable to an examination engagement when management refuses to provide a written assertion:

> Attestation standards established by the American Institute of Certified Public
>
> Accountants require that we request a written statement from management of XYZ Company that XYZ Company's description of its medical claims processing system throughout the period [*date*] to [*date*] is fairly presented and the controls included in the description were suitability designed and operating effectively to achieve the related control objectives stated in the description, based on the criteria identified in XYZ Company's assertion. We requested that statement but management of XYZ Company did not provide such a statement.

Adverse Opinion

5.45 When the service auditor has determined that an adverse opinion is appropriate, in addition to adding a separate paragraph to the service auditor's report describing the matter(s) giving rise to the adverse opinion, the service auditor should modify the opinion paragraph of the service auditor's report, assuming an adverse opinion on all three components of the opinion. The following is an example of such a paragraph. New language is shown in boldface italics:

> In our opinion, ***because of the matter referred to in the preceding paragraph,*** in all material respects, based on the criteria described in [*name of service organization's*] assertion in section 2,
>
> - the description ***does not*** fairly present the [*type or name of system*] that was designed and implemented throughout the period.
> - the controls related to the control objectives stated in the description were ***not*** suitably designed to provide reasonable assurance that the control objectives would be achieved if the controls operated effectively throughout the period [*date*] to [*date*].
> - the controls tested, which were those necessary to provide reasonable assurance that the control objectives stated in the description were achieved, ***did not*** operate effectively throughout the period from [*date*] to [*date*].

5.46 A modified opinion on an individual component of the service auditor's opinion (for example, management's description of the service organization's system is not fairly presented in all material respects) may affect the other components of the opinion (the opinion on the suitability of the design or operating effectiveness of controls). For example, a service auditor may determine that a modified opinion on the fair presentation of the description of the service organization's system is appropriate because the description includes a number of controls for each control objective that have not been implemented, and management will not remove those controls from the description. Because controls that are needed to achieve the related control objectives have not been implemented, a modified opinion on the suitability of the design and operating effectiveness of the controls is also appropriate. Another example is a situation in which the service auditor concludes that the description is fairly presented but the opinion on the suitability of the design of the controls is modified because, as designed, certain controls would not achieve the related control objectives. In this situation, the service auditor would conclude that the modification of the opinion also applies to the operating effectiveness of the controls, because even if the controls operate as designed, the controls would not operate effectively to achieve the related control objectives due to their inappropriate design. In all of these situations, the service auditor should include a separate paragraph in the report that describes the matter(s) giving rise to the modification.

5.47 Although the service auditor may modify the opinion on the fairness of the presentation of management's description of the service organization's system due to the omission of a control objective, the omission would not necessarily affect the service auditor's opinion on the suitability of the design or operating effectiveness of the controls because those opinions relate only to control objectives included in management's description. The service auditor cannot report or comment on the suitability of the design or operating effectiveness of controls intended to achieve control objectives that are not included in management's description of the service organization's system. The service auditor is not responsible for identifying or testing controls that might achieve the omitted control objective(s).

Report Paragraphs Describing the Matter Giving Rise to the Modification

Illustrative Separate Paragraphs: Description Is Not Fairly Presented

5.48 A number of situations are presented in chapter 4, "Performing an Engagement Under AT-C section 320," in which the service auditor determines that the description is not fairly presented. In practice, if the service auditor makes such a determination, the service auditor would inform management of the service organization of the changes that need to be made for the description to be fairly presented. If management refuses to amend the description, the service auditor may decide to withdraw from the engagement. If the service auditor decides to continue with the engagement, the service auditor should modify the opinion on the fairness of the presentation of the description. Paragraphs 5.49–.67 of this guide contain examples of a separate paragraph that would be added to the service auditor's report when the description of the service organization's system is not fairly presented.

Description Includes Controls That Have Not Been Implemented

5.49 The following is an example of a separate paragraph that would be added to the service auditor's report when the description includes controls that have not been implemented:

> The accompanying description of the XYZ System states that Example Service Organization uses operator identification numbers and passwords to prevent unauthorized access to its system. Our testing determined that operator identification numbers and passwords are used in applications A and B, but are not used in applications C and D.

Description Includes Information That Is Not Measureable

5.50 The following is an example of a separate paragraph that would be added to the service auditor's report when the description of the service organization's system includes information that is not measurable:

> On page [mn] of the attached description, Example Trust Organization states that its savings system is the industry's best system and is staffed by the most talented IT personnel. Because no criteria have been established for these attributes of the system or personnel, these statements are not relevant to user entities' internal control over financial reporting and are not measureable within the scope of this examination.

Description Omits Control Objectives and Related Controls Required for Other Controls to Be Suitably Designed and Operating Effectively

5.51 The following is an example of a separate paragraph that would be added to the service auditor's report when the description of the service organization's system omits control objectives and related controls needed for other controls included in the description to be suitably designed and operating effectively:

> The description of Example Trust Organization's savings system includes application controls related to the savings system. These controls depend on the effective operation of IT general controls, which have not been included in the description.

Description Omits Information Relevant to User Entities' Internal Control

5.52 The following is an example of a separate paragraph that would be added to the service auditor's report when the description of the service organization's system omits information that may be relevant to user entities' internal control over financial reporting:

> The accompanying description of Example Service Organization's XYZ1 and XYZ2 systems does not include information about the automated interfaces between the XYZ1 and XYZ2 systems. We believe that such information should be included in management's description of its system because that information is relevant to user entities' internal control over financial reporting.

Description Omits Information About Relevant Subsequent Events

5.53 The following is an example of a separate paragraph that would be added to the service auditor's report when the description of the service organization's system omits information about a subsequent event that affects the functions and processing performed by the service organization during the period covered by the service auditor's report:

> Subsequent to the examination, XYZ Service Organization's management discovered that a supervisor had provided all of the programmers with access to the production data files for the month of July. [*Assume that July is included in the period covered by the report.*] This information has been omitted from XYZ's description of its system but should have been included because providing programmers with access to production data files could enable programmers to modify data, which would be relevant to user entities' internal control over financial reporting.

Description Omits Relevant Changes to Controls

5.54 The following is an example of a separate paragraph that would be added to the service auditor's report when the description does not address relevant changes to the service organization's controls:

> The accompanying description states that the quality assurance group reviews a random sample of work performed by input clerks to determine the degree of compliance with the service organization's input requirements. Inquiries of staff personnel indicate that this control was first implemented on July 1, 20X0, which would be relevant to user entities' internal control over financial reporting during the first six months of the year. [*Assume that the period covered by the report is January 1, 20X0, to December 31, 20X0.*]

Description Includes Information Not Relevant to User Entities' Internal Control That Is Not Appropriately Segregated

5.55 The following is an example of a separate paragraph that would be added to the service auditor's report when the description includes information that is not relevant to user entities' internal control over financial reporting and the service organization refuses to place the information in a separate section of the type 1 or type 2 report identified as, for example, "Other Information Provided by XYZ Service Organization," or to otherwise exclude it from the description:

> The accompanying description includes the procedures the organization performs to comply with Health Insurance Portability and Accountability Act (HIPAA) regulations. Such information is not relevant to user entities' internal control over financial reporting and should not be included in the description.

In these circumstances, because management refuses to move the other information to a separate section of the type 1 or type 2 report, the service auditor may wish to disclaim an opinion on that information by adding the words "and, accordingly, we express no opinion on such information" at the end of the separate paragraph.

Other Information Provided by the Service Organization Is Materially Inconsistent With Information in the Description of the Service Organization's System

5.56 The following is an example of a separate paragraph that would be added to the service auditor's report when the description includes other information that is materially inconsistent with the information in the description of the service organization's system and the service organization refuses to correct it or remove it from the description:

> The information in section 5, "Other Information Provided by XYZ Service Organization," that describes the processing of dental claims by XYZ Service Organization is presented by management of XYZ Service Organization to provide additional information and is not a part of XYZ Service Organization's description of its medical claims processing system made available to user entities during the period June 1, 20X0, to May 31, 20X1. Information about XYZ Service Organization's dental claims processing has not been subjected to the procedures applied in the examination of the description of the medical claims processing system and the suitability of the design and operating effectiveness of controls to achieve the related control objectives stated in management's description of the medical claims processing system and, accordingly, we express no opinion on it. However, we noted that information in section 5 indicating that XYZ Service Organization provides in-house dental claims processing is materially inconsistent with XYZ Service Organization's description of its medical claims processing system, which states that dental claims processing is outsourced to another organization.

Description Includes Control Objective Not Relevant to User Entities' Internal Control

5.57 The following is an example of a separate paragraph that would be added to the service auditor's report when the description includes control objectives that are not relevant to user entities' internal control over financial reporting:

> The accompanying description includes control objective 5, "Controls provide reasonable assurance that data will be recovered in the event of a power system failure." This control objective should not be included in the description because it is not relevant to user entities' internal control over financial reporting during the period April 1, 20X1, to May 31, 20X2.

Description Includes Control Objective That Is Not Measureable

5.58 The following is an example of a separate paragraph that would be added to the service auditor's report when the description includes a control objective that is not measurable.[3]

> Page [mn] of the description includes control objective 10, "Controls are adequate to restrict access to computer resources." The wording of this control objective is not sufficiently measureable for use in evaluating the design or operating effectiveness of controls related to the control objective.

---

[3] Measurability is an attribute of suitable criteria as indicated in paragraph .A42 of AT-C section 105, *Concepts Common to All Attestation Engagements* (AICPA, *Professional Standards*). A control objective that is measureable would permit reasonably consistent measurements of whether the control objective has been achieved.

Description Omits Certain Control Objectives Established by an Outside Party

5.59 The following is an example of a separate paragraph that would be added to the service auditor's report when the control objectives have been established by an outside party and the description omits one or more of the control objectives specified by the outside party:

> The set of control objectives specified by Outside User Group includes the control objective "Controls provide reasonable assurance that investment purchases and sales are authorized." Example Trust Organization has not included or addressed this control objective in its description of Example Trust Organization's savings system.

Set of Control Objectives Established by Outside Party Omits a Control Objective Necessary to Achieve Other Control Objectives

5.60 The following is an example of a separate paragraph that would be added to the service auditor's report when the set of control objectives established by an outside party omits control objectives that the service auditor believes are necessary to achieve other control objectives:

> The set of control objectives specified by Outside User Group does not include a control objective that addresses the authorization, testing, documentation, and implementation of changes to existing applications. Such a control objective and the related controls are necessary for other control objectives related to the application to be achieved.

Description Includes an Incomplete Control Objective

5.61 The following is an example of a separate paragraph that would be added to the service auditor's report when the description of the service organization's system includes an incomplete control objective:

> Control objective 5 in Example Service Organization's description of its system is: "Controls provide reasonable assurance that loan payments received from user entities are completely and accurately recorded." This control objective should be amended to address the timeliness of the recording of loan payments because of its relevance to user entities' internal control over financial reporting.

Description Omits a Relevant Control Objective

5.62 The following is an example of a separate paragraph that would be added to the service auditor's report when the service organization's description omits a relevant control objective:

> Example Trust Organization's description of its system does not include a control objective and related controls that address the restriction of logical access to system resources (for example, programs, data, tables, and parameters) to authorized individuals. This control objective should be included in the description because of its relevance to user entities' internal control over financial reporting.

Service Organization Revises a Control Objective During the Engagement Without Reasonable Justification

5.63 The following is an example of a separate paragraph that would be added to the service auditor's report when the service organization revises a control objective during the engagement without reasonable justification for doing so:

> Example Trust Organization's description of its system, dated April 1, 20X1, includes the following control objective: "Controls provide reasonable assurance that changes to existing applications are authorized, tested, documented, and implemented in a complete, accurate, and timely manner." After informing management that the results of our tests indicate that controls over the authorization of changes to existing applications were not suitably designed, management deleted the word "authorized" from the aforementioned control objective. As modified, the control objective is not sufficiently complete.

Service Organization Changes From Inclusive Method to Carve-Out Method Without Reasonable Justification

5.64   The following is an example of a separate paragraph that would be added to the service auditor's report when the service organization changes from the inclusive method to the carve-out method for a subservice organization without reasonable justification:

> As indicated in the description, Example Trust Organization uses a subservice organization for computer processing. Example Trust Organization elected to change from the inclusive method of presentation to the carve-out method after our testing indicated that controls at the subservice organization intended to restrict access to the subservice organization's system to authorized and approved individuals had not been implemented. As a result, this information would be relevant to user entities' internal control over financial reporting.

Description Omits Complementary User Entity Controls

5.65   The following is an example of a separate paragraph that would be added to the service auditor's report when the description omits complementary user entity controls that are required to achieve the control objectives:

> Example Service Organization has omitted from its description a statement indicating that user entities should have controls in place that limit access to user defined indexes to authorized individuals. Such complementary user entity controls are necessary for controls to be considered suitably designed and operating effectively to achieve control objective 11. Information about the need for such complementary user entity controls would be relevant to user entities' internal control over financial reporting.

Description Omits Complementary Subservice Organization Controls

5.66   The following is an example of a separate paragraph that would be added to the service auditor's report when the description omits complementary subservice organization controls that are required to achieve the control objectives:

> Example Service Organization has omitted from its description a statement indicating that subservice organizations should have controls in place that limit access to user defined tables to authorized individuals. Such complementary subservice organization controls are necessary for controls to be considered suitably designed and operating effectively to achieve control objective 10. This information about the

need for such complementary subservice organization controls would be relevant to user entities' internal control over financial reporting.

Description Does Not Disclose That Service Organization Uses a Subservice Organization

5.67 The following is an example of a separate paragraph that would be added to the service auditor's report when the functions and processing performed by a subservice organization are significant to the processing of user entities' transactions, and the service organization has not disclosed the existence of a subservice organization and the functions it performs:

> Example Trust Organization's description does not indicate that it uses a subservice organization for computer processing, which could be significant to user entities' internal control over financial reporting because controls at the subservice organization are relevant to changes to programs as well as logical access to system resources.

Illustrative Separate Paragraphs: Controls Are Not Suitably Designed

Controls Are Not Suitably Designed to Achieve the Control Objectives

5.68 The following is an example of a separate paragraph that would be added to the service auditor's report when the service auditor concludes that controls are not suitably designed to achieve one or more of the related control objectives:

> The accompanying description of the XYZ System states on page [*mn*] that Example Service Organization reconciles the list of loan payments received with the Loan Payment Summary Report. The Organization's reconciliation procedures, however, do not include a control for follow-up on reconciling items and independent review and approval of the reconciliations. As a result, the controls are not suitably designed to achieve the control objective "Controls provide reasonable assurance that output is complete, accurate, reconciled, and independently reviewed and approved."

Part of the Control Objective Is Not Achieved Because Certain Controls Are Missing

5.69 The following is an example of a separate paragraph that would be added to the service auditor's report when certain controls that are needed to achieve a portion of a control objective are missing:

> Example Service Organization has controls in place to ascertain that total contributions received are recorded in the correct amount. However, there are no controls in place to ascertain that contributions received are recorded in the correct user account. As a result, the design of Example Service Organization's controls does not provide reasonable assurance that the control objective "Controls provide reasonable assurance that contributions received are processed and recorded in a complete, accurate, and timely manner" was achieved solely as it relates to the accuracy of processing contributions during the period.

Scope Limitation Related to Suitably of Design of Controls

5.70   The following is an example of a separate paragraph that would be added to the service auditor's report when the service auditor is unable to obtain sufficient appropriate evidence that controls were suitably designed to achieve a specified control objective:

> Page [*mn*] of the accompanying description of the XYZ System states that Example Service Organization reconciles the list of loan payments received with the Loan Payment Summary Report. The Organization's reconciliation procedures changed on July 15, 20X0, and sufficient evidence that independent review and approval of the reconciliations occurred prior to July 15, 20X0, could not be obtained. As a result, we were unable to determine whether controls were suitably designed and operating effectively during the period January 1 to July 14, 20X0, to achieve the control objective "Controls provide reasonable assurance that output is complete, accurate, reconciled, and independently reviewed and approved."

Illustrative Separate Paragraphs: Controls Were Not Operating Effectively

Controls Were Not Operating Effectively to Achieve the Control Objectives

5.71   The following is an example of a separate paragraph that would be added to the service auditor's report when controls were not operating effectively throughout the specified period to achieve one or more control objectives:

> The service organization states in its description that it has controls in place to reconcile securities account master files to subsidiary ledgers, to follow up on reconciling items, to perform surprise annual physical counts, and to independently review its reconciliation procedures. However, as noted at page [*mn*] of the description of tests of controls and results, controls related to the reconciliations and annual physical counts were not performed during the period April 1, 20X1, to December 31, 20X1. As a result, controls were not operating effectively to achieve the control objective "Controls provide reasonable assurance that securities account master files are properly reconciled to subsidiary ledgers and surprise annual physical counts are performed."

Scope Limitation Related to Operating Effectiveness of Controls

5.72   The following is an example of a separate paragraph that would be added to the service auditor's report if the service auditor is unable to obtain sufficient appropriate evidence regarding the operating effectiveness of controls to achieve a specified control objective:

> Example Trust Organization states in its description of its savings system that it has automated controls in place to reconcile loan payments received with the Loan Payment Summary Report. However, electronic records of the performance of this reconciliation for the period January 1, 20X1, to July 31, 20X1, were deleted as a result of a computer processing error and, therefore, tests of operating effectiveness could not be performed for that period. Consequently, we were unable to determine whether the control objective "Controls provide reasonable

assurance that loan payments received are properly recorded," was achieved throughout the period January 1, 20X1, to July 31, 20X1.

Various Control Objectives in Place for Different Periods

5.73 If various control objectives were in place for different periods, the service auditor's report should disclose the applicable periods. The following is an example of (*a*) a separate paragraph that would be added to the service auditor's report and (*b*) the revisions that would be made to the service auditor's opinion when the periods covered by various control objectives differ and the tests of controls cover those differing periods.

As indicated in XYZ Service Organization's description of its system, control objectives 1–10 were implemented and the related controls were in operation during the period January 1, 20X1, to December 31, 20X1, whereas control objectives 11–13 were implemented and the related controls were in operation during the period November 1, 20X1, to December 31, 20X1. Our tests of operating effectiveness covered the period during which the applicable control objectives were implemented and the related controls were in operation.

Opinion

In our opinion, in all material respects, based on the criteria described in XYZ Service Organization's assertion in section 2,

    a. the description fairly presents the [*type or name of*] system that was designed and implemented throughout the period January 1, 20X1, to December 31, 20X1, as it relates to control objectives 1 through 10, and throughout the period November 1, 20X1, to December 31, 20X1, as it relates to control objectives 11 through 13.

    b. the controls related to the control objectives stated in the description were suitably designed to provide reasonable assurance that the control objectives would be achieved if the controls operated effectively throughout the period January 1, 20X1, to December 31, 20X1, for control objectives 1 through 10 and throughout the period November 1, 20X1, to December 31, 20X1, for control objectives 11 through 13.

    c. the controls tested, which were those necessary to provide reasonable assurance that the control objectives stated in the description were achieved, operated effectively throughout the period January 1, 20X1, to December 31, 20X1, for control objectives 1 through 10 and operated effectively throughout the period November 1, 20X1, to December 31, 20X1, for control objectives 11 through 13.

Controls Did Not Operate During the Period Covered by the Report

5.74 In some cases, controls included in the description of the service organization's system do not operate during the period covered by the report because the circumstances that warrant their operation do not occur during that period. For example, the service organization has implemented controls related to the setup of new clients on a particular application in a period in which no new clients were added to this application. The following is an example of a paragraph that may be added to the service auditor's report in these circumstances:

> As indicated on page [*mn*] of XYZ Service Organization's description of its Trust System, no new accounts were established for the ABC application during the period January 1, 201X, to September 30, 201X; therefore, we did not perform any tests of the design or operating effectiveness of controls related to the control objective "Controls provide reasonable assurance that new accounts are authorized and set up on the system in a complete, accurate, and timely manner."

Illustrative Separate Paragraphs: Disclaimer of Opinion

5.75 A disclaimer of opinion states that the service auditor does not express an opinion on the fairness of the presentation of the description of the service organization's system or on the suitably of the design and operating effectiveness of the controls. Paragraphs 5.40–.41 of this guide describe the elements of a disclaimer of opinion, and paragraph 5.42 contains an illustrative service auditor's report in which the service auditor disclaims an opinion because of a scope limitation. As noted in paragraph 5.40, when the service auditor disclaims an opinion, the service auditor's report should include a paragraph that describes the respects in which the examination did not comply with attestation standards applicable to an examination engagement. A disclaimer is appropriate when the service auditor has not performed an examination sufficient in scope to enable the service auditor to form an opinion on whether the description is fairly presented and the controls were suitably designed and operating effectively.

Management Will Not Provide Written Representations

5.76 Paragraph 5.42 of this guide contains an illustrative type 2 report in which the service auditor disclaims an opinion because management will not provide one or more of the written representations requested by the service auditor.

Other Matters Related to a Service Auditor's Engagement

Intended Users of the Report

5.77 Paragraphs .40*m* and .41*m* of AT-C section 320 indicate that a service auditor's report should contain an alert restricting the use of the report to specified parties, including management of the service organization, user entities of the service organization's system, and the independent auditors of such user entities. The user entities to whom use of the report is restricted include user entities of the service organization ("during some or all of the period covered by the report" for a type 2 report and "as of [date]" for a type 1 report). However, it does not include *potential* users of the service organization.

5.78 Paragraph .A70 of AT-C section 320 states that a user entity of a service organization is also considered a user entity of the service organization's subservice organization if controls at the subservice organization are relevant to the user entity's internal control over financial reporting. In such case, the user entity is referred to as an *indirect* or *downstream* user entity of the subservice organization. Consequently, an indirect or downstream user entity may be included in the group to whom use of the service auditor's report is restricted.

An organization that is considered an indirect user entity ordinarily would not have a contract with the subservice organization but would have a contract with the primary service organization.

5.79 For example, a user entity (customer) contracts with a medical claims processing service organization to process its medical and pharmacy claims. The medical claims processor, in turn, contracts with a separate pharmacy claims processing subservice organization to process the pharmacy claims. The pharmacy claims processor has a type 2 report covering its pharmacy claims processing. In this situation, the medical claims processor is a user entity of the pharmacy claims processor's type 2 report because it has contracted to use the pharmacy claims processor's services. The customer of the medical claims processor is considered an indirect user entity of the pharmacy claims processor's type 2 report because the report is relevant to the customer's internal control over financial reporting. Both would be users of the pharmacy claims processor's type 2 report.

Determining Whether an Entity Is an Indirect User Entity

5.80 The following are factors to consider in determining whether an entity is an indirect user entity:

- Whether the service provided by the subservice organization is relevant to the potential indirect user entity's internal control over financial reporting
- The significance of the services provided by the subservice organization to the potential indirect user entity
- The nature and materiality of the transactions processed or accounts or financial reporting processes affected by the subservice organization's services
- The degree of interaction between the activities of the subservice organization and those of the service organization
- Whether the primary service organization implements effective user entity controls and monitoring that are sufficient for the indirect user entity and therefore negate the need for the subservice organization's type 1 or type 2 report

5.81 For example, Primary Service Organization outsources the retention, testing, and recovery of its backed-up tapes to a subservice organization. Primary Service Organization also outsources its back-office processing to another subservice organization. The controls performed by both subservice organizations are likely to be relevant to the internal control over financial reporting of the user entities of Primary Service Organization, and for that reason those user entities might be considered indirect user entities. However, Primary Service Organization implements effective user entity controls and monitoring of the services provided by the tape retention, testing, and recovery subservice organization. For that reason, the controls implemented by the tape retention, testing, and recovery subservice organization may not be significant to indirect user entities. The services provided by the back-office processing subservice organization are significant to Primary Service Organization and its user entities because the back-office processing subservice organization records the user entities' transactions and reconciles the data. Because of the significance of the services provided by the back-office processing subservice organization to user entities' internal control over financial reporting and the likelihood that Primary Service Organization would not have controls in place sufficient to meet the necessary control objectives important to the user entities, the user entities of Primary Service Organization and their user auditors would likely have a greater need for a type 2 report on the back-office processing subservice organization for the audit of the user entities' financial statements.

5.82 As another example, certain user entities of a medical claims processing service organization submit both medical and pharmacy claims to the medical claims processing service organization. Other user entities submit only medical claims. The medical claims processor contracts with a separate pharmacy claims processing subservice organization to process the pharmacy claims. Only those user entities (customers) of the medical claims processor that submit pharmacy claims for processing would be considered indirect user entities of the pharmacy claims processor's type 1 or type 2 report. Customers of the medical claims processor that do not submit pharmacy claims for processing would not be considered indirect user entities and would not be entitled to the type 1 or type 2 report.

5.83 The following are some illustrations of when a potential user entity would or would not be an indirect user entity:

- A trust services organization provides a type 2 report to user entities and indicates in its description of the service organization's system that it has carved out the back-office processing to a subservice organization. The back-office processing subservice organization maintains the records of the trading performed by the trust services organization, including the recordkeeping of transactions in user entities' accounts. The back-office processor provides a type 2 report to its user entities. The user entities of the trust services organization and their financial statement auditors would need the information contained in the back-office processor's type 2 report to complete their overall assessment of internal control over financial reporting and thus would be considered indirect users of the back-office processor's type 2 report.

- An asset management organization outsources its IT function to a subservice organization and provides user entities with a type 2 report on the asset manager's business controls. The IT general controls are covered in the subservice organization's type 2 report. The IT general controls are integral to the effectiveness of the asset manager's business process controls; therefore, the user entities of the asset manager's services would need the information contained in the type 2 report covering the IT general controls and would be considered indirect user entities.

- A pension plan hires a recordkeeper to administer its defined contribution plan. The pension plan is a user entity of the recordkeeper's type 2 report. The recordkeeper processes trades in various mutual funds through the mutual funds' transfer agents on behalf of the pension plan. The transfer agents of the mutual funds provide the recordkeeper with a type 2 report covering the processing and recording of trades in the mutual funds. The pension plan is an indirect user entity of the transfer agent's type 2 report because the processing performed by the transfer agent is relevant to the pension plan's internal control over financial reporting. However, the plan participants of the pension plan are not indirect user entities because they are not subject to financial statement audits and therefore would not have a need for a type 1 or type 2 report.

- A mutual fund hires an investment management organization that is responsible for managing the assets and executing all of the trades on behalf of the mutual fund. The investment manager provides the mutual fund with its type 2 report. The mutual fund has a number of individual investors that have purchased shares of the mutual fund. The investors are not considered indirect user entities of the investment manager's type 2 report because the mutual fund does not meet the definition of a service organization. (It does not provide services to user entities.) The investors would only be a user entity of a service organization that the investors had hired. Therefore, the investors would not be considered indirect users or be entitled to the investment manager's type 2 report.

- In its type 2 report, a credit card payment processing service organization identifies a data center hosting service organization as a subservice organization. A prospective customer of the credit card payment processor requests the type 2 report of the credit card payment processor and of the data center hosting service organization. The prospective customer is not considered a user entity or an indirect user entity of either the credit card payment processor or the data center hosting service organization because neither of these service organizations are providing services to the prospective customer, and therefore the type 2 reports do not relate to the prospective customer's internal control over financial reporting. However, once the prospective customer becomes a customer of the credit card payment processor, the customer would be considered a user entity of the credit card payment processor and an indirect user of the data center hosting service organization and would be entitled to both type 2 reports covering the period during which it is a customer of the credit card payment processor.

5.84 The requirement to restrict the use of the report is based on paragraph .64*a* of AT-C section 205, which requires that use of a practitioner's report be restricted to specified parties when the criteria used to evaluate or measure the subject matter are available only to specified parties or appropriate only for a limited number of parties who either participated in their establishment or can be presumed to have an adequate understanding of the criteria. Paragraph .A67 of AT-C section 320 indicates that the criteria used for engagements to report on controls at a service organization are relevant only for the purpose of providing information about the service organization's system, including controls, to those who have an understanding of how the system is used for financial reporting by user entities.

Report Date

5.85 As stated in paragraphs .40*p* and .41*p* of AT-C section 320, the service auditor should date the service auditor's report no earlier than the date on which the service auditor has obtained sufficient appropriate evidence to support the service auditor's opinion, including evidence that

    a. management's description of the service organization's system has been prepared, *b.* management has provided a written assertion, and

    c. the attestation documentation has been reviewed.

Subsequent Events and Subsequently Discovered Facts

5.86 In applying paragraph .48 of AT-C section 205, the service auditor should inquire whether management is aware of any events subsequent to the period (or point in time) covered by the type 2 (or type 1) report up to the date of the service auditor's report that could have a significant effect on the fairness of the presentation of the description of the service organization's system, the suitability of the design of the controls, the operating effectiveness of the controls (in a type 2 engagement), or on management's assertion, and should apply other appropriate procedures to obtain evidence regarding such events.

5.87 Procedures a service auditor may perform to identify subsequent events include inquiring about and considering information

- contained in relevant reports issued during the subsequent period by internal auditors, other practitioners, or regulatory agencies.

- obtained through other professional engagements for that entity.

5.88 If the service auditor becomes aware, through inquiry or otherwise, of such an event, or any other event that is of such a nature and significance that its disclosure is necessary to prevent users of the report from being misled, the service auditor would request that management disclose the event in the description of the service organization's system or in management's assertion. If information about that event is not adequately disclosed by management, the practitioner should take appropriate action.

5.89 If management refuses to disclose a subsequent event for which disclosure is necessary to prevent users of the service auditor's report from being misled, appropriate actions the practitioner may take include

- disclosing the event in the service auditor's report and modifying the practitioner's opinion.

- withdrawing from the engagement.

5.90 After the date of the service auditor's report, the service auditor has no responsibility to perform any procedures regarding

- the fairness of the presentation of the description of the service organization's system, the suitability of the design of the controls included in the description, or in a type 2 engagement, the operating effectiveness of those controls or

- management's assertion.

Nevertheless, the service auditor should respond appropriately to facts that become known to the service auditor after the date of the service auditor's report that, had they been known to the service auditor at that date, may have caused the service auditor to revise the report.

Distribution of the Report by Management

5.91 When engaged by the service organization, the service auditor provides the report to management of the service organization, and management distributes the report to the parties to whom use of the report is restricted.

                                                                ©2017, AICPA

5.92 In most cases, the service auditor is engaged by the service organization to perform the service auditor's engagement. However, in some cases the service auditor may be engaged by one or more user entities. A service auditor should distribute the service auditor's report only to the party that engaged the service auditor.

5.93 Paragraph .A100 of AT-C section 205 indicates that a practitioner may consider informing the responsible party and, if different, the engaging party or other specified parties that the report is not intended for distribution to parties other than those specified in the report. The practitioner may, in connection with establishing the terms of the engagement, reach an understanding with the responsible party or, if different, the engaging party that the intended use of the report will be restricted, and the service auditor may obtain the responsible party's agreement that the responsible party and specified parties will not distribute such report to parties other than those identified therein. A practitioner is not responsible for controlling, and cannot control, distribution of the report after its release.

Service Auditor's Recommendations for Improving Controls

5.94 Although it is not the objective of a service auditor's engagement, a service auditor may develop recommendations to improve a service organization's controls. The service auditor and management of the service organization agree on whether and how such recommendations will be communicated. Typically, the service auditor includes this information in a separate written communication provided only to the service organization's management. If recommendations are included in the service auditor's type 1 or type 2 report, they are typically placed in a separate section entitled, "Other Information Provided by the Service Organization." Management's responses to such recommendations may also be included in this separate section. Communication of recommended control improvements is most effective if it takes place within a short timeframe after issuance of the service auditor's report.

Modifying Management's Written Assertion

5.95 Paragraph 3.80 of this guide indicates that management's assertion generally would be expected to align with the service auditor's opinion, including modification of the assertion to reflect modifications to the service auditor's opinion. If the service auditor's report is modified because the description is not fairly stated or because controls are not suitability designed or operating effectively, it would be expected that management's written assertion would also be modified.

5.96 The following is an example of a separate paragraph that the service auditor has added to the service auditor's report because of a misstatement in the fairness of the presentation of management's description of the service organization's system:

> Example Service Organization has not included the following control objective and related controls in its description, which we believe are relevant to user entities internal control over financial reporting: "Controls provide reasonable assurance that logical access to system resources (for example, programs, data, table, and parameters) is restricted to authorized and appropriate individuals."

The following is a modification to the illustrative assertion presented in example 1 of paragraph .A76 of AT-C section 320 to reflect the misstatement in the description of the service organization's system that is identified in the service auditor's report. New language is shown in boldface italics:

  a. ***Except for the matter described in the following paragraph,*** the description fairly presents the [*type or name of*] system made available to user entities of the system during some or all of the period [*date*] to [*date*] for processing their transactions [*or identification of the function performed by the system*]. The criteria we used in making this assertion were that the description....

(*At the end of the portion of management's written assertion that addresses the fairness of the presentation of management's description of the service organization's system, management would add a paragraph such as the following*:)

  The description of Example Service Organization's system does not include the control objective "Controls provide reasonable assurance that logical access to system resources (for example, programs, data, table, and parameters) is restricted to authorized and appropriate individuals," nor have we included the controls designed to achieve that control objective. That control objective is relevant to user entities' internal control over financial reporting. As a result, the description is not fairly presented.

5.97   The following is an example of a modification to the illustrative management assertion presented in example 1 of paragraph .A76 of AT-C section 320 that would be used when controls were not operating effectively. New language is shown in boldface italics:

  c. ***Except for the matter described in the following paragraph,*** the controls related to the control objectives stated in the description were suitably designed and operating effectively throughout the period December 1, 20X0, to November 30, 20X1, to achieve those control objectives. The criteria we used in making this assertion were that

  1. the risks that threaten the achievement of the control objectives stated in the description have been identified;

  2. the controls identified in the description would, if operating as described, provide reasonable assurance that those risks would not prevent the control objectives stated in the description from being achieved; and

  3. the controls were consistently applied as designed, and manual controls were applied by individuals who have the appropriate competence and authority.

  As noted on page [mn], controls related to reconciliations and annual physical counts were not performed from [date] to [date]. As a result, controls were not operating effectively to achieve the control objective "Controls provide reasonable assurance that securities account master files are properly reconciled to subsidiary ledgers and surprise physical counts are performed."

5.98   In some situations, management of the service organization may choose not to revise its assertion. For example, management may disagree with the service auditor's recommendation to revise or delete information in the description of the service organization's system. In other situations, management may agree with the service auditor's recommendation but may prefer not to delay the issuance of the type 1 or type 2 report while modifications to the description are made or additional testing is performed. In such circumstances, management of the service organization would be more likely to modify its written assertion.

Appendix A

Illustrative Type 2 Reports

This appendix is nonauthoritative and is included for informational purposes only.

Although AT-C section 320, *Reporting on an Examination of Controls at a Service Organization Relevant to User Entities' Internal Control Over Financial Reporting* (AICPA, *Professional Standards*), specifies the components of a type 1 and type 2 report[1] and the information to be included in each component, it does not specify how the components should be organized within the type 1 or type 2 report. Service organizations and service auditors may organize and present the required information in a variety of formats. The format presented in this appendix is meant to be illustrative rather than prescriptive.

This appendix contains two illustrative type 2 reports that contain all of the required components of a type 2 report; however, for brevity, the illustrative reports do not include all the elements that might be described in a type 2 report. Ellipses (...) or parenthetical notes to readers indicate places where detail has been omitted from the illustrative reports.

The control objectives and controls specified by the service organization in examples 1 and 2, as well as the tests performed by the service auditor, are presented for illustrative purposes only. They are not intended to represent a complete or standard set of control objectives, controls, or tests of controls that would be appropriate for all service organizations. The determination of the appropriate control objectives, controls, and tests of controls for a specific service organization can be made only in the context of specific facts and circumstances. Accordingly, it is expected that actual type 2 reports will contain differing control objectives, controls, and tests of controls that are tailored to the service organization that is the subject of the engagement.

In examples 1 and 2 of this appendix, the components of the illustrative type 2 reports are referred to as "sections"; for example, section 2 contains management's assertion.

The following table identifies features of each illustrative type 2 report included in this appendix.

---

[1] The required components of a type 1 report are the service auditor's report, management of the service organization's written assertion, and management's description of the service organization's system. The required components of a type 2 report are the service auditor's report, management of the service organization's written assertion, management's description of the service organization's system, and the service auditor's description of tests of controls and results thereof.

Summary of Features of Illustrative Type 2 Reports in Appendix A

Number of Example and Name of Service Organization	Type of System Provided by the Service Organization	Name of Subservice Organization(s) and Method of Presentation	Service Provided by the Subservice Organization(s)	Are Complementary User Entity Controls or Complementary Subservice Organization Controls Required by the Service Organization?	Format of the Type 2 Report
1. XYZ Service Organization	Defined contribution recordkeeping system	N/A	N/A	Service organization requires complementary user entity controls	Narrative containing five report components referred to as sections 1, 2, 3, 4, and 5[2]
2. Example Service Organization	Defined contribution recordkeeping system	Computer Subservice Organization Carve-out method	Hosting services	Service organization requires complementary user entity controls and complementary subservice organization controls	Narrative containing five report components referred to as sections 1, 2, 3, 4, and 5[3]

[2] Section 5, "Other Information Provided by XYZ Service Organization," of this type 2 report includes other information not covered by the service auditor's report.

[3] Section 5, "Other Information Presented by Management of Example Service Organization," of this type 2 report includes other information provided by Example Service Organization that is not covered by the service auditor's report.

Example 1: Service Organization Requires Complementary User Entity Controls

Report on XYZ Service Organization's Description of Its Defined Contribution Recordkeeping System and on the Suitability of the Design and Operating Effectiveness of Its Controls

In example 1, XYZ Service Organization informs report users that complementary user entity controls are required to achieve specific control objectives. Changes to this type 2 report related to the need for complementary user entity controls are shown in boldface italics. This type 2 report includes the following five sections:

Section 1: The independent service auditor's report

Section 2: Management of XYZ Service Organization's assertion

Section 3: Management of XYZ Service Organization's description of its system

Section 4: The service auditor's description of tests of controls and results

Section 5: Other information provided by XYZ Service Organization

Table of Contents

Section Number	Title of Section
1	Independent Service Auditor's Report
2	XYZ Service Organization's Assertion
3	Description of XYZ Service Organization's Defined Contribution Recordkeeping System Overview of XYZ Service Organization Scope of the Description Internal Control Framework Control Environment Risk Assessment Process Monitoring Activities Information and Communications Control Activities Defined Contribution Plan Setup Control Objectives and Related Controls[4] ***Complementary User Entity Controls***
4	Description of XYZ Service Organization's Control Objectives and Related Controls, and Independent Service Auditor's Description of Tests of Controls and Results
5	Other Information Provided by XYZ Service Organization

---

[4] In this illustrative type 2 report, the control objectives and related controls are included in section 4, "Description of XYZ Service Organization's Control Objectives and Related Controls, and Independent Service Auditor's Description of Tests of Controls and Results." This avoids the need to repeat the control objectives and related controls in two sections.

Section 1: Independent Service Auditor's Report

To: XYZ Service Organization

Scope

We have examined XYZ Service Organization's description of its defined contribution recordkeeping system entitled "Description of XYZ Service Organization's Defined Contribution Recordkeeping System" for processing user entities' transactions throughout the period January 1, 201X, to December 31, 201X, (description) and the suitability of the design and the operating effectiveness of controls included in the description to achieve the related control objectives stated in the description, based on the criteria identified in "XYZ Service Organization's Assertion" (assertion). The controls and control objectives included in the description are those that management of XYZ Service Organization believes are likely to be relevant to user entities' internal control over financial reporting, and the description does not include those aspects of the defined contribution recordkeeping system that are not likely to be relevant to user entities' internal control over financial reporting.

The information included in section 5, "Other Information Provided by XYZ Service Organization," is presented by management of XYZ Service Organization to provide additional information and is not a part of XYZ Service Organization's description of its defined contribution recordkeeping system made available to user entities during the period January 1, 201X, to December 31, 201X. Information about XYZ Service Organization's business continuity planning and management's response to exceptions identified in the report has not been subjected to the procedures applied in the examination of the description of the defined contribution recordkeeping system and of the suitability of the design and operating effectiveness of controls to achieve the related control objectives stated in the description of the defined contribution recordkeeping system and, accordingly, we express no opinion on it.

The description indicates that certain control objectives specified in the description can be achieved only if complementary user entity controls assumed in the design of XYZ Service Organization's controls are suitably designed and operating effectively, along with related controls at the service organization. Our examination did not extend to such complementary user entity controls and we have not evaluated the suitability of the design or operating effectiveness of such complementary user entity controls.

Service Organization's Responsibilities

In section 2, XYZ Service Organization has provided an assertion about the fairness of the presentation of the description and suitability of the design and operating effectiveness of the controls to achieve the related control objectives stated in the description. XYZ Service Organization is responsible for preparing the description and its assertion, including the completeness, accuracy, and method of presentation of the description and the assertion, providing the services covered by the description, specifying the control objectives and stating them in the description, identifying the risks that threaten the achievement of the control objectives, selecting the criteria stated in the assertion, and designing, implementing, and documenting controls that are suitably designed and operating effectively to achieve the related control objectives stated in the description.

Service Auditor's Responsibilities

Our responsibility is to express an opinion on the fairness of the presentation of the description and on the suitability of the design and operating effectiveness of the controls to achieve the related control objectives stated in the description, based on our examination.

Our examination was conducted in accordance with attestation standards established by the American Institute of Certified Public Accountants. Those standards require that we plan and perform the examination to obtain reasonable assurance about whether, in all material respects, based on the criteria in management's assertion, the description is fairly presented and the controls were suitably designed and operating effectively to achieve the related control objectives stated in the description throughout the period January 1, 201X, to December 31, 201X. We believe that the evidence we obtained is sufficient and appropriate to provide a reasonable basis for our opinion.

An examination of a description of a service organization's system and the suitability of the design and operating effectiveness of controls involves

- performing procedures to obtain evidence about the fairness of the presentation of the description and the suitability of the design and operating effectiveness of the controls to achieve the related control objectives stated in the description, based on the criteria in management's assertion.

- assessing the risks that the description is not fairly presented and that the controls were not suitably designed or operating effectively to achieve the related control objectives stated in the description.

- testing the operating effectiveness of those controls that management considers necessary to provide reasonable assurance that the related control objectives stated in the description were achieved.

- evaluating the overall presentation of the description, suitability of the control objectives stated therein, and suitability of the criteria specified by the service organization in its assertion.

Inherent Limitations

The description is prepared to meet the common needs of a broad range of user entities and their auditors who audit and report on user entities' financial statements and may not, therefore, include every aspect of the system that each individual user entity may consider important in its own particular environment. Because of their nature, controls at a service organization may not prevent, or detect and correct, all misstatements in processing or reporting transactions. Also, the projection to the future of any evaluation of the fairness of the presentation of the description, or conclusions about the suitability of the design or operating effectiveness of the controls to achieve the related control objectives, is subject to the risk that controls at a service organization may become ineffective.

Description of Tests of Controls

The specific controls tested and the nature, timing, and results of those tests are listed in section 4.

Opinion

In our opinion, in all material respects, based on the criteria described in XYZ Service Organization's assertion

    a.   the description fairly presents the defined contribution recordkeeping system that was designed and implemented throughout the period January 1, 201X, to December 31, 201X.

    b.   the controls related to the control objectives stated in the description were suitably designed to provide reasonable assurance that the control objectives would be achieved if the controls operated effectively throughout the period January 1, 201X, to December 31, 201X, *and user entities applied the complementary user entity controls assumed in the design of XYZ Service Organization's controls throughout the period January 1, 201X, to December 31, 201X.*

    c.   the controls operated effectively to provide reasonable assurance that the control objectives stated in the description were achieved throughout the period January 1, 201X, to December 31, 201X, *if complementary user entity controls assumed in the design of XYZ Service Organization's controls operated effectively throughout the period January 1, 201X, to December 31, 201X.*

Restricted Use

This report, including the description of tests of controls and results thereof in section 4, is intended solely for the information and use of XYZ Service Organization, user entities of XYZ Service Organization's defined contribution recordkeeping system during some or all of the period January 1, 201X, to December 31, 201X, and their auditors who audit and report on such user entities' financial statements or internal control over financial reporting and have a sufficient understanding to consider it, along with other information, including information about controls implemented by user entities themselves, when assessing the risks of material misstatement of user entities' financial statements. This report is not intended to be and should not be used by anyone other than these specified parties.

[*Service auditor's signature*]

[*Service auditor's city and state*]

[*Date of the service auditor's report*]

Section 2: XYZ Service Organization's Assertion

We have prepared the description of XYZ Service Organization's defined contribution recordkeeping system entitled "Description of XYZ Service Organization's Defined Contribution Recordkeeping System" for processing user entities' transactions throughout the period January 1, 201X, to December 31, 201X, (description) for user entities of the system during some or all of the period January 1, 201X, to December 31, 201X, and their auditors who audit and report on such user entities' financial statements or internal control over financial reporting and have a sufficient understanding to consider it, along with other information, including information about controls implemented by user entities of the system themselves, when assessing the risks of material misstatement of user entities' financial statements.

The description indicates that certain control objectives specified in the description can be achieved only if complementary user entity controls assumed in the design of XYZ Service Organization's controls are suitably designed and operating effectively, along with related controls at the service organization. The description does not extend to controls of the user entities.

We confirm, to the best of our knowledge and belief, that

    a. the description fairly presents the defined contribution recordkeeping system made available to user entities of the system during some or all of the period January 1, 201X, to December 31, 201X, for processing their transactions as it relates to controls that are likely to be relevant to user entities' internal control over financial reporting. The criteria we used in making this assertion were that the description

        i. presents how the system made available to user entities of the system was designed and implemented to process relevant user entity transactions, including, if applicable,

            (1) the types of services provided including, as appropriate, the classes of transactions processed.

            (2) the procedures, within both automated and manual systems, by which those services are provided including, as appropriate, procedures by which transactions are initiated, authorized, recorded, processed, corrected as necessary, and transferred to the reports and other information prepared for user entities of the system.

            (3) the information used in the performance of the procedures including, if applicable, related accounting records, whether electronic or manual, and supporting information involved in initiating, authorizing, recording, processing, and reporting transactions; this includes the correction of incorrect information and how information is transferred to the reports and other information prepared for user entities.

            (4) how the system captures and addresses significant events and conditions other than transactions.

            (5) the process used to prepare reports and other information for user entities.

            (6) services performed by a subservice organization, if any, including whether the inclusive method or the carve-out method has been used in relation to them.

            (7) the specified control objectives and controls designed to achieve those objectives including, as applicable, complementary user entity controls assumed in the design of the service organization's controls.

            (8) other aspects of our control environment, risk assessment process, information and communications (including the related business processes),

control activities, and monitoring activities that are relevant to the services provided.

    ii. includes relevant details of changes to the service organization's system during the period covered by the description.

    iii. does not omit or distort information relevant to the service organization's system, while acknowledging that the description is prepared to meet the common needs of a broad range of user entities of the system and their user auditors, and may not, therefore, include every aspect of the defined contribution recordkeeping system that each individual user entity of the system and its auditor may consider important in its own particular environment.

b. the controls related to the control objectives stated in the description were suitably designed and operating effectively throughout the period January 1, 201X, to December 31, 201X, to achieve those control objectives *if user entities applied the complementary user entity controls assumed in the design of XYZ Service Organization's controls throughout the period January 1, 201X, to December 31, 201X.* The criteria we used in making this assertion were that

    i. the risks that threaten the achievement of the control objectives stated in the description have been identified by management of the service organization.

    ii. the controls identified in the description would, if operating effectively, provide reasonable assurance that those risks would not prevent the control objectives stated in the description from being achieved.

    iii. the controls were consistently applied as designed, including whether manual controls were applied by individuals who have the appropriate competence and authority.

Section 3: Description of XYZ Service Organization's Defined Contribution Recordkeeping System

Overview of XYZ Service Organization

XYZ Service Organization is located in Los Angeles, California, and provides defined contribution plan recordkeeping services to corporations, unions, and nonprofit customers (user entities) across the U.S. These services are provided using a proprietary ABC Recordkeeping application developed and maintained by XYZ Service Organization.

Services provided as part of its defined contribution plan recordkeeping services include the following:

- Benefit plan setup and maintenance
- ......
- ......

Scope of the Description

This description addresses only XYZ Service Organization's defined contribution recordkeeping system provided to user entities and excludes other services provided by XYZ Service Organization. The description is intended to provide information for user entities of the defined contribution recordkeeping system and their independent auditors who audit and report on such user entities' financial statements or internal control over financial reporting, to be used in obtaining an understanding of the defined contribution recordkeeping system and the controls over that system that are likely to be relevant to user entities' internal control over financial reporting. The description of the system includes certain business process controls and IT general controls that support the delivery of XYZ Service Organization's defined contribution recordkeeping system.

Internal Control Framework

This section provides information about the five interrelated components of internal control at XYZ Service Organization, including XYZ Service Organization's

- control environment,
- risk assessment process,
- monitoring activities,
- information and communications, and
- control activities.

Control Environment

The control environment sets the tone of an organization, influencing the control awareness of the organization. The control environment is embodied by the organization's awareness of the need for controls and the emphasis given to the appropriate controls through management's actions supported by its policies, procedures, and organizational structure.

The following are the primary elements of the service organization's control environment:

1. Commitment to integrity and ethical values
2. Oversight responsibility of the board of directors
3. Assignment of authority and responsibility
4. Commitment to competence
5. Accountability

Commitment to Integrity and Ethical Values

The service organization operates in a highly regulated environment. To this end, the service organization has developed a formal code of ethics available on its intranet that contains rules about employee conduct while under the employ of XYZ Service Organization. Employees are required to read and evidence their knowledge and receipt of the service organization's code of ethics upon hire and annually thereafter.

The service organization offers its employees a number of channels through which potential breaches of ethical behavior may be reported. These channels include....

Oversight Responsibility of the Board of Directors

The control environment at XYZ Service Organization originates with and is the responsibility of the board of directors (board), chief executive officer (CEO), and executive management. The board provides oversight of XYZ Service Organization operations and activities including oversight of the service organization's investment and audit committees. The investment committee supervises and controls the service organization's investment and related financial matters, approves service organization investment policies and guidelines, and reviews the service organization's investment strategies and investment performance. The audit committee is responsible for reviewing the service organization's policies and practices related to accounting, financial, and operational controls, and financial reporting. The audit committee is also responsible for directing the activities of XYZ Service Organization's internal audit department and coordinating the activities of the service organization's external financial auditors.

The internal audit department performs internal audits that help the service organization maintain an effective system of internal control, manage risk, improve customer service, and enhance business performance. The internal audit department follows a risk-based audit approach including ....

In addition to the internal audit department, the service organization has established several other compliance groups dedicated to effective risk management and oversight, including .....

Assignment of Authority and Responsibility

Executive management recognizes its responsibility for directing and controlling operations, managing risks, and establishing, communicating, and monitoring control policies and procedures, under the ultimate oversight of the board. Management recognizes its responsibility for establishing and maintaining sound internal control and promoting integrity and ethical values to all personnel on a day-to-day basis.

.....

Commitment to Competence

The service organization's commitment to employee competence begins with background checks for all employee candidates and formal hiring practices designed to ensure that new employees are qualified for their job responsibilities. Management has established written competence and performance levels for each job function, including formal promotion and development criteria that help foster professional development for its employees. These criteria are also used to measure employee performance and identify areas for improvement and additional training.

The service organization follows regulatory rules concerning the licensing of personnel in the securities business. Compliance teams monitor license renewals and send update reminders to employees and their supervisors regarding license renewal dates.

The service organization also offers a comprehensive training program including ....

Accountability

XYZ Service Organization's commitment to an effective system of internal control begins with the service organization's board and its audit committee. The audit committee meets four times a year to fulfill its oversight responsibilities related to the financial reporting process, the system of internal control, internal and external audit activities, and the service organization's process for managing risk and monitoring compliance with applicable laws, regulations, and internal policies and procedures.

The service organization's executive committee meets periodically to oversee critical business operations. In addition ...

Risk Assessment Process

The service organization operates in an environment faced with a variety of risks from internal and external sources.

Objectives

The service organization's risk assessment approach involves an iterative process for identifying and assessing risks to the achievement of the service organization's objectives. This approach forms the basis for determining how risks will be managed by the service organization.

Identification and Analysis of Risks

Risk management is primarily the responsibility of individual business units, which perform periodic risk assessments that identify and document the significant risks facing the service organization, including any fraud risks. The results of these risk assessments determine how the business units develop and implement controls, operating procedures, and compliance processes for addressing and mitigating such risks. Service organization policies require that any instances of suspected or actual fraud be brought to the immediate attention of senior management, the internal audit department, and the service organization's legal department. In addition ...

Monitoring Activities

XYZ Service Organization employs a combination of ongoing and periodic monitoring activities to monitor that controls are functioning effectively and that risks are appropriately mitigated.

Ongoing Monitoring

The service organization uses a variety of reports and monitoring mechanisms to help ensure that controls are functioning as intended; these include

- electronic display of pending transactions and their status,
- deficiency and incident reporting,
- suspense account reporting,
- daily pricing variances,
- financial reconciliations,
- quality review results and reporting,
- system processing monitoring and reporting, and
- logical security incident logging and review.

Management regularly reviews and assesses business operations to determine that reporting and monitoring mechanisms are used and effective in managing the operations of the business, controls, and related risks.

Periodic Assessments and Monitoring

In addition to ongoing monitoring activities described above, each business unit conducts specific evaluations of risks and controls to maximize the effectiveness of its operations.

The internal audit department performs internal audits of operations and controls to assess the effectiveness of controls. The results of audits and any identified deficiencies are reported to management as well as the audit committee. Management prepares and implements corrective measures to address any significant deficiencies.

Information and Communications

XYZ Service Organization communicates its policies and procedures and other information necessary to help achieve the service organization's business objectives through several means, including the service organization's intranet, emails, newsletters, memoranda, meetings, and training sessions. The service organization's policies and procedures enforce the importance of adherence to and compliance with rules and regulations that govern its business and operations.

XYZ Service Organization has also implemented various methods of communication to inform user entities of the role and responsibilities of XYZ Service Organization in processing their transactions and to communicate significant events to user entities in a timely manner. These methods include XYZ Service Organization's active participation in quarterly user group meetings; the monthly XYZ Service Organization newsletter, which summarizes the significant events and changes during the month and planned for the following month; and the user liaison, who maintains contact with designated user entity representatives to inform them of new issues and developments. User entities are also encouraged to communicate questions and problems to their liaison, and such matters are logged and tracked until resolved, with the resolution also reported to the user entity.

For information provided to user entities, such as reports, statements, data, and other information provided to user entities, service organization policies and procedures require that all such information be tested to ensure it is sufficiently complete and accurate.

Information Systems Overview

The service organization employs the following IT applications and hardware to provide its defined plan contribution recordkeeping services to its user entities:

    1.   ABC Recordkeeping Application—This system...

    2.   ......

    3.   ....

[*Note to readers: Paragraph 3.26 of this guide indicates that the description of the service organization's system may be presented using various formats such as narratives, flowcharts, tables, or graphics, or a combination thereof. For illustrative purposes, this description would include a flowchart.*]

The following flowchart provides an overview of transaction processing for the defined contribution recordkeeping system.

[*Note to readers: The flowchart would be inserted here.*]

Control Activities

The service organization has developed a variety of policies and procedures including related control activities to help ensure the service organization's objectives are carried out and risks are mitigated. These control activities help ensure that defined contribution plans are administered in accordance with the service organization's policies and procedures.

Control activities are performed at a variety of levels throughout the organization and at various stages during the relevant business process. Controls may be preventive or detective in nature and may encompass a range of manual and automated controls, including authorizations, reconciliation, and IT controls. Duties and responsibilities—such as duties related to the processing and recording of transactions, investment trading, reconciliation activities, application development, compliance, and control monitoring—are allocated among personnel to ensure that a proper segregation of duties is maintained.

A formal program is in place to review and update the service organization's policies and procedures on at least an annual basis. Any changes to the policies and procedures are reviewed and approved by management and communicated to employees.

Defined Contribution Plan Setup

Plan Setup

The new accounts team works with plan sponsors, prior recordkeeping service providers, and third-party administrators to facilitate the setup and conversion of the plan in the ABC Recordkeeping application. After receipt of a signed and authorized administrative services agreement from the plan sponsor, a member of the service organization's new accounts team begins the process of preparing the file for upload into the ABC Recordkeeping application. The new accounts team member uses a new accounts setup checklist to ensure that the plan is completely and accurately set up in the ABC Recordkeeping application. Once the plan is ready for upload, a new accounts team manager reviews the checklist and related documentation to determine whether the plan is completely and accurately set up in the ABC Recordkeeping application and ready for upload. The new accounts team manager signs the checklist as evidence of approval.

After the plan has been set up in the system, the new accounts team manager compares the date the plan was implemented in the system to the date in the administrative service agreement to ensure that the plan was implemented timely. The new accounts team manager also reconciles the dollar total of the plan entered in the system to the dollar total provided by the plan sponsor or prior recordkeeper. Any differences are investigated and resolved. The new accounts team manager completes the checklist to evidence that the reconciliation was performed and that the dollar totals were reconciled.

After the plan has been set up in the ABC Recordkeeping application, a second new accounts team manager reviews the plan information entered in the ABC Recordkeeping application and compares that information to the information in the supporting document provided by the plan sponsor or prior recordkeeper to ensure that the plan was completely and accurately set up in the system. The second new accounts team manager also completes the checklist to evidence that the dollar totals were reconciled and signs the checklist to evidence that the review was performed.

Plan Conversions

For plans set up on the ABC Recordkeeping application from prior recordkeepers, the new accounts team works with...

Plan Changes

For any changes to plans already set up on the ABC Recordkeeping application, the ....

[Note to readers: For brevity, the following aspects of the defined contribution recordkeeping system are not presented in this illustrative type 2 report.]

Plan administration

Participant administration

Transfers and changes in investment allocation

Contributions and loan payments

Plan distributions and payments

Loan requests

Fees

Investment income

New fund setup and changes

Asset purchases and redemption

Plan and participant statement reporting

Reconciliations

System development and change management

Logical security

Network infrastructure

Computer operations

Data transmission

Physical security

Data backup

Control Objectives and Related Controls

XYZ Service Organization has specified the control objectives and identified the controls that are designed to achieve the related control objectives. The specified control objectives, related controls, and complementary user entity controls are presented in section 4, "Description of XYZ Service Organization's Control Objectives and Related Controls, and Independent Service Auditor's Description of Tests of Controls and Results," and are an integral component of XYZ Service Organization's description of its defined contribution recordkeeping system.

Complementary User Entity Controls

XYZ Service Organization's controls related to the defined contribution recordkeeping system cover only a portion of overall internal control for each user entity of XYZ Service Organization. It is not feasible for the control objectives related to recordkeeping services to be achieved solely by XYZ Service Organization. Therefore, each user entity's internal control over financial reporting should be evaluated in conjunction with XYZ Service Organization's controls and the related tests and results described in section 4 of this report, taking into account the related complementary user entity controls identified under each control objective, where applicable.[5] In order for user entities to rely on the controls reported on herein, each user entity must evaluate its own internal control to determine whether the identified complementary user entity controls have been implemented and are operating effectively.

Section 4: Description of XYZ Service Organization's Control Objectives and Related Controls, and Independent Service Auditor's Description of Tests of Controls and Results

Information Provided by the Independent Service Auditor

This report, when combined with an understanding of the controls at user entities, is intended to assist auditors in planning the audit of user entities' financial statements or user entities' internal control over financial reporting and in assessing control risk for assertions in user entities' financial statements that may be affected by controls at XYZ Service Organization.

Our examination was limited to the control objectives and related controls specified by XYZ Service Organization in sections 3 and 4 of the report, and did not extend to controls in effect at user entities.

It is the responsibility of each user entity and its independent auditor to evaluate this information in conjunction with the evaluation of internal control over financial reporting at the user entity in order to assess total internal control. If internal control is not effective at user entities, XYZ Service Organization's controls may not compensate for such weaknesses.

XYZ Service Organization's internal control represents the collective effect of various factors on establishing or enhancing the effectiveness of the controls specified by XYZ Service Organization. In planning the nature, timing, and extent of our testing of the controls to achieve the control objectives specified by XYZ Service Organization, we considered aspects of XYZ Service Organization's control environment, risk assessment process, monitoring activities, and information and communications.

The following table clarifies certain terms used in this section to describe the nature of the tests performed:

Test	*Description*
Inquiry	Inquiry of appropriate personnel and corroboration with management
Observation	Observation of the application, performance, or existence of the control
Inspection	Inspection of documents and reports indicating performance of the control
Reperformance	Reperformance of the control

In addition, as required by paragraph .35 of AT-C section 205, *Examination Engagements* (AICPA, *Professional Standards*), and paragraph .30 of AT-C section 320, when using information produced (or provided) by the service

---

[5] There is no prescribed format for presenting the complementary user entity controls. They may be listed in section 4 following the service organization's description of control objectives and related controls, and the service auditor's description of tests of controls and results, to which they apply, or they may be listed in the description of the service organization's system in section 3. If listed in section 3, the complementary user entity controls should identify the control objectives to which they apply.

organization, we evaluated whether the information was sufficiently reliable for our purposes by obtaining evidence about the accuracy and completeness of such information and evaluating whether the information was sufficiently precise and detailed for our purposes.

Control Objective 1—Defined Contribution Plan Setup

Controls provide reasonable assurance that defined contribution plans set up on the ABC Recordkeeping application are authorized by plan sponsors and completely and accurately processed and recorded in a timely manner.[6]

Controls Specified by XYZ Service Organization	Tests of Controls	Results of Tests
1.1 New plans or plans from prior recordkeepers are accepted and entered in the ABC Recordkeeping application only after receipt of a signed and authorized administrative services agreement from the plan sponsor. A member of the service organization's new accounts team uses a new accounts setup checklist to ensure that plans are • set up completely and accurately in the ABC Recordkeeping application, based on the information in the supporting document provided by the plan sponsor or prior recordkeeper. • set up and implemented by the date specified in the administrative services agreement. A new accounts team manager is assigned to the plan and signs the checklist to evidence that the plan was completely and accurately set up and implemented by the date specified in the administrative services agreement.	For a sample of new plans, • inspected the administrative services agreement to determine whether the agreement was signed and authorized by the plan sponsor. • inspected the new accounts setup checklist to determine whether the checklist was completed and signed by the new accounts team manager. • ...	No exceptions noted.

---

[6] For illustrative purposes the phrase "in a timely manner" is used in this control objective. However, in order for the control objective to be measurable, the service organization would need to define "in a timely manner," for example, "the transaction was entered in the ABC Recordkeeping application within 10 business days of receipt."

Control Objective 1—Defined Contribution Plan Setup—*continued*

Controls Specified by XYZ Service Organization	Tests of Controls	Results of Tests
1.2 After the plan is set up in the ABC Recordkeeping application, the new accounts team manager compares the plan information entered in the ABC Recordkeeping application to the information in the related administrative services agreement and supporting document provided by the plan sponsor or prior recordkeeper to ensure that the plan was completely and accurately set up and implemented by the date specified in the administrative services agreement.	For a sample of new plans set up in the ABC Recordkeeping application, • inspected the related administrative services agreement to determine whether the implementation date per the ABC Recordkeeping application was no later than the implementation date per the administrative services agreement. • reperformed the control by comparing the plan information entered in the ABC Recordkeeping application to the plan information included in the supporting document provided by the plan sponsor or prior recordkeeper to ensure that the plan was completely and accurately set up.	No exceptions noted.
1.3 After the plan is set up in the ABC Recordkeeping application, the new accounts team manager reconciles the total plan dollars entered in the ABC Recordkeeping application to the total plan dollars per the supporting document provided by the plan sponsor or prior recordkeeper and includes the reconciliation in the checklist. Any differences are investigated and resolved.	For a sample of new plans set up in the ABC Recordkeeping application, inspected the checklist to determine whether the new accounts team manager • prepared a reconciliation of the total plan dollars entered in the ABC Recordkeeping application to the total plan dollars per the supporting document provided by the plan sponsor or prior recordkeeper. • investigated and resolved any differences between the two amounts. For a sample of new plans, reperformed the reconciliation of the total plan dollars entered in the ABC Recordkeeping application to the total plan dollars per the supporting document provided by the plan sponsor or prior recordkeeper to determine whether the two amounts reconciled and whether reconciling items had been investigated and resolved.	No exceptions noted.

(continued)

Control Objective 1—Defined Contribution Plan Setup—*continued*

Controls Specified by XYZ Service Organization	Tests of Controls	Results of Tests
1.4 Using the new accounts setup checklist, a second new accounts team manager compares the plan information entered in the ABC Recordkeeping application to the information in the administrative services agreement and supporting document provided by the plan sponsor or prior recordkeeper to ensure that the plan was completely and accurately set up in the ABC Recordkeeping application and implemented by the date specified in the administrative services agreement. The second new accounts team manager also • reviews the reconciliation of the total plan dollars entered in the ABC Recordkeeping application to the total plan dollars per the supporting document provided by the plan sponsor or prior recordkeeper to ensure that the reconciliation was performed and that the two amounts were reconciled. • signs the checklist to evidence that the review was performed.	For a sample of new plans set up in the ABC Recordkeeping application, inspected the related new accounts setup checklist to determine whether it was signed by a second new accounts team manager.	No exceptions noted.
1.5 ...		
1.6...		

Complementary User Entity Controls

1. *Plan sponsors are responsible for ensuring that plan information provided to XYZ Service Organization is complete and accurate and provided on a timely basis.*

2. *Plan sponsors are responsible for ensuring that administrative agreements are signed by authorized plan sponsor personnel and provided to XYZ Service Organization.*

3. *Plan sponsors are responsible for ensuring that any changes to plans already set up in the ABC Recordkeeping application are sent to XYZ Service Organization from authorized personnel on a timely basis and that such changes are complete and accurate.*

4. ...

Control Objective 2—Plan Administration

Controls provide reasonable assurance that changes to plan data are authorized and are processed and recorded in an accurate, complete, and timely manner.

Controls Specified by XYZ Service Organization	Tests of Controls	Results of Tests
2.1 For changes to plans set up in the ABC Recordkeeping application and originating from plan sponsors, a member of the service organization's account changes team verifies that the change was received from a person authorized by the plan sponsor, updates the plan information in the ABC Recordkeeping application based on the document requesting the change, and completes and signs the account changes checklist to ensure that the change was accurately entered in the ABC Recordkeeping application. Using the account change checklist, a second member of the account changes team reviews the change entered in the ABC Recordkeeping application and compares it to the information in the document requesting the change to ensure that the change was accurately entered no later than 10 business days after the receipt of the change request. The second member of the account changes team signs the checklist to evidence that the review was performed.	For a sample of plan changes originating from plan sponsors and entered in the ABC Recordkeeping application, • inspected the documents requesting the change and the account changes checklist to determine whether the change was authorized by a person authorized by the plan sponsor and the checklist was completed and signed by a member of the account changes team. • reperformed the control by comparing the change made to the plan in the ABC Recordkeeping application to the document from the plan sponsor requesting the change to determine whether the change was entered accurately in the ABC Recordkeeping application no later than 10 business days after the receipt of the change request. • inspected the account changes checklist to determine whether the second member of the account changes team signed the checklist.	No exceptions noted.
2.2...		
2.3...		

Complementary User Entity Controls

    1. *Plan sponsors are responsible for submitting complete and accurate plan changes to XYZ Service Organization on a timely basis.*

    2. *Plan sponsors are responsible for verifying any changes to their respective account or plan information and notifying XYZ Service Organization of any errors or discrepancies on a timely basis.*

    3. ...

    4. ...

Control Objective 3—Participant Administration

Controls provide reasonable assurance that participant enrollments and changes to participant data are authorized and completely and accurately processed and recorded in a timely manner.

Controls Specified by XYZ Service Organization	Tests of Controls	Results of Tests
3.1 Participant enrollment forms or participant change requests received via mail, email, or fax are logged and reviewed by an account processing specialist for completeness, authorization (a signature on or accompanying the form), and accuracy prior to entering the information in the ABC Recordkeeping application. Service organization policy requires that all information in the participant enrollment form or change request be completely and accurately entered in the ABC Recordkeeping system within 10 business days of receipt. After entry of the information in the ABC Recordkeeping application and prior to production implementation, the account processing specialist signs the participant enrollment form or change request and forwards the form or request to a second account processing specialist for review. The second account processing specialist • compares the information entered in the ABC Recordkeeping application with the information in the participant enrollment form or change request to ensure that the information was entered accurately and completely within 10 business days of receipt. • resolves any differences and indicates on the participant enrollment form or change request any changes that need to be made to the information previously entered in the ABC Recordkeeping application.	For a sample of participant enrollment forms and participant change requests, inspected • the log to determine whether the form or change request was logged. • the participant enrollment form or change request to determine whether it was signed by — an account processing specialist to evidence that the form or change request was reviewed for completeness, authorization, and accuracy prior to entry in the ABC Recordkeeping application. — a second account processing specialist to evidence that the specialist compared the information entered in the ABC Recordkeeping application with the information in the participant enrollment form or change request to ensure that the information was entered completely and accurately within 10 business days of receipt of complete and accurate data. For a sample of participant enrollment forms and change requests received via mail, email, or fax, reperformed the control by comparing the participant enrollment or change information in the ABC	No exceptions noted.

Control Objective 3—Participant Administration—*continued*

Controls Specified by XYZ Service Organization	Tests of Controls	Results of Tests
• if applicable, sends the participant enrollment form or change request back to the first account processing specialist with instructions for correcting the information in the ABC Recordkeeping application. • signs the participant enrollment or change request to evidence that the review and related procedures were performed.	Recordkeeping application to the information in the participant enrollment form or change request submitted by the participant or plan sponsor to determine whether the information in the application was entered completely and accurately within 10 business days of receipt.	
3.2 For participant enrollment requests received electronically, the plan sponsor must sign on to the XYZ Service Organization plan sponsor web portal and submit the electronic file of participant enrollment information. Plan sponsors are required to authenticate themselves to the web portal via a valid user ID and password. Files uploaded via the XYZ Service Organization web portal are uploaded via file transfer protocol (FTP) or secure FTP.	Inspected the configuration of logical security over the web portal to determine whether authentication to the portal requires a valid user ID and password. For a sample of dates, inspected the FTP or secure FTP configuration for transfer or upload of files to the web portal to determine whether FTP is required.	No exceptions noted.
3.3 For plans that enroll participants electronically, participants are identified in a data file that is transmitted by upload of the file to the XYZ Service Organization web portal. Participants are added to the ABC Recordkeeping application based on plan eligibility requirements and plan parameters. After upload of the file, validation routines are run against the file to identify any errors or incomplete information. Any errors or incomplete participant information that is not corrected is returned to the plan sponsor for correction.	For a sample of participant data files received via electronic file upload, • inspected the participant information in the ABC Recordkeeping application to determine whether the information was completely and accurately loaded into the application. • inspected whether validation routines were run to identify any errors or incomplete data and whether any remaining errors or incomplete data were returned to the plan sponsor for correction.	No exceptions noted.

(continued)

Control Objective 3—Participant Administration—*continued*

Controls Specified by XYZ Service Organization	Tests of Controls	Results of Tests
3.4 Participant access to the voice response system, the participant web portal, and the XYZ Service Organization call center requires entry of a valid personal identification number (PIN).	Observed that access to the voice response system, the participant web portal, and the call center requires entry of a valid PIN.	No exceptions noted.
3.5 For participant changes received via the call center, the automated telephone voice response system, or participant web portal, a change notification is generated and mailed to the participant.	For a selection of participant changes received via the call center, automated telephone voice response system, or participant web portal, inspected the related notification sent to the participant to determine that the notification accurately reflects the change made to the participant's information.	No exceptions noted.
3.6 ...		
3.7 ...		

Complementary User Entity Controls

1. *Plan sponsors are responsible for submitting complete and accurate employee enrollment information to XYZ Service Organization on a timely basis.*
2. *Plan sponsors and participants are responsible for submitting complete and accurate participant change information to XYZ Service Organization on a timely basis.*
3. *Plan sponsors and participants are responsible for verifying any changes to the respective participant account information and notifying the XYZ Service Organization of any errors or discrepancies on a timely basis.*
4. ...
5. ...

[*Note to readers: For brevity, the controls and test of controls and results for control objectives 4–13 are not presented in this illustrative report.*]

Control Objective 4—Transfers and Changes in Investment Allocations

Controls provide reasonable assurance that participant-initiated transfers and changes in investment allocations are authorized and completely and accurately processed and recorded in a timely manner.

Control Objective 5—Contributions and Loan Payments

Controls provide reasonable assurance that contributions and loan payments are authorized and completely and accurately processed and recorded in a timely manner.

Control Objective 6—Plan Distributions and Payments

Controls provide reasonable assurance that plan distributions and payments to participants are authorized and completely and accurately processed and recorded in a timely manner.

Control Objective 7—Loan Requests

Controls provide reasonable assurance that loan requests are authorized and completely and accurately processed and recorded in a timely manner.

Control Objective 8—Fees

Controls provide reasonable assurance that requests for new fee setup, changes, corrections, terminations, and reversals are completely and accurately processed and recorded in the ABC Recordkeeping application in a timely manner.

Control Objective 9—Investment Income

Controls provide reasonable assurance that investment income, dividends, corporate actions, and participant account values are completely and accurately calculated, processed, and recorded in a timely manner.

Control Objective 10—New Fund Setup and Changes

Controls provide reasonable assurance that new funds and changes to funds are authorized and completely and accurately implemented in a timely manner.

Control Objective 11—Asset Purchases and Redemption

Controls provide reasonable assurance that asset purchase and redemption transactions are authorized and completely and accurately traded and recorded in a timely manner.

Control Objective 12—Plan and Participant Statement Reporting

Controls provide reasonable assurance that plan and participant statements are accurate, complete, and provided to or sent to the plan sponsors or participants in a timely manner, in accordance with contractual agreements.

Control Objective 13—Reconciliations

Controls provide reasonable assurance that cash and security positions are completely and accurately reconciled between the ABC Recordkeeping application and the depositories in a timely manner.

Control Objective 14—Systems Development and Change Management

Controls provide reasonable assurance that changes to the ABC Recordkeeping application, other programs, and related data management systems are authorized, tested, documented, approved, and implemented to result in complete, accurate, and timely processing and reporting of transactions and balances relevant to user entities' financial reporting and to support user entities' internal control over financial reporting.

Controls Specified by XYZ Service Organization	Tests of Controls	Results of Tests
14.1 The service organization has established written policies and procedures for systems development and change management.	Inspected the service organization's systems development and change management policies and procedures to determine whether written policies and procedures have been established.	No exceptions noted.
14.2 Requests for new development or changes to existing applications must be documented in a change request form and approved by the business owner (as appropriate) and IT management.	For a sample of new development or changes to existing applications, inspected the change request form to determine whether the request was approved by the business owner and IT management.	No exceptions noted.
14.3 For large projects, change requests are assigned to a system analyst to assess and document the nature and extent of the work and number of project hours required to complete the task. IT management must approve such change requests and indicate approval on the change request form.	For a sample of large projects, inspected the change request form for evidence that a system analyst had assessed and documented the nature and extent of the work and number of project hours required to complete the task, and that the change request form was approved by IT management.	No exceptions noted.
14.4 Upon completion of development, the completed code is tested by the quality assurance department in the test environment. Approval by the quality assurance department is documented on the change request form.	For a sample of program changes implemented into production, inspected the change request form to determine whether testing was performed and approved by the quality assurance department.	No exceptions noted.

Control Objective 14—Systems Development and Change Management—*continued*

Controls Specified by XYZ Service Organization	Tests of Controls	Results of Tests
14.5 Upon approval by the quality assurance department, the change request form is forwarded to the change control board for approval. Approval by the change control board is documented on the change request form.	For a sample of program changes implemented into production, inspected the change request form to determine whether the request was approved by the change control board.	No exceptions noted.
14.6 All changes approved for production implementation are moved to the staging environment and implemented into production by the IT configuration group. When this occurs the change control board team member notes this on the checklist.	For a sample of program changes implemented into production, inspected the change request form to determine whether the change was moved to the staging environment and implemented into production by the IT configuration group.	No exceptions noted.
14.7 Separate environments exist for the development, testing, staging, and production of changes.	Inspected the URLs to determine whether separate environments exist for the development, testing, staging, and production of changes.	No exceptions noted.
14.8 Change control software is used to implement changes into production and to maintain version control over program source code. Any changes to the production code are logged by the software.	Inspected the change control software and related logs to determine whether change control software is used to implement changes into production, maintain version control over program source code, and log changes to the production code.	No exceptions noted.
14.9 Access to the production environment and the change control software is restricted to authorized IT configuration personnel.	On multiple occasions during the period, inspected the security permissions for the change control software and production environment to determine whether access to implement changes into production is restricted to authorized IT configuration personnel.	No exceptions noted.
14.10 ...		
14.11 ...		

Control Objective 15—Logical Security

Controls provide reasonable assurance that logical access to programs, data, the ABC Recordkeeping application, and computer resources that may affect user entities' internal control over financial reporting is restricted to authorized and appropriate users and such users are restricted to performing authorized and appropriate actions.

Controls Specified by XYZ Service Organization	Tests of Controls	Results of Tests
15.1 The service organization has established formal policies and procedures related to logical security and controls over access to and use of service organization applications.	Inspected the service organization's IT security policies and procedures to determine whether formal policies and procedures have been established.	No exceptions noted.
15.2 Requests for new user access to the service organization's system are initiated by the human resources department and the employee's hiring manager by completing an online system access form. The form is forwarded to the IT security group for setup of user access to the service organization's system. User entities are assigned access rights in the ABC Recordkeeping application based on job responsibilities, and security groups are used in the system to segregate and restrict user access.	For a selection of new employee hires, inspected the employee's associated ABC Recordkeeping application access form and the level of access granted to the employee to determine whether the user's access was properly approved and provisioned and that the level of access granted was commensurate with the user's job responsibilities.	No exceptions noted.
15.3 System administrator access to the network and ABC Recordkeeping application is restricted to authorized personnel.	Inspected the list of users with administrative access to the network and the ABC Recordkeeping application and reviewed the list with IT management to determines whether administrative access is appropriately restricted to authorized personnel.	No exceptions noted.
15.4 The access of terminated employees is removed or disabled by the IT security group based on notification from the human resources department. The human resources department completes a ticket in the help desk ticketing system that requests the removal of the employee's system access on a specific date.	For a selection of terminated employees, inspected the employee's access to the network and ABC Recordkeeping application to determine whether the employee's access was properly removed or disabled on or before the date specified by the human resources department.	For 1 out of 25 terminated employees selected for testing, the employee's access to the ABC Recordkeeping application was not removed from the system.

Control Objective 15—Logical Security—*continued*

Controls Specified by XYZ Service Organization	Tests of Controls	Results of Tests
15.5 User access to the network and ABC Recordkeeping application is reviewed twice a year for appropriateness by the IT security group and the application owner. Any access deemed inappropriate is removed or modified by the IT security group.	Inspected a selection of semi-annual user access reviews performed by the IT security group and the application owner to determine whether user access was reviewed for appropriateness and whether the access of any user with inappropriate access was removed or modified.	No exceptions noted.
15.6 Access to the network and ABC Recordkeeping application requires a valid user ID and password.	Inspected the security configuration of the network and application on multiple occasions during the period and observed the login process to determine that a valid user ID and password are required to authenticate the user.	No exceptions noted.
15.7 Password security parameters for the network have been established for the following areas in accordance with service organization policy: *Network* • Minimum password length • Password complexity • Minimum password age • Password history • Number of invalid login attempts *ABC Recordkeeping Application* • Minimum password length • Password complexity • Minimum password age • Password history • Number of invalid login attempts	Inspected the security configuration of the network and ABC Recordkeeping application to determine whether parameters have been configured for the specified areas in accordance with service organization policy.	No exceptions noted.

(continued)

Control Objective 15—Logical Security—*continued*

Controls Specified by XYZ Service Organization	Tests of Controls	Results of Tests
15.8 Direct access to the ABC Recordkeeping application database is restricted to authorized personnel. Administrators are required to "SU" to root[7] to obtain root privileges.	For a sample of administrators with access to the ABC Recordkeeping application database, inspected the related security configuration to determine whether direct access is restricted to authorized personnel and whether administrators are required to SU to root.	No exceptions noted.
15.9 Firewalls are implemented on the network to filter traffic and protect the network from external threats and vulnerabilities.	Inspected the configuration of the firewall to determine whether access rulesets are configured to filter traffic and to protect the network.	No exceptions noted.
15.10 Access to the firewall requires a user ID and password with access to the firewall ruleset[8] and configuration restricted to authorized IT personnel.	Observed that access to the firewall requires a user ID and password. Inspected the firewall configuration to determine whether administrative access is restricted to authorized IT personnel.	No exceptions noted.
15.11 A Point-to-Point Tunneling Protocol (PPTP) based virtual private network (VPN) is used to provide employees with remote access to the internal network. The VPN uses Windows active directory authentication and Microsoft PPTP 128-bit encryption.	Inspected the PPTP-based VPN configuration to determine whether remote user access is controlled via VPN technology and whether Windows authentication and 128-bit encryption is used to access the network.	No exceptions noted.
15.12 Antivirus software is installed on all servers and workstations to protect against viruses and malware. Antivirus software is configured to download virus definition updates every 90 minutes.	Inspected the configuration of the antivirus software to determine whether it is installed on servers and workstations and whether it is configured to receive virus updates every 90 minutes.	No exceptions noted.

Complementary User Entity Controls

1. **Plan sponsors are responsible for ensuring that logical access to ABC Recordkeeping application for their personnel is appropriate based on job responsibility.**

2. ...

3. ...

---

[7] *SU to root* is a way by which privileged access is assigned to a user ID.

[8] *Firewall ruleset* are the rules that govern what the firewall will allow or disallow.

Control Objective 16—Computer Operations

Controls provide reasonable assurance that application and system processing are authorized and completely and accurately executed in a timely manner and deviations, problems, and errors are identified, tracked, recorded, and resolved in a complete, accurate, and timely manner, with respect to user entities' internal control over financial reporting.

Controls Specified by XYZ Service Organization	Tests of Controls	Results of Tests
16.1 All computer jobs are scheduled using job scheduling software.	Inspected the job processing software to determine whether computer jobs are processed using job scheduling software.	No exceptions noted.
16.2 Access to the job scheduling software is restricted to authorized IT personnel. Any changes to job schedules must be approved by the vice president of IT operations.	Inspected the configuration of security over the job scheduling software to determine whether access is restricted to authorized personnel. Inspected the job scheduler to determine whether computer jobs were changed during the examination period.	No exceptions noted. The operating effectiveness of the control related to approval of changes to job schedules could not be tested because no changes were made to computer jobs during the examination period.
16.3 The job processing software logs the processing of all computer jobs and provides status alerts of job completions and failures.	For a selection of completed and failed computer jobs, inspected the computer logs to determine whether the jobs were logged and whether status alerts were produced.	No exceptions noted.
16.4 Job processing is monitored by IT operations personnel using the job scheduling software. Any job errors or deviations from scheduled processing are resolved as appropriate.	On multiple occasions during the period, observed IT operations personnel monitoring computer jobs and the actions taken to resolve processing errors.	No exceptions noted.
16.5...		

[*Note to readers: For brevity, the controls and tests of controls and results for control objectives 17–20 are not presented in this illustrative report.*]

Control Objective 17—Network Infrastructure

Controls provide reasonable assurance that network infrastructure is configured as authorized, with respect to user entities' internal control over financial reporting, to support the effective functioning of application controls to result in valid, complete, accurate, and timely processing and reporting of transactions and balances and to protect data from unauthorized changes.

Control Objective 18—Data Transmissions

Controls provide reasonable assurance that data transmissions between the service organization and its user entities and other outside entities are from authorized sources and are complete, accurate, secure, and timely, with respect to user entities' internal control over financial reporting.

Control Objective 19—Physical Security

Controls provide reasonable assurance that physical access to computer and other resources, with respect to user entities' internal control over financial reporting, is restricted to authorized and appropriate personnel.

Control Objective 20—Data Backup

Controls provide reasonable assurance that data and systems are backed up regularly and available for restoration in the event of processing errors or unexpected processing interruptions, with respect to user entities' internal control over financial reporting.

Section 5: Other Information Provided by XYZ Service Organization

- Business Continuity Planning
- ...
- Management's Response to Exceptions Identified
- ...

Example 2: Service Organization Uses Carve-Out Method for Subservice Organization, Service Organization Requires Complementary User Entity Controls and Complementary Subservice Organization Controls

Example Service Organization

Report on Example Service Organization's Description of Its Defined Contribution Recordkeeping System and on the Suitability of the Design and Operating Effectiveness of Its Controls

In example 2, Example Service Organization outsources aspects of its computer processing to a subservice organization, Computer Subservice Organization, and elects to use the carve-out method of presentation. In addition, complementary user entity and complementary subservice organization controls are required to achieve certain control objectives. Changes to this type 2 report related to Example Service Organization's use of a subservice organization and the need for complementary user entity and complementary subservice organization controls are shown in boldface italics. This report is written in narrative format and includes the following five sections:

Section 1: The independent service auditor's report

Section 2: Management of Example Service Organization's assertion

Section 3: Management of Example Service Organization's description of its system

Section 4: The service auditor's description of tests of controls and results

Section 5: Other information provided by Example Service Organization

Table of Contents

Section Number	Title of Section
1	Independent Service Auditor's Report
2	Example Service Organization's Assertion

3	Description of Example Service Organization's Defined Contribution Recordkeeping System
	    Overview of Example Service Organization
	    Scope of the Description
	    Internal Control Framework
	        Control Environment
	        Risk Assessment Process
	        Monitoring Activities
	        Information and Communications
	        Control Activities
	    Defined Contribution Plan Setup
	    Control Objectives and Related Controls[9]
	    Complementary Subservice Organization Controls
	    Complementary User Entity Controls

(continued)

---

[9] In this illustrative report, the control objectives and related controls are included in section 4, "Description of Example Service Organization's Control Objectives and Related Controls, and Independent Service Auditor's Description of Tests of Controls and Results." This avoids the need to repeat the control objectives and related controls in two sections.

Table of Contents—*continued*

Section 1: Independent Service Auditor's Report

To: Example Service Organization

Scope

We have examined Example Service Organization's description of its defined contribution recordkeeping system entitled "Example Service Organization's Description of its Defined Contribution Recordkeeping System" for processing user entities' transactions throughout the period January 1, 201X, to December 31, 201X, (description) and the suitability of the design and operating effectiveness of controls included in the description to achieve the related control objectives stated in the description, based on the criteria identified in "Example Service Organization's Assertion" (assertion). The controls and control objectives included in the description are those that management of Example Service Organization believes are likely to be relevant to user entities' internal control over financial reporting, and the description does not include those aspects of the defined contribution recordkeeping system that are not likely to be relevant to user entities' internal control over financial reporting.

The information included in section 5, "Other Information Provided by Example Service Organization," is presented by management of Example Service Organization to provide additional information and is not a part of Example Service Organization's description of its defined contribution recordkeeping system made available to user entities during the period January 1, 201X, to December 31, 201X. Information about Example Service Organization's business continuity planning and management's response to exceptions identified in the report has not been subjected to the procedures applied in the examination of the description of the defined contribution recordkeeping system and of the suitability of the design and operating effectiveness of controls to achieve the related control objectives stated in the description of the defined contribution recordkeeping system and, accordingly, we express no opinion on it.

Example Service Organization uses Computer Subservice Organization, a subservice organization, to provide hosting services. The description includes only the control objectives and related controls of Example Service Organization and excludes the control objectives and related controls of the subservice organization. The description also indicates that certain control objectives specified by Example Service Organization can be achieved only if complementary subservice organization controls assumed in the design of Example Service Organization's controls are suitably designed and operating effectively, along with the related controls at Example Service Organization. Our examination did not extend to controls of the subservice organization and we have not evaluated the suitability of the design or operating effectiveness of such complementary subservice organization controls.

The description indicates that certain control objectives specified in the description can be achieved only if complementary user entity controls assumed in the design of Example Service Organization's controls are suitably designed and operating effectively, along with related controls at the service organization. Our examination did not extend to such complementary user entity controls and we have not evaluated the suitability of the design or operating effectiveness of such complementary user entity controls.

Service Organization's Responsibilities

In section 2, Example Service Organization has provided an assertion about the fairness of the presentation of the description and suitability of the design and operating effectiveness of the controls to achieve the related control objectives stated in the description. Example Service Organization is responsible for preparing the description and its assertion, including the completeness, accuracy, and method of presentation of the description and assertion, providing the services covered by the description, specifying the control objectives and stating them in the description, identifying the risks that threaten the achievement of the control objectives, selecting the criteria stated in the assertion, and designing, implementing, and documenting controls that are suitably designed and operating effectively to achieve the related control objectives stated in the description.

Service Auditor's Responsibilities

Our responsibility is to express an opinion on the fairness of the presentation of the description and on the suitability of the design and operating effectiveness of the controls to achieve the related control objectives stated in the description, based on our examination.

Our examination was conducted in accordance with attestation standards established by the American Institute of Certified Public Accountants. Those standards require that we plan and perform the examination to obtain reasonable assurance about whether, in all material respects, based on the criteria in management's assertion, the description is fairly presented and the controls were suitably designed and operating effectively to achieve the related control objectives stated in the description throughout the period January 1, 201X, to December 31, 201X. We believe that the evidence we obtained is sufficient and appropriate to provide a reasonable basis for our opinion.

An examination of a description of a service organization's system and the suitability of the design and operating effectiveness of controls involves

- performing procedures to obtain evidence about the fairness of the presentation of the description and the suitability of the design and operating effectiveness of the controls to achieve the related control objectives stated in the description, based on the criteria referenced above.

- assessing the risks that the description is not fairly presented and that the controls were not suitably designed or operating effectively to achieve the related control objectives stated in the description.

- testing the operating effectiveness of those controls that management considers necessary to provide reasonable assurance that the related control objectives stated in the description were achieved.

- evaluating the overall presentation of the description, suitability of the control objectives stated therein, and suitability of the criteria specified by the service organization in its assertion.

Inherent Limitations

The description is prepared to meet the common needs of a broad range of user entities and their auditors who audit and report on user entities' financial statements and may not, therefore, include every aspect of the system that each individual user entity may consider important in its own particular environment. Because of their nature, controls at a service organization may not prevent, or detect and correct, all misstatements in processing or reporting transactions. Also, the projection to the future of any evaluation of the fairness of the presentation of the description, or conclusions about the suitability of the design or operating effectiveness of the controls to achieve the related control objectives, is subject to the risk that controls at a service organization may become ineffective.

Description of Tests of Controls

The specific controls tested and the nature, timing, and results of those tests are listed in section 4.

Opinion

In our opinion, in all material respects, based on the criteria described in Example Service Organization's assertion,

   a. the description fairly presents the defined contribution recordkeeping system that was designed and implemented throughout the period January 1, 201X, to December 31, 201X.

   b. the controls related to the control objectives stated in the description were suitably designed to provide reasonable assurance that the control objectives would be achieved if the controls operated effectively throughout the period January 1, 201X, to December 31, 201X, *and the subservice organization and user entities applied the complementary controls assumed in the design of Example Service Organization's controls throughout the period January 1, 201X, to December 31, 201X.*

   c. the controls operated effectively to provide reasonable assurance that the control objectives stated in the description were achieved throughout the period January 1, 201X, to December 31, 201X, *if complementary subservice organization and user entity controls assumed in the design of Example Service Organization's controls operated effectively throughout the period January 1, 201X, to December 31, 201X.*

Restricted Use

This report, including the description of tests of controls and results thereof in section 4, is intended solely for the information and use of Example Service Organization, user entities of Example Service Organization's defined contribution recordkeeping system during some or all of the period January 1, 201X, to December 31, 201X, and their auditors who audit and report on such user entities' financial statements or internal control over financial reporting and have a sufficient understanding to consider it, along with other information, including information about controls implemented by user entities themselves, when assessing the risks of material misstatement of user entities' financial statements. This report is not intended to be and should not be used by anyone other than these specified parties.

[*Service auditor's signature*]

[*Service auditor's city and state*]

[*Date of the service auditor's report*]

Section 2: Example Service Organization's Assertion

We have prepared the description of Example Service Organization's defined contribution plan recordkeeping system entitled "Example Service Organization's Description of its Defined Contribution Recordkeeping System" for processing user entities' transactions throughout the period January 1, 201X, to December 31, 201X, (description) for user entities of the system during some or all of the period January 1, 201X, to December 31, 201X, and their auditors who audit and report on such user entities' financial statements or internal control over financial reporting and have a sufficient understanding to consider it, along with other information, *including information about controls implemented by the subservice organization and user entities of the system themselves,* when assessing the risks of material misstatement of user entities' financial statements.

Example Service Organization uses Computer Subservice Organization, a subservice organization, to provide hosting services. The description includes only the control objectives and related controls of Example Service Organization and excludes the control objectives and related controls of the subservice organization. The description also indicates that certain control objectives specified by Example Service Organization can be achieved only if complementary subservice organization controls assumed in the design of Example Service Organization's controls are suitably designed and operating effectively, along with the related controls at Example Service Organization. The description does not extend to controls of the subservice organization.

The description indicates that certain control objectives specified in the description can be achieved only if complementary user entity controls assumed in the design of Example Service Organization's controls are suitably designed and operating effectively, along with related controls at the service organization. The description does not extend to controls of the user entities.

We confirm, to the best of our knowledge and belief, that

a. the description fairly presents the defined contribution recordkeeping system made available to user entities of the system during some or all of the period January 1, 201X, to December 31, 201X, for processing their transactions as it relates to controls that are likely to be relevant to user entities' internal control over financial reporting. The criteria we used in making this assertion were that the description

    i. presents how the system made available to user entities of the system was designed and implemented to process relevant user entity transactions, including, if applicable,

        (1) the types of services provided, including, as appropriate, the classes of transactions processed.

(2) the procedures, within both automated and manual systems, by which those services are provided, including, as appropriate, procedures by which transactions are initiated, authorized, recorded, processed, corrected as necessary, and transferred to the reports and other information prepared for user entities of the system.

(3) the information used in the performance of the procedures, including, if applicable, related accounting records, whether electronic or manual, and supporting information involved in initiating, authorizing, recording, processing, and reporting transactions; this includes the correction of incorrect information and how information is transferred to the reports and other information prepared for user entities.

(4) how the system captures and addresses significant events and conditions other than transactions.

(5) the process used to prepare reports and other information for user entities.

(6) services performed by a subservice organization, if any, including whether the inclusive method or the carve-out method has been used in relation to them.

(7) the specified control objectives and controls designed to achieve those objectives including, as applicable, complementary user entity controls assumed in the design of the service organization's controls.

(8) other aspects of our control environment, risk assessment process, information and communications (including the related business processes), control activities, and monitoring activities that are relevant to the services provided.

    ii. includes relevant details of changes to the service organization's system during the period covered by the description.

    iii. does not omit or distort information relevant to the service organization's system, while acknowledging that the description is prepared to meet the common needs of a broad range of user entities of the system and their user auditors and may not, therefore, include every aspect of the defined contribution recordkeeping system that each individual user entity of the system and its auditor may consider important in its own particular environment.

  b. the controls related to the control objectives stated in the description were suitably designed and operating effectively throughout the period January 1, 201X, to December 31, 201X, to achieve those control objectives *if the subservice organization and user entities applied the complementary controls assumed in the*

design of Example Service Organization's controls through-
out the period January 1, 201X, to December 31, 201X. The
criteria we used in making this assertion were that

    i. the risks that threaten the achievement of the control ob-
jectives stated in the description have been identified by
management of the service organization.

    ii. the controls identified in the description would, if oper-
ating effectively, provide reasonable assurance that those
risks would not prevent the control objectives stated in the
description from being achieved.

    iii. the controls were consistently applied as designed, includ-
ing whether manual controls were applied by individuals
who have the appropriate competence and authority.

Section 3: Description of Example Service Organization's Defined Contribution Recordkeeping System

Overview of Example Service Organization

Example Service Organization is located in Los Angeles, California, and provides defined contribution plan recordkeeping services to corporations, unions,
and nonprofit customers (user entities) across the U.S. These services are provided using a proprietary ABC Recordkeeping application developed and maintained by Example Service Organization.

Services provided as part of its defined contribution plan recordkeeping services
include the following:

- Benefit plan setup and maintenance
- ......
- ......

Scope of the Description

This description of Example Service Organization's defined contribution recordkeeping system addresses only Example Service Organization's defined contribution recordkeeping system provided to its user entities and excludes other
services provided by the Example Service Organization. The description is
intended to provide information for user entities of the defined contribution
recordkeeping system and their independent auditors who audit and report on
such user entities' financial statements to be used in obtaining an understanding of the defined contribution recordkeeping system and the controls over that
system that are likely to be relevant to user entities' internal control over financial reporting. The description of the system includes certain business process
controls and IT general controls that support the delivery of Example Service
Organization's defined contribution recordkeeping system.

Example Service Organization uses Computer Subservice Organiza-
tion, a subservice organization, to provide hosting services. The de-
scription includes only the control objectives and related controls of
Example Service Organization and excludes the control objectives and
related controls of the subservice organization.

Internal Control Framework

This section provides information about the five interrelated components of
internal control at Example Service Organization, including Example Service
Organization's

- control environment,
- risk assessment process,
- monitoring activities,
- information and communications, and
- control activities.

[*Note to readers: For brevity, and except as noted below for monitoring activities, the internal control framework of Example Service Organization would be the same as that provided in example 1 and is not repeated here.*]

Monitoring Activities

Example Service Organization employs a combination of ongoing and periodic monitoring activities to monitor that controls are functioning effectively and that risks are appropriately mitigated.

Ongoing Monitoring

The service organization uses a variety of reports and monitoring mechanisms to help ensure that controls are functioning as intended; these include

- electronic display of pending transactions and their status,
- deficiency and incident reporting,
- suspense account reporting,
- daily pricing variances,
- financial reconciliations,
- quality review results and reporting, and
- system processing monitoring and reporting.

Management regularly reviews and assesses business operations to determine that reporting and monitoring mechanisms are used and effective in managing the operations of the business, controls, and related risks.

Periodic Assessments and Monitoring

In addition to the ongoing monitoring activities described above, each business unit conducts specific evaluations of risks and controls to maximize the effectiveness of its operations.

The internal audit department performs internal audits of operations and controls to assess the effectiveness of controls. The results of audits and any identified deficiencies are reported to management as well as the audit committee. Management prepares and implements corrective measures to address any significant deficiencies.

Monitoring of the Subservice Organization

Example Service Organization uses Computer Subservice Organization, a subservice organization, to provide hosting services.

Management and the internal audit department of Example Service Organization receive and review the type 2 SOC 1® report of Computer Subservice Organization on an annual basis. In addition, through its daily operational activities, management of Example Service Organization monitors the services performed by Computer Subservice Organization to ensure that operations and controls expected to be implemented at the subservice organization are functioning effectively. Management also holds periodic calls with the subservice organization to monitor compliance with the service level agreement, stay abreast of changes planned at the hosting facility, and relay any issues or concerns to subservice organization management.

Defined Contribution Plan Setup

Plan Setup

The new accounts team works with plan sponsors, prior recordkeeping service providers, or third-party administrators to facilitate the setup and conversion of the plan in the ABC Recordkeeping application. After receipt of a signed and authorized administrative services agreement from the plan sponsor, a member of the new accounts team begins the process of preparing the file for upload into the ABC Recordkeeping application. The member of the new accounts team uses a checklist to ensure that plans are completely and accurately set up in the ABC Recordkeeping application. Once the plan is ready for upload, a new accounts team manager approves the file upload and signs the checklist as evidence that the plan was completely and accurately set up in the system.

After the plan has been set up in the system, the new accounts team manager compares the date the plan is to be implemented in the system to the date in the administrative service agreement to ensure that the plan will be implemented timely. The new accounts team manager also reconciles the dollar total of the plan entered in the system to the dollar total provided by the plan sponsor or prior recordkeeper. Any differences are investigated and resolved. The new accounts team manager completes the checklist to evidence that the reconciliation was performed and that the two dollar totals were reconciled.

After the plan has been set up in the ABC Recordkeeping application, a second new accounts team manager reviews the plan information entered in the ABC Recordkeeping application and compares information entered to plan documents to ensure the plan was completely and accurately set up in the system. The second new accounts team manager also completes the checklist to evidence that the dollar totals were reconciled. The second new accounts team manager signs the checklist to evidence that the review was performed.

[*Note to readers: For brevity, the remainder of "Example Service Organization's Description of Its Defined Contribution Recordkeeping System" is not presented in this illustrative type 2 report.*]

Control Objectives and Related Controls

Example Service Organization has specified the control objectives and identified the controls that are designed to achieve the related control objective. The specified control objectives, related controls, and complementary user entity controls are presented in section 4, "Description of Example Service Organization's Control Objectives and Related Controls, and Independent Service Auditor's Description of Tests of Controls and Results," and are an integral component of Example Service Organization's description of its defined contribution recordkeeping system.

Complementary Subservice Organization Controls (CSOC)

Example Service Organization's controls related to the defined contribution recordkeeping system cover only a portion of overall internal control for each user entity of Example Service Organization. It is not feasible for the control objectives related to recordkeeping services to be achieved solely by Example Service Organization. Therefore, each user entity's internal control over financial reporting must be evaluated in conjunction with Example Service Organization's controls and the related tests and results described in section 4 of this report, taking into account the related complementary subservice organization controls expected to be implemented at the subservice organization as described below.

	Complementary Subservice Organization Controls (CSOCs)	Related Control Objective
	Computer Subservice Organization	
1.	*Computer Subservice Organization is responsible for maintaining logical security over the servers and other hardware devices upon which the ABC Recordkeeping application is hosted.*	CO 15
2.	*Computer Subservice Organization is responsible for notifying Example Service Organization of any security incidents related to security over the servers and other hardware devices upon which the ABC Recordkeeping application is hosted.*	CO 15
3.	*Computer Subservice Organization is responsible for maintaining physical security over its data center in which the servers used to host the ABC Recordkeeping application are housed.*	CO 19
4.	.....	

Complementary User Entity Controls

Example Service Organization's controls related to the defined contribution recordkeeping system cover only a portion of overall internal control for each user entity of Example Service Organization. It is not feasible for the control objectives related to recordkeeping services to be achieved solely by Example Service Organization. Therefore, each user entity's internal control over financial reporting should be evaluated in conjunction with Example Service Organization's controls and the related tests and results described in section 4 of this report, taking into account the related complementary user entity controls identified under each control objective, where applicable.[10] In order for user entities to rely on the controls reported on herein, each user entity must evaluate its own internal control to determine whether the identified complementary user entity controls have been implemented and are operating effectively.

Section 4: Description of Example Service Organization's Control Objectives and Related Controls, and Independent Service Auditor's Description of Tests of Controls and Results

Information Provided by the Independent Service Auditor

[Note to readers: For brevity, the details of "Information Provided by the Independent Service Auditor" are not presented in this illustrative type 2 report.]

---

[10] There is no prescribed format for presenting complementary user entity controls. They may be listed in section 4 following the control objectives, tests of controls, and results of tests to which they apply or they may be listed in the description of the service organization's system in section 3. If listed in section 3, the complementary user entity controls should identify the control objectives to which they apply.

Control Objective 1—Defined Contribution Plan Setup

Controls provide reasonable assurance that defined contribution plans set up on the ABC Recordkeeping application are authorized by plan sponsors and completely and accurately processed and recorded in a timely manner.

Controls Specified by Example Service Organization	Tests of Controls	Results of Tests
1.1 New plans or plans from prior recordkeepers are accepted and entered in the ABC Recordkeeping application only after receipt of a signed and authorized administrative services agreement from the plan sponsor. A member of the service organization's new accounts team uses a new accounts setup checklist to ensure that plans are • set up completely and accurately in the ABC Recordkeeping application, based on the information in the supporting document provided by the plan sponsor or prior recordkeeper. • set up and implemented by the date specified in the administrative services agreement. • A new accounts team manager is assigned to the plan and signs the checklist to evidence that the plan was completely and accurately set up and implemented by the date specified in the administrative services agreement.	For a sample of new plans, • inspected the administrative services agreement to determine whether the agreement was signed and authorized by the plan sponsor. • inspected the new accounts setup checklist to determine whether the checklist was completed and signed by the new accounts team manager. • ...	No exceptions noted.
1.2...		

Complementary User Entity Controls

1. *Plan sponsors are responsible for ensuring that plan information provided to Example Service Organization is complete and accurate and provided on a timely basis.*

2. *Plan sponsors are responsible for ensuring that administrative agreements are signed by authorized plan sponsor personnel and provided to Example Service Organization.*

3. *Plan sponsors are responsible for ensuring that any changes to plans already set up in the ABC Recordkeeping application are sent to Example Service Organization from authorized personnel on a timely basis and that such changes are complete and accurate.*

4. *...*

[*Note to readers: For brevity, Example Service Organization's description of its controls and the independent service auditor's description of tests of controls and results for control objectives 2–20 are not presented in this illustrative type 2 report.*]

Control Objective 2—Plan Administration

Controls provide reasonable assurance that changes to plan data are authorized and completely and accurately processed and recorded in a timely manner.

Control Objective 3—Participant Administration

Controls provide reasonable assurance that participant enrollments and changes to participant data are authorized and completely and accurately processed and recorded in a timely manner.

Control Objective 4—Transfers and Changes in Investment Allocations

Controls provide reasonable assurance that participant-initiated transfers and changes in investment allocations are authorized and completely and accurately processed and recorded in a timely manner.

Control Objective 5—Contributions and Loan Payments

Controls provide reasonable assurance that contributions and loan payments are authorized and completely and accurately processed and recorded in a timely manner.

Control Objective 6—Plan Distributions and Payments

Controls provide reasonable assurance that plan distributions and payments to participants are authorized and completely and accurately processed and recorded in a timely manner.

Control Objective 7—Loan Requests

Controls provide reasonable assurance that loan requests are authorized and completely and accurately processed and recorded in a timely manner.

Control Objective 8—Fees

Controls provide reasonable assurance that requests for new fee setup, changes, corrections, terminations, and reversals are completely and accurately processed and recorded in the ABC Recordkeeping application in a timely manner.

Control Objective 9—Investment Income

Controls provide reasonable assurance that investment income, dividends, corporate actions, and participant account values are completely and accurately calculated, processed, and recorded in a timely manner.

Control Objective 10—New Fund Setup and Changes

Controls provide reasonable assurance that new funds and changes to funds are authorized and completely and accurately implemented in a timely manner.

Control Objective 11—Asset Purchases and Redemption

Controls provide reasonable assurance that asset purchase and redemption transactions are authorized and completely and accurately traded and recorded in a timely manner.

Control Objective 12—Plan and Participant Statement Reporting

Controls provide reasonable assurance that plan and participant statements are accurate, complete, and provided to or sent to the plan sponsors or participants in a timely manner in accordance with contractual agreements.

Control Objective 13—Reconciliations

Controls provide reasonable assurance that cash and security positions are completely and accurately reconciled between the ABC Recordkeeping application and the depositories in a timely manner.

Control Objective 14—System Development and Change Management

Controls provide reasonable assurance that changes to the ABC Recordkeeping application, other programs, and related data management systems are authorized, tested, documented, approved, and implemented to result in complete, accurate, and timely processing and reporting of transactions and balances relevant to user entities' financial reporting and to support user entities' internal control over financial reporting.

Control Objective 15—Logical Security

Controls provide reasonable assurance that logical access to programs, data, the ABC Recordkeeping application, and computer resources that may affect user entities' internal control over financial reporting is restricted to authorized and appropriate users and such users are restricted to performing authorized and appropriate actions.

Control Objective 16—Computer Operations

Controls provide reasonable assurance that application and system processing are authorized and completely and accurately executed in a timely manner and that deviations, problems, and errors are identified, tracked, recorded, and resolved in a complete, accurate, and timely manner, with respect to user entities' internal control over financial reporting.

Control Objective 17—Network Infrastructure

Controls provide reasonable assurance that network infrastructure is configured as authorized, with respect to user entities' internal control over financial reporting, to support the effective functioning of application controls to result in valid, complete, accurate, and timely processing and reporting of transactions and balances and to protect data from unauthorized changes.

Control Objective 18—Data Transmissions

Controls provide reasonable assurance that data transmissions between the service organization and its user entities and other outside entities are from authorized sources and are complete, accurate, secure, and timely, with respect to user entities' internal control over financial reporting.

Control Objective 19—Physical Security

Controls provide reasonable assurance that physical access to computer and other resources, with respect to user entities' internal control over financial reporting, is restricted to authorized and appropriate personnel.

Control Objective 20—Data Backups

Controls provide reasonable assurance that data and systems are backed up regularly and available for restoration in the event of processing errors or unexpected processing interruptions, with respect to user entities' internal control over financial reporting.

Section 5: Other Information Presented by Management of Example Service Organization

- Business Continuity Planning
- ......
- Management's Response to Exceptions Identified
- ......

Appendix B

Illustrative Type 2 Reports—Inclusive Method, Including Illustrative Management Representation Letters

This appendix is nonauthoritative and is included for informational purposes only.

This appendix contains two illustrative type 2 reports. In example 1, the service organization uses one subservice organization and presents that subservice organization using the inclusive method. In example 2, the service organization uses two subservice organizations and presents one subservice organization using the inclusive method and the other subservice organization using the carve-out method.

The two illustrative type 2 reports in this appendix contain all of the required components[1] of a type 2 report; however, for brevity, the illustrative reports do not include all the elements that might be described in a type 2 report. Ellipses (...) or parenthetical notes to readers indicate places where detail has been omitted from the illustrative reports.

The control objectives and controls specified by the service organizations in examples 1 and 2, as well as the tests performed by the service auditor, are presented for illustrative purposes only. They are not intended to represent a complete or standard set of control objectives, controls, or tests of controls that would be appropriate for all service organizations. The determination of the appropriate control objectives, controls, and tests of controls for a specific service organization can be made only in the context of specific facts and circumstances. Accordingly, it is expected that actual type 2 reports will contain differing control objectives, controls, and tests of controls that are tailored to the service organization that is the subject of the engagement.

This appendix also contains illustrative representation letters for the service organization and subservice organization following each example.

The following chart identifies features of each illustrative type 2 report included in this appendix.

---

[1] The required components of a type 1 report are the service auditor's report, management of the service organization's written assertion, and management's description of the service organization's system. The required components of a type 2 report are the service auditor's report, management of the service organization's written assertion, management's description of the service organization's system, and the service auditor's description of tests of controls and results thereof.

Summary of Features of Illustrative Type 2 Reports in Appendix B

Example Number and Name of Service Organization	Type of System Provided by the Service Organization	Name of Subservice Organization and Method of Presentation	Service Provided by the Subservice Organization(s)	Are Complementary User Entity Controls or Complementary Subservice Organization Controls Required by the Service Organization?	Format of the Type 2 Report
1. XYZ Service Organization	Defined contribution recordkeeping system	ABC Subservice Organization—Inclusive method	Maintenance and support of ABC Recordkeeping application	Service Organization requires complementary user entity controls	Narrative containing four report components referred to as sections 1, 2, 3, and 4
2. XYZ Service Organization	Defined contribution recordkeeping system	ABC Subservice Organization—Inclusive method and Computer Subservice Organization—Carve-out method	Maintenance and support of ABC Recordkeeping application Hosting services	Service Organization requires complementary user entity controls and complementary subservice organization controls	Narrative containing four report components referred to as sections 1, 2, 3, and 4

In example 1, XYZ Service Organization provides defined contribution record-keeping services and uses the ABC Recordkeeping application. It outsources aspects of the maintenance and support of the ABC Recordkeeping application to ABC Subservice Organization and uses the inclusive method to present ABC Subservice organization.

The following is some information about the responsibilities of the service organization and subservice organization and the features of this type 2 report with respect to the use of the inclusive method for ABC Subservice Organization:

- ABC Subservice Organization prepares a description of its application maintenance and support services; that description is included in XYZ Service Organization's description of its defined contribution recordkeeping system.

- The title of the description of the service organization's system is "Description of XYZ Service Organization's Defined Contribution Recordkeeping System"; the title of the description does not mention ABC Subservice Organization.

- "Description of XYZ Service Organization's Defined Contribution Recordkeeping System" includes the control objectives and related controls of XYZ Service Organization and the relevant controls of ABC Subservice Organization.

- The service auditor's report indicates that

  — the service auditor examined XYZ Service Organization's description of its defined contribution recordkeeping system and ABC Subservice Organization's description of its application maintenance and support services, both of which are included in the "Description of XYZ Service Organization's Defined Contribution Recordkeeping System" for processing user entities' transactions throughout the period January 1, 201X, to December 31, 201X, (description) and the suitability of the design and operating effectiveness of controls included in the description to achieve the related control objectives stated in the description, based on the criteria identified in "XYZ Service Organization's Assertion" and "ABC Subservice Organization's Assertion" (assertions).

  — ABC Subservice Organization is a subservice organization that provides application maintenance and support services to XYZ Service Organization. XYZ Service Organization's description of its defined contribution recordkeeping system includes a description of ABC Subservice Organization's application maintenance and support services used by XYZ Service Organization.

- XYZ Service Organization's assertion states that

  — XYZ Service Organization uses ABC Subservice Organization for application maintenance and support services.

  — XYZ Service Organization's description includes a description of ABC Subservice Organization's application maintenance and support services used by XYZ Service Organization.

- ABC Subservice Organization's assertion states that

  — ABC Subservice Organization provides application maintenance and support services to XYZ Service Organization and that those services are part of XYZ Service Organization's defined contribution recordkeeping system.

  — ABC Subservice Organization is responsible for the description of ABC Subservice Organization's application maintenance and support services provided to XYZ Service Organization and user entities of XYZ Service Organization's defined contribution recordkeeping system, which is included in "Description of XYZ Service Organization's Defined Contribution Recordkeeping System" ...

Example 1: Service Organization Presents Subservice Organization Using the Inclusive Method, Complementary User Entity Controls Are Required, and Description Includes Other Information

XYZ Service Organization

Report on XYZ Service Organization's Description of Its Defined Contribution Recordkeeping System and on the Suitability of the Design and Operating Effectiveness of Its Controls

Changes to this type 2 report related to the use of the inclusive method and the need for complementary user entity controls are shown in boldface italics; deleted language is indicated by strikethrough. This type 2 report includes the following sections:

Section 1: The independent service auditor's report

Section 2: Management of XYZ Service Organization's assertion, Management of ABC Subservice Organization's assertion[2]

Section 3: Management of XYZ Service Organization's description of its system, which includes aspects of ABC Subservice Organization's services

Section 4: The service auditor's description of tests of controls and results

Table of Contents

Section Number	Title of Section
1	Independent Service Auditor's Report
2	XYZ Service Organization's Assertion ABC Subservice Organization's Assertion

3	Description of XYZ Service Organization's Defined Contribution Recordkeeping System
	    Overview of XYZ Service Organization
	    Scope of the Description
	    Internal Control Framework—XYZ Service Organization
	        Control Environment
	        Risk Assessment Process
	        Monitoring Activities
	        Information and Communications
	        Control Activities
	    Internal Control Framework—ABC Subservice Organization
	    Defined Contribution Plan Setup
	    Control Objectives and Related Controls[3]
	    Complementary User Entity Controls

4	Description of XYZ Service Organization's Control Objectives and Related Controls, and Independent Service Auditor's Description of Tests of Controls and Results

---

[2] In example 1 of appendix B, there are two versions of management of ABC Subservice Organization's assertion. Version 1 of the assertion is predicated on the assumption that the service organization is responsible for evaluating whether the controls in the description, including the subservice organization's controls, are suitably designed and operating effectively to achieve the related control objectives. Version 2 of the assertion is predicated on the assumption that the subservice organization is responsible for evaluating the suitability of the design and operating effectiveness of its controls to achieve one or more related control objectives.

[3] In this illustrative report, the control objectives and related controls are included in section 4, "Description of XYZ Service Organization's Control Objectives and Related Controls, and Independent Service Auditor's Description of Tests of Controls and Results." This avoids the need to repeat the control objectives and related controls in two sections.

Section 1: Independent Service Auditor's Report

To: XYZ Service Organization

Scope

We have examined XYZ Service Organization's description of its defined contribution recordkeeping system *and ABC Subservice Organization's description of its application maintenance and support services, both of which are included in* ~~entitled~~ "Description of XYZ Service Organization's Defined Contribution Recordkeeping System" for processing user entities' transactions throughout the period January 1, 201X, to December 31, 201X, (description), and the suitability of the design and operating effectiveness of *XYZ Service Organization's and ABC Subservice Organization's* controls included in the description to achieve the related control objectives stated in the description, based on the criteria identified in "XYZ Service Organization's Assertion" *and "ABC Subservice Organization's Assertion"* (assertions). *ABC Subservice Organization is a subservice organization that provides application maintenance and support services to XYZ Service Organization. XYZ Service Organization's description includes a description of ABC Subservice Organization's application maintenance and support services used by XYZ Service Organization to process transactions for user entities, including controls relevant to the control objectives stated in the description.*[4] The controls and control objectives included in the description are those that management of XYZ Service Organization *and management of ABC Subservice Organization* believe are likely to be relevant to user entities' internal control over financial reporting, and the description does not include those aspects of the defined contribution recordkeeping system that are not likely to be relevant to user entities' internal control over financial reporting.

The description indicates that certain control objectives specified in the description can be achieved only if complementary user entity controls assumed in the design of XYZ Service Organization's controls are suitably designed and operating effectively, along with related controls at the service organization and the subservice organization. Our examination did not extend to such complementary user entity controls and we have not evaluated the suitability of the design or operating effectiveness of such complementary user entity controls.

Service Organization's Responsibilities

In section 2, XYZ Service Organization *and ABC Subservice Organization* ~~has~~ *have provided* ~~an~~*their* assertions about the fairness of the presentation of the description and suitability of the design and operating effectiveness of the controls to achieve the related control objectives stated in the description. XYZ Service Organization *and ABC Subservice Organization* ~~is~~ *are* responsible for preparing the description and *their* assertions, including the completeness, accuracy, and method of presentation of the description and assertions, providing the services covered by the description, specifying the control objectives and stating them in the description, identifying the risks that threaten the achievement of the control objectives, selecting the criteria stated in the assertions, and

---

[4] If the subservice organization's control objectives were presented separately in the description, the wording of this sentence would read: "XYZ Service Organization's description includes a description of ABC Subservice Organization's application maintenance and support services used by XYZ Service Organization to process transactions for its user entities as well as relevant control objectives and related controls of ABC Subservice Organization."

designing, implementing, and documenting controls that are suitably designed and operating effectively to achieve the related control objectives stated in the description.

Service Auditor's Responsibilities

Our responsibility is to express an opinion on the fairness of the presentation of the description and on the suitability of the design and operating effectiveness of the controls to achieve the related control objectives stated in the description, based on our examination.

Our examination was conducted in accordance with attestation standards established by the American Institute of Certified Public Accountants. Those standards require that we plan and perform the examination to obtain reasonable assurance about whether, in all material respects, based on the criteria in management's assertions, the description is fairly presented and the controls were suitably designed and operating effectively to achieve the related control objectives stated in the description throughout the period January 1, 201X, to December 31, 201X. We believe that the evidence we obtained is sufficient and appropriate to provide a reasonable basis for our opinion.

An examination of a description of a service organization's system and the suitability of the design and operating effectiveness of controls involves

- performing procedures to obtain evidence about the fairness of the presentation of the description and the suitability of the design and operating effectiveness of the controls to achieve the related control objectives stated in the description, based on the criteria in management's assertions.

- assessing the risks that the description is not fairly presented and that the controls were not suitably designed or operating effectively to achieve the related control objectives stated in the description.

- testing the operating effectiveness of those controls that management considers necessary to provide reasonable assurance that the related control objectives stated in the description were achieved.

- evaluating the overall presentation of the description, suitability of the control objectives stated therein, and suitability of the criteria specified by the service organization *and subservice organization* in *their* ~~its~~ assertionss.

Inherent Limitations

The description is prepared to meet the common needs of a broad range of user entities and their auditors who audit and report on such user entities' financial statements and may not, therefore, include every aspect of the system that each individual user entity may consider important in its own particular environment. Because of their nature, controls at a service organization *or subservice organization* may not prevent, or detect and correct, all misstatements in processing or reporting transactions. Also, the projection to the future of any evaluation of the fairness of the presentation of the description, or conclusions about the suitability of the design or operating effectiveness of the controls to achieve the related control objectives, is subject to the risk that controls at a service organization *or subservice organization* may become ineffective.

Description of Tests of Controls

The specific controls tested and the nature, timing, and results of those tests are listed in section 4.

Opinion

In our opinion, in all material respects, based on the criteria described in XYZ Service Organization's assertion *and ABC Subservice Organization's assertion,*

a. the description fairly presents XYZ Service Organization's defined contribution recordkeeping system *and ABC Subservice Organization's application maintenance and support services* that ~~was~~ *were* designed and implemented throughout the period January 1, 201X, to December 31, 201X.

b. the controls *of XYZ Service Organization and ABC Subservice Organization* related to the control objectives stated in the description were suitably designed to provide reasonable assurance that the control objectives would be achieved if the controls operated effectively throughout the period January 1, 201X, to December 31, 201X, *and user entities applied the complementary user entity controls assumed in the design of XYZ Service Organization's controls throughout the period January 1, 201X, to December 31, 201X.*

c. the controls *of XYZ Service Organization and ABC Subservice Organization* operated effectively to provide reasonable assurance that the control objectives stated in the description were achieved throughout the period January 1, 201X, to December 31, 201X, *if complementary user entity controls assumed in the design of XYZ Service Organization's controls operated effectively throughout the period January 1, 201X, to December 31, 201X.*

Restricted Use

This report, including the description of tests of controls and results thereof in section 4, is intended solely for the information and use of XYZ Service Organization, user entities of XYZ Service Organization's defined contribution recordkeeping system during some or all of the period January 1, 201X, to December 31, 201X, and their auditors who audit and report on such user entities' financial statements or internal control over financial reporting and have a sufficient understanding to consider it, along with other information, including information about controls implemented by user entities themselves, when assessing the risks of material misstatement of user entities' financial statements. This report is not intended to be and should not be used by anyone other than these specified parties.

[*Service auditor's signature*]

[*Service auditor's city and state*]

[*Date of the service auditor's report*]

Section 2: XYZ Service Organization's Assertion

We have prepared the description of XYZ Service Organization's defined contribution recordkeeping system entitled "Description of XYZ Service Organization's Defined Contribution Recordkeeping System" for processing user entities' transactions throughout the period January 1, 201X, to December 31, 201X, (description) for user entities of the system during some or all of the period January 1, 201X, to December 31, 201X, and their auditors who audit and report on such user entities' financial statements or internal control over financial reporting and have a sufficient understanding to consider it, along with other information, including information about controls implemented by user entities of the system themselves, when assessing the risks of material misstatement of user entities' financial statements.

XYZ Service Organization uses ABC Subservice Organization, a subservice organization, to provide application maintenance and support services. XYZ Service Organization's description includes a description of ABC Subservice Organization's application maintenance and support services used by XYZ Service Organization to process transactions for user entities, including controls relevant to the control objectives stated in the description.[5] *ABC Subservice Organization's assertion is presented in section 2.*

The description indicates that certain control objectives specified in the description can be achieved only if complementary user entity controls assumed in the design of XYZ Service Organization's controls are suitably designed and operating effectively, along with related controls at the service organization. The description does not extend to controls of the user entities.

We confirm, to the best of our knowledge and belief, that

    a.   the description fairly presents the defined contribution recordkeeping system made available to user entities of the system during some or all of the period January 1, 201X, to December 31, 201X, for processing their transactions as it relates to controls that are likely to be relevant to user entities' internal control over financial reporting. The criteria we used in making this assertion were that the description

        i.   presents how the system made available to user entities of the system was designed and implemented to process relevant user entity transactions including, if applicable,

           (1)   the types of services provided including, as appropriate, the classes of transactions processed.

           (2)   the procedures, within both automated and manual systems, by which those services are provided including, as appropriate, procedures by which transactions are initiated, authorized, recorded, processed, corrected as necessary, and transferred to the reports and other information prepared for user entities of the system.

           (3)   the information used in the performance of the procedures, including, if applicable, related accounting records, whether electronic or manual,

---

[5] If the subservice organization's control objectives and related controls are presented separately in the description, the wording of this sentence would read: "XYZ Service Organization's description includes a description of ABC Subservice Organization's application maintenance and support services used by XYZ Service Organization to process transactions for user entities, including relevant control objectives and related controls of ABC Subservice Organization."

and supporting information involved in initiating, authorizing, recording, processing, and reporting transactions; this includes the correction of incorrect information and how information is transferred to the reports and other information prepared for user entities.

(4) how the system captures and addresses significant events and conditions other than transactions.

(5) the process used to prepare reports and other information for user entities.

(6) services performed by a subservice organization, if any, including whether the carve-out method or the inclusive method has been used in relation to them.

(7) the specified control objectives and controls designed to achieve those objectives, including, as applicable, complementary user entity controls assumed in the design of the service organization's controls.

(8) other aspects of our control environment, risk assessment process, information and communications (including the related business processes), control activities, and monitoring activities that are relevant to the services provided.

ii. includes relevant details of changes to the service organization's system during the period covered by the description.

iii. does not omit or distort information relevant to the service organization's system, while acknowledging that the description is prepared to meet the common needs of a broad range of user entities of the system and their user auditors, and may not, therefore, include every aspect of the defined contribution recordkeeping system that each individual user entity of the system and its auditor may consider important in its own particular environment.

b. the controls related to the control objectives stated in the description were suitably designed and operating effectively throughout the period January 1, 201X, to December 31, 201X, to achieve those control objectives *if user entities applied the complementary user entity controls assumed in the design of XYZ Service Organization's controls throughout the period January 1, 201X, to December 31, 201X.* The criteria we used in making this assertion were that

i. the risks that threaten the achievement of the control objectives stated in the description have been identified by management of the service organization.

ii. the controls identified in the description would, if operating effectively, provide reasonable assurance that those risks would not prevent the control objectives stated in the description from being achieved.

    iii. the controls were consistently applied as designed, including whether manual controls were applied by individuals who have the appropriate competence and authority.

Section 2: ABC Subservice Organization's Assertion

Version 1: Illustrative Assertion by Management of Subservice Organization; Service Organization Is Responsible for Evaluating All Controls in the Description

Version 1 of ABC Subservice Organization's assertion is predicated on the assumption that the service organization is responsible for evaluating whether the controls included in the description, including the subservice organization's controls, are suitably designed and operating effectively to achieve the related control objectives.

ABC Subservice Organization's Assertion

ABC Subservice Organization provides application maintenance and support services to XYZ Service Organization. The services provided by ABC Subservice Organization are part of XYZ Service Organization's defined contribution recordkeeping system. We are responsible for the description of ABC Subservice Organization's application maintenance and support services provided to XYZ Service Organization and user entities of XYZ Service Organization's defined contribution record keeping system, which is included in "Description of XYZ Service Organization's Defined Contribution Recordkeeping System" for processing user entities' transactions throughout the period January 1, 201X, to December 31, 201X, (description) for user entities of the system during some or all of the period January 1, 201X, to December 31, 201X, and their auditors who audit and report on such user entities' financial statements or internal control over financial reporting and have a sufficient understanding to consider it, along with other information, including information about controls implemented by user entities of the system themselves, when assessing the risks of material misstatement of user entities' financial statements.

We confirm, to the best of our knowledge and belief, that

    a. the description fairly presents ABC Subservice Organization's application maintenance and support services made available to XYZ Service Organization and user entities of XYZ Service Organization's defined contribution recordkeeping system during some or all of the period January 1, 20X1, to December 31, 201X, for processing their transactions, as it relates to controls that are likely to be relevant to user entities' internal control over financial reporting. The criteria we used in making this assertion were that the description

        i. presents how the application maintenance and support services made available to XYZ Service Organization and user entities of XYZ Service Organization's defined contribution recordkeeping system were designed and implemented to process relevant user entity transactions, including, if applicable,

            (1) the types of services provided by ABC Subservice Organization including, as appropriate, the classes of transactions processed.

            (2) the procedures, within both automated and manual systems, by which those services are provided, including, as appropriate, procedures by which

transactions are initiated, authorized, recorded, processed, corrected as necessary, and transferred to the reports and other information prepared for user entities of the system.

(3) the information used in the performance of ABC Subservice Organization's procedures, including, if applicable, related accounting records, whether electronic or manual, and supporting information involved in initiating, authorizing, recording, processing, and reporting transactions; this includes the correction of incorrect information and how information is transferred to the reports and other information prepared for user entities.

(4) how the application maintenance and support services capture and address significant events and conditions other than transactions.

(5) the process used to prepare reports and other information for user entities.

(6) services performed by a subservice organization, if any, including whether the carve-out method or the inclusive method has been used in relation to them.

(7) the specified control objectives and controls designed to achieve those objectives, including, as applicable, complementary user entity controls assumed in the design of the service organization's controls.

(8) other aspects of our control environment, risk assessment process, information and communications (including the related business processes), control activities, and monitoring activities that are relevant to the services provided.

ii. includes relevant details of changes to ABC Subservice Organization's services during the period covered by the description.

iii. does not omit or distort information relevant to ABC Subservice Organization's services, while acknowledging that the description is prepared to meet the common needs of a broad range of user entities of the system and their user auditors, and may not, therefore, include every aspect of the defined contribution recordkeeping system that each individual user entity of the system and its auditor may consider important in its own particular environment.

b. ABC Subservice Organization's controls related to the control objectives stated in the description were operating as described throughout the period January 1, 201X, to December 31, 201X. The criteria we used in making this assertion were that

i. the controls were consistently applied as described, including whether manual controls were applied by individuals who have the appropriate competence and authority.

Version 2: Illustrative Assertion by Management of Subservice Organization; Subservice Organization Is Responsible for Evaluating Subservice Organization's Controls Included in Description

Version 2 of ABC Subservice Organization's assertion is predicated on the assumption that the subservice organization is responsible for evaluating the design and operating effectiveness of its controls to achieve one or more related control objectives.

To illustrate the differences in this version of the assertion as compared to version 1 of the assertion, new language is shown in boldface italics and deleted language is shown by strikethrough.

ABC Subservice Organization's Assertion

ABC Subservice Organization provides application maintenance and support services to XYZ Service Organization. The services provided by ABC Subservice Organization are part of XYZ Service Organization's defined contribution recordkeeping system. We are responsible for the description of ABC Subservice Organization's application maintenance and support services provided to XYZ Service Organization and user entities of XYZ Service Organization's defined contribution recordkeeping system, which is included in "Description of XYZ Service Organization's Defined Contribution Recordkeeping System" for processing user entities' transactions throughout the period January 1, 201X, to December 31, 201X, (description) for user entities of the system during some or all of the period January 1, 201X, to December 31, 201X, and their auditors who audit and report on such user entities' financial statements or internal control over financial reporting and have a sufficient understanding to consider it, along with other information, when assessing the risks of material misstatement of user entities' financial statements.

We confirm, to the best of our knowledge and belief, that

    a. the description fairly presents ABC Subservice Organization's application maintenance and support services made available to XYZ Service Organization and user entities of XYZ Service Organization's defined contribution recordkeeping system during some or all the period January 1, 20X1, to December 31, 201X, for processing their transactions, as it relates to controls that are likely to be relevant to user entities' internal control over financial reporting. The criteria we used in making this assertion were that the description

        i. presents how the application maintenance and support services made available to XYZ Service Organization and user entities of XYZ Service Organization's defined contribution recordkeeping system were designed and implemented to process relevant user entity transactions, including, if applicable,

            (1) the types of services provided by ABC Subservice Organization, including, as appropriate, the classes of transactions processed.

            (2) the procedures, within both automated and manual systems, by which those services are provided, including, as appropriate, procedures by which transactions are initiated, authorized, recorded, processed, corrected as necessary, and transferred

to the reports and other information prepared for user entities of the system.

 (3) the information used in the performance of ABC Subservice Organization's procedures, including, if applicable, related accounting records, whether electronic or manual, and supporting information involved in initiating, authorizing, recording, processing, and reporting transactions; this includes the correction of incorrect information and how information is transferred to the reports and other information prepared for user entities.

 (4) how the application maintenance and support services capture and address significant events and conditions other than transactions.

 (5) the process used to prepare reports and other information for user entities.

 (6) services performed by a subservice organization, if any, including whether the carve-out method or the inclusive method has been used in relation to them.

 (7) ~~the~~ *XYZ Service Organization's* specified control objectives and *ABC Subservice Organization's* controls designed to achieve those objectives, including, as applicable, complementary user entity controls assumed in the design of the subservice organization's controls.

 (8) other aspects of our control environment, risk assessment process, information and communications (including the related business processes), control activities, and monitoring activities that are relevant to the services provided.

 ii. includes relevant details of changes to ABC Subservice Organization's services during the period covered by the description.

 iii. does not omit or distort information relevant to ABC Subservice Organization's services, while acknowledging that the description is prepared to meet the common needs of a broad range of user entities of the system and their user auditors, and may not, therefore, include every aspect of the application maintenance and support services that each individual user entity of the system and its auditor may consider important in its own particular environment.

 b. ABC Subservice Organization's controls related to the control objectives stated in the description were suitably designed and operating effectively throughout the period January 1, 201X, to December 31, 201X. The criteria we used in making this assertion were that

  i. the risks that threaten the achievement of the control objectives stated in the description have been identified by management of ABC Subservice Organization.

ii. *ABC Subservice Organization's controls identified in the description would, if operating effectively, provide reasonable assurance that those risks would not prevent those control objectives stated in the description from being achieved.*

iii. ABC Subservice Organization's controls were consistently applied as designed, including whether manual controls were applied by individuals who have the appropriate competence and authority.

Section 3: Description of XYZ Service Organization's Defined Contribution Recordkeeping System

Overview of XYZ Service Organization

XYZ Service Organization is located in Los Angeles, California, and provides defined contribution plan recordkeeping services to corporations, unions, and nonprofit customers (user entities) across the U.S. These services are provided using a proprietary ABC Recordkeeping application developed and maintained by XYZ Service Organization.

Services provided as part of its defined contribution plan recordkeeping services include the following:

- Benefit plan setup and maintenance
- ......
- ......

XYZ Service Organization uses ABC Subservice Organization, a subservice organization, to provide application maintenance and support services for the ABC Recordkeeping application. The description includes the control objectives and related controls of XYZ Service Organization and the relevant controls of ABC Subservice Organization.

ABC Subservice Organization is located in Phoenix, Arizona, and provides application maintenance and support services for the ABC Recordkeeping application used by XYZ Service Organization. The ABC Recordkeeping application resides on servers in the XYZ Service Organization data center. ABC Subservice Organization provides application maintenance and support services for the ABC Recordkeeping application used by XYZ Service Organization including software enhancements or change requests originating from XYZ Service Organization.

Scope of the Description

This description of XYZ Service Organization's defined contribution recordkeeping system *and ABC Subservice Organization's application maintenance and support services used by XYZ Service Organization addresses* only XYZ Service Organization's defined contribution recordkeeping system *and ABC Subservice Organization's application maintenance and support services used by XYZ Service Organization* provided to user entities and excludes other services provided by XYZ Service Organization. The description is intended to provide information for user entities of the defined contribution recordkeeping system and their independent auditors, who audit and report on such user entities' financial statements (or internal control over financial reporting), to be used in obtaining an understanding of the defined contribution recordkeeping system and the controls over that system that are likely to be relevant to user entities' internal control over financial reporting. The description of the system includes certain business process controls and IT general controls that support the delivery of XYZ Service Organization's defined contribution recordkeeping system.

Internal Control Framework—XYZ Service Organization

This section provides information about the five interrelated components of internal control at XYZ Service Organization, including XYZ Service Organization's

- control environment,
- risk assessment process,
- monitoring activities,
- information and communications, and
- control activities.

[*Note to readers: For brevity, the remainder of XYZ Service Organization's description of the components of its internal control framework is not included here. Assume that the description of the components of XYZ Service Organization's internal control framework would be the same as the description provided in example 1 of appendix A.*]

Internal Control Framework—ABC Subservice Organization

This section provides information about the five interrelated components of internal control at ABC Subservice Organization, including ABC Subservice Organization's

- control environment,
- risk assessment process,
- monitoring activities,
- information and communications, and
- control activities.

[*Note to readers: For brevity, the remainder of ABC Subservice Organization's description of the components of its internal control framework is not included here. Assume that the description of the components of ABC Subservice Organization's internal control framework would follow the same approach used in example 1 of appendix A, with content that is tailored to the services provided by ABC Subservice Organization.*]

Defined Contribution Plan Setup

Plan Setup

The new accounts team works with plan sponsors, prior recordkeeping service providers, and third-party administrators to facilitate the setup and conversion of the plan in the ABC Recordkeeping application. After receipt of a signed and authorized administrative services agreement from the plan sponsor, a member of the service organization's new accounts team begins the process of preparing the file for upload into the ABC Recordkeeping application. The new accounts team member uses a new accounts setup checklist to ensure that the plan is completely and accurately set up in the ABC Recordkeeping application. Once the plan is ready for upload, a new accounts team manager approves the file upload and signs the checklist as evidence of approval.

After the plan has been set up in the system, the new accounts team manager compares the date the plan is to be implemented in the system to the date in the administrative services agreement to ensure that the plan will be implemented timely. The new accounts team manager also reconciles the dollar total of the plan entered in the system to the dollar total provided by the plan's sponsor or prior recordkeeper. Any differences are investigated and resolved. The new accounts team manager completes the checklist to evidence that the reconciliation was performed and that the dollar totals were reconciled.

After the plan has been set up in the ABC Recordkeeping application, a second new accounts team manager reviews the plan information entered in the ABC Recordkeeping application and compares that information to the information in the supporting document provided by the plan sponsor or prior recordkeeper to ensure that the plan was completely and accurately set up in the system. The second new accounts team manager also completes the checklist to evidence that the dollar totals were reconciled and signs the checklist to evidence that the review was performed.

Plan Conversions

For plans set up on the ABC Recordkeeping application from prior recordkeepers, the new accounts team works with...

Plan Changes

For any changes to plans already set up on the ABC Recordkeeping application, the ....

[*Note to readers: For brevity, the following aspects of XYZ Service Organization's description of its defined contribution recordkeeping system are not presented in this illustrative type 2 report.*]

Plan administration

Participant administration

Transfers and changes in investment allocation

Contributions and loan payments

Plan distributions and payments

Loan requests

Fees

Investment income

New fund setup and changes

Asset purchases and redemption

Plan and participant statement reporting

Reconciliations

System development and change management

XYZ Service Organization uses the ABC Recordkeeping application to support its defined contribution recordkeeping services provided to user entities. The ABC Recordkeeping application was developed by ABC Subservice Organization, which is located in Phoenix, AZ. XYZ Service Organization uses a licensed version of the software from ABC Subservice Organization, which is responsible for providing ongoing maintenance and support of the application through the issuance of periodic software releases. Software releases are issued at least two times a year and patches or other less significant programming changes are issued on an as-needed basis. The ABC Recordkeeping application resides on servers located in the XYZ Service Organization's data center at its Los Angeles, CA, corporate headquarters. ABC Subservice Organization's application development activities follow a standard system development life cycle (SDLC), which is outlined in ABC Subservice Organization's change management policy.

ABC Recordkeeping application changes can be initiated to (1) enhance the ABC Recordkeeping software product, (2) correct software defects, and (3) address specific requests originating from licensed users of the software, for example, XYZ Service Organization. All ABC software enhancements or change requests must be formally documented on a change request form, entered into the IT ticketing system, approved by authorized ABC personnel, and forwarded to ABC Subservice Organization's product development group for approval. All change requests initiated by XYZ Service Organization must be approved by the XYZ Service Organization chief information officer and submitted to the ABC client service representative for processing by ABC personnel.

After review by the product development group, an evaluation is performed to determine whether the nature of the change requires the completion of a requirements analysis. Once the requirements analysis is completed and reviewed, the request is either approved or denied by the product development group. If approved, the approval is documented in the ticketing system and the request is forwarded to the programming development group for development and coding. Any requests originating from user entities are returned to the user entity for approval prior to proceeding with any development activities. All such requests affecting XYZ Service Organization must be approved by the XYZ Service Organization chief information officer.

The programming development group focuses on the development and coding of the request to meet its overall design and system requirements. All development activity is performed in the development environment. Once development or coding has been completed, the change is tested in the development environment. Upon successful completion of testing, the quality assurance group is notified that the request is ready for quality assurance testing and review.

Upon notification by the development group, the quality assurance group moves the change into the quality assurance environment for testing. Testing is performed and documented by quality assurance staff and test results are reviewed and approved by quality assurance management. ABC Subservice Organization maintains separate environments for development, quality assurance testing, and production. Major system changes require user acceptance testing to determine whether the program change satisfies the user's requirements. XYZ Service Organization requires user acceptance testing for all major enhancements and changes to the ABC Recordkeeping software prior to production implementation of any such changes or releases into its production environment. All such testing is performed by the XYZ quality assurance group and must be approved by the XYZ chief information officer. The XYZ Service Organization maintains separate environments for testing and production.

If any defects or issues are found during the quality assurance testing process, they are tracked in the ABC ticketing system. Once testing is satisfactorily completed, the ABC quality assurance director approves the program change for production implementation and records the approval in the ticketing software.

The ABC technical services group is then notified that the change is ready for production implementation. Any changes ready for production implementation for XYZ Service Organization must be approved by the XYZ chief information officer before implementation into the XYZ production environment. Developers do not have access to the production environment to implement changes. ABC Subservice Organization uses the version control software tool to maintain version control over the ABC Recordkeeping program source code, and any changes to the production code are logged by the software. Access to the version control software is restricted to authorized personnel.

If an ABC Recordkeeping software problem or issue is reported by a user entity, the ABC customer service group is responsible for receiving and processing all such requests or incidents. When a call is received from the user entity, the client service representative logs the incident in the ticketing software, describes the problem, and issues a ticket. Issues are then escalated to the appropriate departments, and the problem or issue is prioritized, assigned to personnel for resolution, and documented in the ticketing application. If the problem requires a program change, the above process is followed for any IT programming requests. After the problem is resolved, the client service team notifies the customer and closes the ticket.

[Note to readers: For brevity, the following aspects of XYZ Service Organization's description of its defined contribution recordkeeping system are not presented in this illustrative type 2 report.]

Logical security

Network infrastructure

Computer operations

Data transmission

Physical security

Data backup

Control Objectives and Related Controls

XYZ Service Organization has specified the control objectives and identified the controls that are designed to achieve the related control objectives. The specified control objectives, related controls, and complementary user entity controls are presented in section 4, "Description of XYZ Service Organization's Control Objectives and Related Controls, and Independent Service Auditor's Description of Tests of Controls and Results," and are an integral component of XYZ Service Organization's description of its defined contribution recordkeeping system.

Complementary User Entity Controls

XYZ Service Organization's controls related to the defined contribution recordkeeping system cover only a portion of overall internal control for each user entity of XYZ Service Organization. It is not feasible for the control objectives related to recordkeeping services to be achieved solely by XYZ Service Organization. Therefore, each user entity's internal control over financial reporting should be evaluated in conjunction with XYZ Service Organization's controls and the related tests and results described in section 4 of this report, taking into account the related complementary user entity controls identified under each control objective, where applicable.[6] In order for user entities to rely on the controls reported on herein, each user entity must evaluate its own internal control to determine whether the identified complementary user entity controls have been implemented and are operating effectively.

Section 4: Description of XYZ Service Organization's Control Objectives and Related Controls, and Independent Service Auditor's Description of Tests of Controls and Results

Information Provided by the Independent Service Auditor

[Note to readers: For brevity, the details of "Information Provided by the Independent Service Auditor" are not presented in this illustrative report. An example of the detail in that section is included in section 4 of example 1 in appendix A.]

[Note to readers: For brevity, XYZ Service Organization's description of its controls and the independent service auditor's description of tests of controls and results for control objectives 1–13 are not presented in this illustrative type 2 report.]

Control Objective 1—Defined Contribution Plan Setup

Controls provide reasonable assurance that defined contribution plans set up on the ABC Recordkeeping application are authorized by plan sponsors and completely and accurately processed and recorded in a timely manner.

Control Objective 2—Plan Administration

Controls provide reasonable assurance that changes to plan data are authorized and completely and accurately processed and recorded in a timely manner.

Control Objective 3—Participant Administration

Controls provide reasonable assurance that participant enrollments and changes to participant data are authorized and completely and accurately processed and recorded in a timely manner.

Control Objective 4—Transfers and Changes in Investment Allocations

Controls provide reasonable assurance that participant-initiated transfers and changes in investment allocations are authorized and completely and accurately processed and recorded in a timely manner.

Control Objective 5—Contributions and Loan Payments

Controls provide reasonable assurance that contributions and loan payments are authorized and completely and accurately processed and recorded in a timely manner.

Control Objective 6—Plan Distributions and Payments

Controls provide reasonable assurance that plan distributions and payments to participants are authorized and completely and accurately processed and recorded in a timely manner.

---

[6] There is no prescribed format for presenting the complementary user entity controls. They may be listed in section 4 following the control objectives, tests of controls, and results of tests to which they apply, or they may be listed in the description of the service organization's system in section 3. If listed in section 3, the complementary user entity controls should identify the control objectives to which they apply.

Control Objective 7—Loan Requests

Controls provide reasonable assurance that loan requests are authorized and completely and accurately processed and recorded in a timely manner.

Control Objective 8—Fees

Controls provide reasonable assurance that requests for new fee setup, changes, corrections, terminations, and reversals are completely and accurately processed and recorded in the ABC Recordkeeping application in a timely manner.

Control Objective 9—Investment Income

Controls provide reasonable assurance that investment income, dividends, corporate actions, and participant account values are completely and accurately calculated, processed, and recorded in a timely manner.

Control Objective 10—New Fund Setup and Changes

Controls provide reasonable assurance that new funds and changes to funds are authorized and completely and accurately implemented in a timely manner.

Control Objective 11—Asset Purchases and Redemption

Controls provide reasonable assurance that asset purchase and redemption transactions are authorized and completely and accurately traded and recorded in a timely manner.

Control Objective 12—Plan and Participant Statement Reporting

Controls provide reasonable assurance that plan and participant statements are accurate, complete, and provided to or sent to the plan sponsors or participants in a timely manner, in accordance with contractual agreements.

Control Objective 13—Reconciliations

Controls provide reasonable assurance that cash and security positions are completely and accurately reconciled between the ABC Recordkeeping application and the depositories in a timely manner.

Control Objective 14—Systems Development and Change Management

Controls provide reasonable assurance that changes to the ABC Recordkeeping application, other programs, and related data management systems are authorized, tested, documented, approved, and implemented to result in complete, accurate, and timely processing and reporting of transactions and balances relevant to user entities' financial reporting and to support user entities' internal control over financial reporting.

Controls Specified by XYZ Service Organization	*Tests of Controls*	*Results of Tests*
14.1 All ABC Recordkeeping software enhancements or change requests must be formally documented on a change request form and approved by authorized ABC Subservice Organization IT personnel. *(Control performed by ABC Subservice Organization)*	For a selection of ABC Recordkeeping changes implemented into production, inspected the change request form to determine whether the request was approved by the authorized ABC IT personnel.	No exceptions noted.

(continued)

Control Objective 14—Systems Development and Change Management—*continued*

Controls Specified by XYZ Service Organization	Tests of Controls	Results of Tests
14.2 All ABC Recordkeeping software change requests originating from XYZ Service Organization must be approved by the XYZ Service Organization CIO.	For a selection of ABC Recordkeeping changes implemented into production and initiated by the XYZ Service Organization, inspected the change request form to determine whether the request was approved by the XYZ Service Organization CIO.	No exceptions noted.
14.3 Once a requirements analysis is performed and documented (if required), the request is either approved or denied by the ABC product development group and documented in the ticketing system. **(Control performed by ABC Subservice Organization)**	For a selection of ABC Recordkeeping changes implemented into production, inspected the change request form to determine whether the request was approved or denied by the ABC product development group in the ticketing system.	No exceptions noted.
14.4 Any change requests approved for development (and impacting XYZ Service Organization) must be approved by XYZ CIO before development activities can commence.	For a selection of ABC Recordkeeping changes implemented into production, inspected related change documentation to determine whether the change was approved by the XYZ CIO before any development activities commenced.	No exceptions noted.
14.5 ABC Subservice Organization maintains separate environments for development, quality assurance and testing, and production. **(Control performed by ABC Subservice Organization)**	Inspected the ABC Subservice Organization URLs to determine whether separate environments exist for development, testing, and production.	No exceptions noted.
14.6 Testing of the software change is performed in the ABC quality assurance test environment by ABC QA personnel and, once testing is satisfactorily completed, the ABC QA director approves the change for production implementation and documents approval in the ticketing software. **(Control performed by ABC Subservice Organization)**	For a selection of ABC Recordkeeping changes implemented into production, inspected related change documentation to determine whether testing was performed by QA and whether the change was approved by the ABC QA director for production implementation.	No exceptions noted.

(continued)

Control Objective 14—Systems Development and Change Management—*continued*

Controls Specified by XYZ Service Organization	Tests of Controls	Results of Tests
14.7 XYZ Service Organization requires user acceptance testing for all major enhancements and changes to the ABC Recordkeeping software prior to production implementation of any ABC Recordkeeping software changes or releases into its production environment. All such testing is performed by the XYZ QA group and must be approved by the XYZ CIO. XYZ Service Organization maintains separate environments for testing and production.	For a selection of ABC Recordkeeping changes implemented into production, inspected related change documentation to determine whether user acceptance testing was performed by XYZ QA personnel and approved by the XYZ CIO prior to implementation into the XYZ production environment. Inspected the XYZ Service Organization URLs to determine whether separate environments exist for testing and production.	No exceptions noted.
14.8 ABC Subservice Organization uses version control software to implement changes into production and to maintain version control over program source code. Any changes to the production code are logged by the software. ***(Control performed by ABC Subservice Organization)***	Inspected the change control software and related logs to determine whether change control software is used to (1) implement changes into production and to maintain version control over program source code and (2) to log changes to production software.	No exceptions noted.
14.9 ...		
14.10 ...		
14.11 ...		

[*Note to readers: For brevity, XYZ Service Organization's description of its controls and the independent service auditor's tests of controls and results for control objectives 15–20 are not presented in this illustrative type 2 report.*]

Control Objective 15—Logical Security

Controls provide reasonable assurance that logical access to programs, data, the ABC Recordkeeping application, and computer resources that may affect user entities' internal control over financial reporting is restricted to authorized and appropriate users and such users are restricted to performing authorized and appropriate actions.

Control Objective 16—Computer Operations

Controls provide reasonable assurance that application and system processing are authorized and completely and accurately executed in a timely manner and deviations, problems, and errors are identified, tracked, recorded, and resolved in a complete, accurate, and timely manner, with respect to user entities' internal control over financial reporting.

Control Objective 17—Network Infrastructure

Controls provide reasonable assurance that network infrastructure is configured as authorized, with respect to user entities' internal control over financial reporting, to support the effective functioning of application controls to result in valid, complete, accurate, and timely processing and reporting of transactions and balances and to protect data from unauthorized changes.

Control Objective 18—Data Transmissions

Controls provide reasonable assurance that data transmissions between the service organization and its user entities and other outside entities are from authorized sources and are complete, accurate, secure, and timely, with respect to user entities' internal control over financial reporting.

Control Objective 19—Physical Security

Controls provide reasonable assurance that physical access to computer and other resources, with respect to user entities' internal control over financial reporting, is restricted to authorized and appropriate personnel.

Control Objective 20—Data Backup

Controls provide reasonable assurance that data and systems are backed up regularly and available for restoration in the event of processing errors or unexpected processing interruptions, with respect to user entities' internal control over financial reporting.

Illustrative Representation Letter from Management of the Service Organization for Example 1: Management of the Service Organization Presents the Subservice Organization Using the Inclusive Method

[*XYZ Service Organization's Letterhead*]

[*Date*][7]

[*Service Auditor's Name*]

[*Address*]

In connection with your engagement to report on XYZ Service Organization's description of its defined contribution recordkeeping system and ABC Subservice Organization's description of its application maintenance and support services, both of which are included in "Description of XYZ Service Organization's Defined Contribution Recordkeeping System" for processing user entities' transactions throughout the period January 1, 201X, to December 31, 201X, (description)[8] and the suitability of the design and operating effectiveness of controls included in the description to achieve the related control objectives stated in the description, based on the criteria in "XYZ Service Organization's Assertion" and "ABC Subservice Organization's Assertion" (assertions), we recognize that obtaining representations from us concerning the information contained in this letter is a significant procedure in enabling you to form an opinion about whether the description fairly presents the system that was designed and implemented throughout the period January 1, 201X, to December 31, 201X, and whether the controls related to the control objectives stated in the description were suitably designed and operating effectively throughout the period January 1, 201X, to December 31, 201X, to achieve those control objectives, based on the criteria described in the assertions.

ABC Subservice Organization is a subservice organization that provides application maintenance and support services to XYZ Service Organization. The

---

[7] This representation letter should be dated as of the date of the service auditor's report.

[8] The title of management's description of the service organization's system included in management's representation letter should be the same as the title included in management's description of the service organization's system, in management's assertion, and in the service auditor's report.

services provided by ABC Subservice Organization are part of our defined contribution recordkeeping system. The description includes a description of ABC Subservice Organization's services, including controls of ABC Subservice Organization relevant to the control objectives stated in the description. ABC Subservice Organization has provided a separate assertion attached to the description relevant to the services provided by ABC Subservice Organization.

We confirm, to the best of our knowledge and belief, as of [*date of this letter*], the following representations made to you during your examination:[9]

1. We reaffirm our assertion attached to the description.

2. We have evaluated the fairness of the presentation of the description and the suitability of the design and operating effectiveness of our controls and ABC Subservice Organization's controls to achieve the related control objectives stated in the description, and all relevant matters have been considered and reflected in our evaluation and in our assertion.

3. We have disclosed to you any of the following of which we are aware:

   a. Misstatements including omissions in the description

   b. Instances in which our controls or ABC Subservice Organization's controls were not suitably designed and implemented

   c. Instances in which our controls or ABC Subservice Organization's controls did not operate effectively or as described

   d. Any communications from regulatory agencies, user entities, or others affecting the fairness of the presentation of the description or the suitability of the design or operating effectiveness of the controls to achieve the related control objectives stated in the description, including communications received between the end of the period addressed in our assertion and the date of your report

   e. All other known matters contradicting the fairness of the presentation of the description, the suitability of the design or operating effectiveness of the controls to achieve the related control objectives stated in the description, or our assertion

4. We acknowledge responsibility for our assertion and for

   a. the fairness of the presentation of the description and the suitability of the design and operating effectiveness of the controls to achieve the related control objectives stated in the description.

   b. selecting the criteria stated in our assertion and determining that the criteria are appropriate for our purposes.

5. We have disclosed to you any known events subsequent to the period covered by the description up to the date of this letter that would have a material effect on the fairness of the presentation of

---

[9] If management does not provide one or more of the written representations requested by the service auditor, the service auditor should discuss the matter with management, evaluate the effect of such exclusions, and take appropriate action, which may include disclaiming the opinion or withdrawing from the engagement.

the description, the suitability of the design or operating effectiveness of the controls to achieve the related control objectives stated in the description, or our assertion.

6. We have disclosed to you any changes in the controls that are likely to be relevant to user entities' internal control over financial reporting occurring through the date of this letter.

7. We have provided you with all information and access that is relevant to your examination and to our assertion.

8. We believe the effects of uncorrected misstatements, if any, are immaterial, individually and in the aggregate, to the fairness of the presentation of the description or the suitability of the design or operating effectiveness of the controls to achieve the related control objectives stated in the description.

9. We have responded fully to all inquiries made to us by you during the examination.

10. We have disclosed to you any of the following of which we are aware:

    a. Actual, suspected, or alleged fraud or noncompliance with laws or regulations affecting the fairness of the presentation of the description or the suitability of the design or operating effectiveness of the controls to achieve the related control objectives stated in the description

    b. Instances of noncompliance with laws and regulations or uncorrected misstatements attributable to the service organization that may affect one or more user entities

    c. Knowledge of any actual, suspected, or alleged fraud by our management or the service organization's employees that could adversely affect the fairness of the presentation of the description of the service organization's system or the completeness or achievement of the control objectives stated in the description

[*Add any other representations about matters the service auditor deems appropriate or matters relevant to special circumstances, such as industry-specific matters.*]

We understand that your examination was conducted in accordance with attestation standards established by the American Institute of Certified Public Accountants and was designed for the purpose of expressing an opinion on the fairness of the presentation of the description and on the suitability of the design and operating effectiveness of the controls to achieve the related control objectives stated in the description, based on your examination, and that your procedures were limited to those that you considered necessary for that purpose.

_____
[*Name and title of appropriate member of management*]

_____
[*Name and title of appropriate member of management*]

_____
[*Name and title of appropriate member of management*]

Illustrative Representation Letter From Management of the Subservice Organization for Example 1: Management of the Service Organization Presents the Subservice Organization Using the Inclusive Method

[*ABC Subservice Organization's Letterhead*]

[*Date*][10]

[*Service Auditor's Name*]

[*Address*]

In connection with your engagement to report on XYZ Service Organization's description of its defined contribution recordkeeping system and ABC Subservice Organization's description of its application maintenance and support services, both of which are included in "Description of XYZ Service Organization's Defined Contribution Recordkeeping System" for processing user entities' transactions throughout the period January 1, 201X, to December 31, 201X, (description)[11] and the suitability of the design and operating effectiveness of controls included in the description to achieve the related control objectives stated in the description, based on the criteria identified in "XYZ Service Organization's Assertion" and "ABC Subservice Organization's Assertion" (assertions), we recognize that obtaining representations from us concerning the information contained in this letter is a significant procedure in enabling you to form an opinion about whether the description fairly presents XYZ Service Organization's defined contribution recordkeeping system and ABC Subservice Organization's application maintenance and support services that were designed and implemented throughout the period January 1, 201X, to December 31, 201X, and whether the controls related to the control objectives stated in the description were suitably designed and operating effectively throughout the period January 1, 201X, to December 31, 201X, to achieve those control objectives, based on the criteria identified in the assertions.

The description includes certain services provided by ABC Subservice Organization to or on behalf of XYZ Service Organization. We are responsible for the portion of the description that describes ABC Subservice Organization's services and activities.

We confirm, to the best of our knowledge and belief, as of [*date of this letter*], the following representations made to you during your examination:[12]

1. We reaffirm our assertion attached to the description.

2. We have evaluated the fairness of the presentation of our portion of the description and the suitability of the design and operating effectiveness of our controls as described,[13] and all relevant matters have been considered and reflected in our evaluation and in our assertion.

---

[10] This representation letter should be dated as of the date of the service auditor's report.

[11] The title of management's description of the service organization's system included in management's representation letter should be the same as the title included in management's description of the service organization's system, in management's assertion, and in the service auditor's report.

[12] If management does not provide one or more of the written representations requested by the service auditor, the service auditor should discuss the matter with management, evaluate the effect of such exclusions, and take appropriate action, which may include disclaiming the opinion or withdrawing from the engagement.

[13] The representations in this letter are predicated on the assumption that the service organization is responsible for evaluating whether the controls, including the subservice organization's

(continued)

3. We have disclosed to you any of the following of which we are aware:

   a. Misstatements including omissions in the description

   b. Instances in which controls were not suitably designed and implemented

   c. Instances in which controls did not operate effectively or as described

   d. Any communications from regulatory agencies, user entities, or others affecting the fairness of the presentation of our portion of the description or the suitability of the design or operating effectiveness of our controls as described, including communications received between the end of the period addressed in our assertion and the date of your report

   e. All other known matters contradicting the fairness of the presentation of our portion of the description, the suitability of the design or operating effectiveness of our controls as described, or our assertion

4. We acknowledge responsibility for our assertion and for

   a. the fairness of the presentation of our portion of the description and the suitability of the design and operating effectiveness of our controls as described.

   b. selecting the criteria stated in our assertion and determining that the criteria are appropriate for our purposes.

5. We have disclosed to you any known events subsequent to the period covered by the description up to the date of this letter that would have a material effect on the fairness of the presentation of the description, the suitability of the design or operating effectiveness of our controls as described, or our assertion.

6. We have disclosed to you any changes in our controls that are likely to be relevant to user entities' internal control over financial reporting occurring through the date of this letter.

7. We have provided you with all information and access that is relevant to your examination and to our assertion.

8. We believe the effects of uncorrected misstatements, if any, are immaterial, individually and in the aggregate, to the fairness of the presentation of our portion of the description or the suitability of the design or operating effectiveness of our controls as described.

9. We have responded fully to all inquiries made to us by you during the examination.

10. We have disclosed to you any of the following of which we are aware:

    a. Actual, suspected, or alleged fraud or noncompliance with laws or regulations affecting the fairness of the presentation of the description or the suitability of the design or operating effectiveness of our controls as described

---

(footnote continued)

controls, are suitably designed and operating effectively to achieve the related control objectives. The wording of the representations should be modified to reflect the relevant responsibilities, for example, if the subservice organization were responsible for evaluating the design and operating effectiveness of its controls to achieve one or more related control objectives.

b. Instances of noncompliance with laws and regulations or uncorrected misstatements attributable to the subservice organization that may affect one or more user entities

c. Knowledge of any actual, suspected, or alleged fraud by our management or the subservice organization's employees that could adversely affect the fairness of the presentation of our portion of the description

[Add any other representations about matters the service auditor deems appropriate or matters relevant to special circumstances, such as industry-specific matters.]

We understand that your examination was conducted in accordance with attestation standards established by the American Institute of Certified Public Accountants and was designed for the purpose of expressing an opinion on the fairness of the presentation of the description and on the suitability of the design and operating effectiveness of the controls to achieve the related control objectives stated in the description, based on your examination, and that your procedures were limited to those that you considered necessary for that purpose.

_____

[Name and title of appropriate member of management]

_____

[Name and title of appropriate member of management]

_____

[Name and title of appropriate member of management]

Example 2: Service Organization Presents One Subservice Organization Using the Inclusive Method and Another Subservice Organization Using the Carve-out Method, Complementary User Entity and Complementary Subservice Organization Controls Are Required

In example 2, XYZ Service Organization outsources aspects of the maintenance and support of the ABC Recordkeeping application to ABC Subservice Organization and elects to use the inclusive method of presentation for ABC Subservice Organization. XYZ Service Organization also uses Computer Subservice Organization to provide hosting services and elects to use the carve-out method of presentation for the Computer Subservice Organization. In addition, complementary user entity and complementary subservice organization controls are required to achieve certain control objectives.

The following is some information about the responsibilities of XYZ Service Organization and ABC Subservice Organization and the features of this type 2 report with respect to the use of the inclusive method for ABC Subservice Organization:

- ABC Subservice Organization prepares a description of its application maintenance and support services; that description is included in XYZ Service Organization's description of its defined contribution recordkeeping system.

- The title of the description of the service organization's system is "Description of XYZ Service Organization's Defined Contribution Recordkeeping System"; the title does not mention ABC Subservice Organization.

- "Description of XYZ Service Organization's Defined Contribution Recordkeeping System" includes the control objectives and related controls of XYZ Service Organization and the relevant controls of ABC Subservice Organization.

- The service auditor's report indicates that

  — the service auditor examined XYZ Service Organization's description of its defined contribution recordkeeping system and ABC Subservice Organization's description of its application maintenance and support services, both of which are included in "Description of XYZ Service Organization's Defined Contribution Recordkeeping System" for processing user entities' transactions throughout the period January 1, 201X, to December 31, 201X, (description) and the suitability of the design and operating effectiveness of controls included in the description to achieve the related control objectives stated in the description, based on the criteria identified in "XYZ Service Organization's Assertion" and "ABC Subservice Organization's Assertion" (assertions).

  — ABC Subservice Organization is a subservice organization that provides application maintenance and support services to XYZ Service Organization. XYZ Service Organization's description of its defined contribution recordkeeping system includes a description of ABC Subservice Organization's application maintenance and support services used by XYZ Service Organization.

- XYZ Service Organization's assertion states that

  — XYZ Service Organization uses ABC Subservice Organization for application maintenance and support services.

  — XYZ Service Organization's description includes a description of ABC Subservice Organization's application maintenance and support services used by XYZ Service Organization.

- ABC Subservice Organization's assertion states that

  — ABC Subservice Organization provides application maintenance and support services to XYZ Service Organization and that those services form a part of XYZ Service Organization's defined contribution recordkeeping system.

  — ABC Subservice Organization is responsible for the description of ABC Subservice Organization's application maintenance and support services provided to XYZ Service Organization and user entities of XYZ Service Organization's defined contribution recordkeeping system, which is included in the "Description of XYZ Service Organization's Defined Contribution Recordkeeping System" ...

Changes to this type 2 report related to the use of the inclusive method and the need for complementary user entity and complementary subservice organization controls are shown in boldface italics; deleted language is indicated by strikethrough. This type 2 report includes the following sections:

Section 1: The independent service auditor's report

Section 2: Management of XYZ Service Organization's assertion, Management of ABC Subservice Organization's assertion

Section 3: Management of XYZ Service Organization's description of its system and aspects of ABC Subservice Organization's services

Section 4: The service auditor's description of tests of controls and results

Report on XYZ Service Organization's Description of Its Defined Contribution Recordkeeping System and on the Suitability of the Design and Operating Effectiveness of Its Controls

Table of Contents

Section 1: Independent Service Auditor's Report

To: XYZ Service Organization

Scope

We have examined XYZ Service Organization's description of its defined contribution recordkeeping system and ***ABC Subservice Organization's description of its application maintenance and support services, both of which are included in*** ~~entitled~~ "Description of XYZ Service Organization's Defined Contribution Recordkeeping System" for processing user entities' transactions throughout the period January 1, 201X, to December 31, 201X, (description) and the suitability of the design and operating effectiveness of ***XYZ Service Organization's and ABC Subservice Organization's*** controls included in the description to achieve the related control objectives stated in the description, based on the criteria identified in "XYZ Service Organization's Assertion" ***and "ABC Subservice Organization's Assertion"*** (assertion**s**). ***ABC***

---

[14] In this illustrative report, the control objectives and related controls are included in section 4, "Description of XYZ Service Organization's Control Objectives and Related Controls, and Independent Service Auditor's Description of Tests of Controls and Results." This avoids the need to repeat the control objectives and related controls in two sections.

Subservice Organization is a subservice organization that provides application maintenance and support services to XYZ Service Organization. XYZ Service Organization's description includes a description of ABC Subservice Organization's application maintenance and support services used by XYZ Service Organization to process transactions for its user entities, including controls relevant to control objectives stated in the description. The controls and control objectives included in the description are those that management of XYZ Service Organization *and management of ABC Subservice Organization* believes are likely to be relevant to user entities' internal control over financial reporting, and the description does not include those aspects of the defined contribution recordkeeping system that are not likely to be relevant to user entities' internal control over financial reporting.

XYZ Service Organization uses Computer Subservice Organization, a subservice organization, to provide hosting services. The description includes only the control objectives and related controls of XYZ Service Organization and ABC Subservice Organization and excludes the control objectives and related controls of the Computer Subservice Organization. The description also indicates that certain control objectives specified by XYZ Service Organization can be achieved only if complementary subservice organization controls assumed in the design of XYZ Service Organization's controls are suitably designed and operating effectively, along with the related controls at XYZ Service Organization. Our examination did not extend to controls of the Computer Subservice Organization, and we have not evaluated the suitability of the design or operating effectiveness of such complementary Computer Subservice Organization controls.

The description indicates that certain control objectives specified in the description can be achieved only if complementary user entity controls assumed in the design of XYZ Service Organization's controls are suitably designed and operating effectively, along with related controls at the service organization. Our examination did not extend to such complementary user entity controls, and we have not evaluated the suitability of the design or operating effectiveness of such complementary user entity controls.

Service Organization's Responsibilities

In section 2, XYZ Service Organization *and ABC Subservice Organization* ~~has~~ *have* provided ~~an~~ *their* assertions about the fairness of the presentation of the description and suitability of the design and operating effectiveness of the controls to achieve the related control objectives stated in the description. XYZ Service Organization *and ABC Subservice Organization* ~~is~~ *are* responsible for preparing the description and *their* assertions, including the completeness, accuracy, and method of presentation of the description and assertions, providing the services covered by the description, specifying the control objectives and stating them in the description, identifying the risks that threaten the achievement of the control objectives, selecting the criteria stated in the assertions, and designing, implementing, and documenting controls that are suitably designed and operating effectively to achieve the related control objectives stated in the description.

Service Auditor's Responsibilities

Our responsibility is to express an opinion on the fairness of the presentation of the description and on the suitability of the design and operating effectiveness of the controls to achieve the related control objectives stated in the description, based on our examination.

Our examination was conducted in accordance with attestation standards established by the American Institute of Certified Public Accountants. Those standards require that we plan and perform the examination to obtain reasonable assurance about whether, in all material respects, based on the criteria in management's assertions, the description is fairly presented and the controls were suitably designed and operating effectively to achieve the related control objectives stated in the description throughout the period January 1, 201X, to December 31, 201X. We believe that the evidence we obtained is sufficient and appropriate to provide a reasonable basis for our opinion.

An examination of a description of a service organization's system and the suitability of the design and operating effectiveness of controls involves

- performing procedures to obtain evidence about the fairness of the presentation of the description and the suitability of the design and operating effectiveness of the controls to achieve the related control objectives stated in the description, based on the criteria in management's assertions.

- assessing the risks that the description is not fairly presented and that the controls were not suitably designed or operating effectively to achieve the related control objectives stated in the description.

- testing the operating effectiveness of those controls that management considers necessary to provide reasonable assurance that the related control objectives stated in the description were achieved.

- evaluating the overall presentation of the description, suitability of the control objectives stated therein, and suitability of the criteria specified by the service organization *and subservice organization* in *their* ~~its~~ assertions.

Inherent Limitations

The description is prepared to meet the common needs of a broad range of user entities and their auditors who audit and report on user entities' financial statements and may not, therefore, include every aspect of the system that each individual user entity may consider important in its own particular environment. Because of their nature, controls at a *service organization or a subservice organization* may not prevent, or detect and correct, all misstatements in processing or reporting transactions. Also, the projection to the future of any evaluation of the fairness of the presentation of the description, or conclusions about the suitability of the design or operating effectiveness of the controls to achieve the related control objectives, is subject to the risk that controls at a service organization *or a subservice organization* may become ineffective.

Description of Tests of Controls

The specific controls tested and the nature, timing, and results of those tests are listed in section 4.

Opinion

In our opinion, in all material respects, based on the criteria described in XYZ Service Organization's assertion *and ABC Subservice Organization's assertion*

    a. the description fairly presents XYZ Service Organization's defined contribution recordkeeping system *and ABC Subservice Organization's application maintenance and support services used by XYZ Service Organization* that ~~was~~ *were* designed and implemented throughout the period January 1, 201X, to December 31, 201X.

    b. the controls *of XYZ Service Organization and ABC Subservice Organization* related to the control objectives stated in the description were suitably designed to provide reasonable assurance that the control objectives would be achieved if the controls operated effectively throughout the period January 1, 201X, to December 31, 201X, *and subservice organizations and user entities applied the complementary controls assumed in the design of XYZ Service Organization's controls throughout the period January 1, 201X, to December 31, 201X.*

    c. the controls *of XYZ Service Organization and ABC Subservice Organization* operated effectively to provide reasonable assurance that the control objectives stated in the description were achieved throughout the period January 1, 201X, to December 31, 201X, *if complementary subservice organization and user entity controls assumed in the design of XYZ Service Organization's controls operated effectively throughout the period January 1, 201X, to December 31, 201X.*

Restricted Use

This report, including the description of tests of controls and results thereof in section 4, is intended solely for the information and use of XYZ Service Organization, user entities of XYZ Service Organization's defined contribution recordkeeping system during some or all of the period January 1, 201X, to December 31, 201X, and their auditors who audit and report on such user entities' financial statements or internal control over financial reporting and have a sufficient understanding to consider it, along with other information, including information about controls implemented by user entities themselves, when assessing the risks of material misstatement of user entities' financial statements. This report is not intended to be and should not be used by anyone other than these specified parties.

[*Service auditor's signature*]

[*Service auditor's city and state*]

[*Date of the service auditor's report*]

Section 2: XYZ Service Organization's Assertion

We have prepared the description of XYZ Service Organization's defined contribution recordkeeping system entitled "Description of XYZ Service Organization's Defined Contribution Recordkeeping System" for processing user entities' transactions throughout the period January 1, 201X, to December 31, 201X, (description) for user entities of the system during some or all of the period January 1, 201X, to December 31, 201X, and their auditors who audit and report on such user entities' financial statements or internal control over financial reporting and have a sufficient understanding to consider it, along with other information, including information about controls implemented by user entities of the system themselves, when assessing the risks of material misstatement of user entities' financial statements.

XYZ Service Organization uses ABC Subservice Organization, a subservice organization, to provide application maintenance and support services. XYZ Service Organization's description includes a description of ABC Subservice Organization's application maintenance and support services used by XYZ Service Organization to process transactions for user entities, including controls relevant to the control objectives stated in the description.[15] *ABC Subservice Organization's assertion is presented in section 2.*

XYZ Service Organization also uses Computer Subservice Organization, a subservice organization, to provide hosting services. The description includes only the control objectives and related controls of XYZ Service Organization and ABC Subservice Organization and excludes the control objectives and related controls of the hosting subservice organization. The description also indicates that certain control objectives specified by XYZ Service Organization in the description can be achieved only if complementary subservice organization controls assumed in the design of XYZ Service Organization's controls are suitably designed and operating effectively, along with the related controls at XYZ Service Organization. The description does not extend to controls of the Computer Subservice Organization.

The description indicates that certain control objectives specified in the description can be achieved only if complementary user entity controls assumed in the design of XYZ Service Organization's controls are suitably designed and operating effectively, along with related controls at the service organization. The description does not extend to controls of the user entities.

We confirm, to the best of our knowledge and belief, that

    a. the description fairly presents the defined contribution recordkeeping system made available to user entities of the system during some or all of the period January 1, 201X, to December 31, 201X, for processing their transactions as it relates to controls that are likely to be relevant to user entities' internal control over financial reporting. The criteria we used in making this assertion were that the description

        i. presents how the system made available to user entities of the system was designed and implemented to process relevant user entity transactions including, if applicable,

            (1) the types of services provided, including, as appropriate, the classes of transactions processed.

---

[15] If the control objectives and related controls for the subservice organization are presented separately in the description, the service auditor may consider changing the wording of this sentence to read: "XYZ Service Organization's description includes a description of ABC Subservice Organization's application maintenance and support services used by XYZ Service Organization to process transactions for user entities, including relevant control objectives and related controls of ABC Subservice Organization."

(2) the procedures, within both automated and manual systems, by which those services are provided, including, as appropriate, procedures by which transactions are initiated, authorized, recorded, processed, corrected as necessary, and transferred to the reports and other information prepared for user entities of the system.

(3) the information used in the performance of the procedures, including, if applicable, related accounting records, whether electronic or manual, and supporting information involved in initiating, authorizing, recording, processing, and reporting transactions; this includes the correction of incorrect information and how information is transferred to the reports and other information prepared for user entities.

(4) how the system captures and addresses significant events and conditions other than transactions.

(5) the process used to prepare reports and other information for user entities.

(6) services performed by a subservice organization, if any, including whether the inclusive method or the carve-out method has been used in relation to them.

(7) the specified control objectives and controls designed to achieve those objectives, including, as applicable, complementary user entity controls assumed in the design of the service organization's controls.

(8) other aspects of our control environment, risk assessment process, information and communications (including the related business processes), control activities, and monitoring activities that are relevant to the services provided.

ii. includes relevant details of changes to the service organization's system during the period covered by the description.

iii. does not omit or distort information relevant to the service organization's system, while acknowledging that the description is prepared to meet the common needs of a broad range of user entities of the system and their user auditors, and may not, therefore, include every aspect of the defined contribution recordkeeping system that each individual user entity of the system and its auditor may consider important in its own particular environment.

b. the controls related to the control objectives stated in the description were suitably designed and operating effectively throughout the period January 1, 201X, to December 31, 201X, to achieve those control objectives *if subservice organizations and user entities applied the complementary controls assumed in the design of*

XYZ Service Organization's controls throughout the period January 1, 201X, to December 31, 201X. The criteria we used in making this assertion were that

    i. the risks that threaten the achievement of the control objectives stated in the description have been identified by management of the service organization.

    ii. the controls identified in the description would, if operating effectively, provide reasonable assurance that those risks would not prevent the control objectives stated in the description from being achieved.

    iii. the controls were consistently applied as designed, including whether manual controls were applied by individuals who have the appropriate competence and authority.

Section 2: ABC Subservice Organization's Assertion

This assertion is predicated on the assumption that the service organization is responsible for evaluating whether the controls included in the description, including the subservice organization's controls, are suitably designed and operating effectively to achieve the related control objectives.

ABC Subservice Organization provides application maintenance and support services to XYZ Service Organization. The services provided by ABC Subservice Organization are part of XYZ Service Organization's defined contribution recordkeeping system. We are responsible for the description of ABC Subservice Organization's application maintenance and support services provided to XYZ Service Organization and user entities of XYZ Service Organization's defined contribution recordkeeping system, which is included in "Description of XYZ Service Organization's Defined Contribution Recordkeeping System" for processing user entities' transactions throughout the period January 1, 201X, to December 31, 201X, (description) for user entities of the system during some or all of the period January 1, 201X, to December 31, 201X, and their auditors who audit and report on such user entities' financial statements or internal control over financial reporting and have a sufficient understanding to consider it, along with other information, when assessing the risks of material misstatement of user entities' financial statements.

We confirm, to the best of our knowledge and belief, that

    a. the description fairly presents ABC Subservice Organization's application maintenance and support services made available to XYZ Service Organization and user entities of XYZ Service Organization's defined contribution recordkeeping system during some or all of the period January 1, 20X1, to December 31, 201X, for processing their transactions as it relates to controls that are likely to be relevant to user entities' internal control over financial reporting. The criteria we used in making this assertion were that the description

        i. presents how the application maintenance and support services made available to XYZ Service Organization and user entities of XYZ Service Organization's defined contribution recordkeeping system were designed and implemented to process relevant user entity transactions including, if applicable,

(1) the types of services provided by ABC Subservice Organization, including, as appropriate, the classes of transactions processed.

(2) the procedures, within both automated and manual systems, by which those services are provided, including, as appropriate, procedures by which transactions are initiated, authorized, recorded, processed, corrected as necessary, and transferred to the reports and other information prepared for user entities of the system.

(3) the information used in the performance of ABC Subservice Organization's procedures, including, if applicable, related accounting records, whether electronic or manual, and supporting information involved in initiating, authorizing, recording, processing, and reporting transactions; this includes the correction of incorrect information and how information is transferred to the reports and other information prepared for user entities.

(4) how the application maintenance and support services capture and address significant events and conditions other than transactions.

(5) the process used to prepare reports and other information for user entities.

(6) services performed by a subservice organization, if any, and whether the carve-out method or the inclusive method has been used in relation to them.

(7) the specified control objectives and controls designed to achieve those objectives including, as applicable, complementary user entity controls assumed in the design of the service organization's controls.

(8) other aspects of our control environment, risk assessment process, information and communications (including the related business processes), control activities, and monitoring activities that are relevant to the services provided.

ii. includes relevant details of changes to ABC Subservice Organization's services during the period covered by the description.

iii. does not omit or distort information relevant to ABC Subservice Organization's services, while acknowledging that the description is prepared to meet the common needs of a broad range of user entities of the system and their user auditors, and may not, therefore, include every aspect of the application maintenance and support services that each individual user entity of the system and its auditor may consider important in its own particular environment.

     b. ABC Subservice Organization's controls related to the control objectives stated in the description were operating as described throughout the period January 1, 201X, to December 31, 201X. The criteria we used in making this assertion were that

         i. ABC Subservice Organization's controls were consistently applied as described, including whether manual controls were applied by individuals who have the appropriate competence and authority.

Section 3: Description of XYZ Service Organization's Defined Contribution Recordkeeping System

Overview of XYZ Service Organization

XYZ Service Organization is located in Los Angeles, California, and provides defined contribution plan recordkeeping services to corporations, unions, and nonprofit customers (user entities) across the U.S. These services are provided using a proprietary ABC Recordkeeping application system that was developed and is maintained by XYZ Service Organization.

Services provided as part of its defined contribution plan recordkeeping services include the following:

- Benefit plan setup and maintenance
- ......
- ......

XYZ Service Organization uses ABC Subservice Organization, a subservice organization, to provide application maintenance and support services. XYZ Service Organization also uses Computer Subservice Organization, a subservice organization, to provide hosting services.

ABC Subservice Organization

ABC Subservice Organization is located in Phoenix, Arizona, and provides application maintenance and support services for the ABC Recordkeeping application used by XYZ Service Organization. The ABC Recordkeeping application resides on servers in the Computer Subservice Organization's data center. ABC Subservice Organization provides the following services to XYZ Service Organization:

- *Application maintenance and support services for the ABC Recordkeeping application used by XYZ Service Organization including software enhancements or change requests originating from XYZ Service Organization*

Computer Subservice Organization

ABC Subservice Organization is located in Los Angeles, California, and provides computer hosting services for XYZ Service Organization. The ABC Recordkeeping application resides on servers hosted by Computer Subservice Organization at its data center in Los Angeles, California.

The description includes the control objectives and related controls of XYZ Service Organization and the relevant controls of ABC Subservice Organization and excludes the control objectives and related controls of the Computer Subservice Organization.

Scope of the Description

In accordance with the criteria in management's assertion, this description includes a description of XYZ Service Organization's defined contribution recordkeeping system provided to its user entities *and ABC Subservice Organization's application maintenance and support services used by XYZ Service Organization and excludes the control objectives and related controls of the Computer Subservice Organization.* The description is intended to provide information for user entities and their independent auditors to obtain an understanding of the system and controls in place over XYZ Service Organization's defined contribution recordkeeping system that are likely to be relevant to a user entity's internal control over financial reporting. The description of the system includes certain business process controls and information technology general controls that support the delivery of XYZ Service Organization's defined contribution recordkeeping system.

Internal Control Framework—XYZ Service Organization

This section provides information about the five interrelated components of control at XYZ Service Organization, including

- control environment,
- risk assessment,
- monitoring activities.
- information and communications, and
- control activities.

[*Note to readers: For brevity, and except as noted below for monitoring activities, the remainder of XYZ Service Organization's description of the components of its internal control framework are not included here. Assume that the description of the components of XYZ Service Organization's internal control framework would be the same as the description provided in example 1 of appendix A.*]

XYZ Service Organization employs a combination of ongoing and periodic monitoring activities to monitor that controls are functioning effectively and that risks are appropriately mitigated.

Ongoing Monitoring

The service organization uses a variety of reports and monitoring mechanisms to help ensure that controls are functioning as intended; these include

- electronic display of pending transactions and their status,
- deficiency and incident reporting,
- suspense account reporting,
- daily pricing variances,
- financial reconciliations,
- quality review results and reporting, and
- system processing monitoring and reporting.

Management regularly reviews and assesses business operations to determine that reporting and monitoring mechanisms are used and effective in managing the operations of the business, controls, and related risks.

Periodic Assessments and Monitoring

In addition to the ongoing monitoring activities described above, each business unit conducts specific evaluations of risks and controls to maximize the effectiveness of its operations.

The internal audit department performs internal audits of operations and controls to assess the effectiveness of controls. The results of audits and any identified deficiencies are reported to management as well as the audit committee. Management prepares and implements corrective measures to address any significant deficiencies.

Monitoring of the Subservice Organization

XYZ Service Organization uses Computer Subservice Organization, a subservice organization, to provide hosting services.

Management and Internal Audit of XYZ Service Organization receive and review the type 2 SOC 1® report of Computer Subservice Organization on annual basis. In addition, through its daily operational activities, management of XYZ Service Organization monitors the services performed by the Computer Subservice Organization to ensure operations and controls expected to be implemented at the subservice organization are functioning effectively. Management also holds periodic calls with the subservice organization to monitor compliance with the service level agreement, stay abreast of changes planned at the hosting facility, and to communicate any issues or concerns to Computer Subservice Organization management.

Internal Control Framework—ABC Subservice Organization

This section provides information about the five interrelated components of control at ABC Subservice Organization, including

- control environment,
- risk assessment,
- monitoring activities,
- information and communications, and
- control activities.

[Note to readers: For brevity, the remainder of ABC Subservice Organization's description of the components of its internal control framework is not included here. Assume that the description of the components of ABC Subservice Organization's internal control framework would follow the same approach used in example 1 of appendix A, with content that is tailored to the services provided by ABC Subservice Organization.]

[Note to readers: For brevity, the description of XYZ Service Organization's defined contribution recordkeeping system is not presented here and would be the same as the description provided in example 1 of appendix B.]

Control Objectives and Related Controls

XYZ Service Organization has specified the control objectives and identified the controls that are designed to achieve the stated control objectives. The specified control objectives, related controls, and complementary user entity controls are presented in section 4, "Description of XYZ Service Organization's Control Objectives and Related Controls, and Independent Service Auditor's Description of Tests of Controls and Results," and are an integral component of XYZ Service Organization's description of its defined contribution recordkeeping system.

Complementary Subservice Organization Controls (CSOC)

XYZ Service Organization's controls relating to the defined contribution recordkeeping system cover only a portion of the overall internal control structure of each user entity of XYZ Service Organization. It is not feasible for the control objectives relating to recordkeeping services to be solely achieved by XYZ Service Organization. Therefore, each user entity's internal control over financial reporting must be evaluated in conjunction with XYZ Service Organization's controls and related testing detailed in section 4 of this report, taking into account the complementary subservice organization controls expected to be implemented at the subservice organization as described below.

	Complementary Subservice Organization Control (CSOCs)	*Related Control Objectives (CO)*
	Computer Subservice Organization	
1.	*The Computer Subservice Organization is responsible for maintaining logical security over the servers and other hardware devices upon which the ABC Recordkeeping application is hosted.*	*CO 16*
2.	*The Computer Subservice Organization is responsible for notifying XYZ Service Organization of any security incidents relating to security over the servers and other hardware devices upon which the ABC Recordkeeping application is hosted.*	*CO 16*
3.	*The Computer Subservice Organization is responsible for maintaining physical security over its data center in which the servers used to host the ABC Recordkeeping application are housed.*	*CO 20*
4.	.....	

Complementary User Entity Controls

XYZ Service Organization's controls relating to the defined contribution recordkeeping system cover only a portion of the overall internal control structure of each user entity of XYZ Service Organization. It is not feasible for the control objectives relating to recordkeeping services to be solely achieved by XYZ Service Organization. Therefore, each user entity's internal control over financial reporting must be evaluated in conjunction with XYZ Service Organization's controls and related testing detailed in section 4 of this report, taking into account the related complementary user entity controls identified under each control objective, where applicable.[16] In order for user entities to rely on the controls reported on herein, each user entity must evaluate its own internal control structure to determine if the identified complementary user entity controls are in place.

---

[16] There is no prescribed format for presenting complementary user entity controls. They may be listed in section 4 following the control objectives, tests of controls, and results of tests to which they apply, or they may be listed in the description of the service organization's system in section 3. If listed in section 3, the complementary user entity controls should identify the control objectives to which they apply.

Section 4: Description of XYZ Service Organization's Control Objectives and Related Controls, and Independent Service Auditor's Description of Tests of Controls and Results

Information Provided by the Independent Service Auditor

[*Note to readers: For brevity, the details of "Information Provided by the Independent Service Auditor" are not presented in this illustrative report. An example of the detail in that section is included in section 4 of example 1 in appendix A.*]

[*Note to readers: For brevity, the XYZ Service Organization's description of its controls and the independent service auditor's description of tests of controls and results for control objectives 1–20 are not presented in this illustrative type 2 report.*]

Control Objective 1—Defined Contribution Plan Setup

Controls provide reasonable assurance that defined contribution plans set up on the ABC Recordkeeping application are authorized by plan sponsors and completely and accurately processed and recorded on a timely basis.

Control Objective 2—Plan Administration

Controls provide reasonable assurance that changes to plan data are authorized and completely and accurately processed and recorded in a timely manner.

Control Objective 3—Participant Administration

Controls provide reasonable assurance that participant enrollments and changes to participant data are authorized and completely and accurately processed and recorded in a timely manner.

Control Objective 4—Transfers and Changes in Investment Allocations

Controls provide reasonable assurance that participant-initiated transfers and changes in investment allocations are authorized and completely and accurately processed and recorded in a timely manner.

Control Objective 5—Contributions and Loan Payments

Controls provide reasonable assurance that contributions and loan payments are authorized and completely and accurately processed and recorded in a timely manner.

Control Objective 6—Plan Distributions and Payments

Controls provide reasonable assurance that plan distributions and payments to participants are authorized and completely and accurately processed and recorded in a timely manner.

Control Objective 7—Loan Requests

Controls provide reasonable assurance that loan requests are authorized and completely and accurately processed and recorded in a timely manner.

Control Objective 8—Fees

Controls provide reasonable assurance that requests for new fee setup, changes, corrections, terminations, and reversals are completely and accurately processed and recorded in the ABC Recordkeeping application in a timely manner.

Control Objective 9—Investment Income

Controls provide reasonable assurance that investment income, dividends, corporate actions, and participant account values are completely and accurately calculated, processed and recorded in a timely manner.

Control Objective 10—New Fund Setup and Changes

Controls provide reasonable assurance that new funds and changes to funds are authorized and completely and accurately implemented in a timely manner.

Control Objective 11—Asset Purchases and Redemption

Controls provide reasonable assurance that asset purchase and redemption transactions are authorized and completely and accurately traded and recorded in a timely manner.

Control Objective 12—Plan and Participant Statement Reporting

Controls provide reasonable assurance that plan and participant statements are complete, accurate, and provided to or sent to the plan sponsors or participants in a timely manner, in accordance with contractual agreements.

Control Objective 13—Reconciliations

Controls provide reasonable assurance that cash and security positions are completely and accurately reconciled between the ABC Recordkeeping application and the depositories in a timely manner.

Control Objective 14—Systems Development and Change Management

Controls provide reasonable assurance that changes to the ABC Recordkeeping application, programs, and related data management systems are authorized, tested, documented, approved, and implemented to result in complete, accurate, and timely processing and reporting of transactions and balances relevant to user entities' financial reporting and to support user entities' internal control over financial reporting.

Control Objective 15—Logical Security

Controls provide reasonable assurance that logical access to programs, data, the ABC Recordkeeping application, and computer resources is restricted, with respect to user entities' internal control over financial reporting, to authorized and appropriate users and such users are restricted to performing authorized and appropriate actions.

Control Objective 16—Computer Operations

Controls provide reasonable assurance that application and system processing are authorized and executed in a complete, accurate, and timely manner and deviations, problems, and errors are identified, tracked, recorded, and resolved in a complete, accurate, and timely manner, with respect to user entities' internal control over financial reporting.

Control Objective 17—Network Infrastructure

Controls provide reasonable assurance that network infrastructure is configured as authorized, with respect to user entities' internal control over financial reporting, to support the effective functioning of application controls to result in valid, complete, accurate, and timely processing and reporting of transactions and balances and to protect data from unauthorized changes.

Control Objective 18—Data Transmissions

Controls provide reasonable assurance that data transmissions between the service organization and its user entities and other outside entities are from authorized sources and are complete, accurate, secure, and timely, with respect to user entities' internal control over financial reporting.

Control Objective 19—Physical Security

Controls provide reasonable assurance that physical access to computer and other resources, with respect to user entities' internal control over financial reporting, is restricted to authorized and appropriate personnel.

Control Objective 20—Data Backup

Controls provide reasonable assurance that data and systems are backed up regularly and available for restoration in the event of processing errors or unexpected processing interruptions, with respect to user entities' internal control over financial reporting.

Illustrative Representation Letter From Management of the Service Organization for Example 2: Management of the Service Organization Presents the Subservice Organization

Using the Inclusive Method

[*XYZ Service Organization's Letterhead*]

[*Date*][17]

[*Service Auditor's Name*]

[*Address*]

In connection with your engagement to report on XYZ Service Organization's description of its defined contribution recordkeeping system and ABC Subservice Organization's description of its application maintenance and support services, both of which are included in "Description of XYZ Service Organization's Defined Contribution Recordkeeping System" for processing user entities' transactions throughout the period January 1, 201X, to December 31, 201X, (description)[18] and the suitability of the design and operating effectiveness of controls included in the description to achieve the related control objectives stated in the description, based on the criteria in "XYZ Service Organization's Assertion" and "ABC Subservice Organization's Assertion" (assertions), we recognize that obtaining representations from us concerning the information contained in this letter is a significant procedure in enabling you to form an opinion about whether the description fairly presents the system that was designed and implemented throughout the period January 1, 201X, to December 31, 201X, and whether the controls related to the control objectives stated in the description were suitably designed and operating effectively throughout the period January 1, 201X, to December 31, 201X, to achieve those control objectives, based on the criteria described in the assertions.

ABC Subservice Organization is a subservice organization that provides application maintenance and support services to XYZ Service Organization. The services provided by ABC Subservice Organization are part of our defined contribution recordkeeping system. The description includes a description of ABC Subservice Organization's services, including controls of ABC Subservice

---

[17] This representation letter should be dated as of the date of the service auditor's report.

[18] The title of management's description of the service organization's system included in management's representation letter should be the same as the title included in management's description of the service organization's system, in management's assertion, and in the service auditor's report.

Organization relevant to the control objectives stated in the description. ABC Subservice Organization has provided a separate assertion attached to the description relevant to the services provided by ABC Subservice Organization.

We confirm, to the best of our knowledge and belief, as of [*date of this letter*], the following representations made to you during your examination:[19]

1. We reaffirm our assertion attached to the description.

2. We have evaluated the fairness of the presentation of the description and the suitability of the design and operating effectiveness of our controls and ABC Subservice Organization's controls to achieve the related control objectives stated in the description, and all relevant matters have been considered and reflected in our evaluation and in our assertion.

3. We have disclosed to you any of the following of which we are aware:

   a. Misstatements including omissions in the description

   b. Instances in which our controls or ABC Subservice Organization's controls were not suitably designed and implemented

   c. Instances in which our controls or ABC Subservice Organization's controls did not operate effectively or as described

   d. Any communications from regulatory agencies, user entities, or others affecting the fairness of the presentation of the description or the suitability of the design or operating effectiveness of the controls to achieve the related control objectives stated in the description, including communications received between the end of the period addressed in our assertion and the date of your report

   e. All other known matters contradicting the fairness of the presentation of the description, the suitability of the design or operating effectiveness of the controls to achieve the related control objectives stated in the description, or our assertion

4. We acknowledge responsibility for our assertion and for

   a. the fairness of the presentation of the description and the suitability of the design and operating effectiveness of the controls to achieve the related control objectives stated in the description.

   b. selecting the criteria stated in our assertion and determining that the criteria are appropriate for our purposes.

5. We have disclosed to you any known events subsequent to the period covered by the description up to the date of this letter that would have a material effect on the fairness of the presentation of the description, the suitability of the design or operating effectiveness of the controls to achieve the related control objectives stated in the description, or our assertion.

---

[19] If management does not provide one or more of the written representations requested by the service auditor, the service auditor should discuss the matter with management, evaluate the effect of such exclusions, and take appropriate action, which may include disclaiming the opinion or withdrawing from the engagement.

6. We have disclosed to you any changes in the controls that are likely to be relevant to user entities' internal control over financial reporting occurring through the date of this letter.

7. We have provided you with all information and access that is relevant to your examination and to our assertion.

8. We believe the effects of uncorrected misstatements, if any, are immaterial, individually and in the aggregate, to the fairness of the presentation of the description or the suitability of the design or operating effectiveness of the controls to achieve the related control objectives stated in the description.

9. We have responded fully to all inquiries made to us by you during the examination.

10. We have disclosed to you any of the following of which we are aware:

   a. Actual, suspected, or alleged fraud or noncompliance with laws or regulations affecting the fairness of the presentation of the description or the suitability of the design or operating effectiveness of the controls to achieve the related control objectives stated in the description

   b. Instances of noncompliance with laws and regulations or uncorrected misstatements attributable to the service organization that may affect one or more user entities

   c. Knowledge of any actual, suspected, or alleged fraud by our management or the service organization's employees that could adversely affect the fairness of the presentation of the description of the service organization's system or the completeness or achievement of the control objectives stated in the description

[*Add any other representations about matters the service auditor deems appropriate or matters relevant to special circumstances, such as industry-specific matters.*]

We understand that your examination was conducted in accordance with attestation standards established by the American Institute of Certified Public Accountants and was designed for the purpose of expressing an opinion on the fairness of the presentation of the description and on the suitability of the design and operating effectiveness of the controls to achieve the related control objectives stated in the description, based on your examination, and that your procedures were limited to those that you considered necessary for that purpose.

_____

[*Name and title of appropriate member of management*]

_____

[*Name and title of appropriate member of management*]

_____

[*Name and title of appropriate member of management*]

Illustrative Representation Letter From Management of the Subservice Organization for Example 2: Management of the Service Organization Presents the Subservice Organization Using the Inclusive Method

[*ABC Subservice Organization's Letterhead*]

[*Date*][20]

[*Service Auditor's Name*]

[*Address*]

In connection with your engagement to report on XYZ Service Organization's description of its defined recordkeeping system and ABC Subservice Organization's description of its application maintenance and support services, both of which are included in "Description of XYZ Service Organization's Defined Contribution Recordkeeping System" for processing user entities' transactions throughout the period January 1, 201X, to December 31, 201X, (description)[21] and the suitability of the design and operating effectiveness of controls included in the description to achieve the related control objectives stated in the description, based on the criteria identified in "XYZ Service Organization's Assertion" and "ABC Subservice Organization's Assertion" (assertions), we recognize that obtaining representations from us concerning the information contained in this letter is a significant procedure in enabling you to form an opinion about whether the description fairly presents the system that was designed and implemented throughout the period January 1, 201X, to December 31, 201X, and whether the controls related to the control objectives stated in the description were suitably designed and operating effectively throughout the period January 1, 201X, to December 31, 201X, to achieve those control objectives, based on the criteria identified in the assertions.

The description includes certain services provided by ABC Subservice Organization to or on behalf of XYZ Service Organization. We are responsible for the portion of the description that describes ABC Subservice Organization's services and activities.

We confirm, to the best of our knowledge and belief, as of [*date of this letter*], the following representations made to you during your examination:[22]

1. We reaffirm our assertion attached to the description.

2. We have evaluated the fairness of the presentation of our portion of the description and the suitability of the design and operating effectiveness of our controls as described,[23] and all relevant matters have been considered and reflected in our evaluation and in our assertion.

---

[20] This representation letter should be dated as of the date of the service auditor's report.

[21] The title of management's description of the service organization's system included in management's representation letter should be the same as the title included in management's description of the service organization's system, in management's assertion, and in the service auditor's report.

[22] If management does not provide one or more of the written representations requested by the service auditor, the service auditor should discuss the matter with management, evaluate the effect of such exclusions, and take appropriate action, which may include disclaiming the opinion or withdrawing from the engagement.

[23] The representations in this letter are predicated on the assumption that the service organization is responsible for evaluating whether the controls, including the subservice organization's controls, are suitably designed and operating effectively to achieve the related control objectives. The wording of the representations should be modified to reflect the relevant responsibilities, for example, if the subservice organization were responsible for evaluating the design and operating effectiveness of its controls to achieve one or more related control objectives.

3. We have disclosed to you any of the following of which we are aware:

    a. Misstatements including omissions in the description

    b. Instances in which controls were not suitably designed and implemented

    c. Instances in which controls did not operate effectively or as described

    d. Any communications from regulatory agencies, user entities, or others affecting the fairness of the presentation of our portion of the description or the suitability of the design or operating effectiveness of our controls as described, including communications received between the end of the period addressed in our assertion and the date of your report

    e. All other known matters contradicting the fairness of the presentation of our portion of the description, the suitability of the design or operating effectiveness of our controls as described, or our assertion

4. We acknowledge responsibility for our assertion and for

    a. the fairness of the presentation of our portion of the description and the suitability of the design and operating effectiveness of our controls as described.

    b. selecting the criteria stated in our assertion and determining that the criteria are appropriate for our purposes.

5. We have disclosed to you any known events subsequent to the period covered by the description up to the date of this letter that would have a material effect on the fairness of the presentation of the description, the suitability of the design or operating effectiveness of our controls as described, or our assertion

6. We have disclosed to you any changes in our controls that are likely to be relevant to user entities' internal control over financial reporting occurring through the date of this letter.

7. We have provided you with all information and access that is relevant to your examination and to our assertion.

8. We believe the effects of uncorrected misstatements, if any, are immaterial, individually and in the aggregate, to the fairness of the presentation of our portion of the description or the suitability of the design or operating effectiveness of our controls as described.

9. We have responded fully to all inquiries made to us by you during the examination.

10. We have disclosed to you any of the following of which we are aware:

    a. Actual, suspected, or alleged fraud or noncompliance with laws or regulations affecting the fairness of the presentation of the description or the suitability of the design or operating effectiveness of our controls as described

    b. Instances of noncompliance with laws and regulations or uncorrected misstatements attributable to the subservice organization that may affect one or more user entities *c.* Knowledge of any actual, suspected, or alleged fraud by our management or the subservice organization's employees that could adversely affect the fairness of the presentation of our portion of the description

[Add any other representations about matters the service auditor deems appropriate or matters relevant to special circumstances, such as industry-specific matters.]

We understand that your examination was conducted in accordance with attestation standards established by the American Institute of Certified Public Accountants and was designed for the purpose of expressing an opinion on the fairness of the presentation of the description and on the suitability of the design and operating effectiveness of the controls to achieve the related control objectives stated in the description, based on your examination, and that your procedures were limited to those that you considered necessary for that purpose.

_____

[Name and title of appropriate member of management]

_____

[Name and title of appropriate member of management]

_____

[Name and title of appropriate member of management]

_____

Appendix C

Illustrative Management Representation Letters

This appendix is nonauthoritative and is included for informational purposes only.

Illustrative Representation Letter for Management of a Service Organization: Type 2 Engagement

[*Service Organization's Letterhead*]

[*Date*][1]

[*Service Auditor's Name*]

[*Address*]

In connection with your engagement to report on [*name of service organization*]'s (service organization) description of its [*type or name of*] system entitled "[*name of service organization*]'s Description of [*type or name of system*] For Processing User Entities' Transactions [*or identification of the function performed by the system*] Throughout the Period [*date*] to [*date*]" (description)[2] and the suitability of the design and operating effectiveness of the controls to achieve the related control objectives stated in the description, we recognize that obtaining representations from us concerning the information contained in this letter is a significant procedure in enabling you to form an opinion about whether the description fairly presents the system that was designed and implemented throughout the period [*date*] to [*date*] and whether the controls related to the control objectives stated in the description were suitably designed and operating effectively throughout the period [*date*] to [*date*] to achieve those control objectives, based on the criteria described in our assertion.

We confirm, to the best of our knowledge and belief, as of [*date of this letter*], the following representations made to you during your examination:[3]

1. We reaffirm our assertion attached to the description.

2. We have evaluated the fairness of the presentation of the description and the suitability of the design and operating effectiveness of the controls to achieve the related control objectives stated in the description, and all relevant matters have been considered and reflected in our evaluation and in our assertion.

3. We have disclosed to you any of the following of which we are aware:

    a. Misstatements including omissions in the description

    b. Instances in which controls were not suitably designed and implemented

---

[1] This representation letter should be dated as of the date of the service auditor's report.

[2] The title of management's description of the service organization's system included in management's representation letter should be the same as the title included in management's description of the service organization's system, in management's assertion, and in the service auditor's report.

[3] If management does not provide one or more of the written representations requested by the service auditor, the service auditor should discuss the matter with management, evaluate the effect of such exclusions, and take appropriate action, which may include disclaiming the opinion or withdrawing from the engagement.

      c. Instances in which controls did not operate effectively or as described

      d. Any communications from regulatory agencies, user entities, or others affecting the fairness of the presentation of the description or the suitability of the design or operating effectiveness of the controls to achieve the related control objectives stated in the description, including communications received between the end of the period addressed in our assertion and the date of your report

      e. All other known matters contradicting the fairness of the presentation of the description, the suitability of the design or operating effectiveness of the controls to achieve the related control objectives stated in the description, or our assertion

4. We acknowledge responsibility for our assertion and for

      a. the fairness of the presentation of the description and the suitability of the design and operating effectiveness of the controls to achieve the related control objectives stated in the description.

      b. selecting the criteria stated in our assertion and determining that the criteria are appropriate for our purposes.

5. We have disclosed to you any known events subsequent to the period covered by the description up to the date of this letter that would have a material effect on the fairness of the presentation of the description, the suitability of the design or operating effectiveness of the controls to achieve the related control objectives stated in the description, or our assertion.

6. We have disclosed to you any changes in the controls that are likely to be relevant to user entities' internal control over financial reporting occurring through the date of this letter.

7. We have provided you with all information and access that is relevant to your examination and to our assertion.

8. We believe the effects of uncorrected misstatements, if any, are immaterial, individually and in the aggregate, to the fairness of the presentation of the description or the suitability of the design or operating effectiveness of the controls to achieve the related control objectives stated in the description.

9. We have responded fully to all inquiries made to us by you during the examination.

10. We have disclosed to you any of the following of which we are aware:

      a. Actual, suspected, or alleged fraud or noncompliance with laws or regulations affecting the fairness of the presentation of the description or the suitability of the design or operating effectiveness of the controls to achieve the related control objectives stated in the description

      b. Instances of noncompliance with laws and regulations or uncorrected misstatements attributable to the service organization that may affect one or more user entities

      c. Knowledge of any actual, suspected, or alleged fraud by management or the service organization's employees that could adversely affect the fairness of the presentation of the description of the service organization's system or the completeness or achievement of the control objectives stated in the description

[*Add any other representations about matters the service auditor deems appropriate or matters relevant to special circumstances, such as industry-specific matters.*]

We understand that your examination was conducted in accordance with attestation standards established by the American Institute of Certified Public Accountants and was designed for the purpose of expressing an opinion on the fairness of the presentation of the description and on the suitability of the design and operating effectiveness of the controls to achieve the related control objectives stated in the description, based on your examination, and that your procedures were limited to those that you considered necessary for that purpose.

_____

[*Name and title of appropriate member of management*]

_____

[*Name and title of appropriate member of management*]

_____

[*Name and title of appropriate member of management*]

Illustrative Representation Letter for Management of a Service Organization: Type 1 Engagement

[*Service Organization's Letterhead*]

[*Date*]⁴

[*Service Auditor's Name*]

[*Address*]

In connection with your engagement to report on [*name of service organization*]'s (service organization) description of its [*type or name of*] system entitled "[*name of service organization*]'s Description of [*type or name of system*] For Processing User Entities' Transactions" [*or identification of the function performed by the system*] as of [*date*] (description)⁵ and the suitability of the design of controls to achieve the related control objectives stated in the description, we recognize that obtaining representations from us concerning the information contained in this letter is a significant procedure in enabling you to form an opinion on whether the description fairly presents the system that was designed and implemented as of [*date*] and whether the controls related to the control objectives stated in the description were suitably designed to provide reasonable assurance that those control objectives would be achieved if the controls operated effectively as of [*date*], based on the criteria described in our assertion.

---

⁴ This representation letter should be dated as of the date of the service auditor's report.

⁵ The title of management's description of the service organization's system included in management's representation letter should be the same as the title included in management's description of the service organization's system, in management's assertion, and in the service auditor's report.

We confirm, to the best of our knowledge and belief, as of [*date of this letter*], the following representations made to you during your examination:[6]

1. We reaffirm our assertion attached to the description.

2. We have evaluated the fairness of the presentation of the description and the suitability of the design of the controls to achieve the related control objectives stated in the description, and all relevant matters have been considered and reflected in our evaluation and in our assertion.

3. We have disclosed to you any of the following of which we are aware:

    a. Misstatements including omissions in the description

    b. Instances in which controls were not suitably designed and implemented

    c. Instances in which controls did not operate effectively or as described

    d. Any communications from regulatory agencies, user entities, or others affecting the fairness of the presentation of the description or the suitability of the design or operating effectiveness of the controls to achieve the related control objectives stated in the description, including communications received between the end of the period addressed in our assertion and the date of your report

    e. All other known matters contradicting the fairness of the presentation of the description, the suitability of the design or operating effectiveness of the controls to achieve the related control objectives stated in the description, or our assertion

4. We acknowledge responsibility for our assertion and for

    a. the fairness of the presentation of the description and the suitability of the design and operating effectiveness of the controls to achieve the related control objectives stated in the description.

    b. selecting the criteria stated in our assertion and determining that the criteria are appropriate for our purposes.

5. We have disclosed to you any known events subsequent to the period covered by the description up to the date of this letter that would have a material effect on the fairness of the presentation of the description, the suitability of the design or operating effectiveness of the controls to achieve the related control objectives stated in the description, or our assertion.

6. We have disclosed to you any changes in the controls that are likely to be relevant to user entities' internal control over financial reporting occurring through the date of this letter.

7. We have provided you with all information and access that is relevant to your examination and to our assertion.

---

[6] If management does not provide one or more of the written representations requested by the service auditor, the service auditor should discuss the matter with management, evaluate the effect of such exclusions, and take appropriate action, which may include disclaiming the opinion or withdrawing from the engagement.

8. We believe the effects of uncorrected misstatements, if any, are immaterial, individually and in the aggregate, to the fairness of the presentation of the description or the suitability of the design or operating effectiveness of the controls to achieve the related control objectives stated in the description.

9. We have responded fully to all inquiries made to us by you during the examination.

10. We have disclosed to you any of the following of which we are aware:

    a. Actual, suspected, or alleged fraud or noncompliance with laws or regulations affecting the fairness of the presentation of the description or the suitability of the design or operating effectiveness of the controls to achieve the related control objectives stated in the description

    b. Instances of noncompliance with laws and regulations or uncorrected misstatements attributable to the service organization that may affect one or more user entities

    c. Knowledge of any actual, suspected, or alleged fraud by management or the service organization's employees that could adversely affect the fairness of the presentation of the description of the service organization's system or the completeness or achievement of the control objectives stated in the description

[*Add any other representations about matters the service auditor deems appropriate or matters relevant to special circumstances, such as industry-specific matters.*]

We understand that your examination was conducted in accordance with attestation standards established by the American Institute of Certified Public Accountants and was designed for the purpose of expressing an opinion on the fairness of the presentation of the description and on the suitability of the design of the controls to achieve the related control objectives stated in the description, based on your examination, and that your procedures were limited to those that you considered necessary for that purpose.

———————————————
[*Name and title of appropriate member of management*]

———————————————
[*Name and title of appropriate member of management*]

———————————————
[*Name and title of appropriate member of management*]

———————————————

Appendix D

Illustrative Control Objectives for Various Types of Service Organizations

This appendix is nonauthoritative and is included for informational purposes only.

This appendix illustrates typical control objectives related to

- general business processes.
- IT general controls.
- specific types of service organizations, including
  - application service providers,
  - claims processors,
  - credit card payment processors,
  - defined contribution plan recordkeepers,
  - investment managers,
  - payroll processors, and
  - transfer agents.
- custodians subject to SEC Rule 206(4)-2, "Custody of Funds or Securities of Clients by Investment Advisers."

The illustrative control objectives in this appendix are not meant to be all-encompassing. Rather, they represent typical control objectives included in descriptions of a service organization's system for service organizations that provide the services listed in the preceding paragraph; these control objectives should be tailored to the particular service organization's business. Additionally, the service organization should review the entire appendix before determining which control objectives best fit its needs. For example, control objectives for transaction processing are presented in a number of ways in this appendix.

To assist the service organization is identifying applicable control objectives, the appendix contains footnotes designed to further explain and clarify the control objectives as written.

Illustrative General Business Process Control Objectives

The illustrative control objectives in this section generally are applicable to many types of service organizations. These control objectives are discussed in tables 4-1 and 4-2, along with the related user entity financial statement assertions and illustrative risks that threaten the achievement of the control objectives as they relate to the user entities' financial statements. The control objectives would be tailored to the facts and circumstances of the service organization and the particular business process service being provided to user entities.

Application Control Objectives Related to Transactions and Events During a Period

Controls provide reasonable assurance that...

- transactions are authorized and received only from authorized sources.[1]
- transactions are validated[2] in a complete, accurate, and timely manner.[3]
- transactions are entered, processed, recorded, and reported in a complete manner.
- transactions are entered, processed, recorded, and reported in an accurate manner.
- transactions are entered, processed, recorded, and reported in a timely manner.[4]
- transactions are recorded and reported in the proper accounts.

Application Control Objectives Related to Account Balances at the Period End

Controls provide reasonable assurance that . . .

- balances represent valid asset, liability, and equity interest balances and are classified properly.
- asset and liability balances relate to rights or obligations of the user entity.
- balances represent all asset, liability, and equity interest balances that should have been recorded.
- asset, liability, and equity interest balances are reported at accurate amounts.

Control Objectives Related to IT General Controls

The illustrative control objectives in this section are applicable to IT general controls and are discussed in table 4-3, along with the related illustrative risks that threaten the achievement of the IT general control objectives. IT general control objectives can be used alone or in combination with the business process control objectives, depending on the nature of the outsourced service. The service organization tailors these control objectives to the services provided, selecting control objectives that are likely to be relevant to controls over financial reporting at user entities.

Illustrative Control Objectives

Information Security

Controls provide reasonable assurance that

---

[1] Transaction data may be received in paper or electronic form or by telephone, for example, by a call center. The service organization may have separate control objectives for each method of receipt.

[2] Validation includes determining that the recorded transaction has occurred and pertains to the user entity. It also includes correcting invalid data and properly reentering corrected data.

[3] A timely manner also includes recording the transaction in the correct period.

[4] See footnote 3.

- logical access[5] to programs, data, and computer resources[6] relevant to user entities' internal control over financial reporting is restricted to authorized and appropriate users and such users are restricted to performing authorized and appropriate actions.[7]

- physical access to computer and other resources[8] relevant to user entities' internal control over financial reporting is restricted to authorized and appropriate personnel.

Change Management

Controls provide reasonable assurance that

- changes to application programs and related data management systems[9] are authorized, tested, documented, approved, and implemented to result in the complete, accurate, and timely[10] processing and reporting of transactions and balances relevant to user entities' internal control over financial reporting.[11]

- network infrastructure[12] is configured as authorized to (1) support the effective functioning of application controls to result in valid, complete, accurate, and timely[13] processing and reporting of

---

[5] In assessing the logical access controls over programs, data, and computer resources, the service organization considers

- logical access controls that may affect the user entities' financial statements. Generally, this would begin with the access controls directly over the application. If the effectiveness of application level security is dependent on the effectiveness of network and operating system controls, these are also considered. Controls over direct access to the databases or data files and tables are considered as well.

- the configuration and administration of security tools and techniques and monitoring controls designed to identify and respond to security violations in a timely manner.

[6] Computer resources include, but are not limited to, computer equipment, network equipment, storage media, and other hardware supporting the services provided by the service organization.

[7] Many service organizations have features enabling customers to directly access programs and data. In assessing the logical access controls over programs and data, the service organization considers the controls over security related to service organization personnel, the service organization's customers, and the customers' clients, as applicable, as well as the likely effect of these controls on user entities' financial statements.

[8] Computer resources include, but are not limited to, computer equipment, network equipment, storage media, and other hardware supporting the services provided by the service organization. Other resources include, but are not limited to, buildings, vaults, and negotiable instruments.

[9] Data management systems include database management systems, specialized data transport or communications software (often called middleware), data warehouse software, and data extraction or reporting software. Controls over data management systems may enhance user authentication or authorization, the availability of system privileges, data access privileges, application processing hosted within the data management systems, and segregation of duties.

[10] Timeliness may be relevant in particular situations, for example, when emergency changes are needed or when changes that would likely affect the user entities' information system are being implemented to meet contractual requirements. Controls for emergency changes typically will be different from those for planned changes.

[11] This control objective is quite broad and should be tailored to the service organization's environment. For example, if the service organization has different controls for developing new applications or for making changes to applications or databases, it might be clearer to have separate control objectives for each of these.

[12] Network infrastructure includes all of the hardware, software, operating systems, and communication components within which the applications and related data management systems operate.

[13] Timeliness may be relevant in particular situations, for example, when emergency changes are needed or when changes are being implemented to meet contractual requirements.

transactions and balances relevant to user entities' internal control over financial reporting; (2) protect data relevant to user entities' internal control over financial reporting from unauthorized changes; and (3) support user entities' internal control over financial reporting.[14]

Computer Operations

- Controls provide reasonable assurance that
- application and system processing[15] relevant to user entities' internal control over financial reporting are authorized and executed in a complete, accurate, and timely manner and deviations, problems, and errors that may affect user entities' internal control over financial reporting are identified, tracked, recorded, and resolved in a complete, accurate, and timely manner.
- data transmissions between the service organization and its user entities and other outside entities that affect user entities' internal control over financial reporting are from authorized sources and are complete, accurate, secure, and timely.[16]
- data relevant to user entities' internal control over financial reporting is backed up regularly and is available for restoration in the event of processing errors or unexpected processing interruptions.

Illustrative Control Objectives for an Application Service Provider

In addition to the illustrative control objectives in this section, the control objectives in the preceding section, "Control Objectives Related to IT General Controls," may be appropriate for an application service provider (ASP).[17] An ASP may perform some or all of the following services for user entities:

- Providing a commonly used application that is accessed using an Internet protocol such as HTTPS or a web browser
- Maintaining and operating the application software on behalf of its clients

---

[14] Program change controls over network infrastructure include, as appropriate, the authorization, testing, documentation, approval, and implementation of changes to network infrastructure. In assessing change management, the service organization considers the configuration and administration of the security tools and techniques, and monitoring controls designed to identify exceptions to authorized network infrastructure applications and data management systems (for example, database structures) and act upon them in a timely manner. If the service organization has different controls for new implementations or for making changes to either the infrastructure, applications, or data management systems, it might be clearer to have separate control objectives that address the controls over each type of infrastructure. There also may be separate control objectives for controls over new implementations and controls over changes to existing resources.

[15] The processing in this control objective refers to the batch processing of data. It typically does not include scheduling of file backups. Should the service organization have significant online, real-time processing, it may tailor this control objective or add a new control objective to address controls over the identification, tracking, recording, and resolution of problems and errors in a complete, accurate, and timely manner.

[16] This control objective may also be presented as part of logical access security or as part of the business operations related to data input or reporting.

[17] An application service provider (ASP) may provide software for functions, such as credit card payment processing or timesheet services, or may provide a particular financial application or solution package for a specific type of customer, such as a dental practice.

- Owning, operating, and maintaining the servers that support the software
- Billing the ASP's clients on a "per use" basis

Illustrative Control Objectives

New Customer Setup and Maintenance

Controls provide reasonable assurance that

- new customers are established on the system in accordance with the applicable contracts and requirements.[18]
- maintenance instructions[19] are properly authorized, recorded completely and accurately, and processed timely.

Transaction Processing

Controls provide reasonable assurance that

- client transactions are initially recorded completely, accurately, and in a timely manner.
- invalid transactions and errors are identified, rejected, and correctly reentered into the system in a timely manner.
- client transactions are processed in a timely manner and reported in accordance with client-specific business rules.
- the contents of data files remain complete and accurate, and the correct versions of all data files are used in processing.[20]

Customer Support

Controls provide reasonable assurance that

- production and business problems[21] are identified, recorded, analyzed, and resolved completely and in a timely manner.
- system availability is monitored and issues are identified and resolved on a timely basis.

Illustrative Control Objectives for a Claims Processor

The illustrative control objectives in this section may be appropriate for a service organization that processes claims for user entities such as health insurers.

---

[18] Because most ASPs provide a service that is flexible and can be tailored to a particular customer, it is important that a new customer's business rules be properly established on the system to ensure that processing of its data is in accordance with expectations and requirements.

[19] Maintenance instructions are required to make changes to customer information.

[20] This control objective includes controls in place to ensure that the correct versions of the files are used to validate and update transactions entered for processing. This control objective can be used as a control objective related to any transaction processing. The service organization determines the nature and extent of the control objective and whether the control objective belongs with the business process controls or with the IT general controls, based on the services provided and the relevance of these controls to the preparation of financial statements.

[21] *Production and business problems* refer to the issues encountered by user entities, the computer systems that support the services, or the general business questions user entities may have regarding the services rendered.

The claims processor may perform some or all of the following services for user entities:

- Maintaining eligibility and enrollment information for customers
- Processing claims, such as insurance or medical benefit claims, on behalf of customers of the user entities based on contractual arrangements
- Adjudicating claims on behalf of their customers
- Processing bills to customers

Illustrative Control Objectives

Groups or Customers[22]

Controls provide reasonable assurance that group and benefits contracts[23] are authorized and that contract terms are established[24] and maintained in a complete, accurate, and timely manner.

Providers

Controls provide reasonable assurance that provider contracts are authorized and provider data is established[25] and maintained in a complete, accurate, and timely manner.

Enrollments[26]

Controls provide reasonable assurance that enrollment and eligibility information received from customers is authorized and processed in a complete, accurate, and timely manner.

Claims Receipts and Adjudication[27]

Controls provide reasonable assurance that

- claims are received only from authorized sources.
- claims received are entered in a complete, accurate, and timely manner.
- claims are validated and adjudicated in a complete, accurate, and timely manner.
- claim adjustments are authorized and processed in a complete, accurate, and timely manner.

---

[22] Group or customer information would include information such as member benefits, global pricing, and reimbursement schedules.

[23] Group and benefits contracts may refer to physician, dental, and other health care provider agreements.

[24] Establishing this information in the application software may also be referred to as installation of the group and customer information.

[25] Establishing this information in the application software may also be referred to as installation of the provider information.

[26] Enrollment information may be received through various channels either electronically via fax, Internet, or specific feeds or as a hard copy. If the controls for each channel are different, the service organization should consider establishing individual control objectives for each channel.

[27] Claims may be received in paper or electronic format. The service organization may establish separate control objectives for each method of receipt, depending on the control activities and the needs of the user entities.

- claim actions for subrogation, coordination of benefits, and other recoveries for submitted claims are processed in a complete, accurate, and timely manner.[28]

Claim Payments and Billing Operations

Controls provide reasonable assurance that

- adjudicated claims are paid in a complete, accurate, and timely manner.
- customer invoices and funding requests are authorized and processed in a complete, accurate, and timely manner.
- reports provided to customers are complete, accurate, and timely.

Illustrative Control Objectives for a Credit Card Payment Processor

The illustrative control objectives in this section may be appropriate for a service organization that processes credit card payments. The credit card payment processor may perform some or all of the following services for user entities:

- Processing transactions initiated by credit card holders at authorized merchants
- Paying merchants for authorized credit card transactions
- Preparing and managing cardholder invoices and payments
- Managing and reporting potential fraudulent transactions
- Managing blank cards and personal identification numbers
- Reporting to the merchants and credit bureaus
- Managing rewards programs

Illustrative Control Objectives

Merchant and Sales Partner Setup

Controls provide reasonable assurance that

- new merchant accounts are authorized and set up completely and accurately, according to the contractual agreement.
- new sales partners are authorized and set up completely and accurately, according to the contracted agreement.
- changes to merchant and sales partner data are authorized and processed completely and accurately and in a timely manner.

Authorization Processing

Controls provide reasonable assurance that authorization requests are received, transmitted to the processing system, properly evaluated based on the

---

[28] This control objective should include controls over the collection and payment to the appropriate parties of any funds recovered. In such cases, the service organization may consider a separate control objective for these controls.

cardholder's available credit and current account status, and that the authorization or denial message received from the processor is transmitted back to the originating merchant.

Transaction Processing

Controls provide reasonable assurance that

- all and only authorized transactions are processed and settled completely, accurately, timely, and only once.
- all data is validated and errors are rejected and reported for user entity follow-up and correction.
- transmissions to and from clearinghouses are accurate, complete, and valid.
- the contents of data files remain complete and accurate, and the correct versions of all data files are used in processing.[29]

Chargebacks and Refunds

Controls provide reasonable assurance that all and only authorized chargeback or refund data received is processed and settled completely, accurately, and in a timely manner.

Merchant Payments

Controls provide reasonable assurance that

- amounts payable to merchants are computed completely and accurately, and amounts due are transferred to the merchant using the appropriate remittance option.
- sales partner residual amounts are calculated completely, accurately, and in a timely manner.

Client Settlement

Controls provide reasonable assurance that

- the system is in balance prior to settlement with the interchange clearinghouses and the client's processing, and net settlement amounts are properly computed.
- all outgoing wire transfers are properly authorized and all incoming wire transfers are received accurately and on a timely basis.

Cardholder Accounting

Controls provide reasonable assurance that

- transactions are processed in accordance with system descriptions and posted completely and accurately to the correct cardholder accounts in a timely manner.

---

[29] This control objective includes controls in place to ensure that the correct versions of the files are used to validate and update transactions entered for processing. This can be used as a control objective related to any transaction processing. The service organization determines the nature and extent of the control objective and whether the control objective belongs with the business process controls or the IT general controls, based on the services provided and the relevance of these controls to the preparation of financial statements.

- problem accounts (for example, accounts that exceed limits or are delinquent) are identified by the system and reported to the client for follow-up.

Cardholder Inquiry Management

Controls provide reasonable assurance that cardholder inquiries are logged and processed to permit a timely response to the inquiry or resolution of the problem.

Cardholder Statements and Communication

Controls provide reasonable assurance that cardholder statements are generated on a timely basis and distributed no more than 10 days after statement generation.

Risk Management

Controls provide reasonable assurance that periodic credit reviews, fraud investigations, and collections are routinely performed, monitored, and reported for follow-up on a timely basis.

Rewards

Controls provide reasonable assurance that cardholder rewards processing functions and calculations are performed in accordance with system descriptions and all and only authorized transactions are posted to the correct cardholder account in the proper accounting period.

Blank Cards

Controls provide reasonable assurance that

- blank cards are safeguarded and protected from unauthorized use.
- blank cards are not lost or duplicated during the personalization process.
- adjustments to inventory levels are authorized by appropriate individuals.

Personal Identification Numbers

Controls provide reasonable assurance that

- personal identification numbers (PINs) used to authenticate cash advance transactions are protected from unauthorized disclosure.
- cardholder PINs generated and mailed during the card-issuance process are protected from unauthorized disclosure.
- access to the information used to produce the PIN mailer, as well as the printed mailers, is restricted to authorized and appropriate individuals.
- client-defined encryption keys are protected from unauthorized disclosure.

Report Statement Generation and Distribution

Controls provide reasonable assurance that client reports are complete, accurate, and distributed on a timely basis.

Credit Bureau Reporting

Controls provide reasonable assurance that month-end credit bureau reporting files are complete, accurate, and transmitted to the appropriate credit bureaus in the agreed-upon timeframes and in accordance with client specifications.

Illustrative Control Objectives for a Defined Contribution Plan Recordkeeper

The illustrative control objectives in this section may be relevant to a service organization that is a defined contribution plan recordkeeper. Selected control objectives may also be relevant to a defined benefit plan recordkeeper.

Illustrative Control Objectives

New Plan Setup and Maintenance

Controls provide reasonable assurance that

- new plan setups, plan mergers, and plan conversions[30] are authorized and processed in a complete, accurate, and timely manner in accordance with instructions from the plan sponsor and specific plan provisions.

- plan parameter changes are authorized and processed in a complete, accurate, and timely manner in accordance with instructions from the plan sponsor.

Enrollments and Changes

Controls provide reasonable assurance that

- enrollments are authorized and processed in a complete, accurate, and timely manner.

- indicative data changes are authorized and processed in a complete, accurate, and timely manner.

Contributions

Controls provide reasonable assurance that contributions[31] are authorized and processed in a complete, accurate, and timely manner.

Distributions

Controls provide reasonable assurance that distributions[32] are authorized and processed in a complete, accurate, and timely manner.

---

[30] Depending on the similarities in the controls, these three areas may be included as one, two, or three control objectives. To the extent controls related to new plans, mergers, and conversions are different, the service organization may want to have separate control objectives for ease of understanding.

[31] Contributions, including the recordkeeping and money movement, commonly include, but may not be limited to, payroll deductions, loan repayments, loan payoffs, rollovers-in and adjustments.

[32] Distributions, including recordkeeping and money movement, commonly include, but may not be limited to, forfeitures, loans, qualified domestic relations orders (QDROs), pension payments (lump sum and periodic), and adjustments.

Investments and related transactions

Controls provide reasonable assurance that

- investment transactions are processed in a complete, accurate, and timely manner.
- fund transfers are authorized and processed in a complete, accurate, and timely manner.

Pricing

Controls provide reasonable assurance that prices and net asset values are received daily from an authorized source and are recorded in a complete, accurate, and timely manner.

Investment income

Controls provide reasonable assurance that investment income (for example, dividends and interest income) is processed and allocated to participant accounts in a complete, accurate, and timely manner.

Corporate Actions

Controls provide reasonable assurance that corporate actions are authorized and processed in a complete, accurate, and timely manner.

Reconciliations

Controls provide reasonable assurance that reconciliations between plan and participant records are performed in a complete, accurate, and timely manner.

Statements

Controls provide reasonable assurance that statements are provided to participants and plan sponsors in a complete, accurate, and timely manner.

Illustrative Control Objectives for an Investment Manager

The illustrative control objectives in this section may be relevant to asset management service organizations. They also can be adapted and used, as appropriate, for investment management organizations, trust organizations, hedge fund advisers, or hedge fund of fund advisers.

The control objectives included in this section would be appropriate for an investment manager that performs some or all of the following functions:

- Initiating and executing purchase and sale transactions, either by specific direction from the client or under discretionary authority granted by the client
- Determining whether transactions comply with guidelines and restrictions
- Reconciling records of security transactions and portfolio holdings, for each client, to statements received from the custodian
- Reporting to the customer on portfolio performance and activities

Illustrative Control Objectives

New Account Setup and Administration

Controls provide reasonable assurance that

- new accounts are authorized and set up in accordance with client instructions and guidelines in a complete, accurate, and timely manner.
- account modifications are authorized and implemented in a complete, accurate, and timely manner.
- new account holdings and cash are reconciled to custodian bank statements in a complete, accurate, and timely manner.[33]

Security Setup

Controls provide reasonable assurance that new securities and changes to existing securities are authorized and entered in the security master file in a complete, accurate, and timely manner.

Investment Transaction Processing

Controls provide reasonable assurance that

- investment transaction instructions are authorized and entered into the system in a complete, accurate, and timely manner.
- portfolio guidelines are monitored and exceptions are identified and resolved in a complete, accurate, and timely manner.[34]
- allocations are approved by a portfolio manager.
- block orders are allocated to clients on a pro rata basis for equity trades and a predetermined allocation for fixed-income trades.

Confirmation, Affirmation, or Settlement

Controls provide reasonable assurance that

- investments are settled in a complete, accurate, and timely manner.
- custodians are informed of transactions in a complete, accurate, and timely manner.

Loans

Controls provide reasonable assurance that

- loans and collateral are authorized and processed and recorded in a complete, accurate, and timely manner.
- collateral on loans is invested in accordance with the lender agreement and recorded and monitored in a complete, accurate, and timely manner.

---

[33] The service organization may consider establishing a separate control objective that covers the applicable controls related to account conversions or new account set up or including these controls as part of the reconciliation control objective listed subsequently.

[34] This control objective may also be combined with the first control objective in this section by including the additional wording "investment transactions are authorized and executed in accordance with the portfolio policies."

- loan repayments are processed and recorded completely, accurately, and in a timely manner.

Pricing

Controls provide reasonable assurance that

- security prices are received from an authorized source and updated in a complete, accurate, and timely manner.
- price overrides are authorized and processed in a complete, accurate, and timely manner.

Corporate Actions

Controls provide reasonable assurance that corporate action notices are identified and received from an authorized source and are updated in the system in a complete, accurate, and timely manner.

Investment Income

Controls provide reasonable assurance that

- interest, dividend, and other income information is received from an authorized source and recorded in a complete, accurate, and timely manner.
- cash received for interest and dividends is processed in a complete, accurate, and timely manner.

Money Movement

Controls provide reasonable assurance that money movement (receipts and disbursements) is authorized and processed in a complete, accurate, and timely manner.[35]

Custodian Reconciliation

Controls provide reasonable assurance that security positions and cash balances reflected in the portfolio accounting system are reconciled in a complete, accurate, and timely manner to actual positions and balances held by custodians.[36]

Fees

Controls provide reasonable assurance that investment management fees and other expenses are authorized, calculated, and recorded in a complete, accurate, and timely manner.[37]

Net Asset Valuation

Controls provide reasonable assurance that net asset values are authorized and calculated in a complete, accurate, and timely manner.

---

[35] The service organization may consider establishing separate control objectives for receipts and disbursements.

[36] The service organization may consider establishing separate control objectives for security positions and cash balances.

[37] A service organization may establish separate control objectives for the accrual of the expense and the payment of the expense.

Account Statements and Client Reports

Controls provide reasonable assurance that account statements and client reports detailing client account holdings and market values are complete, accurate, and provided to clients in a timely manner.

Illustrative Control Objectives for a Payroll Processor

The illustrative control objectives included in this section may be appropriate for a service organization that performs some or all of the following functions:

- Processing various types of payroll
- Calculating payroll tax liabilities for federal, state, and local jurisdictions
- Preparing and submitting payroll tax returns and compliance reports
- Printing and distributing payroll checks
- Calculating workers' compensation, state unemployment, and other benefit costs
- Making payments to appropriate agencies and other third parties

Illustrative Control Objectives

Payroll Processing Setup

Controls provide reasonable assurance that

- client requirements are properly authorized and set up in the system completely, accurately, and timely.
- payroll taxes and other deductions are authorized and set up completely, accurately, and timely.
- payroll tax and other deductions tables are updated completely, accurately, and timely, as required.
- changes to client requirements, payroll taxes, and other deductions are updated completely, accurately, and timely.

Payroll Data Authorization and Recording

Controls provide reasonable assurance that

- payroll data is received from authorized sources.
- payroll data is recorded completely, accurately, and timely.
- rejected transactions and errors are identified, reported to user entities for follow-up, and properly reentered into the system on a timely basis.
- payroll transactions are processed completely, accurately, and timely.
- payroll adjustments are received from authorized sources and processed completely, accurately, and timely.
- data transmissions to or from clients are authorized, complete, accurate, secure, and processed timely.

Payroll Processing

Controls provide reasonable assurance that

- processing is scheduled and performed appropriately in accordance with client specifications; deviations from the schedule are identified and resolved timely.[38]
- payroll deductions and tax withholdings are calculated by the system in accordance with statutory and client specifications.

Reporting

Controls provide reasonable assurance that

- payroll checks, pay statements, and reports are produced completely, accurately, and timely in accordance with client specifications.
- disbursements of direct deposits are authorized, complete, accurate, and processed timely.
- data transmissions of money movement and files from the system to outside parties and to the clients' banks are authorized, complete, accurate, secure, and processed in a timely manner.

Illustrative Control Objectives for a Transfer Agent

The illustrative control objectives in this section may be appropriate for a transfer agent that performs transfer or registrar functions. Transfer agents may also perform securities custodial services or execute trades based on authorized instructions. If this is the case, refer to the control objectives under the heading "Illustrative Control Objectives for an Investment Manager," for control objectives that may apply to these functions.

The transfer function may include any of the following tasks:

- Processing old certificates that are properly presented and endorsed in good deliverable form
- Reviewing legal documents to ensure that they are complete and appropriate, before transferring the securities
- Notifying the presenter if the documents are incomplete, or returning rejected documents that are incorrect, insufficient, or otherwise unexecutable
- Issuing new certificates in the name of the new owner
- Making appropriate adjustments to the issuer's shareholder records

The registrar function may include any of the following tasks:

- Monitoring the issuance of authorized securities

---

[38] This control objective includes controls in place to ensure that the correct versions of the files are used to validate and update transactions entered for processing. This can be used as a control objective related to any transaction processing. The service organization determines the nature and extent of the control objective and whether the control objective belongs with the business process controls or the IT general controls, based on the services provided and the relevance of these controls to the preparation of financial statements.

- Ensuring that the issuance of the new securities will not cause the authorized number of shares in an issue to exceed the total permitted to be issued

- Ensuring that the number of shares transferred corresponds to the number of shares canceled

As part of the transfer and registrar functions previously noted, a transfer agent's functions may also include

- maintaining records of the name and address of each security holder, the number of securities owned by each security holder, the certificate numbers corresponding to a security holder's position, the issue date of the security certificate, and the cancellation date of the security certificate, if applicable.

- logging and tracking shareholder and issuer correspondence and resolving inquiries in the correspondence in a timely manner.

- acting as paying agent for cash dividends, dividend reinvestments, and distributions of stock dividends and stock splits.

- monitoring and controlling the proxy voting process.

Illustrative Control Objectives

Issuer and Shareholder Setup and Maintenance

Controls provide reasonable assurance that

- new clients are authorized and established in the system in a complete, accurate, and timely manner, in accordance with client instructions.

- changes to client data are authorized and updated in the system in a complete, accurate, and timely manner.

- shareholder account information and maintenance instructions are authorized and recorded in a complete, accurate, and timely manner.

Securities Transfers

Controls provide reasonable assurance that

- only eligible securities can be transferred, and stock transfers are processed completely and accurately and on a timely basis.

- subscriptions are authorized and processed in a complete, accurate, and timely manner.

- exchanges are authorized and processed in a complete, accurate, and timely manner.

- redemptions are authorized and processed in a complete, accurate, and timely manner.

- total outstanding share balances are accurately maintained and reconciled in a timely manner.

Dividends

Controls provide reasonable assurance that

- dividend rates are authorized and payments are calculated and distributed to shareholders of record in a complete, accurate, and timely manner.
- dividend reinvestments are processed only for authorized individuals and the processing is complete, accurate, and timely.
- dividend check replacement requests are processed completely, accurately, and in a timely manner.

Safeguarding Assets

Controls provide reasonable assurance that securities and checks in the custody or possession of the transfer agent are protected from loss, misappropriation, or other unauthorized use.

Certificate Replacements

Controls provide reasonable assurance that

- notifications of lost or stolen certificates are authorized and recorded in a complete, accurate, and timely manner.
- certificate replacement requests are authorized and processed completely, accurately, and in a timely manner.

Illustrative Control Objectives for Custodians Subject to SEC Rule 206(4)-2, "Custody of Funds or Securities of Clients by Investment Advisers" [39]

The illustrative control objectives in this section are relevant when performing an engagement under AT-C section 320, *Reporting on an Examination of Controls at a Service Organization Relevant to User Entities' Internal Control Over Financial Reporting* (AICPA, *Professional Standards*), to meet the reporting requirements of SEC Rule 206(4)-2, which amends the custody rule under the Investment Advisers Act of 1940 by requiring advisers that have custody of client funds or securities to maintain those assets with broker-dealers, banks, or other qualified custodians. Paragraph (a)(6) of Rule 206(4)-2 indicates that an investment adviser that maintains, or has custody because a related person maintains, client funds or securities pursuant to Rule 206(4)-2 as a qualified custodian in connection with advisory services provided to clients must obtain or receive from its related person, no less frequently than once each calendar year, a written internal control report prepared by an independent public accountant. The internal control report must include an opinion of an independent public accountant about whether controls have been placed in operation as of a specified date, and are suitably designed and operating effectively to meet control objectives related to custodial services, including the safeguarding of funds and securities held by either the adviser or a related person on behalf of the advisory clients, during the year. In addition to meeting the reporting requirements of SEC Rule 206(4)-2, the illustrative control objectives in this section may also be appropriate for a custodian that is not subject to SEC Rule 206(4)-2 but wishes to undergo an attestation engagement that addresses controls over custody:

Controls provide reasonable assurance that

---

[39] Code of Federal Regulations, Title 17, Section 275.206(4)-2.

- documentation for the opening and modification of client accounts is received, authenticated, and established completely, accurately, and timely on the applicable system(s).
- client transactions, including contributions and withdrawals, are authorized and processed in a complete, accurate, and timely manner.
- trades are properly authorized, settled, and recorded completely, accurately, and timely in the client account(s).
- new securities and changes to securities are authorized and established on the relevant system(s) in a complete, accurate, and timely manner.
- securities income and corporate action transactions are processed to client accounts in a complete, accurate, and timely manner.
- physical securities are safeguarded from loss or misappropriation.
- cash and security positions are reconciled completely, accurately, and on a timely basis between the custodian and depositories.
- account statements reflecting cash and security positions are provided to clients in a complete, accurate, and timely manner.

Appendix E

Comparison of SOC 1®, SOC 2®, and SOC 3® Engagements and Related Reports

This appendix is nonauthoritative and is included for informational purposes only.

AT-C section 320, *Reporting on an Examination of Controls at a Service Organization Relevant to User Entities' Internal Control over Financial Reporting* (AICPA, *Professional Standards*), contains performance and reporting requirements and application guidance for a service auditor examining controls at a service organization that are likely to be relevant to user entities' internal control over financial reporting. However, a practitioner may be engaged to examine and report on controls at a service organization relevant to subject matter other than user entities' internal control over financial reporting, for example, controls that affect the privacy of information processed for the customers of user entities. The applicable attestation standard for such engagements may vary, depending on the subject matter. To make practitioners aware of the various professional standards and guides available to them for examining and reporting on system and organization controls and to help practitioners select the appropriate standard or guide for a particular engagement, the AICPA has introduced the term *system and organization controls* (SOC). The following are designations for three such reports and the source of the guidance for performing and reporting on these engagements:

- SOC 1®: AT-C section 320 and the AICPA Guide *Service Organizations: Applying AT-C Section 320*, Reporting on an Examination of Controls at a Service Organization Relevant to User Entities' Internal Control Over Financial Reporting (SOC 1®)

- SOC 2®: AT-C section 205, *Examination Engagements* (AICPA, *Professional Standards*) and the AICPA Guide *Reporting on Controls at a Service Organization Relevant to Security, Availability, Processing Integrity, Confidentiality, or Privacy (SOC 2®)*

- SOC 3®: AT-C section 205

The following table identifies differences between SOC 1®, SOC 2®, and SOC 3® engagements and related reports:

	SOC 1® Reports	*SOC 2® Reports*	*SOC 3® Reports*
Under what professional standard and interpretive publications is the engagement performed?	AT-C section 320, *Reporting on an Examination of Controls at a Service Organization Relevant to User Entities' Internal Control Over Financial Reporting* (AICPA, *Professional Standards*) The AICPA Guide *Reporting on an Examination of Controls at a Service Organization Relevant to User Entities' Internal Control Over Financial Reporting (SOC 1®)*	AT-C section 205, *Examination Engagements* (AICPA, *Professional Standards*) The AICPA Guide *Reporting on Controls at a Service Organization Relevant to Security, Availability, Processing Integrity, Confidentiality, or Privacy (SOC 2®)*	AT-C section 205
What are the criteria for the engagement and where are they stated?	In AT-C section 320, paragraph .15 contains the minimum criteria for evaluating the description of the service organization's system, paragraph .16 contains the criteria for evaluating the suitability of the design of the controls, and paragraph .17 contains the criteria for evaluating the operating effectiveness of the controls.	Paragraph 1.26 (and paragraph 1.27 if the description addresses controls over privacy) of the AICPA Guide *Reporting on Controls at a Service Organization Relevant to Security, Availability, Processing Integrity, Confidentiality, or Privacy (SOC 2®)* contains the criteria for evaluating the description of the service organization's system. TSP section 100, *Trust Services Principles and Criteria for Security, Availability, Processing Integrity, Confidentiality, and Privacy* (AICPA, *Trust Services Principles and Criteria*), contains the criteria for evaluating the design and operating effectiveness of the controls, as well as the criteria for evaluating the content of a privacy notice.	TSP section 100 contains the criteria for evaluating the design and operating effectiveness of controls, as well as the criteria for evaluating the content of a privacy notice.

	SOC 1® Reports	SOC 2® Reports	SOC 3® Reports
What is the subject matter of the engagement?	Controls at a service organization relevant to user entities' internal control over financial reporting	Controls at a service organization relevant to security, availability, processing integrity, confidentiality, or privacy	Controls at a service organization relevant to security, availability, processing integrity, confidentiality, or privacy
What is the purpose of the report?	To provide management of the service organization, user entities, and the independent auditors of user entities' financial statements with information and a service auditor's opinion about controls at a service organization that are likely to be relevant to user entities' internal control over financial reporting. A SOC 1® report enables the user auditor to perform risk assessment procedures and, if a type 2 report is provided, to use the report as audit evidence that controls at the service organization are operating effectively.	To provide management of a service organization, user entities, and other specified parties with information and a service auditor's opinion about controls at the service organization relevant to security, availability, processing integrity, confidentiality, or privacy.	To provide interested parties with a service auditor's opinion about controls at the service organization relevant to security, availability, processing integrity, confidentiality, or privacy.
What are the components of the report?	**Components of a Type 1 Report** *a.* Management's description of the service organization's system *b.* A written assertion by management of the service organization about whether, based on the criteria in management's assertion,	**Components of a Type 1 Report** *a.* Management's description of the service organization's system *b.* A written assertion by management of the service organization about whether, based on the criteria in management's assertion,	**Components of a SOC 3® Report[1]** *a.* Management's description of the boundaries of the service organization's system and,[2] in the case of a report that addresses the privacy principle, management's description of the boundaries of the service

(continued)

---

[1] Unlike SOC 1® and SOC 2® engagements, there is only one type of report for a SOC 3® engagement.

[2] These descriptions are typically less detailed than the descriptions in SOC 1® or SOC 2® reports and are not covered by the practitioner's opinion.

SOC 1® Reports	SOC 2® Reports	SOC 3® Reports
i. management's description of the service organization's system fairly presents the service organization's system that was designed and implemented as of a specified date ii. the controls related to the control objectives stated in management's description of the service organization's system were suitability designed to achieve those control objectives as of the specified date c. A service auditor's report that expresses an opinion on the matters in (*b*i)–(*b*ii)	i. management's description of the service organization's system fairly presents the service organization's system that was designed and implemented as of a specified date ii. the controls related to the applicable trust services criteria stated in management's description of the service organization's system were suitability designed to meet the applicable trust services criteria as of the specified date c. A service auditor's report that expresses an opinion on the matters in (*b*i)–(*b*ii)	organization's system and a copy of the service organization's privacy notice b. A written assertion by management of the service organization about whether the entity maintained effective controls over its system as it relates to the principle being reported on (that is, security, availability, processing integrity, confidentiality, or privacy), based on the applicable trust services criteria c. A service auditor's report that expresses an opinion on whether the entity maintained effective controls over its system as it relates to the principle being reported on (that is, security, availability, processing integrity, confidentiality, or privacy), based on the applicable trust services criteria
Components of a Type 2 Report a. Management's description of the service organization's system b. A written assertion by management of the service organization about whether, based on the criteria,	**Components of a Type 2 Report** a. Management's description of the service organization's system b. A written assertion by management of the service organization about whether, based on the criteria,	

	SOC 1® Reports	SOC 2® Reports	SOC 3® Reports
	i. management's description of the service organization's system fairly presents the service organization's system that was designed and implemented throughout the specified period	i. management's description of the service organization's system fairly presents the service organization's system that was designed and implemented throughout the specified period	
	ii. the controls related to the control objectives stated in management's description of the service organization's system were suitability designed throughout the specified period to achieve those control objectives	ii. the controls related to the applicable trust services criteria stated in management's description of the service organization's system were suitability designed throughout the specified period to achieve the applicable trust services criteria	
	iii. the controls related to the control objectives stated in management's description of the service organization's system operated effectively throughout the specified period to achieve those control objectives	iii. the controls related to the applicable trust services criteria stated in management's description of the service organization's system operated effectively throughout the specified period to meet the applicable trust services criteria	

(continued)

	SOC 1® Reports	SOC 2® Reports	SOC 3® Reports
	c. A service auditor's report that i. expresses an opinion on the matters in (bi)–(biii) ii. includes a description of the service auditor's tests of the controls and the results of the tests	c. A service auditor's report that i. expresses an opinion on the matters in (bi)–(biii) ii. includes a description of the service auditor's tests of controls and the results of the tests	
Who are the intended users of the report?	Management of the service organization, user entities during some or all of the period covered by the report (for type 2 reports) and user entities as of a specified date (for type 1 reports), and auditors of the user entities' financial statements	Management of the service organization and other specified parties who have sufficient knowledge and understanding of the following: • The nature of the service provided by the service organization • How the service organization's system interacts with user entities, subservice organizations, and other parties • Internal control and its limitations • User entity responsibilities • Complementary user entity controls and how they interact with related controls at the service organization to meet the applicable trust services criteria • The applicable trust services criteria • The risks that may threaten the achievement of the applicable trust services criteria and how controls address those risks	Interested parties

Appendix F

Comparison of Requirements in AT-C Section 320, Reporting on an Examination of Controls at a Service Organization Relevant to User Entities' Internal Control Over Financial Reporting, With Requirements of International Standard on Assurance Engagements 3402, Assurance Reports on Controls at a Service Organization [1]

This appendix is nonauthoritative and is included for informational purposes only.

This analysis was prepared by the AICPA Audit and Attest Standards staff to highlight substantive differences between AT-C section 320, *Reporting on an Examination of Controls at a Service Organization Relevant to User Entities' Internal Control Over Financial Reporting* (AICPA, *Professional Standards*), and International Standard on Assurance Engagements (ISAE) 3402, *Assurance Reports on Controls at a Service Organization*, and to explain the rationale for those differences. This analysis is not authoritative and is prepared for informational purposes only.

1. Fraud by Service Organization Personnel

Paragraph .32 of AT-C section 320 requires the service auditor to investigate the nature and cause of any deviations identified, as does paragraph 28 of ISAE 3402. Paragraph .33 of AT-C section 320 indicates that, if the service auditor becomes aware that such deviations resulted from fraud by service organization personnel, the service auditor should assess the risk that management's description of the service organization's system is not fairly presented, the controls are not suitably designed, and in a type 2 engagement, the controls are not operating effectively. The ISAE does not contain the requirement included in paragraph .33 of AT-C section 320. The Auditing Standards Board (ASB) believes that information about fraud affects the nature, timing, and extent of the service auditor's procedures. Therefore, paragraph .33 provides follow-up action for the service auditor when the service auditor obtains information about fraud as a result of performing the procedures in paragraph .32 of AT-C section 320.

---

[1] When performing an engagement under AT-C section 320, *Reporting on an Examination of Controls at a Service Organization Relevant to User Entities' Internal Control Over Financial Reporting* (AICPA, *Professional Standards*), in addition to complying with AT-C section 320, the service auditor is also required to comply with the following sections in AICPA *Professional Standards*: AT-C section 105, *Concepts Common to All Attestation Engagements*, and AT-C section 205, *Examination Engagements*.

2. Anomalies

Paragraph 29 of ISAE 3402 contains a requirement that enables a service auditor to conclude that a deviation identified in tests of controls involving sampling is not representative of the population from which the sample was drawn. AT-C section 320 does not include this requirement because of concerns about the use of terms such as, "in the extremely rare circumstances" and "a high degree of certainty." These terms are not used in U.S. professional standards and the ASB believes their introduction in AT-C section 320 could have unintended consequences. The ASB also believes that not including this requirement will enhance examination quality because deviations identified by the service auditor in tests of controls involving sampling will be treated in the same manner as any other deviation identified by the practitioner, rather than as an anomaly.

3. Direct Assistance

Paragraphs .39, .41–.42, and .44 of AT-C section 205, *Examination Engagements* (AICPA, *Professional Standards*), contain requirements for a service auditor using internal auditors to provide direct assistance. The ISAEs do not address the use of internal auditors to provide direct assistance.

4. Documentation Completion

Paragraph 50 of the ISAE requires the service auditor to assemble the documentation in an engagement file and complete the administrative process of assembling the final engagement file on a timely basis after the date of the service auditor's assurance report. Paragraph .35 of AT-C section 105, *Concepts Common to All Attestation Engagements* (AICPA, *Professional Standards*), also requires the service auditor to assemble the engagement documentation in an engagement file and complete the administrative process of assembling the final engagement file on a timely basis and, in addition, indicates that a timely basis is no later than 60 days following the service auditor's report release date.

5. Considering Subsequent Events and Subsequently Discovered Facts

Paragraph .48 of AT-C section 205 requires the service auditor, in addition to inquiring whether the responsible party, and if different, the engaging party, is aware of any events subsequent to the period (or point in time) covered by the examination engagement up to the date of the practitioner's report that could have a significant effect on the subject matter or assertion, to also apply other appropriate procedures to obtain evidence regarding such events. ISAE 3402 does not require the service auditor to apply procedures other than inquiry.

6. Reading Reports of the Internal Audit Function and Regulatory Examinations

Paragraph .23 of AT-C section 320 requires the service auditor to read the reports of the internal audit function and regulatory examinations that relate to the services provided to user entities and the scope of the engagement, if any, to obtain an understanding of the nature and extent of the procedures performed and the related findings. These findings are considered as part of the risk assessment and in determining the nature, timing, and extent of the tests.

7. Terms of the Engagement

Paragraph .08 of AT-C section 205 requires that the written agreement that specifies the terms of the engagement include specified matters. Paragraph 13 of ISAE 3402 does not specify the matters that should be included in the written agreement.

8. Required Written Representations

Paragraph .50 of AT-C section 205 and paragraph .36 of AT-C section 320 require the service auditor to request specific written representations from management of the service organization. Some of those representations are not required by ISAE 3000 (Revised), *Assurance Engagements Other Than Audits or Reviews of Historical Financial Information*, or ISAE 3402, including representations that

- all known matters contradicting the subject matter or assertion and any communication from regulatory agencies or others affecting the subject matter or assertion have been disclosed to the practitioner, including communications received between the end of the period addressed in the written assertion and the date of the practitioner's report.

- acknowledge responsibility for

  - the subject matter and the assertion;
  - selecting the criteria, when applicable; and
  - determining that such criteria are appropriate for the responsible party's purposes.

- any known events subsequent to the period (or point in time) of the subject matter being reported on that would have a material effect on the subject matter or assertion have been disclosed to the practitioner.

- if applicable, the responsible party believes the effects of uncorrected misstatements are immaterial, individually and in the aggregate, to the subject matter.

- if applicable, significant assumptions used in making any material estimates are reasonable.

In addition, there are differences between AT-C section 205 and ISAE 3402 with respect to the actions the service auditor is required to take when management refuses to provide written representations.

9. Elements of the Report Required by AT-C Section 320 That Are Not Required by ISAE 3402

Paragraphs .40–.41 of AT-C section 320 contain certain requirements regarding the content of the service auditor's report that are incremental to the requirements in ISAE 3402. These incremental requirements are included in

- paragraphs .40*d* and .41*d*, which require that the report include a statement that the controls and control objectives included in the description are those that management believes are likely to be relevant to user entities' internal control over financial reporting and that the description does not include those aspects of the system that are not likely to be relevant to user entities' internal control over financial reporting.

- paragraphs .40*f*iv–v and .41*f*iv–v, which require that the report include a statement that management is responsible for identifying the risks that threaten the achievement of the control objectives and selecting the criteria.

- paragraphs .40*f*vi and .41*f*vi, which require that the report include a statement that management is responsible for documenting controls that are suitably designed and operating effectively to achieve the related control objectives stated in the description of the service organization's system.

- paragraph .40*i*, which requires that the report include a statement that an examination of management's description of a service organization's system and the suitability of the design and operating effectiveness of the service organization's controls to achieve the related control objectives stated in the description involves

  — performing procedures to obtain evidence about the fairness of the presentation of the description and the suitability of the design and operating effectiveness of the controls to achieve the related control objectives stated in the description, based on the criteria in management's assertion.

  — assessing the risks that management's description of the service organization's system is not fairly presented and that the controls were not suitably designed or operating effectively to achieve the related control objectives.

  — testing the operating effectiveness of those controls that management considers necessary to provide reasonable assurance that the related control objectives stated in management's description of the service organization's system were achieved.

  — evaluating the overall presentation of management's description of the service organization's system, suitability of the control objectives stated in the description, and suitability of the criteria specified by the service organization in its assertion.

- paragraph .41*i*, which requires that the report include a statement that an examination of management's description of a service organization's system and the suitability of the design of the service organization's controls to achieve the related control objectives stated in the description involves

  — performing procedures to obtain evidence about the fairness of the presentation of the description and the suitability of the design and operating effectiveness of the controls to achieve the related control objectives stated in the description, based on the criteria in management's assertion.

  — assessing the risks that management's description of the service organization's system is not fairly presented and that the controls were not suitably designed or operating effectively to achieve the related control objectives.

  — evaluating the overall presentation of management's description of the service organization's system, suitability of the control objectives stated in the description, and suitability of the criteria specified by the service organization in its assertion.

- paragraph .40*k*v, which requires, if the work of the internal audit function has been used in tests of controls to obtain evidence, that the report include a description of the internal auditor's work and of the service auditor's procedures with respect to that work.

- paragraphs .40*l*v and .41*l*iv, which require, if the application of complementary subservice organization controls is necessary to achieve the related control objectives stated in management's description of the service organization's system, a statement to that effect.

- paragraphs .40*m* and .41*m*, which require that the report include a statement indicating that the report is not intended to be and should not be used by anyone other than the specified parties.

10. Elements of the Report Required by ISAE 3402 That Are Not Required by AT-C Section 320

Paragraph 69(i) of ISAE 3000 (Revised), *Assurance Engagements Other Than Audits or Reviews of Historical Financial Information,* which amends ISAE 3402, requires that the service auditor's report include a statement indicating that the firm of which the practitioner is a member applies International Standard on Quality Control (ISQC) 1, *Quality Control for Firms that Perform Audits and Reviews of Financial Statements, and Other Assurance and Related Services Engagements,* or other professional requirements, or requirements imposed by law or regulation, that are at least as demanding as ISQC 1. AT-C section 320 does not contain this requirement.

Paragraph 69(j) of ISAE 3000 (Revised) requires that the service auditor's report include a statement that the practitioner complies with the independence and other ethical requirements of Parts A and B of the *Code of Ethics for Professional Accountants* issued by the International Ethics Standards Board for Accountants (IESBA Code), or other professional requirements, or requirements imposed by law or regulation, that are at least as demanding as Parts A and B of the IESBA Code related to assurance engagements. AT-C section 320 does not contain this requirement.

Appendix G

Illustrative Service Auditor's Report When Reporting Under Both AT-C Section 320, Reporting on an Examination of Controls at a Service Organization Relevant to User Entities' Internal Control Over Financial Reporting, and ISAE 3402, Assurance Reports on Controls at a Service Organization

This appendix is nonauthoritative and is included for informational purposes only.

> The following is an illustrative service auditor's report that meets the requirements related to the contents of the report in AT-C section 320, *Reporting on an Examination of Controls at a Service Organization Relevant to User Entities' Internal Control Over Financial Reporting* (AICPA, *Professional Standards*), and ISAE 3402, *Assurance Reports on Controls at a Service Organization*, when the service auditor is reporting under both standards. This illustrative report is intended for reports dated on or after May 1, 2017.

Example 1: Type 2 Service Auditor's Report

Independent Service Auditor's Report on XYZ Service Organization's Description of its [*Type or name of*] System and the Suitability of the Design and Operating Effectiveness of Controls

To: XYZ Service Organization:

Scope

We have examined XYZ Service Organization's description of its [*type or name of*] system entitled "Description of XYZ Service Organization's [*type or name of*] System," for processing user entities' transactions [or identification of the function performed by the system] throughout the period [*date*] to [*date*] (description) and the suitability of the design and operating effectiveness of controls included in the description to achieve the related control objectives stated in the description, based on the criteria identified in "XYZ Service Organization's Assertion" (assertion). The controls and control objectives included in the description are those that management of XYZ Service Organization believes are likely to be relevant to user entities' internal control over financial reporting, and the description does not include those aspects of the [*type or name of*] system that are not likely to be relevant to user entities' internal control over financial reporting.

Service organization's responsibilities

In [*section number where the assertion is presented*], XYZ Service Organization has provided an assertion about the fairness of the presentation of the description and suitability of the design and operating effectiveness of the controls to achieve the related control objectives stated in the description. XYZ Service Organization is responsible for preparing the description and assertion, including the completeness, accuracy, and method of presentation of the description and assertion, providing the services covered by the description, specifying the control objectives and stating them in the description, identifying the risks that threaten the achievement of the control objectives, selecting the criteria stated in the assertion, and designing, implementing, and documenting controls that are suitably designed and operating effectively to achieve the related control objectives stated in the description.

Service auditor's responsibilities

Our responsibility is to express an opinion on the fairness of the presentation of the description and on the suitability of the design and operating effectiveness of the controls to achieve the related control objectives stated in the description, based on our examination.

Our examination was conducted in accordance with attestation standards established by the American Institute of Certified Public Accountants (AICPA) and International Standard on Assurance Engagements (ISAE) 3402, *Assurance Reports on Controls at a Service Organization*, issued by the International Auditing and Assurance Standards Board. Those standards require that we plan and perform the examination to obtain reasonable assurance about whether, in all material respects, based on the criteria in management's assertion, the description is fairly presented and the controls were suitably designed and operating effectively to achieve the related control objectives stated in the description throughout the period [*date*] to [*date*]. We believe that the evidence we obtained is sufficient and appropriate to provide a reasonable basis for our opinion.

An examination of a description of a service organization's system and the suitability of the design and operating effectiveness of controls involves

- performing procedures to obtain evidence about the fairness of the presentation of the description and the suitability of the design and operating effectiveness of the controls to achieve the related control objectives stated in the description, based on the criteria in management's assertion.

- assessing the risks that the description is not fairly presented and that the controls were not suitably designed or operating effectively to achieve the related control objectives stated in the description.

- testing the operating effectiveness of those controls that management considers necessary to provide reasonable assurance that the related control objectives stated in the description were achieved.

- evaluating the overall presentation of the description, suitability of the control objectives stated in the description, and suitability of the criteria specified by the service organization in its assertion.

Service auditor's independence and quality control

We have complied with the independence and other ethical requirements of the Code of Professional Conduct established by the AICPA.

We applied the Statements on Quality Control Standards established by the AICPA and, accordingly, maintain a comprehensive system of quality control.

Inherent limitations

The description is prepared to meet the common needs of a broad range of user entities and their auditors, who audit and report on user entities' financial statements, and may not, therefore, include every aspect of the system that each individual user entity may consider important in its own particular environment. Because of their nature, controls at a service organization may not prevent, or detect and correct, all misstatements in processing or reporting transactions [*or identification of the function performed by the system*]. Also, the projection to the future of any evaluation of the fairness of the presentation of the description, or conclusions about the suitability of the design or operating effectiveness of the controls to achieve the related control objectives, is subject to the risk that controls at a service organization may become ineffective

Description of tests of controls

The specific controls tested and the nature, timing, and results of those tests are listed in [*section number where the description of tests of controls is presented*].

Opinion

In our opinion, in all material respects, based on the criteria described in XYZ Service Organization's assertion

a. the description fairly presents the [*type or name of*] system that was designed and implemented throughout the period [*date*] to [*date*].

b. the controls related to the control objectives stated in the description were suitably designed to provide reasonable assurance that the control objectives would be achieved if the controls operated effectively throughout the period [*date*] to [*date*].

c. the controls operated effectively to provide reasonable assurance that the control objectives stated in the description were achieved throughout the period [*date*] to [*date*].

Restricted use

This report, including the description of tests of controls and results thereof in [*section number where the description of tests of controls is presented*], is intended solely for the information and use of management of XYZ Service Organization, user entities of XYZ Service Organization's [*type or name of*] system during some or all of the period [*date*] to [*date*], and their auditors who audit and report on such user entities' financial statements or internal control over financial reporting and have a sufficient understanding to consider it, along with other information including information about controls implemented by user entities themselves, when assessing the risks of material misstatement of user entities' financial statements. This report is not intended to be and should not be used by anyone other than the specified parties.

[*Service auditor's signature*]

[*Date of the service auditor's report*]

[*Service auditor's city and state*]

Appendix H

Overview of Statements on Quality Control Standards

This appendix is nonauthoritative and is included for informational purposes only.

This appendix is a partial reproduction of chapter 1 of the AICPA practice aid *Establishing and Maintaining a System of Quality Control for a CPA Firm's Accounting and Auditing Practice*, available at www.aicpa.org/interestareas/frc/pages/enhancingauditqualitypracticeaid.aspx.

This appendix highlights certain aspects of the quality control standards issued by the AICPA. If appropriate, readers should also refer to the quality control standards issued by the PCAOB, available at www.pcaobus.org/Standards/QC/Pages/default.aspx.

1.01   The objectives of a system of quality control are to provide a CPA firm with reasonable assurance[1] that the firm and its personnel comply with professional standards and applicable regulatory and legal requirements, and that the firm or engagement partners issue reports that are appropriate in the circumstances. QC section 10, *A Firm's System of Quality Control* (AICPA, *Professional Standards*), addresses a CPA firm's responsibilities for its system of quality control for its accounting and auditing practice. That section is to be read in conjunction with the AICPA Code of Professional Conduct and other relevant ethical requirements.

1.02   A system of quality control consists of policies designed to achieve the objectives of the system and the procedures necessary to implement and monitor compliance with those policies. The nature, extent, and formality of a firm's quality control policies and procedures will depend on various factors such as the firm's size; the number and operating characteristics of its offices; the degree of authority allowed to, and the knowledge and experience possessed by, firm personnel; and the nature and complexity of the firm's practice.

Communication of Quality Control Policies and Procedures

1.03   The firm should communicate its quality control policies and procedures to its personnel. Most firms will find it appropriate to communicate their policies and procedures in writing and distribute them, or make them available electronically, to all professional personnel. Effective communication includes the following:

- A description of quality control policies and procedures and the objectives they are designed to achieve

---

[1] The term *reasonable assurance*, which is defined as a high, but not absolute, level of assurance, is used because absolute assurance cannot be attained. Paragraph .53 of QC section 10, *A Firm's System of Quality Control* (AICPA, *Professional Standards*), states, "Any system of quality control has inherent limitations that can reduce its effectiveness."

- The message that each individual has a personal responsibility for quality

- A requirement for each individual to be familiar with and to comply with these policies and procedures

Effective communication also includes procedures for personnel to communicate their views or concerns on quality control matters to the firm's management.

Elements of a System of Quality Control

1.04 A firm must establish and maintain a system of quality control. The firm's system of quality control should include policies and procedures that address each of the following elements of quality control identified in paragraph .17 of QC section 10:

- Leadership responsibilities for quality within the firm (the "tone at the top")

- Relevant ethical requirements

- Acceptance and continuance of client relationships and specific engagements

- Human resources

- Engagement performance

- Monitoring

1.05 The elements of quality control are interrelated. For example, a firm continually assesses client relationships to comply with relevant ethical requirements, including independence, integrity, and objectivity, and policies and procedures related to the acceptance and continuance of client relationships and specific engagements. Similarly, the human resources element of quality control encompasses criteria related to professional development, hiring, advancement, and assignment of firm personnel to engagements, all of which affect policies and procedures related to engagement performance. In addition, policies and procedures related to the monitoring element of quality control enable a firm to evaluate whether its policies and procedures for each of the other five elements of quality control are suitably designed and effectively applied.

1.06 Policies and procedures established by the firm related to each element are designed to achieve reasonable assurance with respect to the purpose of that element. Deficiencies in policies and procedures for an element may result in not achieving reasonable assurance with respect to the purpose of that element; however, the system of quality control, as a whole, may still be effective in providing the firm with reasonable assurance that the firm and its personnel comply with professional standards and applicable regulatory and legal requirements and that the firm or engagement partners issue reports that are appropriate in the circumstances.

1.07 If a firm merges, acquires, sells, or otherwise changes a portion of its practice, the surviving firm evaluates and, as necessary, revises, implements, and maintains firm-wide quality control policies and procedures that are appropriate for the changed circumstances.

Leadership Responsibilities for Quality Within the Firm (the "Tone at the Top")

1.08 The purpose of the leadership responsibilities element of a system of quality control is to promote an internal culture based on the recognition that quality is essential in performing engagements. The firm should establish and maintain the following policies and procedures to achieve this purpose:

- Require the firm's leadership (managing partner, board of managing partners, CEO, or equivalent) to assume ultimate responsibility for the firm's system of quality control.

- Provide the firm with reasonable assurance that personnel assigned operational responsibility for the firm's quality control system have sufficient and appropriate experience and ability to identify and understand quality control issues and develop appropriate policies and procedures, as well as the necessary authority to implement those policies and procedures.

1.09 Establishing and maintaining the following policies and procedures assists firms in recognizing that the firm's business strategy is subject to the overarching requirement for the firm to achieve the objectives of the system of quality control in all the engagements that the firm performs:

- Assign management responsibilities so that commercial considerations do not override the quality of the work performed.

- Design policies and procedures addressing performance evaluation, compensation, and advancement (including incentive systems) with regard to personnel to demonstrate the firm's overarching commitment to the objectives of the system of quality control.

- Devote sufficient and appropriate resources for the development, communication, and support of its quality control policies and procedures.

Relevant Ethical Requirements

1.10 The purpose of the relevant ethical requirements element of a system of quality control is to provide the firm with reasonable assurance that the firm and its personnel comply with relevant ethical requirements when discharging professional responsibilities. Relevant ethical requirements include independence, integrity, and objectivity. Establishing and maintaining policies such as the following assist the firm in obtaining this assurance:

- Require that personnel adhere to relevant ethical requirements such as those in regulations, interpretations, and rules of the AICPA, state CPA societies, state boards of accountancy, state statutes, the U.S. Government Accountability Office, and any other applicable regulators.

- Establish procedures to communicate independence requirements to firm personnel and, where applicable, others subject to them.

- Establish procedures to identify and evaluate possible threats to independence and objectivity, including the familiarity threat that may be created by using the same senior personnel on an audit or attest engagement over a long period of time, and to take appropriate action to eliminate those threats or reduce them to an acceptable level by applying safeguards.

- Require that the firm withdraw from the engagement if effective safeguards to reduce threats to independence to an acceptable level cannot be applied.

- Require written confirmation, at least annually, of compliance with the firm's policies and procedures on independence from all firm personnel required to be independent by relevant requirements.

- Establish procedures for confirming the independence of another firm or firm personnel in associated member firms who perform part of the engagement. This would apply to national firm personnel, foreign firm personnel, and foreign-associated firms.[2]

- Require the rotation of personnel for audit or attest engagements where regulatory or other authorities require such rotation after a specified period.

Acceptance and Continuance of Client Relationships and Specific Engagements

1.11 The purpose of the quality control element that addresses acceptance and continuance of client relationships and specific engagements is to establish criteria for deciding whether to accept or continue a client relationship and whether to perform a specific engagement for a client. A firm's client acceptance and continuance policies represent a key element in mitigating litigation and business risk. Accordingly, it is important that a firm be aware that the integrity and reputation of a client's management could reflect the reliability of the client's accounting records and financial representations and, therefore, affect the firm's reputation or involvement in litigation. A firm's policies and procedures related to the acceptance and continuance of client relationships and specific engagements should provide the firm with reasonable assurance that it will undertake or continue relationships and engagements only where it

- is competent to perform the engagement and has the capabilities, including the time and resources, to do so;

- can comply with legal and relevant ethical requirements;

- has considered the client's integrity and does not have information that would lead it to conclude that the client lacks integrity; and

- has reached an understanding with the client regarding the services to be performed.

1.12 This assurance should be obtained before accepting an engagement with a new client, when deciding whether to continue an existing engagement, and when considering acceptance of a new engagement with an existing client.

---

[2] A *foreign-associated firm* is a firm domiciled outside of the United States and its territories that is a member of, correspondent with, or similarly associated with an international firm or international association of firms.

Establishing and maintaining policies such as the following assist the firm in obtaining this assurance:

- Evaluate factors that have a bearing on management's integrity and consider the risk associated with providing professional services in particular circumstances.[3]

- Evaluate whether the engagement can be completed with professional competence; undertake only those engagements for which the firm has the capabilities, resources, and professional competence to complete; and evaluate, at the end of specific periods or upon occurrence of certain events, whether the relationship should be continued.

- Obtain an understanding, preferably in writing, with the client regarding the services to be performed.

- Establish procedures on continuing an engagement and the client relationship, including procedures for dealing with information that would have caused the firm to decline an engagement if the information had been available earlier.

- Require documentation of how issues relating to acceptance or continuance of client relationships and specific engagements were resolved.

Human Resources

1.13 The purpose of the human resources element of a system of quality control is to provide the firm with reasonable assurance that it has sufficient personnel with the capabilities, competence, and commitment to ethical principles necessary (a) to perform its engagements in accordance with professional standards and regulatory and legal requirements, and (b) to enable the firm to issue reports that are appropriate in the circumstances. Establishing and maintaining policies such as the following assist the firm in obtaining this assurance:

- Recruit and hire personnel of integrity who possess the characteristics that enable them to perform competently.

- Determine capabilities and competencies required for an engagement, especially for the engagement partner, based on the characteristics of the particular client, industry, and kind of service being performed. Specific competencies necessary for an engagement partner are discussed in paragraph .A27 of QC section 10.

- Determine the capabilities and competencies possessed by personnel.

---

[3] Such considerations would include the risk of providing professional services to significant clients or to other clients for which the practitioner's objectivity or the appearance of independence may be impaired. In broad terms, the significance of a client to a member or a firm refers to relationships that could diminish a practitioner's objectivity and independence in performing attest services. Examples of factors to consider in determining the significance of a client to an engagement partner, office, or practice unit include (a) the amount of time the partner, office, or practice unit devotes to the engagement, (b) the effect on the partner's stature within the firm as a result of his or her service to the client, (c) the manner in which the partner, office, or practice unit is compensated, or (d) the effect that losing the client would have on the partner, office, or practice unit.

- Assign the responsibility for each engagement to an engagement partner.

- Assign personnel based on the knowledge, skills, and abilities required in the circumstances and the nature and extent of supervision needed.

- Have personnel participate in general and industry-specific continuing professional education and professional development activities that enable them to accomplish assigned responsibilities and satisfy applicable continuing professional education requirements of the AICPA, state boards of accountancy, and other regulators.

- Select for advancement only those individuals who have the qualifications necessary to fulfill the responsibilities they will be called on to assume.

Engagement Performance

1.14   The purpose of the engagement performance element of quality control is to provide the firm with reasonable assurance (*a*) that engagements are consistently performed in accordance with applicable professional standards and regulatory and legal requirements, and (*b*) that the firm or the engagement partner issues reports that are appropriate in the circumstances. Policies and procedures for engagement performance should address all phases of the design and execution of the engagement, including engagement performance, supervision responsibilities, and review responsibilities. Policies and procedures also should require that consultation takes place when appropriate. In addition, a policy should establish criteria against which all engagements are to be evaluated to determine whether an engagement quality control review should be performed.

1.15   Establishing and maintaining policies such as the following assist the firm in obtaining the assurance required relating to the engagement performance element of quality control:

- Plan all engagements to meet professional, regulatory, and the firm's requirements.

- Perform work and issue reports and other communications that meet professional, regulatory, and the firm's requirements.

- Require that work performed by other team members be reviewed by qualified engagement team members, which may include the engagement partner, on a timely basis.

- Require the engagement team to complete the assembly of final engagement files on a timely basis.

- Establish procedures to maintain the confidentiality, safe custody, integrity, accessibility, and retrievability of engagement documentation.

- Require the retention of engagement documentation for a period of time sufficient to meet the needs of the firm, professional standards, laws, and regulations.

- Require that

- — consultation take place when appropriate (for example, when dealing with complex, unusual, unfamiliar, difficult, or contentious issues);
- — sufficient and appropriate resources be available to enable appropriate consultation to take place;
- — all the relevant facts known to the engagement team be provided to those consulted;
- — the nature, scope, and conclusions of such consultations be documented; and
- — the conclusions resulting from such consultations be implemented.

- Require that

  - — differences of opinion be dealt with and resolved;
  - — conclusions reached are documented and implemented; and
  - — the report not be released until the matter is resolved.

- Require that

  - — all engagements be evaluated against the criteria for determining whether an engagement quality control review should be performed;
  - — an engagement quality control review be performed for all engagements that meet the criteria; and
  - — the review be completed before the report is released.

- Establish procedures addressing the nature, timing, extent, and documentation of the engagement quality control review.
- Establish criteria for the eligibility of engagement quality control reviewers.

Monitoring

1.16 The purpose of the monitoring element of a system of quality control is to provide the firm and its engagement partners with reasonable assurance that the policies and procedures related to the system of quality control are relevant, adequate, operating effectively, and complied with in practice. Monitoring involves an ongoing consideration and evaluation of the appropriateness of the design, the effectiveness of the operation of a firm's quality control system, and a firm's compliance with its quality control policies and procedures. The purpose of monitoring compliance with quality control policies and procedures is to provide an evaluation of the following:

- Adherence to professional standards and regulatory and legal requirements
- Whether the quality control system has been appropriately designed and effectively implemented
- Whether the firm's quality control policies and procedures have been operating effectively so that reports issued by the firm are appropriate in the circumstances

1.17 Establishing and maintaining policies such as the following assist the firm in obtaining the assurance required relating to the monitoring element of quality control:

- Assign responsibility for the monitoring process to a partner or partners or other persons with sufficient and appropriate experience and authority in the firm to assume that responsibility.

- Assign performance of the monitoring process to competent individuals.

- Require the performance of monitoring procedures that are sufficiently comprehensive to enable the firm to assess compliance with all applicable professional standards and the firm's quality control policies and procedures. Monitoring procedures consist of the following:

  — Review of selected administrative and personnel records pertaining to the quality control elements.

  — Review of engagement documentation, reports, and clients' financial statements.

  — Summarization of the findings from the monitoring procedures, at least annually, and consideration of the systemic causes of findings that indicate that improvements are needed.

  — Determination of any corrective actions to be taken or improvements to be made with respect to the specific engagements reviewed or the firm's quality control policies and procedures.

  — Communication of the identified findings to appropriate firm management personnel.

  — Consideration of findings by appropriate firm management personnel who should also determine that any actions necessary, including necessary modifications to the quality control system, are taken on a timely basis.

  — Assessment of

    - the appropriateness of the firm's guidance materials and any practice aids;

    - new developments in professional standards and regulatory and legal requirements and how they are reflected in the firm's policies and procedures where appropriate;

    - compliance with policies and procedures on independence;

    - the effectiveness of continuing professional development, including training;

    - decisions related to acceptance and continuance of client relationships and specific engagements; and

    - firm personnel's understanding of the firm's quality control policies and procedures and implementation thereof.

- Communicate at least annually, to relevant engagement partners and other appropriate personnel, deficiencies noted as a result of the monitoring process and recommendations for appropriate remedial action.
- Communicate the results of the monitoring of its quality control system process to relevant firm personnel at least annually.
- Establish procedures designed to provide the firm with reasonable assurance that it deals appropriately with the following:
    — Complaints and allegations that the work performed by the firm fails to comply with professional standards and regulatory and legal requirements.
    — Allegations of noncompliance with the firm's system of quality control.
    — Deficiencies in the design or operation of the firm's quality control policies and procedures, or noncompliance with the firm's system of quality control by an individual or individuals, as identified during the investigations into complaints and allegations.

    This includes establishing clearly defined channels for firm personnel to raise any concerns in a manner that enables them to come forward without fear of reprisal and documenting complaints and allegations and the responses to them.

- Require appropriate documentation to provide evidence of the operation of each element of its system of quality control. The form and content of documentation evidencing the operation of each of the elements of the system of quality control is a matter of judgment and depends on a number of factors, including the following, for example:
    — The size of the firm and the number of offices.
    — The nature and complexity of the firm's practice and organization.
- Require retention of documentation providing evidence of the operation of the system of quality control for a period of time sufficient to permit those performing monitoring procedures and peer review to evaluate the firm's compliance with its system of quality control, or for a longer period if required by law or regulation.

1.18 Some of the monitoring procedures discussed in the previous list may be accomplished through the performance of the following:

- Engagement quality control review
- Review of engagement documentation, reports, and clients' financial statements for selected engagements after the report release date
- Inspection[4] procedures

---

[4] *Inspection* is a retrospective evaluation of the adequacy of the firm's quality control policies and procedures, its personnel's understanding of those policies and procedures, and the extent of the firm's

(continued)

Documentation of Quality Control Policies and Procedures

1.19 The firm should document each element of its system of quality control. The extent of the documentation will depend on the size, structure, and nature of the firm's practice. Documentation may be as simple as a checklist of the firm's policies and procedures or as extensive as practice manuals.

(footnote continued)

compliance with them. Although monitoring procedures are meant to be ongoing, they may include inspection procedures performed at a fixed point in time. Monitoring is a broad concept; inspection is one specific type of monitoring procedure.

Index of Pronouncements and Other Technical Guidance

A

Title	Paragraphs
AT Section 801, *Reporting on Controls at a Service Organization*	Preface
AT-C Section	
105, *Concepts Common to All Attestation Engagements*	3.01, 3.48, 3.74, 3.76, 3.90, 3.96, 3.107, 3.128–.131, 4.12, 4.33, 4.44, 4.165, 4.167, Appendix F
205, *Examination Engagements*	1.06, 3.01, 3.48–.49, 3.61, 3.83, 3.91–.93, 3.98, 3.100, 3.108, 3.112, 3.120, 4.01, 4.19, 4.31, 4.44, 4.47, 4.79, 4.93, 4.108, 4.111, 4.113, 4.117, 4.119, 4.121–.122, 4.125–.127, 4.135, 4.143, 4.164, 4.168–.172, 4.175, 4.178, 4.180, 4.183, 4.186–.188, 4.190–.193, 5.29–.31, 5.35–.36, 5.40, 5.84, 5.86, 5.93, 5.96–.97, Appendix E, Appendix F, Table 1-1 at 1.09
215, *Agreed-Upon Procedures Engagements*	Table 1-1 at 1.09
320, *Reporting on an Examination of Controls at a Service Organization Relevant to User Entities' Internal Control Over Financial Reporting*	1.02, 1.04, 1.06, 1.09, 2.03, 2.12, 2.18–.19, 3.01, 3.08, 3.14, 3.17, 3.19, 3.24, 3.26, 3.28, 3.31–.33, 3.36, 3.38–.39, 3.42, 3.44, 3.48, 3.57–.59, 3.61, 3.66, 3.68, 3.70, 3.72, 3.74–.75, 3.77–.79, 3.82–.83, 3.95, 3.97, 3.102, 3.106, 3.109, 3.130, 4.01–.197, 5.01–.02, 5.09–.11, 5.17–.19, 5.24, 5.33, 5.77–.78, 5.84–.85, Appendix A, Appendix E, Appendix F, Appendix G, Introduction to 3.01, Introduction to 5.01, Table 1-1 at 1.09, Table 5-3 at 5.18

C

I

Title	Paragraphs
Investment Company Act of 1940 Rules	
38a-1	Table 1-1 at 1.09
206(4)-7	Table 1-1 at 1.09

S

Title	Paragraphs
Sec Rules and Regulations	
38a-1	Table 1-1 at 1.09
206(4)-2	Appendix D
206(4)-7	Table 1-1 at 1.09
SOC	
1, *Report on Controls at a Service Organization Relevant to User Entities' Internal Control Over Financial Reporting*	2.19, 3.130, 4.31, Appendix A, Appendix B, Appendix E
2, *Report on Controls at a Service Organization Relevant to Security, Availability, Processing Integrity, Confidentiality, or Privacy*	1.06, 3.130, 4.32, Appendix E, Table 1-1 at 1.09
3, *Trust Services Report for Service Organization*	4.31, Appendix E, Table 1-1 at 1.09
SOP 07-2, *Attestation Engagements That Address Specified Compliance Control Objectives and Related Controls at Entities That Provide Services to Investment Companies, Investment Advisers, or Other Service Providers*	Table 1-1 at 1.09
SSAE No. 18, *Attestation Standards: Clarification and Recodification*	Preface

T

Title	Paragraphs
TSP Section 100, "Criteria, and Illustrations for Security, Availability, Processing Integrity, Confidentiality and Privacy"	Table 1-1 at 1.09

Subject Index